The Crisis of Democratic Pluralism

Brendan Sweetman

The Crisis of Democratic Pluralism

The Loss of Confidence in Reason and the Clash of Worldviews

Brendan Sweetman
Department of Philosophy
Rockhurst University
Kansas City, MO, USA

ISBN 978-3-030-78381-5   ISBN 978-3-030-78382-2 (eBook)
https://doi.org/10.1007/978-3-030-78382-2

© The Editor(s) (if applicable) and The Author(s), under exclusive licence to Springer Nature Switzerland AG 2021

This work is subject to copyright. All rights are solely and exclusively licensed by the Publisher, whether the whole or part of the material is concerned, specifically the rights of translation, reprinting, reuse of illustrations, recitation, broadcasting, reproduction on microfilms or in any other physical way, and transmission or information storage and retrieval, electronic adaptation, computer software, or by similar or dissimilar methodology now known or hereafter developed.

The use of general descriptive names, registered names, trademarks, service marks, etc. in this publication does not imply, even in the absence of a specific statement, that such names are exempt from the relevant protective laws and regulations and therefore free for general use.

The publisher, the authors and the editors are safe to assume that the advice and information in this book are believed to be true and accurate at the date of publication. Neither the publisher nor the authors or the editors give a warranty, expressed or implied, with respect to the material contained herein or for any errors or omissions that may have been made. The publisher remains neutral with regard to jurisdictional claims in published maps and institutional affiliations.

This Palgrave Macmillan imprint is published by the registered company Springer Nature Switzerland AG.
The registered company address is: Gewerbestrasse 11, 6330 Cham, Switzerland

*In memory of my mother, Anna Sweetman,
and of my uncle and aunt, Dennis and Patricia Fagan*

Preface

I attempt to develop in this book a line of inquiry that suggests there is a looming and quite deep crisis facing the liberal democratic form of government. The problems that seem to be leading to a crisis involve the very *foundations* of the democratic system. They have to do with the consequences that result from the operation of freedom and pluralism within a democratic structure over the long term. The supreme prominence placed on, and absolutist interpretation of, human freedom has led to a contentious pluralism, marked by the emergence of incommensurable worldviews and a spirit of relativism that have become characteristic features of modern democratic nations. I call this phenomenon the problem of *worldview pluralism*. It is not a disagreement over this or that economic or social policy, or over the worthiness of a political party or political leader, or about the foreign policy of a particular country, or whatever; it is a far deeper disagreement concerning what are largely incommensurable views on the meaning of life, the nature of human fulfillment, the correct approach to ethics, law, politics, and culture This phenomenon is further compounded by a loss of confidence in the power of human reason to lead to productive dialogue and the discovery of objective truth that might go some way to resolving or at least alleviating our disagreements. Thus, we are concerned with a deeper form of crisis than current critics of democracy focus on today, where recent electoral trends and other disturbing developments have inspired some to bemoan the present state of the democratic system. Contemporary worries about liberal democracy are often inspired by the attitude that the general populace is uninformed, stupid, perhaps even prejudiced and immoral, and that if only we could correct these vices, we would then have an enlightened electorate who would make wise and moral decisions (meaning, often, decisions that accord with those of the critics!).

Our claim is that the crisis goes deeper than such worries would suggest. For even if we had a fully informed, extremely well-educated and perfectly moral general populace, there would still remain serious disagreement on central worldview questions of life and culture, giving rise to a contentious pluralism to which there is no obvious or easy solution. I will develop an argument to illustrate how we ended up with a loss of confidence in reason, and how our difficulties are added to by various relativistic approaches to knowledge that have become widespread, and also by the *practical* failure of public discourse. It is also essential, as we will illustrate, to recognize that a growing and increasingly influential worldview of secularism contributes significantly to the clash of worldviews. In illustrating this latter phenomenon, secularism must be distinguished both from the process of secularization that is occurring in many democratic countries and from the concept of the secular state. Consequently, a subtheme of this book is to clarify the role of religion in democratic societies, especially at the political level, and to show why and how religious worldviews, contrary to the position of liberal political theory, must be allowed some limited role in public discourse in the modern state.

Although our intention is to offer a modest, original reflection on the nature of democracy and its current problems, it will also be important and enlightening to consider along the way the proposed solution to the problems of secular society in recent liberal political theory, and its failure. What we are therefore left with is a clash of worldviews in the modern state, both between various religious worldviews and between religious worldviews and secularist worldviews. Indeed, the rise of the secularist worldview, I will argue, changes completely the conventional understanding of the modern state, changes how we should think about profound disagreements involving defining beliefs, values, and political policy decisions in a democratic society. It also changes the way we should think about the presence and place of religious views. As a result, the time is now ripe for a re-envisioning of the relationship between secularism, religion, and the state.

In discussing these challenging but fascinating themes, I am not writing from the point of view of democracy in the U.S. or any particular country, but more broadly. I wish to consider the nature of the democratic form of government as it has developed over the past fifty years or so, but especially in the past thirty years, in the many states in which it is practiced. Democratic societies around the world are facing the same set of problems, perhaps most especially in the Western hemisphere. Different countries are at different stages in confronting these problems; some nations are behind others with regard to the extent of their experience of various concerns, but all are struggling to deal with similar societal developments, trends, and tensions (which often manifest themselves in intense and acrimonious public disputes, disputes to which there seem to be no obvious resolutions that do not end up violating the principles of democracy themselves). I am mainly concerned with democracy as it is practiced in developed Western countries, the countries of Europe, the U.S., and also in the Southern hemisphere, especially in Australia and New Zealand. The countries of South America are not as advanced on the path of democracy, nor are the countries of Eastern Europe, such as Poland and Slovakia, but nevertheless many of the themes of this book are still relevant to these nations, albeit affecting them at an earlier stage of development. Indeed, some of the same concerns arise even in Asian countries, such as the Philippines and India.

It is my contention that all democratic countries, whether they are fledgling or mature, will have to deal eventually with the problems that arise from worldview pluralism, moral relativism, the loss of confidence in reason, and the rise of secularism, in one form or another, and that these problems will not be easy to resolve. Indeed, part of the crisis is that there does not seem to be an uncomplicated solution, that it is difficult to see an obvious remedy, or hopeful way forward. Nevertheless, I will develop my own approach to pluralist disagreement which requires a rethinking of the relationship between religion, secularism, and politics, and which allows a limited place for all major worldviews in the state, including religious worldviews. I also develop some suggestions for how best to conduct public deliberation today. It is possible that the foundational problems arising in the democratic form of government could lead to major instability in various countries, and perhaps the democratic system may even begin to unravel. This book then is a reflection on the nature of modern pluralist democracy, particularly with regard to its foundational ideas, their origin and development, and the crisis they have led to today.

Chapter 1 introduces the problem of a threatening crisis, then distinguishes my position from other claims that liberal democracy is in crisis. We explain what we mean by democracy, consider briefly its history, and provide an overview of its main values, as well as the distinction between democracy and liberalism. We consider a list of practical problems facing the democratic system that, while serious and irritating, are not fatal to it, and are not what we mean by crisis in this book. The last section introduces the key arguments and issues of the book, which revolve around the following six themes: 1. Freedom as an Absolute Value; 2. The Phenomenon of Relativism; 3. Loss of Confidence in Reason; 4. Secularism as a Worldview; 5. The Presence of Religious Worldviews in the Democratic State; and 6. The Failure of the Liberal Solution. Chapter 2 turns to the gradual shift in the understanding of freedom from the time of John Locke and John Stuart Mill onward. After considering Mill's arguments for freedom of thought and expression, we develop the argument that freedom of expression seems to lead inexorably toward relativism. In Chap. 3, we turn more directly to the loss of confidence in reason that is a characteristic feature of modern democracies. After introducing the notion of a worldview, and considering the phenomenon of pluralism in contemporary democracy, we then present what we call a causal argument/process to explain how we came to a loss of confidence in reason. We survey the causes for this loss of confidence, including the phenomenon of antirealism about knowledge, reflect on how people respond to it, and consider how over time worldviews become ideologies.

Chapter 4 provides a full discussion of the phenomenon of relativism, including an overview of the philosophical approach of postmodernism. We distinguish between relativism as a philosophical thesis and the rhetoric of relativism, illustrating with the postmodernist approach, and other practical examples, before outlining the problems that relativism faces. The chapter goes on to examine the problem of incommensurability, clarifying three types of moral disagreement, before concluding with some guidelines for how to approach the difficulties relativism presents for public discourse in modern democratic culture. We explain how secularism has emerged and has become an influential worldview in Chap. 5. Its presence in society makes the problem of worldview pluralism much worse and forces us to begin to re-envision the relationship between religion and secularism, and democracy and politics. The chapter provides an overview of the Christian worldview and of the secularist worldview, in terms of their main beliefs on central topics, such as human nature. The last section of the chapter considers a sophisticated, serious example of the philosophical case for secularism in the work of philosopher, Philip Kitcher.

It becomes necessary to offer further analysis of the secularizing characteristics of contemporary society, which we do in Chap. 6. After first distinguishing carefully between secularism, secularization, and the secular, we introduce helpful notions of passive and active secularism, before considering the case study of Ireland as a country that has recently undergone a process of fairly radical secularization. Given the phenomena discussed in previous chapters, including the rise of relativism, the loss of confidence in reason leading to a clash of worldviews, in addition to the influence of secularism in modern democracies, the question inevitably arises: how are we to govern and make progress; how are we to navigate through our serious disagreements about morality, politics, and culture? Chapter 7 considers the standard way of thinking about these matters in recent liberal political theory, in the work of philosopher John Rawls. We present an overview of his position and solution to the problem of pluralism, and introduce and explain the notion of public reason—the idea that in public deliberation, one must present arguments that all reasonable people can accept; this excludes religious reasons. Turning then specifically to the argument that religious views should be excluded from the process of democratic deliberation, we examine the work of Robert Audi. We then consider the notion of public reason as a possible solution or way of alleviating the problem of a contentious pluralism in Chap. 8. Distinguishing first between a worldview being reasonable and being true, and how we might decide if a person (or a worldview) is reasonable, we go on to examine various views of public reason, including those of Rawls and Cécile Laborde by means of a consideration of concrete cases.

There is often a general suspicion of the liberal response to the problem of pluralism, especially for its exclusion of religious views from public discourse. In Chap. 9, we illustrate the problems with the proposals of liberal political philosophers further by means of a detailed case study of Martin Luther King Jr.'s religious arguments for civil rights in U.S. society. This leads to an overall critical assessment of Rawls' view, both in the light of and in contrast to our King analysis. The chapter then brings together our views on the role of religion and politics, arguing that all views presented in public political debates need to be reasonable, and providing an overview of what it means to be reasonable. Given our critique of the liberal solution and our conclusions about public reason and our argument that the religious worldview should have some limited place in public discourse, it becomes necessary to re-envision the relationship between religion and the state. We turn to this challenging topic in the last chapter. After a brief overview of the conventional view, both morally and legally, we develop an argument that it is no longer possible to put religion into a separate category (either to its detriment or for its protection). This prompts us to consider the question of the limits of what is allowed in public deliberation and to consider a worry about the tyranny of the majority and the related phenomenon of populism (which is garnering renewed attention today in democratic nations around the world). The chapter concludes with ten suggestions for how best to engage in public discourse in a democracy.

This book is not aimed only at philosophers and specialists, but is intended to be accessible to the general, educated reader. My hope is that it will appeal to non-philosophers who have an interest in the theory of democracy, in the phenomenon of secularization, in freedom and pluralism, and in related topics such as the role of religion in a democratic state, the growing prominence of secularism, and the rise of relativism as a specter hanging over public discourse. My general approach is that of a religious believer who welcomes secular liberal democracy but who is concerned about recent trends of relativism and the attack on reason, and the incommensurability of worldviews that leads to a contentious pluralism. Unlike secular liberals, who wish to exclude religious perspectives from politics, the view I develop does not exclude secularist views from playing a role in political deliberation.

Our study is not intended to be yet another exhaustive reading of liberal political theory, nor does it get bogged down in painstaking reading of original texts or in excessive analysis of secondary sources. While obviously important in their place, such an approach is not appropriate for our topic because it requires delving too much into scholarly minutiae, which not only tests the patience of readers but can become a serious obstacle to the development and understanding of the general argument. Given that philosophy, in particular, is in real danger of becoming too specialized, we need to occasionally seek the indulgence of professional philosophers and academics as we try to discuss broader themes with the aim of making a fascinating and important set of topics accessible to a wider, interested audience. Nevertheless, my aim is to develop a plausible and rigorous argument, while trying hard not to be overly technical or to employ academic jargon to such an extent that the larger questions become obscured and stripped of their interest. From the point of view of the development of the argument, the central chapters of 7 and 8 will likely be the most challenging for the non-specialist.

I have tried to write in an engaging, accessible style, and to use detailed examples in order to make sophisticated arguments more concrete. This study is not intended to be the final word on the topic (God forbid), but aims at a modest set of reflections in order to help us understand the present situation in the modern pluralist state, and to further the discussion about the future of democracy. The book may be of special interest to those who work more directly with issues of democracy, politics, and civic matters on a regular basis such as social workers, judges, lawyers, politicians, teachers, pastors, theologians and students of theology, workers in non-profits and other organizations that wish to have an influence on public policy. My overall aim is to stimulate further reflection on a vitally important topic for our times: the nature of democracy and its (foundational) problems, how it came to be in its present condition, how to understand and respond to that condition, and where it may be heading in the future.

Like all authors, I am indebted to others for helping me bring this book to fruition! I am especially grateful to Philip Getz, and the staff at Palgrave Macmillan, for their encouragement and early support of the project, and for making the editorial process as smooth as possible. I owe my great thanks to Professor Bill Stancil for his rich insights, stimulating conversation, and invaluable feedback on the whole manuscript. I also wish to thank Tina Baceski, Christopher Callaway, Desmond Egan, Doug Geivett, Catherine Green, Curtis Hancock, Mario Ramos Reyes, Craig Sasse, Tom Seaver, John Sheil, and Turner White for insightful discussion and advice along the way. I am grateful also for perceptive feedback from anonymous referees. I have sometimes used a phrase or two, or a couple of paragraphs, from material I have published previously, and I thank InterVarsity Press and the editors of the *International Philosophical Quarterly* for granting permission. Rockhurst University awarded me a summer research grant to work on the project, which was greatly appreciated. I also benefited from efficient, helpful assistance from the library staff at Rockhurst. As always, my greatest debt of gratitude is to my family for their strong support and encouragement, without which this book would not have been possible!

Kansas City, MO, USA   Brendan Sweetman

Contents

Part I Democracy and Freedom: Pluralism, Reason, and
        Relativism   1

1 Introduction: Democracy in Crisis?   3
   What the Crisis Is Not   4
   The Democratic System and Democratic Values   7
   Familiar Practical Problems Facing the Democratic System   18
   Overview of the Crisis: Themes of This Book   29

2 Freedom and Disagreement in a Democracy   41
   Locke and Mill on Freedom   45
   Mill's Arguments for Freedom of Thought and Expression   52
   Does Freedom of Expression Lead to Relativism?   54
   The Temptation to Suppress "Objectionable" Views   62

3 Worldviews, Pluralism, and Loss of Confidence in Reason   71
   Worldviews and Pluralism   72
   *The Problem of Worldview Pluralism and its Origin: A
   Tentative Causal Argument*   78
   Loss of Confidence in Reason: Anti-Realist Views of Knowledge   86
   Pluralism as a Cultural Phenomenon   93

4	Democracy and Relativism	101
	Relativism as a Cultural Phenomenon	102
	A Postmodern World	104
	Relativism as Rhetorical Strategy	107
	Relativism in Ordinary Moral Debate	112
	Problems for Relativism	117
	Disagreement, Incommensurability, and Relativism	119

Part II Secularization and Political Liberalism: The Exclusion of Religion   123

5	Religion, and the Rise of Secularism	125
	The Worldviews of Religion and Secularism	126
	Areas of Disagreement and Some Qualifications	134
	Secularism and Western Societies	137
	Case Study: Philosophical Secularism in the Work of Philip Kitcher	142

6	Secularizing Society	157
	Secularism and Secularization	158
	The Secularization Thesis	160
	Reflections on the Concept of "The Secular"	165
	Passive and Active Secularism	172
	Case Study: Republic of Ireland	174
	Immature and Mature Secularism	182

7	Secular Liberalism and the Exclusion of Religious Worldviews	187
	Assumptions of Modern Secular Liberalism	188
	Reasonable Pluralism in John Rawls	194
	Rawls and Habermas on Public Reason	199
	Audi on Excluding Religious Views from Democratic Politics	206

Part III Reasonable Worldviews and Public Deliberation:
          The Way Ahead   215

8   Public Reason   217
    Reasonable Pluralism and Interpretations of Public Reason 218
    How Would Public Reasoning Work?   224
    Rejecting Public Reason?   233
    Case Study: Arguing About Abortion in the Public Square   236
    The Reasoning Process Versus the Conclusions of Reason   242

9   Worldviews in Politics, and the Failure of Liberalism   253
    Religion in Politics   254
    Case Study: Martin Luther King, Jr. and Civil Rights   262
    Assessment of Rawls and Political Liberalism   268
    Secularism, Religion, and Politics   274

10 Re-envisioning Church and State   283
    Re-envisioning the "Separation" of Church and State   284
    Democracy and Populism   294
    A Worry About the Tyranny of the Majority   304
    Guidelines for Public Discourse: Ten Suggestions   309

Bibliography   319

Index   327

About the Author

Brendan Sweetman is Professor of Philosophy and holds the Sullivan Chair in Philosophy at Rockhurst University, Kansas City, Missouri, USA. A native of Dublin, he is the author or editor of fifteen books, including *Evolution, Chance, and God* (2015), *Religion and Science: An Introduction* (2010), *The Vision of Gabriel Marcel* (2008), *Why Politics Needs Religion: The Place of Religious Arguments in the Public Square* (2006), and *Contemporary Perspectives on Religious Epistemology* (1992). Author of over one hundred articles and critical reviews in a variety of journals, collections, and reference works, Professor Sweetman is an elected Fellow of the *International Society for Science and Religion* (Cambridge, U.K.). His work has been translated into several languages, including Spanish, Portuguese, Italian, Polish, and Persian.

PART I

Democracy and Freedom: Pluralism, Reason, and Relativism

CHAPTER 1

Introduction: Democracy in Crisis?

The political system of democracy, often regarded as one of the most advanced and even perhaps as the only legitimate political arrangement, even possibly as one of the achievements of humankind, may in fact be reaching something of a crisis. The crisis runs deep into the very foundations of the system, and it is difficult to foresee or predict the eventual outcome. The political arrangement of monarchy lasted for more than a thousand years, only to be gradually replaced by democratic forms of government, which have really only existed for two hundred and fifty years, even though a form of democracy actually goes back to the time of ancient Greece (800–400 BC). Yet, several current developments that have become part and parcel of democracy as it is now practiced appear to have begun to slowly undermine it as an effective political arrangement, and raise a question from within it that was almost unthinkable fifty years ago: will the democratic form of government survive? Will it perhaps strengthen its influence in countries across the globe, or will it collapse and self-destruct, and be superseded by new political structures as the twenty-first century unfolds?

Of course, we must be careful and quite clear about what we mean when we say that there is something of a crisis facing modern democracy. Our suggestion that there are looming fault lines must be somewhat tentative, for two reasons. First, the underlying problems that contribute to the crisis are at different stages of development and influence in various democratic countries; general trends may peter out and come to nothing

© The Author(s), under exclusive license to Springer Nature Switzerland AG 2021
B. Sweetman, *The Crisis of Democratic Pluralism*,
https://doi.org/10.1007/978-3-030-78382-2_1

in some or even all of them, or certain defining forces may lead to the undermining and eventual breakup of the democratic form of government. Second, the crisis has its roots in modern developments that concern the *foundations* of democracy; it takes time for such developments to have an obvious influence at the practical level of public discussion and democratic decision-making, and indeed we are only now beginning to see these effects at this level. There is every reason to believe that the consequences at the practical level will only get worse as time goes on and that the crisis will become more evident. But there are enough signs of it now to identify it, discuss its causes and its implications, and talk about a way forward, though I am afraid that at this juncture the problems appear quite intractable and solutions may prove elusive.

What the Crisis Is Not

The suggestion that there is "something of a crisis" surrounding modern democracy is a bit of dramatic claim, so we need to be clear about just what we are saying. It is true that the word crisis is invoked with increasing frequency today to describe difficulties with the democratic political arrangement. Yet, more often than not it is used to convey straightforward, though strong, disagreement over political policy matters, or as a scaremongering tactic to express frustration that the democratic process does not yield the conclusions one thinks it should yield. My claim is that the crisis is deeper than these worries, one that originates in and threatens the very foundations of the democratic system of government. We should distinguish this understanding from several other possible meanings of the claim that democracy is in crisis that have become prominent in recent discussions of the topic.

One way to interpret the claim that democracy is in crisis might be that although countries officially adhere to the democratic political process, and are supposed to make most major decisions through popular sovereignty or representative governmental structures (both at local and national level), they do not in fact do this. One might refer to the Kingdom of Cambodia as an example; the country is officially a constitutional monarchy (like the United Kingdom), but (also like the United Kingdom) operates in practice as a parliamentary democracy, with representative government and national elections. However, despite this, the current Prime Minster (as of 2020), Hun Sen (in power since 1985), is accused of operating a de facto dictatorship, which the people tolerate because of continued economic prosperity after the unstable and murderous prior reign of Pol Pot. Another more recent example of this phenomenon can be found in Venezuela, which is led by Nicholas Maduro, and, despite officially being a democratic country, it is now run as a dictatorship (with some constitutional rights actually suspended in 2017, along with the suspension of the National Assembly). It seems to be the case in Venezuela that many decisions are in fact made without the consent of the people because of voter manipulation, rigging of election results, intimidation tactics, and subtle and not-so-subtle manipulation of the political process with the aim of bypassing the will of the people. However, in developed Western societies, which we are mostly focusing on in our discussion in this book, although the claim is often advanced from time to time that this or that country does not adhere to the democratic process, this is not a major problem facing the democratic arrangement. In most Western countries, people are quite free to vote, and most elections run smoothly and the outcome is accepted by all. Even attempts to deny this fact are usually motivated more by dissatisfaction with the results of an election rather than by any real belief that the process had been compromised. Lamentations about the state of modern democracy are often inspired by a desire to reverse the results of an election rather than a genuine worry that these results were not arrived at democratically! While rigged elections, suppression of votes, and voter intimidation occur in some democratic countries (e.g., in some of the countries in South America), these are not serious problems in Western democracies.

A second meaning is that "special interest groups," especially those that have significant public support and (most importantly) large financial clout, may use their authority and financial might to dictate the agenda of politicians without regard to the wishes of the electorate. (They also dispense largesse to politicians in many other ways, all too familiar to us, such as through dangling lobbyist jobs, future appointments to corporate boards, insider information about company stocks, fact-finding missions to the Bahamas, airline conferences in Tahiti, and other lucrative junkets, large and small!). These are certainly problems with the democratic system, and the word crisis is often used to describe and bemoan them. Yet these drawbacks arise mainly from abuses by people acting in immoral ways within the system, or at least against the spirit of democracy. While it is often very difficult to control and regulate against influence of this type, one of the differences between fledgling, immature democracies and mature, established democracies is that the latter have gotten better at minimizing these kinds of abuses. Perhaps they can never be eliminated completely, and we should always be on guard against them, but I don't regard them as problems that emerge from the *foundations* of democracy itself. So although this failure to adhere to the spirit of the democratic process is worrying, regrettable, and serious, it is not the kind of crisis we are talking about in this book.

A third possible meaning of the phrase "democracy is in crisis," especially understood as a reaction to recent election results in Europe (e.g., the Brexit vote in the U.K. in 2016) and America (the election of Donald Trump as President in the same year), is that a significant and influential minority, or various interest groups or adherents of a particular worldview, do not approve of or support the results of a particular election or referendum. This evocation of the term may perhaps be regarded simply as a parochial dissatisfaction with current election trends, a temper tantrum because a particular election did not bring the outcome one wishes for. Although he identifies several serious problems with the democratic system in an overall insightful discussion, this is the primary meaning of crisis appealed to in the work of philosopher, A.C. Grayling, and others who bemoan the fact that they do not approve of recent outcomes of the democratic process in various countries, and so are tempted to exaggerate their disagreement into a crisis![1] Those who use the word "crisis" to express their disappointment and indeed abhorrence at recent election trends that do not accord with their preferences then sometimes mistakenly conclude that there must be something wrong with the democratic system as a whole! It must be in crisis because it did not arrive at the "right conclusions" (i.e., at my views!). The suggestion is that if only the electorate was more informed, more educated, less fickle, less emotional, less prejudiced, they would have voted for *my* preferred outcome or candidate. (We will return to this general criticism of democracy later in our chapter, and in our discussion of the notion of populism later in the book.)

While this reaction and judgment is perhaps understandable from a human point of view, especially in current democratic settings where there is sharp polarization between the different sides on many issues, it cannot be said to describe a crisis originating in the foundations of democracy. Indeed, in all such cases the democratic process operated smoothly in making decisions about the election of leaders and in the settling of questions of public and social policy. It is an overreaction to conclude that democracy is failing or is in crisis simply because it produced a result with which one disagrees (however wrongheaded one believes the result to be).

Of course, from the point of view of objective truth and especially of objective morality, the majority could vote incorrectly or make a wrong choice, but this is a logical risk one is prepared to endure as part of a democratic arrangement. (It is also important to keep in mind that the person who judges that the democratic majority has made a mistake might themselves be wrong, no matter how sincere or convinced they may be!) And so what we have in this particular case is mostly a political disagreement, not a real crisis with democracy itself. We will see later that part of the deeper crisis is that people who are equally well-informed and equally well-educated still fail to come to agreement on topics of life, law, and culture.

THE DEMOCRATIC SYSTEM AND DEMOCRATIC VALUES

Our topic in this book is the crisis that is emerging gradually in many countries that favor the democratic form of government. So before we attempt to identify the ideas, trends, and cultural, moral, and political developments that are contributing to and leading to this crisis, it will be helpful to remind ourselves of what we mean by the democratic system, with a view particularly to identifying the central beliefs, values, and themes that provide the foundation for this form of government. We need to keep these central themes in mind for our purposes in this book, and they will be reflective of what we understand by democracy in subsequent chapters. There are obviously different versions of the democratic system, and several different theories of democracy as well.[2] The democratic form of government may be exemplified in different structures; indeed, we see this around the world wherever democracy is practiced (e.g., a presidential system vs. a parliamentary system); we also note that its structure occasionally undergoes significant change over time within a nation (e.g., senators to the U.S. Congress were initially appointed by State legislatures; now they are elected by the general population in each state). It may also be paired with different types of economic system, and individual forms of it may emphasize certain values over others in actual practice.

For our purposes, we do not need a precise and exhaustive definition of democracy nor a thorough understanding of the system, if there is such a thing. The word itself comes from two Greek words, *demos*, meaning the people, and *kratia*, meaning rule or power, reflecting the idea of rule by the people. We understand by a democracy a system of government in which the leaders and members of government are elected by the people every few years by popular vote. In this system, every person over the age of 18 (usually) is eligible to vote. In modern democracies, elected leaders are representatives in the sense that they make decisions on behalf of the people and are subject to ongoing accountability (through regular elections). So all government legislation ideally is subject to the will of the people; the notion of *the consent of the governed* is therefore paramount in a democracy, at least ideally (we know that it does not always work out this way in practice). The notion of the consent of the governed (a phrase used in the U.S. Declaration of Independence, but the idea goes back to at least Aristotle[3]) reminds us that democracies decide things by majority vote; it does not mean that *everyone* living in the state must give their consent before a decision can be made at the local or national level, or before a piece of legislation can be passed. Consent also carries with it, crucially, the idea that everyone who is voting age should have a say in decisions that affect them (a key aspect of freedom, as we will see momentarily), but agree to be bound by the majority will. This system recognizes that logically everyone will not agree on every issue, and so those views that can only command minority support always lose out in any election or referendum. Democracy, however, should not be seen as just a matter of the consent of the governed, or of holding regular elections; democratic systems are also usually founded on three crucial moral values, justice, freedom, and equality, in addition to a strong emphasis on some scheme of natural rights, about which more in a moment.

Democratic theory often distinguishes between a democracy and a republic, though the distinction is not universally accepted or used, and is often controversial. The usual way of drawing the distinction is to say that in a republic the rights of minorities are protected in some way in the law and in the constitution, if there is one. For example, a democratic republic with a majority religion would be expected to protect the rights of minorities to practice their religion, at least to some extent. "Minority rights" should be understood to refer to rights that every citizen possesses, but that only a smaller group would exercise. Most modern democracies are republics in this sense, since another feature of them is that they have a scheme of rights in place that all citizens hold by virtue of their nature as human beings, and this would include many of the rights that minorities might claim. Of course, there is often a dispute about what these rights are, a topic that remains contentious today (of which more later). It is possible to have a democracy that might not call itself a republic but in which the rights of minorities are also protected, so it is not a hard and fast distinction. (Indeed, sometimes the term is invoked to describe a democratic nation that does not have a monarchy; it was also used in the past to distinguish between direct and representative democracy—this is how James Madison understood the distinction).

In many democracies there is a necessity for a certain amount of tolerance, since, especially in a pluralist democracy, different views will emerge on defining issues of human nature, morality, and human rights. This matter is a key theme in this book, one we will return to throughout (indeed, the fact that the values of tolerance and free speech are under pressure today, that democratic nations are becoming less tolerant of opposing views and are moving to impose a uniformity of opinion on the whole of society, is further evidence of our current crisis). But for now let us note that one would expect to find an emphasis on tolerance to a significant degree in a democratic society, at least in principle. Modern democracies have also tended to be strongly capitalist in terms of economic system, perhaps with some socialist tendencies, some more than others. Although not a major theme in our discussion, we will understand democracy in its modern forms to include a capitalist economic system, even though it is debatable whether it has to be capitalist in its definition.

In terms of its history, the democratic form of government goes back famously to Ancient Greece, to the time of Plato. The Greeks practiced a form of direct democracy in which the people (adult male citizens who had completed military training) were consulted directly about issues facing the city-states (as they then were), such as the makeup of the city Assembly and regarding the decisions of the Assembly. Plato was famously critical of this system of government in his best known work, *The Republic*, for various reasons. One of his main worries was that the mass of people, made up of ordinary members of the general public, did not have sufficient knowledge to make wise moral and political decisions. He also distrusted what he called "the democratic character" because it involved an unhealthy emphasis on freedom, and he thought it would eventually lead to behavior dominated by selfishness and licentiousness at the expense of the common good. He understands freedom as, or as mainly leading to, license, which encourages us to arrange our lives according to our (capricious) wishes. Hedonism and indolence follow, and eventually severe corruption, even tyranny.[4]

Although there were what might be described as democratic moments in various civilizations throughout ancient and medieval times, the democratic form of government was generally frowned upon throughout the centuries, and we do not see its reappearance in a developed way until the eighteenth century in the United Kingdom, France, and the United States. Its success in the U.S., coupled with the U.S. promotion of it worldwide, has led to the democratic system becoming a popular form of government in the last two hundred years, especially for new nations. Perhaps it can be accurately described as the presumptively most morally desirable form of government today. However, because of its relative newness when compared to other forms of government, its future is far from certain, and the recent trends that we will identify and discuss in this book raise worries about its long-term prospects. At very least, it is no longer alarmist or an overreaction to consider the question of its future, a question that prompts us to focus especially (as we will see) on the foundational values and structure of the democratic system.

The U.S. Founding Fathers (including Thomas Jefferson, John Adams, Alexander Hamilton, John Jay, and James Madison) were influenced by the thought of several thinkers of the seventeenth century, such as Thomas Hobbes, Jean-Jacques Rousseau, Baron Montesquieu, Baruch Spinoza, David Hume, and perhaps especially John Locke.[5] The work of these thinkers began an important debate about the next steps for government after the Reformation, and through the Enlightenment period (1660–1800 approx.). It was a time of political and religious upheaval in Europe and America, which involved not just a fascinating debate about political ideas, but significant political events such as the Thirty Years' War, the growth of democracy in England, and the French and American Revolutions. During this period, democratic values and the democratic form of government began to emerge as a serious political force in the world.[6] It is perhaps too much of a reach to say that the Founding Fathers of the U.S. implemented the political theory of John Locke, but most of the main ideas came from Locke (with some help from other thinkers of the time), and were gradually refined to become associated with the democratic form of government.[7] There are five key ideas that are usually at the heart of the theory of democracy, no matter what form it eventually takes in a particular historical setting: popular sovereignty, natural rights, equality, freedom, and justice.

Democracy is most associated of course with the idea of popular sovereignty, the idea of one person, one vote, or more generally that the people vote directly for their leaders, and that the leaders are held accountable periodically to the will of the people. As Locke argued, the people are ultimately sovereign in this type of government, a view that was a radical break with previous systems, such as monarchy or plutocracy, where the general populace had little or no say in the running of their own affairs.[8] The justification for popular sovereignty, although often not expressed this way, *involves appeal to a certain view of human nature*. It involves the idea that freedom is an essential feature of human nature, that people should have a certain range or sphere of freedom to make their own decisions about important issues that affect them such as who their leaders are to be, which economic policies should be pursued, which laws should be enacted, the content of educational curricula, the culture in which they will rear their children, and so forth. So in this way, democracy and freedom go together. Of course, in early democracies the populace did not initially have a say on many of these issues, but in principle these are the kinds of things on which the individual citizen, both logically and morally, should have a say. There is often debate about the range of topics on which the populace should have direct input; but again the key point in a democratic form of government is that this matter should also ideally be decided by the general population, whether they wish to restrict their own freedom in certain ways by law or by delegating some matters to their representatives.

It was also recognized by Locke and others that representative democracy was a better form of government than direct democracy. Representative democracy requires that the people elect leaders to *represent* them in government decision-making on the issues of the day. Again, the actual structure of representative government varies in different countries, and has changed over time in some countries, as noted above. Each country has arrived at a practice that works well for them, and no doubt there are disadvantages and advantages in each arrangement. With regard to representative democracy, the system also recognizes a general distinction between reactive leadership or representation and proactive leadership or representation. Leadership is often reactive in the sense that the people's representative stays very close to the will of the people, and generally only supports or implements in government policy what the people wish for or agree to as gauged by public opinion and concern, as far as it is possible to do so. Yet there is a proactive dimension to leadership too, where leaders may have their own ideas about what is good for the people and the nation, even though the populace may not be convinced, and then attempts to persuade the electorate of their point of view. The best leaders would employ a combination of both approaches, but the main point is that the people will ultimately judge by virtue of their power of sovereignty which ideas a representative should support. A representative government will obviously be reactive and proactive at different times, and would hope that at election time their proactive policies prove palatable to the electorate. This seems essential to the effective governing of a country, in which, inevitably, the government must occasionally support unpopular policies; for example, implementing an austerity program when a country is in the midst of severe economic distress.[9] So perhaps the central meaning of democracy is that the people have an obvious say in *the running of their own affairs* by means of the exercise of popular sovereignty.

Initially, as we noted earlier with regard to Ancient Greece, the vote was restricted to certain classes of people, usually wealthy men. John Stuart Mill proposed an (elitist) system of plural voting, in which the more educated would receive more votes than the less educated because of their mental superiority.[10] Gradually, however, the franchise was extended to include all men, then women.[11] There is still debate from time to time about the minimum age requirement for voters, and whether or not one should have to pass a literacy or some type of general knowledge test in order to be eligible to vote. Voting is compulsory in some countries (e.g., Peru, Belgium, and Australia), but in most nations the franchise is voluntary.

This brings us to the foundational value of freedom. A central tenet of the democratic approach to government is that people should make key decisions for themselves on important issues that affect their lives, and the lives of their families and children. The justification for this involves a claim about the nature of the human person, although, as already mentioned, it is not usually expressed in quite that way. But freedom has often been looked upon with suspicion by many thinkers and leaders because they believe it has a danger attached to it that could be detrimental to society. One can clearly see this in Plato's critique of democracy. The idea is that too much freedom for citizens is bad for society because people will often make uninformed, usually short-term type, and occasionally destructive, choices, choices that would be deleterious for them and their country. And so ancient societies generally held the view that it is better to have a paternalistic form of government where the ordinary mass of mankind are led by more educated and enlightened people or groups who dictate (if we might use that word!) the "correct" choices rather than allowing the populace to make such decisions for themselves. Plato and others believed that this was the best way not just to keep order in a country, but to produce a society that contributes to human fulfillment.

As we will see in the next chapter in detail, democratic political theory, especially under the influence of John Stuart Mill, challenged this view, and held that because freedom is a key part of human nature, society should respect a large element of (though not total) freedom for the individual. Though, even the constraints on freedom in a democratic society must be understood as constraints that people place (freely through laws) upon *their own choices*, rather than being imposed upon them in some way independently of the democratic process. And so, unlike in many other forms of government, freedom became a central feature of democracy, not just in the exercise of being able to choose one's leaders, but in choosing one's own path in life, one's beliefs, and worldview, within certain limits (which will turn out to be a matter of serious contention). This general approach also led to worries about what Mill called the "tyranny of the majority," the idea (paradoxically) that a majority in a particular nation could democratically, through popular vote, restrict the freedom of minority opinion and practice, another contentious and challenging issue in the democratic system, and one we will return to in the next chapter.

Along with freedom comes an emphasis on equality. Equality is a powerful idea in political history. There is dispute about its origins, whether it comes from the Judeo-Christian view that all people are made equally in the image of God, or whether it comes from the Enlightenment view of the natural rights of the person. In any case, the idea is to be found in both Locke and Hobbes, and expresses the view that all human beings, just by virtue of being human, have a fundamental equality with all other human beings. Of course, such a view was not practiced at the political level until quite recently (nor is there agreement in modern democracies about what it means in particular contexts). But the basic claim is that human beings are all fundamentally the same and so essentially equal, a conclusion that has far-reaching political consequences; for example, it will mean, as Locke noted, that everyone is entitled to a fair trial in a court of law (and not just members of the aristocracy, or the rich and powerful), that everyone has the same set of natural rights (whatever these turn out to be), that everyone is entitled to a certain amount of freedom in society (to practice one's religion, for instance). It is indeed a very powerful claim that there is a fundamental sameness about all human beings that cuts across ethnic, national, and cultural differences, and a claim that obviously has far-reaching implications for how society should be structured.

While equality and freedom are closely related, equality and justice may be even closer, because equality suggests the value of justice, and since justice involves the notion of fairness, then it also demands a certain equality between people. The fundamental idea involved in the concept of justice is fairness, the idea not only that a particular person should be treated fairly (e.g., in the law courts, or with regard to government benefits or salary or tax issues) but the recognition that people be treated fairly in relation to each other, so the concept naturally leads to the idea of equality. Justice also has a broader application, especially in modern democracies, to include the view that economic disadvantages or hardships in society should not affect only one group or class of people, and that society should try to alleviate economic distress in a way that is fairly distributed. Of course, there is no agreement on how to decide or resolve many of these challenging issues in contemporary democratic societies either at the abstract or the concrete level.

This difficulty reminds us of a key truth about the values of freedom, equality, and justice, so central to democratic societies. These are *abstract* values, and problems usually arise when we try to elaborate what they mean in more *concrete* terms, or when we try to develop government or societal policies based on these values (e.g., in areas like economics, education, social welfare programs, tax codes). This was a point some thinkers worried about, such as Edmund Burke, who thought that governments would encounter a serious problem when they tried to express what he called "abstract rights" in a concrete form in a particular cultural context (such as French society after the coming Revolution) because it would likely lead to unfairness or injustice (even, as Burke correctly predicted, to violence).[12] Yet, these values do have some content even at the abstract level; for example, the idea of freedom in a democratic context suggests that individuals should have a significant sphere of freedom to make decisions on issues that affect them (more freedom than one would have in a monarchy or a communist state), and the idea of justice indicates that a person should be treated fairly in his or her dealings with individuals and with state institutions. Nevertheless, problems arise at the practical level because there is often disagreement about how far the sphere of freedom should extend (how far should freedom of religion extend; does the sphere of freedom extend to include legal gun ownership; to a right to euthanasia, etc.?), and also about which policy best expresses that freedom in specific cases (e.g., whether or not a particular tax code is fair to everyone in a society). These are difficult, contentious questions; the important point is that there is no ready-made or built-in answer to them, and so they are frequently the subject of dispute in modern democratic nations.

This brings us then to the last defining theme in the democratic system: the theme of the natural rights of a human being. Thinkers such as Locke and Mill framed much of their political theories, as well as their work on toleration and freedom, in terms of giving expression to the rights of the individual person. Rights (not uncontroversially) might be initially understood as a useful way of translating traditional moral values and virtues into a theory of rights and responsibilities; thus the notion of self-preservation and the value of life, as defended for instance in the natural law theory of St. Thomas Aquinas, could be expressed in the claim that every human being has a right to life. A further important part of the theory of rights is that a human being possesses rights *by virtue of being human*, leading to the implication that a main task of the democratic state is to protect and facilitate human or natural rights. Rights are therefore understood to be part of the nature or essence of what it means to be human; values that define the basic worth of a human being.[13] They are often interpreted as an expression of more traditional religious notions of human dignity and respect. They are not to be confused with legal rights, which refer to rights given to citizens in law in a particular society (these will normally correspond to the set of natural rights in most democratic societies, but they may include other rights, such as a right to hire a lawyer when before the law courts, that is not part of the essence of being human). Over time in modern thinking about rights, the notion of the responsibilities of human beings toward each other along with their duties in society gradually disappeared in favor of an almost exclusive emphasis on individual rights. The main rights Locke and Mill had in mind were the obvious ones, such as the rights to life, property, and certain personal freedoms, but many other rights were later added to the list.

One of the issues that rights theories in the context of a democracy struggled with, and continue to do so, concerns how to determine the range of rights that belong to the individual, and how these rights are justified in a philosophical sense. Where do natural rights come from, and what is the range of rights possessed by human beings? Rights are usually described as "natural" or "human," or sometimes as "moral" rights, which conveys the understanding that they are possessed in virtue of our nature as human beings, and are not earned, or simply given to us by the government, or some other privileged group; so the justification of rights becomes a problem if one denies the existence of human nature. Locke's view was that such rights come from God, but if one rejects a religious origin for natural rights, one will need to find another way to ground rights philosophically. This is a pressing issue because if human beings are to have civil rights, most of these would be based upon natural or moral rights, and so these latter would need to be rationally justified. Whatever theory one puts forward to justify moral rights would need to explain why these rights are good, why human beings ought to have them, and why they should be promoted at the political level. Liberal political philosophers, in particular, have struggled with this question because they have usually wished to deny any metaphysical basis to the justification of rights, either in God or human nature. They have often appealed to a societal consensus to ground them, or to suggest that structural features of democracy itself might somehow contain or reveal a scheme of rights, which might not then require any further independent philosophical justification (we will return to this view in later chapters).

Another difficulty facing thinking about natural rights is whether some rights are absolute (e.g., the right to life), and how to deal with conflicts between rights (e.g., the right to freedom of expression vs. the right to privacy). As our understanding of democracy has increasingly being articulated in recent times around the notion of the rights of the individual, societies have struggled with questions such as whether the unborn have a right to life, whether capital punishment violates the rights of a person, or whether everyone has a right to a job. While democracies are quick to express many of their moral beliefs and their laws in terms of rights, there is considerable disagreement over the overall justification of rights, the range of rights, and their application in particular cases. Nevertheless, the important point we need to emphasize is that rights are now understood to be a central theme of democratic societies, and their protection is seen as one of the main aims of the modern state. We will not defend any theory of rights in this book since that is not our task, but assume that citizens in a democracy will enjoy a basic scheme of rights in the modern understanding of democracy.

These five key values are often referred to as liberalism, or sometimes as classical liberalism, or as the classical view of liberal democracy.[14] Although democracy today is usually referred to as "liberal democracy," we should note that one can distinguish between them to some extent depending on the features and values one wishes to emphasize, though as Josiah Ober has succinctly put it, today "liberalism is the dominant value system in which democracy has been interwoven."[15] But democracy as a political system could be more narrowly defined perhaps to include majority decision-making, representative government, adherence to what has become known as "the rule of law," a concern to design a system to minimize the abuse of power, holding regular elections, the protection of certain minority rights, and so forth. It would also include the essential points that human freedom must be limited and is not absolute, that part of the democratic system is to agree to accept the majority decision with the understanding that the minority is free to challenge results and to try to change people's minds peacefully (thus freedom is necessary). Perhaps the theory of democracy would also include the protection of private property (one of the key themes in Locke), and the attempt to promote economic prosperity.

The definition of democracy (perhaps) need not necessarily include the liberal values of freedom, equality, and justice, though as we have seen it is very hard to elaborate the form of government just described without some reference to liberal values. Joseph Schumpeter, a critic of democracy, argued for a "minimalist" approach, one that did not pay such homage to what he regarded as the unrealistic ideals noted (as we will see further below). It is important to note that we can still distinguish democracy from what we might call philosophical liberalism.[16] This latter worldview would include a commitment to the political system of democracy along with a robust theory of liberal values that includes specifying a particular definition or understanding of each value *before*, rather than after, a process of public deliberation in a particular democratic state. It also tends to be secularist, though it need not be. Since liberals do not always agree among themselves about these definitions, there are several different versions of philosophical liberalism. Modern academics and liberal political philosophers tend to hold a more extreme version of liberalism than the general population in democratic countries. Indeed, a considerable source of difficulty is that while citizens today would mostly describe themselves as liberal democrats, they do not agree on which version of philosophical liberalism one should follow, or indeed on whether we should follow any version of it! One of the problems with liberal political philosophers in particular is that they can be heavy handed in insisting that there is only one version of liberalism, or refuse to respect the disagreement that emerges from the fact that there are different versions, and promote a kind of doctrinaire liberalism. (Indeed, one definition of democracy, especially in the context of liberalism, is that one person, or some elite faction, does not get to determine *what is reasonable* for everybody.) But there are clear disagreements for instance about how values are to be weighted in relation to each other, such as liberty and equality. We should also note that philosophical liberalism is a worldview, which includes metaphysical beliefs, whereas pluralism should be understood more broadly as the presence of many worldviews in the same state, including philosophical liberalism.

In our discussion, we will assume that everyone accepts the classical view of liberal democracy in some form (and indeed it is probably true that it has only existed in a developed form for little more than a hundred years, and the current version of it only for about fifty years). This means we accept popular sovereignty and the key values of freedom, equality, justice, and rights, without necessarily agreeing what these values mean in concrete terms, as noted above. This does not commit us to saying that democracy is necessarily the best possible political system, but, as we will see below, we are suggesting that whatever political system we accept should be based around some version of the key values mentioned. Scholars such as Sarah Conley and Jason Brennan have debated whether some other system might not be better than democracy for realizing such values.[17] We will not get into that interesting debate here. Instead, we will assume that a democratic system of government is in place based around these key values, and our discussion is taking place within this context. My position then is that democracy understood in this way is facing a crisis. Before we identify the crisis a bit more, let us place on the table some of the worst *practical* problems that continually worry us about the democratic form of government.

Familiar Practical Problems Facing the Democratic System

In everyday life in a democratic nation, we often experience and discuss problems that cause us to think that democracy is a seriously flawed set-up! Perhaps even that it is an unjust disgrace that should be abolished! These practical problems remind us of Winston Churchill's famous remark to the British House of Commons that some think democracy is the worst form of government, except for all the others! It frequently seems that the values inherent in the democratic system are often more honored in the breach that in the observance (as in most areas of life, perhaps). It will be good for us to identify briefly some of these problems in this section both to acknowledge them and to distinguish them from the problems already noted in the first part of the chapter, and also from the problems affecting the foundations of democracy that will be introduced in the next section and that will be our main focus in this book. Often when we reflect negatively on the democratic form of government the problems that we will identify in this section are the ones that irritate us, and occasionally it crosses our minds that democracy is indeed a seriously flawed arrangement because of them. Yet these problems do not stem from the *foundations* of the system. They seem akin to the kinds of problems we encounter as car owners. While we enjoy the great advantages that come with a car, we are also irritated regularly by the problems it brings, such as the need for regular (and expensive) repairs that cause inconvenience, frustration, and distress; the rising cost of insurance; the headache of traffic congestion; and so forth. Few would think of getting rid of their cars to avoid these problems; we just put up with them as the cost of enjoying the indispensable benefits of a car, and indeed sometimes our vehicle will even run smoothly for a welcome period of time!

These everyday problems that we run into at the practical level of living in a democratic country are not usually based on any deeper foundational or indeed ideological position. Yet, it is a fact that serious practical problems have emerged in many democratic countries, problems that perhaps cannot be fixed. This then prompts some to wonder whether these problems are so serious that democracy overall is starting a period of decline that may well lead to its end as a political system. It would take us too far away from our present task to discuss these problems here in detail but we can at least identify them and acknowledge that they are serious enough to cause great concern.

1. The first is the corruption of government leaders, politicians, and those involved in politics in an intimate way as advisors, appointees, election agents, consultants, those who seek government contracts, and so forth. Plato's concern about those with political power and influence succumbing to the temptation to increase their personal fortunes is an unfortunate reality in most democracies of the world. Moreover, it seems to be a systemic problem, and no matter how many rules and regulations we introduce to try to curb it, the abuse continues, from kickbacks, bogus consultancy fees, insider trading on the stock market, the awarding of contracts to friends or for financial gain, misuse of campaign funds, abuse of expense accounts, abuse of government patronage, bribery, retainers, "sweeteners" in relation to government business, junkets, and so forth. Despite tons of new rules and regulations, implementation of "best practices" and a slew of oversight procedures, we have not managed to stamp

out corruption, and every day we read of a new scandal involving a kickback scheme, political influence for financial gain, or misuse of campaign funds. No doubt all of this is partly due to the fact that we are dealing with flawed human beings, but the endemic corruption in democratic systems often prompts us to wonder whether some other political system would manage the problem of flawed human nature better!

2. Second, the need for politicians to pander to the electorate to win office is another serious concern that seems again systemic to this political arrangement. The strong temptation to offer short-term fixes to long-term problems that often succeeds only in making the problems worse, the reluctance to work with other political parties and rivals once elected, and the practice of constantly criticizing one's opponents for political gain, all seem to be problems that are getting worse not better. These flaws have played a significant contributory role in bringing some countries to the edge of financial (and by extension moral) bankruptcy. Allied to all of this is the fact that the emphasis on getting and then staying elected, along with the often brutal nature of political campaigns, seems to attract the wrong type of people to run for office, and leaves many of us quite sympathetic to Plato's observation that democratic governments are in the main run by incompetent idiots rather than qualified experts! The populace can become resigned to the view that the motivating factors in the democratic system are greed and a lust for power, and that the ideal—leadership based on vision and expertise, guided by morality and a desire to serve—is unattainable.

3. This issue is closely related to a third predicament, the fact that politicians need significant and sometimes even novel political issues and concerns upon which to base a campaign for office, issues that serve to define their candidacy, and which are too often deliberately developed in opposition to the views of their political rivals. This is particularly true in the race for the U.S. Presidency, where prospective candidates begin to formulate their campaign strategy and begin to seize on political issues and opportunities at least two years before election day! This desire for political power encourages candidates to carve out issues that they don't really believe in; it also tempts people to interpret or adapt an issue for political means to gain an advantage over their opponent. Indeed, some politicians as we know only too well would rather have a societal problem than its solution, especially coming into an election season! So it seems as if the democratic system actually encourages politicians to spend more time playing politics than governing.

4. A fourth problem is the extent of civil service power. There is a layer of decision-making in every democracy just below that of the elected representatives—the civil service and bureaucrats—who officially are supposed to implement policy but who usually have a large role in the making of it as well (this layer also includes powerful government agencies and entities such as the military, the law courts, various regulatory and state bodies). Indeed, there is always a worry that the civil service has too much power in policy-making in most democracies (while recognizing also that many civil servants are experts and contribute greatly to their nations). And this means that an unelected group makes many of the policy decisions that affect people's day-to-day lives in their jobs and in their communities (in recent times, this layer of decision-making is referred to in some countries derogatorily as the "deep state," and has come under increased scrutiny). This problem is particularly acute in the European Union, with its huge bureaucracy operating at a level far removed from official decision-making in member states. It is one of reasons for current widespread dissatisfaction with the impact of faceless policies coming from Brussels on member states, and one of the reasons that contributed to the U.K.'s vote to leave the E.U. in 2016. Regular elections that bring in new politicians, and so new bosses for the civil service, is one check on this power, but not a very effective one, since elections do not always bring change. Indeed, the civil service often has significant leverage over politicians, who are beholden to them for the implementation of their policies, the running of their office, and sometimes their reelection campaigns.

5. Related to this concern, fifth, is the increasing bureaucracy that seems to accompany modern democracy and be an inevitable part of it. This is a growing and disconcerting problem and a source of constant irritation for many. Indeed, it was first seriously identified as a growing problem by the sociologist, Max Weber, in his reflections on democracy (of which more in a moment). The escalating amount of paperwork and necessity to document every part of modern life is becoming a staple of Western societies. When coupled with the litigious nature of such societies, bureaucracy has led to a spate of deeper problems affecting the human spirit which many twentieth-century philosophers, such as Gabriel Marcel, Herbert Marcuse, and Miguel de Unamuno, have perceptively written about, of treating human beings as numbers or units, leading to identifying people with their functions. The bureaucratization of modern society has contributed to a sense of alienation and loss of meaning for many, and at the same time has allowed government agencies and private

corporations to treat human beings in a manner that regards them as means rather than as ends. Bureaucracies also cost a fortune to operate, thereby creating a beast that feeds itself! This phenomenon seems to be getting worse, not better. As an example, one might consider the burdensome paperwork required to purchase a house today, or to take up an offer of employment. The number of forms one is typically asked to add one's signature to, about which one has little knowledge, that are written in gobbledygook and that are often designed to protect a company legally, while masquerading as concern for the person, is truly shocking, even though over time we have become somewhat inured to it. Bureaucracies (particularly government, state, or municipal, or those in public bodies) are also quite renowned for significant amounts of waste and fraud.

6. Sixth, we must consider the increasing gap between rich and poor in democratic countries, between the haves and have-nots. While many people enjoy good paying jobs, significant savings and a pension for the future, others have none of these things and often have to work at more than one job just to make ends meet. This is a difficult issue to be clear about, and I do not want to say that it is a necessary consequence of democracy. Perhaps one could say that it is a necessary consequence of democracy together with a capitalist system, and that things would be better if we had a democracy coupled with a more socialist system, or with a blend of capitalism and socialism. We will not take a position on this challenging topic here but simply note two things: that a significant and increasing gap between rich and poor seems to be a feature of many democracies, and that it is not clear that the democratic system is capable of solving this dilemma.[18] Of course, there are other issues at play as well. The phenomenon of the underclass, as it is often referred to in modern societies, involves and leads to many undesirable social consequences and hardships, such as growing up in poverty, lack of family structure, failing schools, lack of job skills, depressed areas without jobs, lack of proper housing, dysfunctional behavior that leads to criminal records. The breakdown of the family, which is the root cause or a significant contributory cause, for many of these problems is a direct result of many liberalizing trends in modern culture, and this can be laid at the door of some form of secular liberalism. One could devote a whole book to a discussion of this topic but my main point is that these are very difficult problems in a democracy that are not easy to solve (indeed to many they seem intractable). Sometimes today when people become exasperated with democracy, they may be thinking of problems of this sort.

Aristotle noted that a democracy requires a large middle class, a large number of people that are reasonably well off. This is because, among other problems that can arise such as instability and lack of consensus, the presence of too many wealthy people can result in disproportionate economic and political influence, as we noted above, and a high number living in poverty has the result of marginalizing many from the political process because people are too busy trying to survive.[19] Perhaps the value of freedom, particularly the operation of free markets, is responsible for the gap between rich and poor, because as well as generating wealth in a general sense, free enterprise also enables particular individuals to make very large personal fortunes and therefore gain significant economic and political influence. Whatever the reason, and the issue is no doubt complicated, the gap between rich and poor seems to be a very disturbing feature of modern culture, and so one might conclude that economic reasons contribute in a significant way to the difficulties facing modern democracy (and might in the end fatally compromise democratic values). We should also note the ability of wealthy corporations and business trend setters to exploit people in various ways (such as creating false "needs" through manipulative advertising), and the apparent inability of the democratic system to prevent such exploitation.

7. Plato's general concerns about democracy are more serious than those already mentioned. They continue to be a source of frustration for many, and move our focus away from practical-type problems to more theoretical flaws facing the democratic model of government. Indeed, his concerns have engaged many thinkers, including Weber, Schumpeter, Lecky, and others, to varying degrees.[20] Earlier critics of the democratic system tended to adopt a more cynical outlook with regard to the democratic values and ideals championed by Locke, Mill, and the U.S. Founding Fathers. Influenced by Marx's critique of democracy and capitalism, Weber and Schumpeter, in particular, extended Plato's critique, though these thinkers seem to have believed that democracy might be saved if we approached it with more realistic, honest expectations, and if its aims were not so loftily conceived (as in classical liberalism). Weber, and later Schumpeter, thought it was somewhat naive to begin with foundational ideas, such as freedom and equality, and then decide how one could best realize them in society. Instead, we should examine how the democratic system works in practice, and then hone our theoretical understanding with a view to preserving the system's strengths. So, following Plato's line, they argued that at the practical level, the mass of people have little say in

governing, but suggested that this outcome was not as undesirable as it might initially seem, thereby moving the conception of the modern state in what would now be described as an elitist direction.

Weber understood the state as being less concerned with bringing about certain aims, and more as one that claimed (legitimate) authority to monopolize the use of violence within its territory, which was the source of its centralized power to enforce its decisions and laws. As he put it: "the state cannot be defined in terms of its ends ... [rather] today we have to say that a state is a human community that (successfully) claims the monopoly of the legitimate use of physical force within a given territory."[21] He seems to have regarded this power rather narrowly, not so much as a means to an end, but as a defining feature of the state itself. The main problem that faces the development of the modern state, for Weber, especially following the extension of the franchise, is that gradually political parties become dominant, and the voice of the individual voter grows more remote. Over time, winning elections and manipulation of voters becomes paramount, and very little democratic deliberation is actually carried out in parliament. He also lamented the fact that accompanying these trends is the rise of an electorate that is subject to emotional appeal and that is too easily swayed; so, what is needed are strong leaders who are more rational and wiser than the ordinary citizens. In short, what we need to cultivate, according to Weber, is a leadership class. He argued that we must recognize and indeed accept that the function of the electorate is not to actually govern, but to choose strong leaders who will govern! Elections then can be seen as a kind of referendum on our leaders; yet he believed that this understanding still maintains (what we can only describe as a semblance of) popular sovereignty. So Weber played down democratic values like rational deliberation, sovereignty, and freedom in favor of an elite leadership by those who were better educated, more reflective, and wiser than the masses.

These ideas were extended by Joseph Schumpeter in his influential book, *Capitalism, Socialism, and Democracy*. Adopting a practical, down to earth, and some would say, more cynical approach, Schumpeter argued that democracy is best understood as a method rather than as a theory of ideals. If we look at the political system honestly and observe carefully how it actually works, a more accurate definition is that "the democratic method is that institutional arrangement for arriving at political decisions in which individuals acquire the power to decide by means of a competitive struggle for the people's vote."[22] Understood this way, its aim is not necessarily to promote the democratic ideals of Locke and Mill (even though it could be used for this purpose, or part of this purpose). The tradition of democratic theory, especially in its contemporary expressions, has a tendency to see democracy as an end in itself, not as a procedure or as a method. Schumpeter gives short shrift to this understanding, arguing that it cannot be an end in itself because of the fickle and often irrational electorate that is an unavoidable part of how it works. Moreover, he thought that this latter problem could not be fixed because people are simply too far removed in their ordinary lives from political issues, especially at the national and international level. The masses concern themselves only with local matters; this is why they give more attention to their jobs and their hobbies than to national affairs. Unlike some contemporary thinkers, he believed that more education would not help correct this problem (indeed, those who are more educated tend to be even more absorbed with their private and local affairs).[23]

A consequence of Schumpeter's approach is that democracy could be used to promote other values, including some that are regarded as antidemocratic, such as curtailments on free speech or on equality. Indeed, he went on to defend an elitist view of leadership, under the influence of Weber's thought. In a clever analysis, he held that the ordinary person was not fit to rule, was often prejudiced, irrational and emotional, and argued eloquently in a famous passage that "the typical citizen drops down to a lower level of mental performance as soon as he enters the political field. He argues and analyzes in a way which he would readily recognize as infantile within the sphere of his real interests. He becomes a primitive again."[24] In a move clearly reminiscent of Plato, Schumpeter openly argued for a theory of "competitive leadership," the cultivation of a ruling class from which political leaders would be selected by regular elections (he regarded the leadership exemplified in English aristocratic society, including the civil service, as the best example of this). Such leaders would be people of education and wisdom, of high moral character and with excellent leadership skills.

Schumpeter believed that this is how democracy works in practice; he was not open to the view that it could be reformed to iron out its problems in order to realize the classical ideal. The ideals of earlier democratic theory are a bit of sham in any case because the people do not rule, he argued; rather the majority does, and even then, it is really the politicians that rule. Moreover, elections are simply a way for the people to choose who will lead, not a way of leading or ruling, as Weber had suggested.

Rule by the people made no sense in any case, according to Schumpeter, because there is no agreement on the nature of the common good (he regards his enemy throughout his work as the then popular theory of classical utilitarianism, with its emphasis on rationalization, calculation, and discerning the common good for all), yet he does not seem to have considered that this problem would also emerge among the leadership class (one of the deeper issues of this book). Like Weber, he thought that there was still a place for popular sovereignty in the democratic system, because elections were referendums on the leadership party, and a good amount of freedom of speech is necessary to ensure accountability. Schumpeter's view does foreshadow the problem that there is no agreed-upon view of the common good, the problem of pluralism that we are talking about in this book, yet he relies on the common good in another way, since the leadership class must themselves be committed to some vision of the good in order to rule.

There are echoes of these more theoretical worries in some recent contemporary criticisms of the democratic system. A common criticism today, raised by Grayling, Brennan, and others, is that the general populace in most democracies has two big vices: it is uninformed (some might say stupid and irrational) and often given to what we might call immoral impulses![25] This means that the average voter is not well-informed, well-educated, and reflective enough to make wise decisions and, moreover, is often motivated by self-interest, and even sometimes by prejudice or other undesirable emotions and attitudes that do not lead to good government. In addition, politicians and elected representatives, and other interest groups, including very powerful media forces, play and pander to these vices during political campaigns and public debates with the result that we end up with more bad leaders and bad decisions than good ones! These problems seem legitimate to many, and they appear to be getting worse. What is the solution? There are two avenues to think about. One is better civic education in schools and universities, and more emphasis on the democratic process and on the importance of making informed decisions (this latter would have to be a societal, not just an educational, task). The other perhaps is to try to put in place mechanisms and procedures aimed at reducing attempts to manipulate voters, such as better media standards, more responsible use of opinion polls, perhaps even reforms of the electoral system, and/or the structure of government (such as adopting a system of proportional representation rather than a first past the post system, requiring an absolute majority rather than a plurality to pass a measure or a law, making voting compulsory), all considerations that have pros and cons, and that would need to be subject to careful deliberation and refinement.

These critical reflections on the nature of democracy, both past and present, though insightful and thought-provoking, differ from the arguments we are making in this book. As I will come to in the next section, none of these worries concerning our understanding of democracy or measures for improvement get to the heart of the problem in which I am interested. For the fact is that *even if we had a fully informed, perfectly educated and extremely moral general populace, people will still disagree on central worldview questions of life, morality, politics, and culture.*[26] Perhaps the claim that the general populace today (especially those who actually vote) is uninformed and lacking in moral virtue is likely exaggerated in any case; some will find the lamentation that the ordinary person is irrational, stupid, and immoral perhaps a bit hard to take. This is a frequent complaint, particularly of those on the left side of the political spectrum, especially when the majority does not see things the way the left sees them. Perhaps we should not exaggerate this problem and should take it with a grain of salt, especially since the left has an unfortunate tendency today to immediately label anyone who disagrees with them as uninformed, immoral, or racist (even to sometimes propose psychological causes for why people don't see eye to eye with them!). It is getting harder today to distinguish between coming to think that those who arrive at what one might regard as the wrong or bad decisions nevertheless do so based on independent, rational, indeed often empirical, grounds, and the position that they are *bad* decisions just because I *disagree* with those decisions (Brexit being, I think, a textbook example)! It is common today to say that "people do not know their own interests" but then to judge their interests as being identical with the political views of their critics! This is a difficult problem to navigate through in a contentious political atmosphere, and one even sees it creeping into academic discussions where there is a tendency to *advocate* political views in the way terms are defined, in how issues are framed, and even with regard to the type of views one deigns to discuss, another clear sign of the problem we wish to identify in this book.

We can agree that democracy needs a well-educated and informed electorate to function well, but it is not a serious criticism today in mature civilized nations with developed educational, economic, scientific and political systems to suggest that the people are too ignorant to govern. This charge may be true of unstable, second or third world democracies (and it was true in Plato's time), but again the question must be, if the people are not to make the important political decisions in such countries, who should make them?[27] Even Weber and Schumpeter did not give enough attention to how an informed electorate can make good decisions. There is a clear disdain for the masses in their approach, a condescension which is not well analyzed or defended against serious objections. Indeed, one of the great virtues of the democratic system is that it may be regarded as the ultimate check on possible abuses of power, as containing the ultimate mechanism to produce a critique and rejection of the power of elites, or any other group that wishes to subject the general populace to its will. Perhaps there is something "populist" about the very essence of democracy. (I will return to the notion of populism in Chap. 10, a notion much in the news today and one that gets to the heart of the relationships between popular sovereignty, rational discourse, elitism, and representative government.)

8. Other problems that are cause for serious anxiety include the fact that there is often one law for the wealthy and one for the ordinary person in a democratic state. Not only are the wealthy much less likely to be prosecuted for committing the same crimes as people of ordinary means, but even if they are prosecuted they are likely to escape with a lighter punishment because they can use their financial resources to manipulate the legal system. Indeed, the legal system in many countries cries out for reform because of its soul-destroying bureaucracy, cost, and relegation of justice to the manipulation of procedures and regulations, allied with a too subjective approach to the interpretation and application of laws. In addition, while it is supposed to be a strength and a unique feature of democracy—that everyone is subject to the law—it is an ideal rarely practiced, to put it charitably! As an example, the criterion for applying the law to politicians who are believed to be in violation is often political rather than legal or moral (this is especially true in the U.S.), as it is for the wealthy, or those with significant social standing. Perhaps again this is human nature to some extent, but it is a reality that the ordinary person has to contend with in a democratic society.

While all of these problems are very serious, and might themselves lead to the end of democracy, they are not the problems I am interested in, except in an indirect way, where they may bear on the foundational problems I will focus on. Indeed, despite them, as Robert B. Talisse has noted, "no matter how hard democracy is to love, we do love it....Democracy is often presented as a necessary precondition for all other social and political goods, such as freedom, fairness, equality and justice to security, peace, and prosperity."[28] So while these vexing problems could get worse, and may be even hasten the end of democracy since they could possibly lead to a series of social crises or even social unrest, they are not what we have in mind in this book.

Overview of the Crisis: Themes of This Book

The line of inquiry I wish to develop is that there is a deeper crisis facing liberal democracy than is reflected in any of the problems described above, serious though these worries undoubtedly are. The foundational problems I will identify here and develop in the rest of the book have to do with the consequences that result from pluralism and freedom operating within a democratic structure over the long term. We will see that the democratic emphasis on and interpretation of the concept of freedom leads to a *contentious pluralism*, marked by the emergence of incommensurable worldviews (including an increasingly influential worldview of secularism), and thus leading to a phenomenon of relativism that has become a characteristic feature of modern democratic societies. This phenomenon is further compounded by *a loss of confidence in reason* to lead to productive dialogue that might go some way to resolving or at least alleviating our disagreements. Our general argument also includes an overview of one prominent solution to some of these problems proposed in recent liberal political theory, and its failure. We are therefore left with a *clash of worldviews* in the modern state, both between various religious worldviews, and between religious worldviews and secularist worldviews (indeed voting *against*, rather than *for*, a position, or candidate, or political party has become a common motivation in recent elections in *many* democratic countries). Moreover, the rise of the secularist worldview, I will argue, changes completely the conventional understanding of the modern state, changes how we should think about our disagreements concerning our cherished beliefs and values, and changes also the way we should think about the presence and place of religious views. One consequence is that the time has come to re-envision our understanding of the relationship between religion and the state. As we work through these themes, I will offer some suggestions for how it is best for us to proceed, while also emphasizing that an unfortunate feature of the crisis is that there is no obvious way out of it.

As noted in the Preface, in discussing these challenging themes I am not writing from the point of view of liberal democracy in the U.S. or the European Union, or any particular country, but more broadly. We are interested in liberal democracy as it is practiced in modern Western countries, as well as in the Southern hemisphere, especially Australia and New Zealand, and even in countries such as Poland, India, and the Philippines, where democracy is not so well developed. The United States is often regarded as the champion par excellence of the notion of pluralist democracy, not just because it was the first democracy in modern times, but also because of its historical emphasis on the central themes of freedom and pluralism. However, the democratic system has taken root in many countries (often with U.S. support—military, financial, and/or moral) so the problems and trends that I wish to identify and discuss in this book will be found to be common to most modern democracies in some form or other. It would be a very interesting study in itself to examine a particular country in the light of the ideas I raise in this book to explore how it fits into our analysis. But our concern is with a more general analysis, though I will refer to particular democratic nations and their problems to illustrate our arguments and points.

Over the course of our discussion I will attempt to identify the nature of the crisis, and how it arose. Along the way I will consider some possible solutions (including the solution of liberal political theory), but will not pretend that I have the solution. *Indeed, I am contending that part of the crisis is that there is no easy solution, that it is very difficult to see any remedy, or hopeful way forward.* It is possible that the foundational problems arising in the democratic form of government could even lead to major instability in various countries, and perhaps the system may even begin to unravel.

1. Freedom as an Absolute Value: The first problem that has emerged in liberal democracy that I will focus on, and that may be moving us closer to a crisis, is that the emphasis on (indeed some might say obsession with) the notion of freedom has had interesting and far-reaching consequences. I will try to show that the notion of freedom has been developed and interpreted in such a broad and absolutist manner that *we can reasonably trace a series of causal steps where freedom has led to a contentious pluralism.* By pluralism I mean to describe the phenomenon of the existence of a number of different *worldviews* (a term I favor in the general discussion of pluralism and the issues of this book, and which I will introduce more fully in Chap. 3) in the same democratic state. Of course, this phenomenon is not that surprising in itself, since pluralism was one of the motivations for democracy, and, as James Madison shrewdly observed, a society founded on freedom will lead inevitably to the emergence of new religious, philosophical, moral, and political views going forward.[29] However, the strong promotion of individual freedom and the emphasis on individuals choosing their own system of meaning and value, and their own path in life, with increasingly fewer restrictions, has led to the phenomenon in the democratic state of *a plurality of worldviews that conflict with each other on crucial matters. These matters concern the origin and purpose of human life, the nature of morality, and issues relating to education, politics, law, and culture*. More and more, people are sorting themselves into and defining themselves by their worldviews, leading to sharp disagreements. These disagreements are profound, and they cannot be settled by appeals to science or facts, nor can they be settled by appeals to reason. In short, freedom has led to what some philosophers have described as the emergence of *incommensurable* worldviews, *worldviews that are fundamentally in conflict with each other and that cannot be reconciled with each other.*

Moreover, part of the crisis is that this conflict affects all groups and social classes in society; people who are equally well-educated and equally well-informed are as likely to disagree with each other, as they are to disagree with those who are uneducated and uninformed, and the latter group also disagrees strongly among themselves. Another sign of the crisis is that elite opinion in many nations is itself beginning to fracture. We have reached a stage in some democratic countries where people often regard worldviews other than their own as not just wrong but as incomprehensible, and we are fast reaching the point where there no longer exists any clear center of normalcy, where people no longer agree on what the common good is, at least with regard to many issues relating to values. This phenomenon creates therefore an obvious practical problem from the point of view of day-to-day living in a democratic nation, a problem with regard to such crucial issues as the making of laws, the education of children (particularly as regards morality), religious freedom, the place of worldviews not our own in the state, and so forth. This is an extremely difficult problem, and I will argue that it is getting worse, not better. A clash of worldviews is one of the issues that is contributing to the crisis facing liberal democracy. I call this problem *the problem of worldview pluralism*.

2. The Phenomenon of Relativism: A second clear trend in modern democracies is the rise of relativism, prompting a serious reflection on whether democracy leads to relativism, whether relativism is an inevitable consequence of the democratic system. Relativism is the view that there is no objective truth that is independent of human opinion, attitude, individual perspective, viewpoint, conceptual scheme, or cultural background. It is therefore up to the individual to choose his or her own truth from the many possibilities available. From a philosophical point of view, relativism has generated much discussion and can be applied to all knowledge claims in general, or just to a particular area of knowledge. In popular thinking relativism is generally claimed for moral and religious truth claims, and perhaps political truth claims, but not usually for scientific or historical claims (though to be consistent, as we will see later when we discuss the topic further, it must apply in the end to *every* truth claim). Relativism is one of the prominent themes in this book because of its prevalence in democratic societies, especially in the idea that the sphere of legitimate human freedom includes the freedom to choose one's own worldview. This freedom also suggests that, from a practical point of view, there is no objective way to differentiate between worldviews. It is even more urgent to consider the phenomenon of relativism given also the fact that, if allowed free rein, relativism would lead to chaos, especially morally and politically.

Despite the prevalence of relativism in modern pluralist societies, and its strong influence over the way that people approach disagreement and arrive at decisions, it faces many problems; one of the most serious is how to draw a limit to it so that we can pass laws by which to govern ourselves. This problem is also clearly related to the more general worry of where to draw the limits to freedom itself, since total freedom is unthinkable, and would simply lead to anarchy. Yet, we continually disagree in democratic societies about these matters, a debate that pulls us toward relativism. This is a fascinating and challenging topic that we will discuss fully but we should not underestimate its influence in many areas of democratic life. I will also show later that its influence can be subtle rather than obvious. Moreover, we can make a useful distinction between relativism as a philosophical thesis about reality, and what I call the rhetoric of relativism (where a moral objectivist adopts a "posture" of relativism), and how (oddly) this can be an effective strategy in a frayed democratic culture struggling to cope with fractious social, moral, and political debates.

3. Loss of Confidence in Reason: I will try to illustrate that a strong contributory factor to the crisis that is slowly creeping into the democratic form of government is the gradual loss of confidence in reason that is a feature of democratic countries. One of my main claims is that citizens in a modern democracy have *lost confidence in the power of human reason* to help make progress in resolving their differences. Reason is a human tool, part of the objective nature of human beings, relying on the application of logical reasoning and use of evidence, to enable us to solve problems, make rational decisions, and make moral and political progress. I will try to show that this understanding is now gradually being lost, that people no longer think they can persuade others in political debates, and indeed are coming round to the view that discussing one's ideas with others is often a lost cause, even a task not worth pursuing. Citizens in a democracy no longer have confidence that they can persuade others of the merit or truth of their views, that certain views are irrational or false, or that both sides have good points and that we should compromise, that we should be more tolerant of other worldviews we disagree with, or whatever. The loss of confidence in reason is more obvious at the social and political level, but I will try to show that it is connected in a *causal* way to the themes of freedom and relativism, and also that it has deeper philosophical roots. Indeed, it is not just a feature of modern political and social life in many democratic nations (reflected also in the fact that new political parties and movements are emerging, and that traditional parties are failing to hold the allegiance of their supporters), it is now also an important trend in academic life as well. This is one reason why academic life exhibits many of the same trends as political life, why some university professors are abandoning reasonable debate and are becoming more political in their approach to teaching and education.

4. Secularism as a Worldview: There is a notable oversight in recent works that discuss democracy and pluralism—they do not give enough emphasis to the growing phenomenon of *the emergence of secularism as a major worldview and influential cultural player in modern pluralist democracies*.[30] A key theme of my study is that a developing trend in modern democracy, which we can also relate to the notion of freedom, is the rise of secularism as a very significant worldview. Perhaps this trend was not inevitable; however, part of my argument is that it is a *reality*. I am not referring here to the notion of "the secular," a term often used to convey the idea of a neutral secular state, a state in which all worldviews can somehow function together, and where the state is not supposed to favor any worldview in particular. I am referring to the worldview of secularism, and to its growth and deep influence on modern society, to secularism as a philosophical view of reality, one that challenges religion, one that wishes to have political and moral influence. It is this worldview that I will focus on, and we must also be careful to distinguish it both from the notion of the secular state, and of the process of secularization which is often understood as a movement away from religion, but not necessarily one that involves embracing or taking up an *alternative* worldview (that of secularism). I am interested in identifying what secularism is, its beliefs and values, and its approach to the meaning of life. I will argue that it now has a quite influential role, and that it is contributing to a clash of worldviews, partly because of its hostility to religion, which is almost part of its essence, a clash that is not easily revolved. Indeed, this clash of worldviews, in which we must also include religious views that are hostile to each other, could lead to social breakdown, or at the very least to political repression of certain undesirable views by those with the power to enforce this repression (thereby, as we will see, violating democratic principles, yet another illustration of the crisis facing the democratic system).

5. The Role of Religious Worldviews in the Democratic State: Another central argument in my analysis of the fermenting crisis is that the emergence of secularism as an influential worldview, as well as its inevitable clash with religious worldviews, forces us *to re-envision the conventional understanding of the relationship between religion and the state*. Indeed, the relationship between religion and the state has always been quite contentious in the democratic system and contains within it some of the general problems we have mentioned (problems that are often approached *through the lens of one's own politics* rather than by application of agreed-upon, and consistently applied, democratic principles). A key claim of our argument is that given the contentious nature of modern pluralism, as well as the rise of secularism, *the notion of the relationship between church and state has to be rethought*. I will explain why this is so later and also offer some guidelines for how it might be done. This may seem a radical idea, but it is one I believe whose time has come because of modern pluralism. It is no longer plausible to place all religious worldviews into a separate category today and to advocate treating them in a different way to secularist worldviews, either to their gain or detriment. I will also suggest that religious views have a legitimate, if limited, role in the modern pluralist democratic state, comparable to that given to other worldviews, especially secularist ones.

6. Failure of the Liberal Solution: As our discussion unfolds over these topics, I will also consider the "liberal solution" to some of the problems that I have been discussing and show why it should be rejected. The liberal solution refers to the central ideas of liberal political theory, and particularly to the work of influential American political philosopher, John Rawls (1921–2002), and some of those he has influenced, such as Ronald Dworkin, Thomas Nagel, Robert Audi, Gerald Gaus, and Cécile Laborde (thinkers we will return to from time to time). As explained in the Preface, this book is not yet another exposition and discussion of the ideas of recent liberal political philosophers, but is rather an attempt to make a modest contribution from a philosophical point of view to the current state of modern democracy, particularly its foundational ideas and themes, and how these lead to some of its most serious current problems. But it can be quite helpful by way of contrast to consider along the way the solution proposed by Rawls and his followers. Not only is Rawls' solution clever and fascinating in its own right but consideration and indeed critique of it will, I believe, help us further clarify many of our main points and arguments. Another important reason for discussing the view of Rawls and some of his followers is that it will enable us to focus on *the notion of public reason* that is a vital part of liberal political theory. An analysis of this notion will help us to understand the general role of reason in democratic public decision-making more clearly, and to see why we have lost confidence in it, one of my key themes. This examination will further help us to see what is involved in formulating and presenting a reasonable argument, whether secularist arguments can be shown to be reasonable, whether the notion of the reasonable excludes the religious, and the general difficulty of applying the notion in concrete cases. The notion of public reason is fascinating, challenging, and can be useful; it is also difficult to interpret and hard to apply, but it is not a concept, I will show (contrary to Rawls) that can solve any of the current crises facing pluralist democracy.

Over the course of this book, we will elaborate on these various themes, claims, and arguments in an attempt to offer a reflective essay on some foundational ideas and trends that are part of the democratic system as it has been developing around the world. I will try to identify the nature of what I think is a gradual but clear situation of crisis and how it arose. As I noted above, although I am trying to identify the main developments that are leading toward a crisis, my discussion is not aimed at setting the stage in order to introduce my own solution. The fact is, I don't see any easy solution, at least one which would not involve a violation of the very principles of democracy that we should be safeguarding. With regard to all of the problems we identified earlier in our discussion, I contend that no matter how well-informed the general population are, no matter how moral they are, and even if we succeeded in removing all the abuses, malpractices, inefficiencies, and other flaws, along with perfecting the electoral process and the structure of government, the crisis that I am identifying would still remain. This is because we would *still* have contentious disagreements at the level of worldviews. The crisis might even be worse if we had a very sophisticated electorate and a well-functioning system due to the fact that people would be more likely to develop and sharpen their worldview beliefs, and this fact would *add* to the strife that pervades modern political life.

Will the democratic form of government begin to unravel? I don't think it is silly to say that the problems I discuss in this book could (and I emphasize *could*) lead to significant instability in various countries, or even civil unrest. One would hope that civil unrest would not be the next step, but it is not ridiculous to consider the possibility. As with many things, the future of democracy is impossible to predict. In this book I wish to offer a few ideas to help us better understand and appreciate the current situation, how we got to this point, and to suggest how we might proceed. That at least is a first step in trying to prevent any possible crisis from becoming a reality.

Notes

1. See A.C. Grayling, *Democracy and Its Crisis* (London: Oneworld, 2017).
2. Robert A. Dahl insists that we should speak of *theories* of democracy; see his masterly works, *Democracy and its Critics* (New Haven, CT.: Yale U.P., 1989) and *A Preface to Democratic Theory* (Chicago: University of Chicago Press, 1989 ed.). See also Ronald J. Terchek and Thomas C. Conte, *Theories of Democracy: A Reader* (Lanham, MD: Rowman and Littlefield, 2000); Frederick G. Whelan, *Democracy in Theory and Practice* (London: Routledge, 2018); David Held, *Models of Democracy* (Stanford, CA.: Stanford U.P. 2006 ed.).
3. See Aristotle, *Politics* (New York: Penguin, 1981 ed.), Book 3: Parts 4 and 15.
4. For Plato's views on democracy, and the democratic character, see *The Republic* (New York: Penguin, 2007 ed.), Book VIII, and *The Laws* (New York: Penguin, 2005 ed.), Book II; also see Josiah Ober, *Demopolis: Democracy Before Liberalism in Theory and Practice* (New York: Cambridge U.P., 2017).
5. The important texts include Thomas Hobbes, *Leviathan* (London: Penguin, 1985 [original: 1651]), Jean-Jacques Rousseau, *The Social*

Contract (London: Penguin, 1968 [1762]); Baron Montesquieu, *The Spirit of the Laws* (New York: Cambridge U.P., 1989 [1748]); Baruch Spinoza, *Theological–Political Treatise* (New York: Cambridge U.P., 2007 [1670]); David Hume, *A Treatise of Human Nature* (London: Penguin, 1985 [1739]); John Locke, *Two Treatises of Government* (New York: Cambridge U.P., 1988 [1689]).

6. Recent work has shown quite decisively that the claim that the modern secular state was developed as a way of moving beyond religious violence is a myth about the origins of secular liberalism; see William T. Cavanaugh, *The Myth of Religious Violence: Secular Ideology and the Roots of Modern Conflict* (New York: Oxford U.P., 2009). Jeremy Waldron has argued that in fact all of the central liberal values come from religion; see his *God, Locke, and Equality: Christian Foundations in Locke's Political Thought* (New York: Cambridge U.P., 2002).

7. See Jonathan Wolff, *An Introduction to Political Philosophy* (Oxford, UK.: Oxford U.P., 2016 ed.), pp. 17–24, 96–100.

8. See John Locke, *Two Treatises of Government*. p. 412 (Section 222); also Benjamin Constant, who made the distinction between the "Liberty of the Ancients" and the "Liberty of the Moderns" (the latter emphasizing human rights and representative government); see Biamcamaria Fontana (ed.), *Constant: Political Writings* (New York: Cambridge U.P., 1988).

9. Grayling places great stock on the idea of representative democracy because he sees it as a check on an uninformed and sometimes immoral electorate. He does not explain how the representatives would themselves come to be above these vices, and seems to think that a representative government could act almost like an oligarchy; see Grayling, *Democracy and Its Crisis*, p. 166. This point is also echoed by James Madison in Federalist Paper No. 10; see Clinton Rossiter (ed.), *The Federalist Papers* (New York: New American Library, 2003), pp. 71–79. There is a clear sense in these writers that the thinking of the ordinary people should be done for them by experts.

10. See John Stuart Mill, *Thoughts on Parliamentary Reform* in J.M. Robson, et al, The *Collected Works of John Stuart Mill* (Toronto: University of Toronto Press 1963–1991), Vol. 19b, pp. 324–325.

11. See Bernard Crick's helpful overview of the gradual increase of the franchise in democratic societies, and of the worries this posed for the aristocratic, wealthy, ruling classes, in his *Democracy: A Very Short Introduction* (Oxford, UK.: Oxford U.P., 2002), pp. 72–76.

12. See Edmund Burke, *Reflections on the Revolution in France* (New York: Cambridge U.P., 2014 [original: 1790]), pp 59–65; see a contrasting view in Thomas Paine, *The Rights of Man* (London: Penguin, 1984 [original: 1791]).

13. For a full discussion of moral rights, see Joseph Raz, *The Morality of Freedom* (New York: Oxford U.P., 1988), Part III.
14. For a historical overview, see Edmund Fawcett, *Liberalism: The Life of an Idea* (Princeton, N.J.: Princeton U.P., 2018).
15. Ober, *Demopolis*, p. xiii.
16. For an informative discussion, see Ober's, *Demopolis*. Among other things, Ober argues that democracy is not necessarily committed to state neutrality, a key (value) claim of many versions of philosophical liberalism that is often itself presented as if it is value neutral!
17. See Sarah Conley, *Against Autonomy: Justifying Coercive Paternalism* (New York: Cambridge U.P., 2013); Jason Brennan, *Against Democracy* (Princeton, NJ: Princeton U.P., 2017).
18. See Thomas Piketty, *Capital in the Twenty-First Century* (Cambridge, MA.: Belknap Press, 2014). Thinkers of the past, of course, especially Karl Marx, and to a lesser extent, Joseph Schumpeter, thought that capitalism would eventually bring about its own destruction (and take democracy along with it).
19. See Aristotle, *Politics*, Book IV, Part XI.
20. See Max Weber, *Economy and Society* (Cambridge, MA.: Harvard U.P, 2019 [orig. pub. 1921]); also his *Political Writings*, ed. by Peter Lassman and Ronald Speirs (New York: Cambridge U.P., 1994); Joseph Schumpeter, *Capitalism, Socialism and Democracy* (New York: Harper, 1975 [1942]); William Lecky, *Democracy and Liberty* (Indianapolis, IN.: Liberty Fund, 1981 [orig. pub. 1896].
21. Max Weber, "Politics as a Vocation," in *Political Writings*, p. 310.
22. Joseph Schumpeter, *Capitalism, Socialism and Democracy*, p. 269.
23. See ibid., pp. 260–263.
24. Ibid., p. 262.
25. For contemporary accounts of the general problems with democracy and possible solutions, there are a number of provocative and helpful studies. See, especially, A.C. Grayling, *Democracy and Its Crisis*; David Van ReyBrouck *Against Elections: The Case for Democracy* (New York: Random House, 2016); Jason Brennan, *Against Democracy*; Carole Pateman, *Participation and Democratic Theory* (New York: Cambridge U.P., 1976); Jeffrey Stout, *Democracy and Tradition* (Princeton, NJ.: Princeton U.P., 2004). It is worth noting, also, that a number of theologians are very critical of democracy, to the point almost of giving up on it; see especially the provocative work of John Milbank and Stanley Hauerwas.
26. Brennan has argued that only more informed citizens should vote, or that government policy should be decided or approved by a more educated, more informed elite group. While his discussion is very interesting, it suffers from one fatal flaw: it skirts around and never comes to terms with the

vital issue that not all disagreements can be settled scientifically and by appeal to "the facts." Many are worldview, foundational value disagreements and these cannot be resolved by privileging the worldviews of certain voters. It is unacceptable from the point of view of the value of freedom for people who may be more informed and more rational with regard to factual and scientific matters to be making judgments for everyone on foundational matters of value, human nature, and the meaning and purpose of life. As I have suggested, perfectly educated, fully rational and extremely moral people will still disagree about *these* matters. This is part of what we mean by the crisis of worldview pluralism.
27. For a defense of majority rule and the collective wisdom of the democratic electorate, along with a critique of elitist approaches, see Hélène Landemore, *Democratic Reason* (Princeton, NJ.: Princeton U.P., 2013). Among other arguments, Landemore thinks that democratic decision-making is more inclusive. See also David Estlund, *Democratic Authority* (Princeton, NJ.: Princeton U.P. 2008).
28. Robert B. Talisse, *Engaging Political Philosophy: An Introduction* (New York: Routledge, 2016), p. 130.
29. See Madison in Clinton Rossiter (ed.), *The Federalist Papers*, pp. 71–79.
30. See, as examples, Martha Nussbaum, *Liberty of Conscience* (New York: Basic Books, 2008); A.C. Grayling, *Democracy and Its Crisis*; Jeffrey Stout, *Democracy and Tradition*—studies that give little attention to the phenomenon of secularism in the modern democratic state.

CHAPTER 2

Freedom and Disagreement in a Democracy

Around about the time of Locke in the seventeenth century, there was a gradual shift in the understanding of freedom among philosophers and political thinkers. Unlike philosophers in the classical tradition who had often looked upon the notion with suspicion, thinkers of the Enlightenment period began to reevaluate the significance of human freedom and to reassess its importance in both ordinary life and for our political arrangements. An important motivating idea in this shift in attitude was a growing acceptance that in some very crucial sense (which had yet to be spelled out) freedom is an essential feature of *the nature of human beings*. It is not the only feature but it was regarded as being on a par with other fundamental human traits and pursuits, perhaps even up there in importance with the value of human life itself. Freedom came to be regarded as part of the essence of what it means to be human, an essential property (in the older metaphysical language), the exercise of which, and the protection of which, is necessary for human fulfillment. It is part of human dignity to be free to make up our own minds about cardinal questions of life and meaning. This new perspective on freedom is in contrast to ancient and medieval views. Thinkers in these traditions were not necessarily hostile to freedom, but they were apprehensive about it, and did not regard its accommodation and promotion as an essential part of human nature or as being indispensable in our political arrangements.[1]

The wariness with which the value of freedom was regarded has been well expressed by Plato in his critique of the democratic approach. There are a number of aspects to this critique with which later thinkers are sympathetic, and even today the points raised by the Greek philosopher are still a cause of concern for many. The foundation of Plato's critique is a distinction that many thinkers make, even if only covertly, implicitly (or occasionally perhaps without even realizing it)—the distinction between informed and uninformed citizens in the state. Informed citizens are those who have some familiarity with current affairs, who have taken the trouble to try to discern the facts, who have engaged in some reflection on the best course of action on a given topic. Their opinion and their vote then in a democratic context can be said to be informed. Of course, informed citizens will still disagree on the correct action to pursue or about the right way forward for society (a key development, as we noted in Chap. 1) but they are alike because they have taken the trouble to educate themselves about the issues of the day, and have arrived at a considered opinion. The uninformed then are those who know little or nothing about the issues of the day, who are ignorant of the facts and who have given scant consideration to the matter at hand. They hold impressionistic or superficial opinions based on what they hear in ordinary conversation or pick up in snippets (unfortunately, a situation all too common today in our sound bite driven media culture). Such citizens are not fully cognizant of the facts, and have given no serious thought to making the best judgment with regard to questions of law, society, and culture, or about which candidate to support for public office, and so forth. The mass of people, the general populace, Plato held, are in the second group. (He famously employed the "ship of state" metaphor in *The Republic* to illustrate this truth.[2])

A second point is that there is high correlation between a person being well-educated and intelligent and being a member of the informed group of citizens. Though, it would be a mistake to conclude that all educated and intelligent people are informed about the political issues of the day (and, of course, that they always make correct and wise decisions)! Indeed, there are many from all walks of life today who have made the decision to give up on politics completely, to tune out coverage of political issues, and who choose not to (even refuse to) vote. But Plato thought that in his time the mass of ignorant and uneducated were in the second group, and let us recall also that he lived in a culture that was largely illiterate, so the lack of familiarity with, and knowledge of, current affairs and of the political process would have been acute in such a society. So it is not really surprising that he held the view that the problem with the democratic approach is that the ignorant, unenlightened masses would have too much power over those who generally know better, know better because they are more educated and more informed, and are therefore more equipped to lead the state. Today, this view would be described as elitism, because it seems to relegate to lesser importance the fundamental value of equality that is part of the essence of a democratic society, and it fails to give due regard to the value of freedom. And it is true that Plato did not think that all opinions were equal; he thought that some opinions were better than others because they were more informed. Of course, modern democracy recognizes such a distinction in principle as well; we do not think that the ordinary person in the street's opinion on health care is as valuable as that of a public official who has spent all of his or her career working on that topic; yet at the practical level of governing both views are equal because they carry the same weight at the ballot box. So, for Plato, that meant that in a democratic system the masses of people would decide most questions, and very likely decide them wrongly, guided by ignorance instead of knowledge!

A third worry facing such a strong emphasis on the value of freedom is the perception that too much freedom can be dangerous for people, and therefore for the direction of society. This is one of the biggest concerns many have about human freedom. It is an ancient problem: recognizing that human beings should have a certain range of freedoms, yet trying to place a limit on this range, with a view to preventing self-destruction and harm to society in general. The fear is that if citizens have a wide range of choices they may not be able to handle such liberty. The general absence of restraints would mean in practice that many people would make destructive decisions, destructive for themselves, their families, and ultimately destructive for society. Freedom can be dangerous in two ways: it leads to independent ideas, not all of which are healthy, and it encourages people to be selfish, which is morally wrong. For example, several thinkers had suggested that couples should be free to dissolve their marriages if they experience what today would be called irreconcilable differences (the poet John Milton was one of the first thinkers to write a sustained refection on this topic, in the face of his own marriage difficulties at a young age). But others were skeptical of this argument. They reasoned that if people were free to divorce they would be less careful about keeping their marriage vows, whereas if marriages could not be dissolved this would place a kind of legal constraint on people's actions that would have the effect in most cases of protecting the institution of marriage. If we just leave it to people's free choice, although in principle of course one could still keep one's marriage vows, in practice it would become more difficult. Over time, it could lead to marriage breakdown becoming a cultural phenomenon, especially after several generations. It might even lead to a new understanding of marriage, one perhaps where it came to be regarded as a convenient arrangement until one's relationship hit difficulties, and so marriage would no longer be understood as a lifelong commitment. Such arguments were advanced in those democratic countries that had a serious debate before divorce was made legal, and indeed many of these worries have come to pass.

The worries accompanying a strong emphasis on freedom and the example of the debate about divorce lead us to identify a deeper concern that many recognized and accepted: that it is neither wise nor possible that people should have total or complete freedom in society because this would only lead to chaos and lack of social control and constraint. So the question became: how much freedom should people have? Plato's view was that people could not be trusted with freedom because they did not have enough knowledge to make wise choices and they also did not have enough will power to resist the inevitable temptations that freedom would bring. He talked of the "democratic character," as we noted in the previous chapter, as a corrupt personality that knew no restraint, and that was drawn toward a materialistic life style caught up in pursuits of comfort and amusement, even hedonism. So to promote this type of freedom in society would be both catastrophic and irresponsible.

Another issue that later democratic thinkers often struggled with as they considered the question of freedom was freedom of religion (today we need to refer to it as "freedom of worldview," for interesting and crucial reasons that we will come to appreciate as our discussion unfolds in this book). Locke considered the question of how much freedom people should have to choose their own religion. He recognized the difficulty of the question and was torn between defending a greater realm of freedom in the area of religious belief than was usual in his own day, and yet at the same time recognizing that there would have to be some restrictions on religious freedom; otherwise we run into a kind of religious relativism. Many were against freedom of religion for just this reason—they believed that not only would it lead people to make false and even immoral choices, but it would also lead to a kind of pluralist chaos that would be destructive for society. Many religious leaders (including Catholic leaders, e.g.) thought that freedom of religion was dangerous because it would give people the opportunity to reject the true (i.e., their!) religion, a worry many had about freedom in general (and still have, as we will see). So the idea that some kind of control, restraint, censorship, or paternalistic style of leadership must be imposed on the mass of people from (usually) an enlightened minority from above to protect people from themselves and to protect us (and society) from each other was common, and hovered in the background of early deliberations about the nature of freedom and democracy.

Locke and Mill on Freedom

John Locke and especially John Stuart Mill were not the only thinkers to consider the question of freedom, but they were two of the most significant, particularly Mill who was one of the first thinkers to attempt a careful philosophical defense of the value of freedom in a democratic society. Whereas Locke is the pre-eminent thinker associated with the theory and structure of democracy, Mill is usually regarded as the unsurpassed defender of freedom. We will briefly consider Locke's views on tolerance before looking in more detail at Mill's very interesting articulation of the scope of, and defense of, freedom in a democratic society.

Locke was one of the first philosophers to think more deeply about the concept of tolerance (along with Voltaire and Pierre Bayle[3]), or "toleration," as he called it, a buzz word today and part of our zeitgeist. In his *A Letter Concerning Toleration* (1689), he considered the question of the range of views society should tolerate in terms of allowing their free expression, and in allowing some element of practice concerning them.[4] Like Mill, and other intellectuals of this era, he was thinking particularly of religious toleration. Mindful of the Reformation and the wars of religion across Europe, and in the aftermath of the Thirty Years' War (1618–1648), Locke was beginning to craft some of the early thinking behind the principle of the separation of church and state. He was especially worried about religious intolerance and persecution in British society, yet he struggled with the question of where to draw the line between what should be tolerated and what should not be tolerated.

Locke argued that the church should be mainly concerned with salvation and the care of souls, and that the state should be occupied with life, liberty, and the protection of property, and things of that sort. Religious believers should be allowed freedom of worship, and a certain latitude in the areas of faith and morals. But he recognized the problem with maintaining a hard and fast distinction immediately when he considered the objection of what to do if a Church was promoting or engaging in immoral practices, such as child sacrifice (a hypothetical example he considered).[5] The problem arises because we cannot simply endorse the view that each religion must be free to put into practice its own beliefs, including moral beliefs. We can appeal, Locke thought, to a realm of objective morality to justify prohibiting certain church practices. He suggested that there was a kind of "universal morality," which most people held, and which could be used to restrain and control other moral belief systems, such as those that might be found in some religions. He pointed out that the problem was not all that pressing because few churches advocated anything too radical in terms of dangerous or violent activity. Nevertheless, he did not sufficiently appreciate the political nature of some religious beliefs.

Locke's position still leaves us with the difficulty of where we would find this "universal morality" to which we must appeal to regulate the moral codes of others. To whose view of "universal morality" do we appeal if there is disagreement on its nature, a very serious problem facing democracies today. Such disagreements could perhaps be addressed through the democratic process, at least in principle; that was supposed to be a vital feature of democracy, that an answer to difficult questions like this one would come from the people themselves—based on their freely given consent—and not from the monarch or an elite class, or some other non-representative group. Locke himself drew the limits of tolerance, famously, at Catholics and atheists! Catholics should not be tolerated, he suggested, because they could not be trusted to give their full allegiance to their state, since they are supposed to obey "a foreign prince" (the Pope).[6] He supported the view that atheism should not be tolerated with two brief arguments. The first is a version of the position that atheists cannot be trusted to follow objective morality, and so "promises, covenants, and oaths, which are the bonds of human society, can have no hold upon or sanctity for an atheist."[7] He seems also to suggest that tolerance is essentially a religious virtue and that one must be religious to practice it. So it would be difficult for atheists to be guided by the virtue.

Influenced by Locke and others, John Stuart Mill in his *On Liberty* (1859), was a pioneering thinker on the nature of democracy, and specifically concerning the meaning and importance of freedom in developing democratic societies. Mill noted that a crucial question facing any democratic nation concerns the nature and limits of the power that can be legitimately exercised by the government and society over the individual person.[8] He believed that the power to rule over others can be dangerous because it is subject to abuse; he noted that the history of political society illustrates that there was a gradual acceptance that it is necessary to have some way of defining or drawing a limit to this power. Earlier forms of rule maintained a central authority as a way of preserving order and stability, but as countries moved to democratic forms of government—to people ruling over themselves—the power of the central authority was greatly diminished and subject to the decisions of popular sovereignty. Mill also recognized that an inevitable feature of fledgling democracies is that majority opinion will be the arbiter of laws and of morality in the state, and that, although it is part of the democratic process to accept the will of the majority, we must also be on our guard against majority opinion becoming tyrannical.

Therefore, a key part of this process is that there should be a considerable sphere of individual liberty in the state so that those who do not agree with majority opinion can try to persuade people to change their minds. More generally, there must be room for free discussion and debate, a practice that is important for bringing about change, improvement, and hopefully progress in society in a number of areas. However, for this kind of change to be possible, considerable freedom must be allowed to the individual. Mill was interested in attempting to offer some rationale that would show why freedom is a very important value. He wished to explore how we might justify the value of freedom in a *philosophical* way. He knew that many people were suspicious of freedom and believed that it could be destructive to both the individual and to society (as we have noted), and he wished to provide arguments against this influential view. Although in the new-found democratic states (Britain, France, and the U.S.), there was an understanding that citizens should have a significant amount of freedom in principle, the people were often reluctant to allow the exercise of this freedom in practice, and it was common to restrict people's liberty in areas such as religion, morality, political affairs, publications, and so forth, and censorship was widely practiced. This was not just because those in power did not want any ideas expressed but their own; it was also because of the widespread view that some ideas (and actions) are dangerous, immoral, obscene, even seditious. Such ideas could give rise to destructive tendencies that would have the consequence of ushering in forms of corruption, contributing to individual unhappiness, and perhaps even undermining the stability of the state.

As we have noted, one of the main arguments of the liberal political tradition from Locke onward is that freedom is a key feature of the nature of man, and this is why it must be a major facet of the modern state. Later thinkers (such as Isaiah Berlin, 1909–1997) sometimes distinguished between negative freedom and positive freedom.[9] Negative freedom is understood as freedom from government interference (the government will not force you to pursue a career, e.g.), and positive freedom is usually defined as the freedom to make your own choices in life (e.g., to decide to become a doctor rather than a lawyer). Mill argued that the modern democratic state should normally provide the individual with a large sphere of (negative) freedom; this would then allow the individual to exercise a large amount of (positive) freedom in his or her autonomous decision-making. The question is: exactly how much freedom should be accorded to individual citizens, and what would it include and exclude? No philosopher has ever agreed that the individual should have total freedom because this position would lead to anarchy; so the question is about where we should draw the line concerning what we will allow (and forbid) ourselves to say and do.

Mill developed a number of interesting and very influential arguments with respect to this question. Initially, he raised a worry about what he called "the tyranny of the majority" in a democracy. This is the fact that in many democracies there is often a large majority that gives its allegiance to the same worldview, moral code, and understanding of the meaning of life. Moreover, they would also in fact have the power to make their views, in whole or in part, the basis of many of the state's laws and practices (they could vote for a law, for instance, that would make religious education compulsory). "The will of the people," as Mill observed, "practically means the will of the most numerous or the most active *part* of the people; the majority, or those who succeed in making themselves accepted as the majority; the people, consequently, *may* desire to oppress a part of their number; and precautions are as much needed against this as against any other abuse of power."[10] He believed it is a natural human tendency to impose one's will on others if one has the power (in this case the votes) to do so. While this may sound like an odd criticism, since democracy works by majority rule, Mill intriguingly argued that, although this is true in general, there are nevertheless *some issues* where the majority should *not* impose their will on the majority, even though they can do so. There is a limit, as he put it, to what the majority can morally ask of the minority; the minority needs protection "against the tyranny of the prevailing opinion and feeling; against the tendency of society to impose, by other means than civil penalties, its own ideas and practices as rules of conduct on those who dissent from them."[11] He had in mind, in particular, the situation of minority religious views, or an atheistic rejection of religion; he argued that if a particular religion has a majority in a democratic state, they should not use their superior numbers to restrict smaller religions, or to force citizens into the majority religion.[12] Yet, this is a very complicated issue; it raises questions concerning whether, if the majority thinks an action is immoral, they should make it illegal even if there is a significant minority who think that it is not immoral?

Influenced by Locke and others, Mill developed a quite sophisticated philosophical defense of the notion of freedom in his famous work, *On Liberty*. His account is brilliant, thought-provoking, controversial, and has been extremely influential in modern democracies. We will confine ourselves to an exposition of his view here, and will then raise several critical issues (in the next section) as we examine the application of his ideas in the modern democratic context. Mill wished to defend the thesis that human beings should be accorded a large area of personal freedom in their day-to-day lives, and he wished to develop good persuasive philosophical arguments for this position. He was juggling several difficulties that human freedom must confront in the democratic context, and he came up with ingenious ways of solving them. The difficulties included Plato's general worry, which many shared, that too much freedom for people is dangerous, that freedom can be quite destructive both for individuals and for society. The deeper point behind this worry is perhaps that we all have a strong temptation to guide other people's decisions along the right path, not because of a desire to dominate necessarily but because one strongly wishes for the other person's own good. One then makes a judgment that one knows best concerning what is good for people, better than they often know themselves, especially if one is older or wiser, and has authority over those whom one wishes to influence (such as parental or supervisory authority and guidance over children and young people, and perhaps also political or social authority). The second issue Mill had to think about is that there is a lot of truth to the view that it is not possible to grant to people total or complete freedom; that position is simply impractical and would lead to chaos and all sorts of harm. So we must have some method or set of criteria for drawing a limit to the sphere of personal freedom that can be accorded to individuals (e.g., should we allow the practice of divorce in society?). We need to remind ourselves also that in the democratic setting, this means that we are trying to draw a limit to the amount of freedom *we give to ourselves*. We may operate through the government to impose the limits, but ideally it is not the government who decides the limit on freedom, nor some enlightened, elite group, but *the people themselves*, since the populace must consent to the limits, and can change these limits, through the democratic process.

Mill addressed the second question about placing a limit on the range of human freedom by introducing his famous harm principle. Although the principle is most associated with Mill, it did not originate with him. There is a similar principle included in the *Declaration of Rights of Man and of the Citizen*, adopted as part of the French Revolution in 1789 (the Declaration was written by Thomas Jefferson, Lafayette, and Abbé Sieyès). Mill's version proposes, "That the only purpose for which power can be rightfully exercised over any member of a civilized community, against his will, is to prevent harm to others. His own good, either physical or moral, is not a sufficient warrant."[13] The basic idea is now a very familiar one in modern democracy, even though most may be unaware of its origins: that the individual should be free to do as he or she wishes as long as it does not harm others. Mill thought that this principle, which later became known as the harm principle, was a reasonable way to draw the line between what should be permitted and what should not be permitted. From a moral point of view, he is saying that if any action or even verbal expression harms another person then a person could be prevented by law from doing that action or saying those words. This principle is intended to apply in the area of personal liberty, but would have a much wider application in many areas of society since many laws forbidding crimes, for example, assault, embezzlement, would fall under it.

Mill framed the principle deliberately and carefully so that it did not cover cases of self-harm; it only applies to actions that harm others. He did this so as to limit interference in a person's actions that others might deem as harmful to that person, for example, pursuing an immoral lifestyle, or not practicing one's religion, or to use a modern day example, taking up smoking or skydiving, and so forth. Mill recognized that if one included self-harm in the definition of harm (which many people would be strongly inclined to do), it would open up a minefield and make the harm principle practically useless because it could be used to restrict all kinds of behavior on the grounds that it is harmful to the individual engaging in it. Many of Mill's critics think that it is unreasonable to allow people to harm themselves (e.g., by smoking or not wearing a seatbelt), but Mill thought that this price was a necessary part of freedom; otherwise, the realm of personal freedom would be too severely restricted. And there is also the real risk of abuse. For every case of restricting freedom to prevent people from harming themselves, Mill thought there would be a case where one was simply imposing one's views because one disagreed with or disapproved of the beliefs or lifestyles of others, even though the other was not being harmed, or where the question of harm was disputed. And in cases of dispute, Mill thought we must err on the side of freedom. Even in cases where there is perhaps no doubt about whether an action is harmful (such as smoking), Mill argued that we should not take the step of legally trying to prevent people from harming themselves. Mill, a utilitarian in ethics, thought that this was preferable from the point of view of promoting the overall good—the harm that would come to people from allowing them to smoke, for instance, is outweighed by the harm that would come to society if we allowed our freedom to be restricted with regard to these kinds of matters. What if one pursued the wrong worldview? Millians reply by saying either that (1) there are no wrong worldviews (a position that embraces relativism), or that (2) there are wrong worldviews, but choosing wrongly is better than being compelled toward the correct view (so it would seem that choosing unhappiness freely is better than being forced to follow the true path, assuming that false views lead to unhappiness).

Mill believed that mature democracies, those with longevity and political stability, should adopt the harm principle. But the principle raises an essential question concerning what harm means, or how it is to be defined. Are we referring to physical harm only, or perhaps also to moral harm, psychological harm, or what? Surely all of these types of harm are real and we should do our best to prevent them? Mill's general view is that we are mostly talking about physical harm, and perhaps also harm that involves a violation of the rights of the individual (the sphere of rights would have to be clearly defined). But Mill realized that if one extended the principle to include moral harm this would make it unworkable, because, as we have seen with regard to self-harm, it would result in restrictions on all kinds of behavior that seem to harm people morally even if no physical harm is apparent (though he does not seem to have considered the view that in many cases moral harm to one person often results in physical or moral harm to others). And while he accepted that it is possible to harm people morally, he thought there was too much disagreement about which beliefs, ideas, actions, or circumstances contributed to moral harm. If we try to legislate for moral harm, it would involve far too many restrictions on personal freedom that are incompatible with the truth that freedom is part of the nature of man. So again one of the prices of freedom is that we have to tolerate a certain amount of moral harm in society, a price many early critics of Mill were reluctant to pay. Two other qualifications to Mill's view are also important. First, the harm principle does not apply to children and people of immature mentality, but only to adults; second, it does apply also to some extent to words as well as to actions. Mill knew that we could not be as liberal with actions as with words, but he did agree that words could be libelous and slanderous, and so these forms of speech may be restricted by law under the harm principle (even though libel and slander do not cause physical harm), another example of the difficulties of defining a consistent position on this matter that would cover every type of case.

MILL'S ARGUMENTS FOR FREEDOM OF THOUGHT AND EXPRESSION

Mill took up in Chap. 2 of *On Liberty* the question of freedom of speech in a democracy.[14] First, he proposed that there should be a general sphere of personal freedom, and then he turned more specifically to the philosophical case that one might make for freedom of opinion in a society, something that many were deeply suspicious of, and regarded as dangerous. Mill elaborates his argument by proposing three areas of freedom that should be accorded to the individual: the inward domain of consciousness, the liberty of tastes and pursuits, and the freedom to unite (or of association). The inward domain of consciousness refers to freedom of conscience, the liberty of thought and feeling, and includes freedom of opinion on all subjects (including theological, moral, philosophical, and scientific), and on publishing these opinions. One can imagine that in Mill's time this was quite a radical proposal. The individual person, Mill contended, should also be free to decide on his or her own path in life, again as long as it does not harm others. This liberty of tastes and pursuits would include such activities as becoming a doctor, taking up golf, developing an interest in World War II, collecting stamps or becoming a punk rocker! This understanding of freedom is founded on the belief that the individual has priority over the common good of society (a claim about the nature of the human person), as does Mill's general position with regard to the role of freedom in the democratic state. The third area involves the freedom to set up political parties, interest groups, and organizations of like-minded people for political, moral, or other purposes, again subject to the limits of the harm principle.

Mill gave special attention to the controversial area of freedom of discussion and free speech and developed three distinct and very influential arguments for why freedom of speech (which includes freedom to publish) should be allowed in a society.[15] His first argument is that the opinion we might want to suppress could be true, and so by suppressing it we may be depriving society of benefiting from true ideas. Of course, many people might think the idea is not true, but Mill says that the majority is not infallible. While this is an interesting reason, it would seem to apply to ideas about which there might be a legitimate dispute (which ideas fit into this category is itself a key, and by no means uncontentious, question), but it would not apply to ideas that are definitely false, such as, for instance, racist or Nazi ideas. Why not suppress *false* ideas? Mill does not want to reply to this objection in the way many of his later disciples are tempted to—by denying that there is any objective truth, and adopting a position of relativism about morality and politics (a problem we will return to in the next section). He agrees that some ideas are definitely false, and so he does not argue that the reason we should allow false ideas to be expressed is because we can never be really sure that they are false.[16] If he adopted this view, he would have to admit that racism, for example, might be moral, that we just don't see or agree about its truth now, but that we might eventually. He argues instead that there are two reasons for why we should allow false ideas to be expressed: the true view is strengthened in the collision with error, and the true view becomes more of a living truth rather than a dead dogma if it is occasionally challenged by other views, no matter how wrong or absurd (or dangerous?) these other views are. He expresses his general position in this way: "If the opinion is right, they are deprived of the opportunity of exchanging error for truth: if wrong, they lose, what is almost as great a benefit, the clearer perception and livelier impression of truth, produced by its collision with error."[17] His third reason is that it is often the case, especially for complex subjects, that different individuals and perspectives have part of the truth, but not the whole truth, and so by allowing free expression of each view the entire truth has a better chance of gradually emerging.

This point reminds us of another central claim of Mill's, that in allowing freedom of speech in this way there is more likelihood of the truth emerging on any given topic that there is if we suppress some views, for whatever well-intentioned reasons, and allow only certain favored views to be expressed. Mill's disciples later argued that another problem with suppressing certain views in a society is that there seems to be no practical way to decide which ideas should be censored (which books or films, e.g.), or who would do the censoring. Moreover, any form of censorship may lead eventually to the problem of the "slippery slope," where we begin today by censoring pornography but end up tomorrow censoring Shakespeare! So the solution is to allow no or very limited censorship, which is the lesser of two evils even though we know that some destructive, obscene, and degrading material will be published as a result of this freedom (obscene, gratuitously violent, deliberately shocking, sensationalist movies will be made as well as wholesome, uplifting, improving ones, and so forth). But on the positive side, we are always free to criticize the products of free speech, and in many cases we can simply avoid material that we find objectionable.

Mill did think that one could try to persuade, cajole, remonstrate with, or criticize someone whose expression, or indeed, whose actions, one disagreed with, or believed to be harmful to themselves. But he argued that the harm principle meant that one could not prevent that person *by law* from expressing their ideas or from their chosen pursuits. For example, one should be free to publish a book critiquing the majority religion in the state, according to Mill, because it would not violate the harm principle. People often mistakenly think protecting freedom of expression means that we should not be able to criticize the views of others (even strong champions of free speech sometimes labor under this misapprehension). However, it means only that one is free to express one's view, but not that one's view is immune from criticism, though we must be careful not to create such a critical atmosphere that people become afraid to express themselves. That is why it is better today as a general policy to criticize a view by saying, "It is my opinion that your view is odious" than to say, "Your view is odious" because the latter sounds as if you are speaking for everyone, whereas the former makes it clear that you are and can only speak for yourself! Let us now turn to further elaboration of this topic.

Does Freedom of Expression Lead to Relativism?

The question of freedom of speech is a vexed one in modern democracy and raises all kinds of problems and contentious debate when it comes to developing a consistent position on the matter, both morally and legally.

There is a constant struggle involved in getting the balance right between what is allowed under free speech and what is not allowed, and unfortunately it is increasingly common today that one's politics (i.e., one's *own personal views* on various issues) is often the (unacceptable) criterion that is used to draw the line. As soon as we try to put free speech into practice it becomes quite difficult for us to tolerate views that we do not agree with, and we are tempted to employ all sorts of means, some subtle, some not so subtle, to restrict the speech of others, especially those with whom we disagree sharply.

We must also be careful to distinguish between the moral question of free speech and the legal question; the latter refers to what is permitted in a legal sense in a particular democratic nation. Individual democratic states often have particular traditions with regard to this matter, and frequently it is legal actions, and judicial decisions, that decide which forms of speech are permitted under the law. This judicial route can be very controversial; public opinion is often enjoined on one side or the other, frequently not based on an appeal to principle but guided by the politics of those doing the approving, and, in the case of the press, those who form public opinion. There is often little consistency with regard to the legal question in particular contexts, and it is hard to have confidence that any principles are being upheld steadfastly.[18] It is probably naïve to approach contemporary democratic culture with the expectation that any kind of principle will be applied consistently. It seems that principles succumb to partisan politics on a regular basis. Surprisingly, this seems to be especially true the more educated a person is, and everyone seems susceptible to this temptation, no matter how high-minded we like to think we are! Principles become further weapons in a pluralist battle; unfortunately everything gets dragged into the worldview conflict. The increasing polarization in some democratic societies, where each side on certain issues regards the other side as irrational, stupid, depraved, or worse, only makes this problem particularly acute. But it is important to draw a clear distinction between the moral and the legal question with regard to the question of free speech. We are concerned with how freedom of thought and expression operates from a descriptive point of view in public discussions and how *it eventually leads to a relativism about knowledge and morality in a democratic, free society*.

One overall problem facing the type of arguments offered by Mill in defense of free speech is that while these arguments are quite convincing in theory, and he clearly makes a strong and interesting case for why freedom of expression, including of thought and speech, on a wide range of topics, seems to be good and productive, it has proved very difficult in practice to put Mill's arguments into effect. Even those who regard themselves as most committed to free speech are frequently tempted to suppress views with which they disagree, whenever they have the chance. The reason for this is, I believe, an obvious one: *it is one of the strongest instincts of the human heart to tell people what is good for them, and then to try to force them to follow our advice!* This instinct often prompts a suppression of the speech of others if they are inclined to take a different line or to ignore our counsel. Mill recognized that many routinely believe they have a better understanding of what is good for people than the people know themselves! But he believed that we must accept as a working principle in the application of freedom that A does not know B's interests as well as B knows them, despite perhaps A's best intentions (even though A may not always have the best intentions).[19] Mill thought A would sometimes abuse power over B if she had it, rather than just using it for what she (A) thought was best for B. This seems a good principle, and yet we have found it very hard indeed to put it into practice. This is why some thinkers argue that Mill's position implies a selfish and very individualistic view of the human person, one that is, moreover, inaccurate.[20] He does not seem to have considered sufficiently the view that many people have no real idea of their own good, or whether there is, for instance, an *objective* account of human goodness (such as one finds in the work of Aristotle and St. Thomas Aquinas), and if there is not, whether we are then faced inevitably with a relativism about the goals and meaning of human life. Indeed, most forms of liberalism hold that one must be free to choose one's own path in life, even if one chooses a life that is debasing in the eyes of others. Popular opinion in most countries rejects such a view as extreme, but liberal thinkers who support Mill are not content to allow popular opinion to decide how debasement is to be defined, because they believe that the ordinary mass of people are not fit to judge this matter. Mill's view sets up a tension between democracy and individualism, because although in a democratic setting individual freedom is encouraged, in the end majority decision rules, and remains then a restraint on individualism, either through law or public opinion. Individualism is therefore limited to some degree in a democratic setting.

This is why one of Mill's main concerns, as we have seen, was a worry about the tyranny of the majority; he did not trust the judgment or wisdom of the majority, and seems to believe, very similar to Plato, that the (or a) minority were more likely to be enlightened, to know better than the majority. There is little doubt that he is one of those philosophers who, ideally, would like the enlightened minority to rule over the unenlightened majority (we noted his recommendation of a system of "plural voting" in Chap. 1). One of the irritating problems with the democratic system, at least from the point of view of those who regard themselves as enlightened, is that it gives the ordinary person too much political power, including the power to decide (by majority vote) for those who disagree with them! (A related problem is that there is no viewpoint–independent way to arrive at an objective definition of what we mean by an "enlightened minority.")

This brings us to another, and perhaps the central, difficulty with the notion of free speech and freedom of expression, the fact that in order to develop a consistent policy with regard to it we are pushed toward an *absolutist understanding*, so that it becomes difficult in practice to distinguish between correct and incorrect views, between right and wrong views. As Mill put it, "unless the reasons [for freedom of speech] are good for an extreme case, they are not good for any case."[21] In short, arguments defending freedom of expression seem to lead us into a position of *relativism* in society, for all practical purposes. As we noted above, one of the strong objections to freedom of expression from its critics is the fact that it can be used to express views that are false or morally wrong or dangerous, and also that it would *encourage* the expression of false views, views that originate not just because of mistakes or ignorance, but also due to human folly. The advantage of Mill's view is that no idea is protected from criticism; a disadvantage seems to be that that no idea can stick, even true ones. In a culture dominated by the absolutizing of freedom, it can be quite difficult to find an anchor for any view that claims to be true. In a liberal culture taken to its logical conclusion, what is complete idiocy or evil to one person may be philosophically cogent and morally impressive to another!

Mill could have replied to this objection in the way that many of his closest disciples today respond to it by saying that we should not suppress false views because this would require us to know in advance which views are false and which are true, and we cannot know this. It also means that someone would have to decide which views are true and which are false in advance, and this is not compatible with the essence of freedom of speech. Mill agreed that some views are definitely false, so he rejected the temptation to defend this position by appealing to relativism. He argued for the free expression of false views, as we have seen, by saying that they strengthen the true view in the clash with error and make the true view stronger and more dynamic. But there is a worrying objection to this reply—that it would be better to suppress such views because if we allow their expression there is a danger that people will come to believe them (and come to act on them). Would it not be better to suppress or censor false views, rather than allowing their expression and taking a great risk that open discussion and debate will then lead to their rejection?

To see the difficulty confronting Mill's position more clearly and also how it will eventually push a society toward moral relativism, it is helpful to distinguish between three categories of beliefs. The first category contains those beliefs (ideas, opinions, arguments, positions, etc.) on various topics that the vast majority in a society accepts as true (in modern society this would include the following beliefs {wouldn't it?}): that all people are equal, that we should be good neighbors to our fellow human beings, that society should provide a safety net for the less fortunate, and so forth). The second category refers to beliefs about issues that are recognized in a society as being in dispute; in contemporary democratic societies, for example, this category may include topics concerning the content of educational curricula, abortion, climate change, how to tackle various social problems, and so forth. The third category contains beliefs that modern society regards as false, for example, that racial segregation is moral, that women should be subordinate to men, that incest between adults is moral, and so forth. Given these categories, one might then argue that beliefs in the first two categories can be freely expressed, but that beliefs in the third category can be restricted or censored. The problem with this proposal is that a general commitment to the value of freedom of thought and of speech cannot support such a threefold division of beliefs; in particular it *cannot support a distinction between categories two and three.*

To illustrate this point further, consider the following belief: that gender is a social construct, a widely held belief in the university academy, particularly among feminist scholars, and perhaps in the humanities more generally, but one still widely rejected by many academics, and by a large majority of the general population. Does this belief belong to category two or three? The fact that it is a disputed belief is not by itself enough to place it in category two because presumably we could have a belief in a society that although disputed by some was regarded as clearly false by the vast majority so that from a practical point of view the society does not take it seriously (what would be an example of this kind of belief?). Of course, the fact that the vast majority do not take a belief seriously is not enough to dismiss the belief from the logical point of view (there were many beliefs that fell into this category in history, across a range of subjects, including science and medicine, that turned out to be true!). However, suppose some people think the belief is definitely false—they are totally convinced of it, absolutely sure, and are inclined to ridicule anyone who accepts it. This is not enough to place it in category three, because there may be lots of people who have exactly the same attitude and assurance but who think the belief is true! So the fact that there is a clear disagreement about the belief would place it in category two.

What follows from this is that it is very difficult to place *any* belief in category three in a free society no matter how false, silly, stupid, or irrational it may appear to many people. The whole point of freedom of expression, as Mill noted, is that the majority are not infallible (even though they are very tempted to think they are) and that unusual, strange, offensive, and radical ideas can get a hearing, after which they may or may not catch on. Remember that Mill called for *absolute* freedom of expression on all topics, including moral topics. This presumably includes the freedom to argue that some forms of terrorism or Nazi views are justified. Even if (and perhaps especially if) there is disagreement over whether a belief belongs to category two or three, it only serves to show that no belief can be put in category three from a practical point of view (even if we might agree or think that it should go in that category from the point of view of objective truth). The upshot is that once we allow people the freedom to arrive at their own beliefs, and their own worldviews, we cannot decide in advance which beliefs and worldviews (within a certain range) *count* and which do not count (even though from the point of view of objective truth we do make such a judgment). But deciding in advance which beliefs, or which categories of beliefs, are acceptable violates the cardinal principle of the freedom of the individual in a democratic setting. The problem with excluding certain views from the range of free speech is that someone will have to decide what these exceptions are, and the worry is that this only succeeds in privileging some worldviews over others. This problem is particularly acute in the context of worldview pluralism. *This means that free speech inevitably, it seems to me, moves society toward a moral and epistemological relativism over time.* So Mill's argument that his approach would have the opposite effect—that it would lead to the truth emerging over time—seems to be wrong.[22]

Does this mean then that one cannot hold that one's view on a certain topic is objectively true and that other views are false, and should not have influence on law, society, and culture? Of course not, but it is very important to understand what it means to say that someone's view is wrong *in a democratic context*. The first point to make is that to agree that people should enjoy a wide sphere of freedom, especially in the area of free speech, automatically carries with it a certain respect for how they exercise their freedom. Commitment to such values seems to require us to recognize that other people have in good faith tried to arrive at their views on key issues relating to worldviews, morality, and the meaning of life in just the same way that we ourselves have. Just as our views should be respected, so should theirs (this is in fact a key facet in the articulation of modern liberal political theory, as we will see later in the book—that we must recognize that others approach many topics in the same way that we do, and so there is a certain parity among free people, which automatically has the result of undermining any priority one might, for whatever reason, feel one's views have over those of others). The second point is that showing respect for the views of others does not mean that I have to *agree* with those views (though one can easily see that the first point suggests, even if it does not require, the second point, and is one reason why democratic society over time has become more relativistic). However, third, when I say that those who hold the opposite view to mine on a specific issue are wrong, I don't just mean that I disagree with them, but that they could be right. Although I hold that others are entitled to arrive at and to hold their own views in a free society, just as I am, *I do not hold that the views others arrive at must therefore in some way be actually true*. In fact, I often believe that such views are false. In addition, I do not mean by this simply that "I happen to think that their view is false" but since it is *their* view, it is true *for them*, despite what I think. This would be to become a philosophical relativist, where one thinks there is no objective truth with regard to these kinds of questions. In saying that democratic culture moves toward relativism, I do not mean that people become philosophical relativists (though we will see later that many do in fact move closer to this position because a spirit of relativism does begin to emerge, where people begin to doubt their views, are tempted to regard their view as "just one among many," a fact that might undermine one's confidence in proposing objective truth claims). No, I can believe that the opposite view to mine is false—objectively false (e.g., that gender is a social construct)—that it is not the way things are in reality, despite what a person or a culture or a society may believe.

However, this gets us to the heart of the fundamental problem stemming from the notion of freedom in a democratic society. This problem is that although I hold that other people's views may be objectively false, I realize that because of the democratic values and setting, *I cannot speak for them on this matter*. I must accept that they have come to a different conclusion than me, and that the way they have arrived at it is just as legitimate as mine. This is why the democratic system seems to move toward relativism about knowledge and morality in an inexorable way. In a setting where there is a very large emphasis on freedom of expression and where arriving at one's own views is not only an option, but is encouraged and expected of citizens, it is very difficult to say things like "this view is false," or "many people hold the wrong view" or "She was the wrong person to be elected." What one might more accurately say is that "*I think* that this view is false," or "*It is my belief* that many people hold the wrong view on this question," or "*It is my opinion* that she was the wrong person to be elected," etc.! In short, I have my view on the matter but cannot speak for others. In addition, there is the presumption not only that others may come to a different view to mine, but that I would prefer them to come to *their own view freely*, even if wrong, than for me to somehow force my view on them. I can try to persuade them, but if I fail, I must then accept that their views differ from mine.

Of course, this in itself will often put pressure on my certainty with regard to my view from the point of view of objective truth, in the sense that, in an honest moment, I might start questioning my certainty because many people that I generally regard as being as reasonable and as well informed as me come to a different conclusion! *The opposite can also happen*; because disagreements appear irresolvable, I might be tempted to dig in on my view, to become almost fanatical with regard to it, to portray those who disagree as irrational and/or immoral (indeed, this is now a common phenomenon). We see both consequences in modern democratic society, a fact that starts to push the society toward relativism, and that also leads to the contentious problem of pluralism described in Chap. 1. (The difficulty is further compounded by the prevalence and influence of anti-realist views of knowledge, which we will discuss in the next chapter.) So while one may not officially hold the position of (philosophical) relativism, society in general is moving toward relativism in one crucial sense: that I recognize that I cannot speak for others on the questions of the day, however much I would like to. I must accept that I cannot adopt the position that everyone needs to share my foundational metaphysical commitments. I may wish others did accept these commitments, and I can try to persuade them of their truth, but the reality of pluralism is that *I must accept that this is not how things work anymore*. Freedom of expression leads toward relativism in the sense that we realize we cannot speak for others, and we tend because of this to flirt with philosophical relativism (a topic we will explore in Chap. 4, after we have first looked at pluralism and loss of confidence in reason in more detail in the next chapter).

The Temptation to Suppress "Objectionable" Views

It can be very disconcerting to experience strong disagreement with others, quite difficult to admit that other people are as reasonable or as well informed as we are but come to different conclusions. This is where the temptation to develop an animus toward those with different views can enter into the picture. The democratic emphasis on freedom leads to a dangerous tension between the fact that other people who appear to be as equally rational and sincere as me nevertheless arrive at different conclusions on the same issues, and favor different laws in society. I may then become reluctant to admit that there seems to be no simple way to resolve these disagreements and perhaps hesitant to confront the deeper foundational problem now facing democracy—that many reasonable people hold very diverse views that lead to increasingly contentious arguments, polarization, perhaps even giving rise to feelings of revulsion. I may be tempted whenever I have the opportunity to disparage the convictions of others and to deny to others the freedom to arrive at and hold their convictions simply because they are different from mine. Worldview pluralism places this temptation before us. The temptation to curtail the freedom of others can occur in a variety of ways, some subtle, some more obvious, all of which, I contend, we see in some form or other creeping into modern democracies around the world.

One move is to adopt the posture that *I am more reasonable* that those I disagree with, that others are stupid, irrational, lazy, have not taken the time to consider the facts, or think issues through, perhaps because they are not educated properly, or do not spend enough time thinking clearly! While personal faults like these may be a factor in some individual cases, they are not at play in most cases because of a simple fact about democratic pluralism: *that equally educated and well-informed people freely arrive at incommensurable views* (as we saw in Chap. 1). Let us not forget that the phenomenon of incommensurability may be understood to include three factors: views that are *different* from each other, views that are so different that they *cannot be reconciled*, and (we should also add at least initially) views that have been arrived at in a *reasonable* way, that other people are acting in good faith just as we are (we will come back to the concept of incommensurability in more detail in Chap. 8). This last point is crucial because it means that many people believe sincerely that their views are reasonable; in addition, acceptance of the value of freedom in a democracy means that *others may not speak for me* with regard to any topic (however much they may be tempted to). So portraying others as unreasonable when compared to me, while correct in some cases, is generally just a way of avoiding the unpleasant truth that incommensurable views are a consequence of pluralism. It is also a way of avoiding debate and discussion, and can also be used in some contexts as a way of bullying people who disagree with me into suppressing their views.

A second way to call into question the freedom of those we disagree with is a variation of the first. This is to adopt the position that people who disagree with me are being manipulated, maneuvered, hoodwinked, even brainwashed, by some powerful forces in society and are not thinking for themselves. If they were thinking for themselves, they would adopt my view! Manipulation may occur by an individual with great rhetorical skills, someone we describe for good measure as a demagogue even; perhaps demagoguery would be engaged in by the media in a society, or by means of university educational programs, or some political party or interest group or charismatic individual, or by powerful economic forces through insidious advertising techniques, and so forth. Again such a thing is possible from a theoretical point of view, even in a democratic society where it would perhaps be less likely to have much effect because of the freedom of not only the press but of individuals to interrogate and critique various positions. However, in this case the charge of manipulation, in particular, is usually just a device to express frustration at the fact that *educated people do not agree with me*! (Of course, the general charge also raises the question as to whether critically reflective people are not themselves capable of, and indeed susceptible to, manipulation and demagoguery, questions that our experience of the democratic process has not clearly resolved!)

A third tactic is to encourage the suppression of free thinking in specific contexts like academia, and to promote by force and intimidation the "correct" views, which through filtering down would have a big impact on society. In this instance, there is no rule, procedure, or law banning the discussion of certain ideas, but one can send a clear message by constructing a certain type of social environment that entertaining ideas that one disfavors will not be tolerated. So those who might be inclined to raise them get the message to keep quiet, or risk problems, discrimination certainly and perhaps even dismissal. This is a particularly hypocritical tactic if it is employed, say in a university setting, which has as one of its foundational guiding principles the free exchange of ideas in order to arrive at truth! Modern universities are getting more political and it is becoming more common on campuses to suppress dissent, especially when it comes to discussing ideas regarded as "politically incorrect." An example of this tactic occurred at Wilfrid Laurier University in Canada in 2017 when a young adjunct professor was discussing in class the arguments for and against the use of certain pronouns to describe transgender people. This professor was subjected to a very intimidating cross-examination later by two of her departmental colleagues, during which one of them asked her if she would discuss the arguments for and against Nazi ideology side by side in the classroom. This is a very interesting case because it shows a kind of attempt at what I call social censorship where one creates a special climate with the aim of silencing views one does not agree with, while still being able to claim that there are no actual forms of censorship in place.[23] The adjunct professor later sued the University, claiming among other things that the incident made her unemployable in academia, a charge which, if true, suggests that many university educators agreed with her treatment by her supervisors.

This case also instructively raises the question of which ideas one is free to discuss in the classroom.[24] It is true that in the above situation the professor would not discuss in a neutral way both sides of Nazi ideology. This reminds us of our three categories of beliefs, discussed above. The transgender pronoun issue would go into the category of topics that are in dispute in our democratic societies, but Nazi ideas would go into the category of beliefs that are rejected. But suppose there is considerable disagreement about which category the transgender issue should be in (which there is), then this by itself would mean that the issue is not settled, and so would fall under the heading of disputed beliefs. One can see the danger of having separate categories for disputed beliefs and for false beliefs, which is why I noted that Mill's general arguments cannot support such a distinction. In any case, a good protocol has gained acceptance in the democratic setting for handling problems of this type—that we should err on the side of freedom if there is any doubt about whether a belief should be expressed. I will return to this general issue later because this kind of absolutist approach to free speech, which is standard in democratic societies in recent times, especially when it is being invoked to defend liberal ideas that are aimed at attacking traditional ideas, should now, some are suggesting, be rethought (i.e., we should not allow absolute freedom of thought and expression). The phenomenon of "cancel culture" that is beginning to emerge in Western democratic nations is a good example of this recent phenomenon. (Indeed, who would have thought that we would see the day when one of the world's most prestigious newspapers, the *New York Times*, would apologize for publishing an opinion piece and force out the editor who published it?[25]) These direct threats to free speech are instructive, I believe, and another argument to show that the important value of freedom, and with it the democratic process in which freedom is a founding principle, *is beginning to strain along the edges*, as pluralism becomes more acute.

A fourth way to attempt to suppress or control the views of others with whom one disagrees is to seek to do an "end run" around the democratic process. This means either to overturn the democratic votes of the majority by some procedural maneuver or to orchestrate a situation where issues that play a key role in the direction of life and culture that should be put to a vote of the people in a democracy are decided in some other way, perhaps by parliament. The first way occurs regularly in the U.S. where the Supreme Court by tradition has the authority of a second government and has the power (unlike in most countries, the United Kingdom, Belgium, Canada, and New Zealand, e.g.) to overturn a piece of legislation passed by the U.S. Congress if they judge that it is not consistent with the U.S. Constitution. This is a very tricky judgment to make of course in individual cases, since these issues are open to (subjective, i.e., political) interpretation and debate. So the charge is often made that the U.S. courts can and do decide many issues that are in dispute in society according to the political views of (unelected and unrepresentative) judges. To be sure, overturning the will of the people is a serious matter, and is one of the reasons many believe such laws lack legitimacy.[26] It can only be done if the courts have the support of a significant tranche of public opinion, with the help of the media and the establishment classes, on the issues that they are deciding from the bench. The U.S. Supreme Court has decided many issues in recent years that would normally be decided by the people in a democracy, for example, on abortion, affirmative action, campaign finance, capital punishment, and gay marriage.

A significantly disenfranchised or apathetic electorate also helps with the manipulation of public opinion. The media can use its power as opinion makers to try to manipulate and to pacify public opinion, especially if it is inclined to take sides on matters that are under dispute, and if it speaks with largely one voice. Indeed, one of the features of modern pluralism is that the media *takes sides* on contentious issues that are in dispute in society, and so are less able to, and not often interested in, fulfilling their duties as watchdogs on government power, and in the task of educating the public through informed and balanced reporting. It was inevitable that this would happen as a consequence of pluralism, and we are now right in the midst of an increasingly politicized media in many democratic countries, making it harder than ever for the public to navigate its way through the issues of the day.

How the issues of the day are to be decided, let us remind ourselves, is not our concern here; our focus is on the temptation to suppress views one disagrees with, and who gets to decide such issues in a free society—the people, the government, the judges, the media, or perhaps an elite or other non-representative group? Usurping the democratic process is not without consequences though. In the U.S., for instance, the Supreme Court is now regarded as just another branch of politics, and the ideal of the objectivity and indeed majesty of the law has been lost (if it ever existed)! There is now a hugely partisan and rancorous battle (bringing out the very worst in people) every time there is a vacancy on the Court. The battle is fought over the (perceived) *political* views of the judicial nominees. This is another symptom of the breakdown of democracy, the fact that the courts become political entities, and take sides in the dispute between worldviews in a state, in addition to the fact that every worldview, political party and interest group will try to use the courts to avoid the democratic process if they are in a position to do so. Overturning laws that have been put in place democratically and attempting to decide contentious issues in non-democratic ways because we have become disillusioned with democratic principles and with the power of reason to solve disagreement is now *a clear trend, I contend, in modern states.*

All sides now know that it is unlikely that they will be able to convince others to accept their views in a public deliberation, so forcing these views through the courts on those who disagree with them is regarded, correctly, as being more politically expedient in some democratic countries. The European Union is often perceived to work in a similar way because many of its laws are passed in the abstract by the European Parliament. It is in their concrete interpretation and implementation, which is often done by civil servants in Brussels, that laws are imposed on the citizens of individual member states who had virtually no say in them and often no advance knowledge of them (e.g., regarding health policy, economic regulations, labor policies, funding for education, road safety regulations, and property rights). This is one of the reasons that there is unrest in some countries with regard to the vital issue of their sovereignty in the E.U., and was one of the reasons behind the British decision to leave. The consternation among those on the wrong end of this decision and the frequent suggestion in the years after the vote that it might be possible to find some way to overturn the views of the majority, perhaps by mounting a new campaign and forcing a new referendum, also confirms my general point that democracy in the face of pluralism and freedom is beginning *to creak at the seams.*

The final way we wish to consider of forcing one's views on others who disagree with them is that one might attempt to define democracy (particularly liberal democracy, our concern in this book) in such a way that it can only be expressed in one set of values, that these lead to one correct and true way of seeing things, support only one worldview in fact. This will usually be the worldview of the person providing the definition, of course! This approach is now a prevailing view in contemporary liberal political philosophy in the western world, ever since the influential political theory of Harvard philosopher, John Rawls. There is a genuine philosophical question, of course, about how democracy should be defined (as we noted in Chap. 1), but there is also a temptation in a pluralist context especially, which is becoming increasingly polarized and where a number of incommensurable beliefs, views, and opinions emerge, to define liberal democracy in such a way as to exclude views one finds objectionable (and to pave the way then for one's own view!). For example, one might try to *define* the freedom of the individual as including the freedom to have an abortion, thereby coming to the table with a built-in answer to a complex question, suggesting that we can avoid the debate altogether because the definition of freedom settles the matter. I will not belabor this point here but do want to note that I believe that modern political philosophy is guilty of this charge. Pursuit of this strategy may or may not be one of the motivations of Rawls' political theory, but it may be one of the main reasons it has become widely accepted among western academics, at least. We will return to a full discussion of this fascinating topic in Chaps. 8 and 9.

Notes

1. For a full discussion of the views of a number of thinkers throughout history, and the contrast with modern liberalism, see Robert P. Kraynak, *Christian Faith and Modern Democracy* (South Bend, IN.: University of Notre Dame Press, 2001).
2. See Plato, *The Republic*, 481–489d.
3. See Voltaire's 1763 work, *A Treatise on Tolerance* (New York: Barnes and Noble, 2009); also Pierre Bayle, *Political Writings*, ed. by Sally Jenkinson (Cambridge, UK.: Cambridge U.P., 2000). Also, Perez Zagorin, *How the Idea of Religious Toleration Came to the West* (Princeton, NJ.: Princeton U.P., 2003).
4. See John Locke, *A Letter Concerning Toleration*, ed. James Tully (Indianapolis, IN.: Hackett, 1983).
5. See *A Letter*, p. 27.
6. Although Locke does not mention Catholics specifically, these passages are understood to be referring to them; see *A Letter*, p. 40.
7. *A Letter*, p. 40.
8. See Mill's *On Liberty* (Indianapolis, IN.: Hackett, 1978), pp. 1–2.
9. See Isaiah Berlin, "Two Concepts of Liberty" in his *Four Essays on Liberty* (London: Oxford U.P., 2002). This distinction can be complicated, and is subject to a number of interpretations; see Ian Carter, *A Measure of Freedom* (New York: Oxford U.P., 1999). See also Benjamin Constant, "The Liberty of the Ancients Compared with that of the Moderns," in B. Fontana (ed.), *Constant: Political Writings*.
10. See J.S. Mill, *On Liberty*, p. 4.
11. Ibid., p. 4.
12. See ibid., p. 84.
13. Ibid., p. 9.
14. See ibid., pp. 15–52.
15. See ibid., pp. 16ff.
16. See ibid., pp. 32ff.
17. Ibid., p. 16.
18. See the sobering discussion in Sandra Day O'Connor, *The Majesty of the Law* (New York: Random House, 2003), pp. 99–112, concerning shifting and subjective court opinions concerning free speech cases in the history of the U.S. Supreme Court.
19. See Mill, *On Liberty*, p. 74.
20. See Michael Sandel (ed.), *Liberalism and its Critics* (New York: New York U.P., 1984), especially pp. 1–11.
21. Mill, *On Liberty*, p. 20.

22. Some thinkers have argued that the modern university is a microcosm of this problem that faces liberal society in general; see Patrick Dineen, *Why Liberalism Failed* (New Haven, CT.: Yale U.P., 2018), pp. 110–130.
23. See "Wilfred Laurier University TA claims censure over video clip on gender pronouns," available at the *globeandmail.com*; also "Lindsay Shepherd sues Wilfred Laurier," available at *nationalpost.com*.
24. For a thought-provoking discussion, see Stanley Fish, *The First: How to think about Hate Speech, Campus Speech, Religious Speech, Fake News, Post-Truth, and Donald Trump* (New York: Atria, 2019).
25. See "New York Times editorial page editor resigns after uproar over Cotton op–ed," *The Washington Post*, June 7th, 2020.
26. See Mitchell Muncy (ed.), *The End of Democracy?* (Dallas, TX: Spence Pub., 1997).

CHAPTER 3

Worldviews, Pluralism, and Loss of Confidence in Reason

In 2016, the Oxford Dictionary's word of the year was "post-truth," which the dictionary's website defines as an adjective "relating to or denoting circumstances in which objective facts are less influential in shaping public opinion than appeals to emotion or personal beliefs." While the editors of the Dictionary explain that they were mainly thinking of the word in the context of recent political and social trends, it is clear that it has a much wider application, reminding us of the incommensurability of worldviews in western societies, and of the practical failure of public deliberation to settle on objective truths. Democracies began with an emphasis on popular sovereignty and on the freedom of the individual; now they are moving slowly but surely toward a situation that might be described as post-truth, which is a form of relativism (both epistemological, and especially moral). I will argue that this problem is compounded by a crisis of confidence with regard to the power of human reason. There is a critical loss of confidence in our ability to solve our differences by means of reason, in the hope that reason can be an effective tool and guide for democratic society. This is especially true with regard to moral, political, social, religious, and cultural questions that play such a role in our understanding of ourselves as human beings, our purpose in life, our responsibilities toward our families, other people, and even nature itself. In this chapter, I will try to explain clearly how this loss of confidence has come about. In the next chapter, we will then turn to the emergence and pervasive

© The Author(s), under exclusive license to Springer Nature
Switzerland AG 2021
B. Sweetman, *The Crisis of Democratic Pluralism*,
https://doi.org/10.1007/978-3-030-78382-2_3

influence of moral relativism as a cultural phenomenon in modern democratic societies.

I believe that we can trace the current crisis of confidence in human reason in a kind of *causal* way from the very beginnings of democratic society. I hope to be able to illustrate a tentative causal story for how we got to where we are today (even though social causation is, admittedly, notoriously difficult to trace or predict). It was perhaps inevitable that a free and open democratic society would eventually lead to pluralism, understood mainly in a relativistic sense, though it was not really predictable before the fact. A democratic arrangement might have developed in several different directions than the path it actually took, but I contend that we can trace the main causal forces, if we might put it like that, that led to the loss of confidence in reason as a consequence, and that also led to the crisis concerning objective truth that is now a feature of modern democratic culture. This crisis in turn gave rise to related trends concerning contentious clashes of views, tolerance and intolerance, bullying as a tactic in moral and political argument, and the abandonment of principle in intellectual debate. I shall say something about all of these and related issues in this and later chapters. But first we need to take a moment to introduce more fully the concept of a worldview.

Worldviews and Pluralism

The rise of pluralism in the modern democratic state, I contend, leads to what I am calling the problem of worldview pluralism. I am using the term pluralism in a descriptive way to refer to the fact that there now exist several distinctive, and incommensurable, worldviews in the same state. In many democratic nations, there are now present a number of distinct worldviews or philosophies of life that command significant allegiance from people in those nations and that therefore have considerable influence when it comes to decision-making about the issues of the times concerning moral, political, religious, social, economic, and cultural questions. Many states either currently have a number of diverse worldviews or are on their way to having a number of them. Before we come to our discussion of pluralism and the undermining of reason, we need to provide an overview of what we mean by a worldview, a term I introduced in detail in an earlier work.[1] The term "worldview" is very valuable when discussing substantive questions of meaning, freedom, culture, and politics that arise within democratic states. It is more neutral than the term "religion," and so helps us to see the key concepts and what is at stake in a substantively clearer light. I encourage everyone to make this their preferred term when referring to a person's foundational and defining beliefs on moral, political, and social questions, and when considering the role these beliefs play or should play in the context of democratic pluralism.

Let us begin with a number of points aimed at clarifying further the notion of a worldview. First, it is intended to describe a person's philosophy of life, those key beliefs and values which regulate how one lives, and which influence the way in which one raises one's family. In the philosophical sense, the beliefs of one's worldview can be organized for convenience under three general headings: beliefs about the nature of reality, beliefs about the nature of the human person, and beliefs about social, moral, and political matters. Beliefs in the first category are more abstract, and may not be considered much of the time by most people, though they play a central role in one's worldview because they usually provide the philosophical foundations for more familiar practical beliefs. This category would include foundational beliefs such as whether or not one believes in God or a supreme power behind the universe, what one believes about the nature of the physical universe (its structure, size, age, current state, future development, etc.), and what one holds to be true about other abstract topics to which most people do not give much thought. These would include such topics as the type of causation that operates in the universe, the laws of the universe, the categories of things that exist, whether there exist physical and non-physical things, the role of chance and freedom in the universe, and so forth.

The second set of beliefs concerns the human person. Traditionally, the nature of the human person has been an important topic in the work of many thinkers because of its centrality to questions about the meaning and purpose of human life, including questions about our place in the grand scheme of things, and about the nature of human fulfillment and happiness. So this general area would include beliefs about the makeup of human beings; for instance, whether we consist of body and soul, whether we have free will, whether our species, *Homo sapiens*, differs in kind or in degree from other species, what our place in nature is, whether there is such a thing as *human nature*, whether human beings can obtain objective knowledge of the external world, and so on. The last set of beliefs covers more practical areas of culture and society, morality, and politics. This is where people are more directly engaged with their beliefs and so would recognize their worldview more clearly and would be aware of how it plays a central role in their day-to-day lives. This third category would include one's beliefs on ordinary moral and political topics, such as, for example, one's position on euthanasia, on whether health care should be provided by the government, on whether businesses should be taxed to combat climate change, and so forth. It may also include one's *moral theory*, for example, a theory based on the virtues like that of Aristotle and St. Thomas Aquinas, or a utilitarian theory inspired by the thought of John Stuart Mill, or a religious (e.g., Christian) moral theory. One's moral theory might also be classified under one's view of the human person; it is also the case that many people may have given little or no thought to an overall theory, though their general moral beliefs, crucially, can still be organized under a theory, and can be shown to fit largely into one theory or another. The same is true for one's political theory. In addition to holding a position on this or that political issue, one might also hold a political theory (such as democracy) that supports one's political views, and that one also believes is the best system by which to organize society. Or one might subscribe to such a theory only in a general way, but be unable, and perhaps not interested in trying, to work out the details at a theoretical level, for example, on the difficult question of how much freedom a democratic society (i.e., the people) should give to its citizens (i.e., to themselves), or how exactly governing bodies are to be structured, and so forth. It is also sometimes possible to work out a person's worldview from observation of their beliefs and actions, to some extent.

The second point to make is that it is more accurate to say that most people *live* their worldview first and think about their beliefs, how they might justify or defend these beliefs, and about the structure and makeup of their worldview, second, if at all. People make decisions, moral and otherwise, as they are confronted with situations in their everyday lives, and perhaps seldom think about how the decisions fit into their moral theory, which moral theory they hold, what it says about their overall worldview, how this worldview is justified, and so forth. Although increasingly I think one of the trends in democratic pluralist societies is that people are now *more aware of their worldview than ever before*; they recognize more than ever that not everyone shares their worldview, and that the disagreement between worldviews, especially at the moral and political level, can cause great consternation and conflict in society. They likely experience this conflict and tension in their own circle of family and friends, in the work place, and at the societal level, including at the national level. This is one of the consequences of pluralism. Indeed, in some countries public discussion and debate of important topics is becoming very difficult to conduct and is leading to polarization; even public institutions, such as academia, the law courts, and the media, are becoming overtly political. The very fact of pluralism prompts people to give more attention to what they believe. Pluralism prompts us to realize that others do not have the same beliefs as we do, and this in turn forces us to think about what our beliefs are and also hopefully why we hold them.

Given this modern climate, I would like to encourage everyone, thirdly, to give more attention to one's own worldview, and its structure as outlined above. I believe that everyone has a worldview, whether they realize it or not or give it much thought, or even if they deny that they have a worldview! One's beliefs and practices can always be organized under the headings above and classified as belonging in whole or in part to a particular worldview. There are four clarifying questions that can help us think further about our worldview: 1. *What is your worldview?* This question asks not only for the name of your worldview, but also about your beliefs concerning the three areas mentioned above. One may have to think hard about some of these beliefs, but it is a very useful exercise to explore one's position in these general categories, which can sometimes be aided by thinking about what one's everyday moral and political beliefs might imply for larger questions. For example, what does one's everyday beliefs (and resulting actions) imply about one's view of the human person, or about where one might stand on the question of whether human beings differ in degree or in kind from other species, and so forth? 2. *Is your worldview reasonable?* This may be a hard question to answer, of course, though it is a crucial matter in much theoretical work about modern democracy, and we will give it full attention later in Chaps. 8 and 9. But for now I have in mind common sense questions such as: are you able to back up your main beliefs with reason and evidence, could you present an argument defending your beliefs to those who reject them, do you know the critical issues involved in a debate concerning your beliefs and the beliefs of others, have you considered the overall philosophical justification of your views?

The subject matter of worldviews—the nature of reality, the nature of the human person, and the nature of moral and political values—is not typically discernable in black and white, of course, which only further complicates things. Another worry is that in many democratic societies we are increasingly coming to regard views different from our own as not just incorrect, mistaken, or wrong, but as irrational or even immoral. But nevertheless it is important for people to try to put their worldview on a reasonable footing which means at very least getting some clarity about what one believes, why one believes it, and also why one's view may be better reasoned than other views that a person of good will holds on the other side, perhaps even in one's own family. This second question also requires one to give some attention to whether one would regard oneself as generally a reasonable person! Are you the kind of person who attempts to think things through logically and who takes account of any evidence that is available on a topic; do you keep yourself informed of the facts, and consider the objections of those with different convictions? One should consider these questions when thinking about whether in general one adopts a reasonable approach to things. It is vitally important in a pluralist context that one strives to be reasonable in both the articulation of one's worldview, and in the democratic exchange with other worldviews. We shall devote a considerable part of our later discussion to what it means to be reasonable, and the question of how to assess the rationality of worldviews.

Our third question then is: 3. *Does your worldview have political implications?* I do think that most worldviews have political implications, especially those that are involved in pluralist debates in democratic societies. So perhaps we could rephrase the question to ask: what are the political implications of your worldview? And then the question would also involve asking if you vote according to your worldview when you go to the polling booth? Most worldviews have political consequences in one key sense: they contain at least some beliefs concerning the way in which human beings should live and conduct themselves in society, about how society should be organized, about which beliefs and behaviors with regard to various issues are morally appropriate, about how we should inculcate these beliefs in our children, so that the next generation learns them, accepts them, practices them, and so forth. Not all beliefs in a worldview have political implications, but some do. Two examples will help to illustrate. The first is a central belief of many worldviews: that all people are equal. One may hold this belief whether one is a secularist, a religious believer, or a Marxist, for instance. One of my own central beliefs is that God created all people equally, a belief that has clear social and political significance. One political implication is that the state should mandate laws and policies that force employers to treat people equally in job applications; it also mandates laws, I believe, that ensure that every person is entitled to a fair trial in a court of law, that everyone is entitled to a basic education or basic health care, and so forth. There may be disagreement about which particular political policy is correct or most appropriate in a certain cultural and political context for implementing the belief that all human beings are created equal, but this is a secondary issue. The crucial point is that the belief has political significance, and just as important, one would feel that one was seriously remiss at a moral level if one ignored its political nature. Most of us would feel that we are not really living out our worldview with moral integrity if we just ignore some of its political implications. The belief in equality was a key belief of Martin Luther King, Jr. in his crusade for civil rights in the U.S., as we will see in our case study of his view in Chap. 9.

The belief that it is part of God's moral law that we are our brother's keeper is another religious belief that has important political implications. This means that we must look after people who are in difficulty, or facing hardship, even if their problems are self-inflicted (though it does not mean that we should not judge people's behavior, or condone irresponsible behavior). From the political point of view, this belief would have implications for social welfare programs and policies, as well as for health care, employment and in other areas. Again, the bare belief is initially understood somewhat at an abstract level so it might not settle the issue of which particular policy we should pursue in a certain context but this is a disagreement about how the belief is to be implemented, not a disagreement about whether it should be implemented. There are many beliefs in our worldviews similar to the two mentioned where one simply could not live with integrity if one were to ignore their political implications. This will be a strong argument, as we will see later, against a commonly expressed view today in some circles in democratic societies that religious believers should practice their beliefs privately, but not bring them into the political arena. We might add a fourth question that underlies the fact of pluralism. 4. *What is one's attitude to worldviews not one's own?* Do you regard these worldviews as reasonable? Wrong in whole or in part, or perhaps as irrational and/or immoral, or what? Are you the kind of person who thinks that when it comes to these matters, most people are stupid and their worldviews irrational, and your worldview is (*obviously*) the correct one?! These are challenging questions that we must focus on as the phenomenon of pluralism moves to the front burner.

The final point we wish to underscore is that the term "worldview"— when used to identify, describe, and call attention to different ways of looking at the world in a democratic state—is a *transformative* term. It is not only transformative on a personal level, but also at the level of politics and society. This is because of its power to help us to see the foundational issues involving the nature of democracy, as well as disagreements within democratic societies, in a completely new, fresh way. It is also immensely helpful when trying to appreciate and understand the role of religious worldviews and secularist worldviews in the modern state, as well as in showing that the way we have been thinking about these topics up to now is no longer adequate. Consequently a sub-theme of this book is to clarify the role of religion in democratic societies, especially at the political level, and to show why and how the religious worldview should not be denied a role in democratic states. The same arguments will also apply to the worldview of secularism which is often mistakenly given a privileged position in some democratic societies, at least at the level of theory.

The Problem of Worldview Pluralism and its Origin: A Tentative Causal Argument

We traced in a broad sense in previous chapters the beginnings of democratic society, especially the emphasis on the foundational values of popular sovereignty, natural rights, freedom, equality, and justice. These values are first embraced in the abstract and then gradually particularized and implemented over time in various countries. For example, equality conveys the notion that people are essentially equal in their nature and their essence and so everyone should be treated in the same way under the law, but it still needs to be worked out more specifically what this means in particular cases (for instance, are all people entitled to a free education?). It is also a considerable challenge to actually implement these theoretical values in real life, as we know. Many democracies failed at this task for the longest time, and continue to fail. Justice means that people should be treated fairly, but again we need to figure out how to realize this in specific cases, for example, with regard to economic policy (which tax policy is fair?).

Of the foundational democratic values, the important one for our discussion in this section is freedom. The abstract meaning of freedom is that people should be allowed to make important decisions for themselves about issues that affect their own lives (and those of their children). That is the basic point concerning freedom, and as we noted above, the more general justification for this understanding of freedom is that freedom appears to be part of human nature, part of who we are as human beings.

Nevertheless, this abstract understanding does not tell us whether freedom extends to all areas of life, whether there are any limits to it, how these limits are decided, and so forth. Such matters still have to be settled, and as we know they are often the subject of intense debate and controversy, and indeed there are a variety of answers to them across different democracies.

I have indicated that attempting to trace a kind of causal process through developments in democratic society is extremely difficult, perhaps something of a minefield. This is because of the idiosyncratic twists and turns in the history of individual countries, not to mention the greater upheavals caused by wars, various political struggles, and occasional political instability, along with straitened economic circumstances, all of which have an impact on the course and pace of social change. Nevertheless, I believe the argument we present here is broadly correct, and is an accurate description of how things did in fact develop in many countries, especially as they became more politically stable and mature in terms of their implementation of democratic values. Our argument here adopts a strategy similar to Locke's in his description of the state of nature (from which, he claimed, societies emerged to form social contracts). It is an attempt to envisage in the abstract how a state of affairs developed without claiming that it actually did develop in just this way in every affected country, and without trying to lay out a series of necessary steps that must be fulfilled in a country so that it satisfies the causal argument (and while also noting that social change is brought about in specific countries by events that are often unique to those countries).

In addition, the timeline of this causal process runs from the beginnings of democracy in a particular country down to today (it is indeed an ongoing process, as we have been arguing). As the argument indicates, the particular implementation and understanding of the value of freedom proceeded at different paces in individual nations, and it is only in the last generation or so that the last steps have been realized or are beginning to be realized in most mature democracies. Even though there were interruptions along the way in many democracies, such as, for example, in those very directly affected in their internal affairs by World War II, these nations eventually settled back down on the course of democracy, and the movement toward freedom continued apace (this is even true of those countries in Eastern Europe which gained their independence only comparatively recently, such as Poland and Slovakia, but which are clearly on the same trajectory as their more Western neighbors). We are tracing the main outlines of some broad developments while recognizing that there are individual differences along the way, aberrations here and there, and catalytic events in specific countries, including sometimes clashes of values, that would not fit easily into our story. We can trace broad and largely correct outlines in history, I believe, while recognizing that, however much we might wish it, there is never a neat story to be told. So with these qualifications in mind, let us turn to our tentative causal argument.[2]

Step 1. Democratic societies were free in principle but not in practice: The first step to identify in the tentative causal process I wish to trace is that democratic society started out with an emphasis on the value of freedom, but mainly in a theoretical sense, and not in the sense we understand it today. One might say that although democratic society aspired to freedom of the individual, it moved very slowly toward realization of this goal, and was often quite reluctant to put it into practice. In fact it was only quite late in the game that the practice of freedom with regard to individual decision-making began to take off, with very far-reaching consequences. The reason democratic society was slow to practice the value of freedom in its fullest expression is because it is surely part of the nature of a society that lives together with a deeply shared culture that such a society would be reluctant to, and very cautious about, changing the way it does things. Most people tended to share a philosophy of life, and so there was a cultural presumption in favor of one set of foundational beliefs, one religion, one morality, one shared understanding of the function of law, one set of cultural traditions, mores, and so forth. In early democratic culture, people were free in theory to change their religion, to adopt a different moral point of view, to express a radical political position, to pursue a different worldview or a different path. Yet in practice this was easier said than done, for a variety of reasons: severe cultural pressure to conform, negative consequences if one rocked the boat too much, and even legal sanction if one went too far. People and so societies are also cautious or even frightened of change; the exercise of free human expression is by nature a slow process; it also takes time for new ideas to catch on; and it takes time for human desires, in particular, to be unshackled, for us to free ourselves from our inhibitions so that we can express ourselves differently from others. Legal sanction for different views perhaps could not be justified under democratic theory but one can get away with it if one has public will on one's side.

The upshot of this conformity is that although in theory people were free to arrive at their own ideas even with regard to defining matters in religion, morality, and politics, in practice most people adhered to the established and majority view in the state, and most countries therefore were quite monolithic in their beliefs and worldview. This was especially evident in the area of religious and sexual morality, as we know only too well. The dominant worldview was also strongly enforced and reinforced by the institutions of the state in the educational system, the courts, the media, the universities, and by educated, elite opinion. Democracies functioned like this for a long time; indeed, in some countries right up until the latter half of the twentieth century.

Step 2. Freedom led gradually to the emergence of different (but not yet incommensurable) beliefs and values: The second step in our causal story is that eventually a significant change began to occur when people started to exercise in practice the freedom they possessed in theory. It is difficult to say exactly why people started to exercise this freedom; as noted above, this is a fascinating question for sociologists and historians (see Endnote 2). The main point however for our discussion is that people *did* begin to express themselves more freely. Gradually, the attention, sometimes notoriety, even stigma that came with challenging well-established beliefs, advancing new ideas, and pursuing new paths in thought and behavior, especially in the areas of religion, morality, and politics, began to lessen, and new ways of thinking and living began to spring up. Over a very long period of time, perhaps more than a hundred to one hundred and fifty years, and rapidly gaining ground especially in recent decades (perhaps since the 1960s in America, the 1980s in Ireland and the 2000s in Poland—the time line is relative to the culture of each democratic state), *a pluralism of views began to materialize*. This means that what started out as a monolithic culture underwent a process of gradual change that eventually led to a pluralistic culture. A pluralistic culture is one in which there are a variety of diverse views held by significantly large numbers of people with regard to the general area of worldviews and the meaning of life, particularly as they affect the issues of the day. These different views also give rise, of course, to different ways of living. So for example there may be different views on religious, moral, political, and cultural topics. One may even have different religions springing up and gaining some cultural recognition. This might happen as a result of immigration, but also because people may be drawn to, and experiment with, alternative religions both as a way of rejecting the religion they grew up with, the religion of their culture, but also as a way of trying something new. The motivation for trying something new can vary and can be hard to identify, but it could include a moral dissatisfaction with the main beliefs of one's culture or religion, moral weakness in the face of a morally demanding religion, a loss of meaning that prompts a new search for fulfillment, abandonment of restrictive beliefs, a search for a rationalization for one's behavior, an attempt to deal with a practical problem, or because one has close ties to a new community, and so forth. These developments are some of the many consequences of the exercise of freedom in democratic society.

Step 3. Plurality of views initially received a mixed reaction: fear, bemusement, curiosity, and was even welcomed as intriguing!: The initial reaction to the appearance of novel beliefs, strange views, and ways of living was also varied, but it had one key characteristic among a broad range of people, perhaps especially among the intelligentsia and the elites. As well as a reaction of dismay, bemusement, and even fear, it was also regarded with some curiosity, even as an intriguing phenomenon! For some it was a novel, even welcome, experience to see various people challenge mainstream religious, moral, political, and cultural beliefs and practices (perhaps especially religious ones), and to propose, defend, and pursue alternative opinions and patterns of living. It is probably true to say that it was often the intelligentsia that were the very ones in the vanguard of this new trend, and who also observed and followed with great interest those of their own circle and class who exhibited this attitude! Gradually, many people found it novel and interesting that growing numbers were beginning to challenge their supposedly sacrosanct religious teachings, to see people flouting social mores (e.g., in the area of sexual morality, the practice of co-habitation as an alternative to marriage started to gain ground, and so forth). One might liken the initial effect to a graduate seminar in literature in which some of the participants begin proposing new-fangled ways of reading a standard literary text; one's initial response perhaps is that the new readings are wrong, or cannot be defended, but there is also a seductive attraction to the process, and one may even find the fanciful interpretations interesting, novel, and yes, intriguing! As it is in the literature course, so it is in the culture at large! Indeed, it is a natural human reaction perhaps for many to be intrigued by the possibilities inherent in the practice of an increasingly less restrained understanding of freedom, and attracted to them themselves, even if inhibited to take the next step, as many were of course at first. I am claiming that over a very long period of time, the result was the appearance of a variety of different and conflicting views and practices with regard to the serious business of living in society, such as in morality, politics, and social and religious matters.

The emergence of this phenomenon did not affect everyone in democratic society, and it was more obvious in some nations than others, and, as noted above, did not occur as the shortest distance between two points in any country; nevertheless, many became involved in it or caught up in it in some way, and eventually it showed up in most democratic settings.

Step 4. Pluralism became troubling, irritating, and contentious: The early novelty and intriguing nature of the presence of a plurality of views began to wear off eventually and the phenomenon of pluralism started to trouble the increasing numbers of people that were caught up in it. Pluralism started to become contentious and frustrating for two main reasons. The first reason is that after the novelty and excitement began to wear off people came to realize that they had serious disagreements about momentous issues of morality and politics, culture, and life with family members, their friends, in their communities, and at the national political level. Gradually, it became clear that nothing less that the future direction of society was at stake, along with the shaping of culture. This was not immediately a problem when new and novel beliefs, attitudes, and practices began to appear, but as they gained clout and cultural influence, and significant numbers started agitating more directly for societal reform based on their worldview, something of a crisis situation began to form.

The second reason is critical to our argument in this book. This was the growing realization not only that one's differences with others on important matters of life and culture were serious, but that *nothing could really be done about solving these disagreements.* People gradually began to realize that an increasingly educated general public, along with rational debate, logical argument, and consideration of evidence, could not succeed in resolving differences. It slowly became evident that others with different views were not persuaded by our arguments, in either private discussions and debates or in public deliberations. Of course, many adopted the position that *their* views were best for society! It is common for people to think that "If only people would listen to me, then we would be all much better off, and society would take the correct path forward!" We sometimes adopt the attitude that if only we could educate others well, then they would agree with us, because we are more informed, more reasonable, more moral, less weak, less emotional, can see things more clearly than other mere mortals! However, this general approach is naive, and fails to appreciate and respect the fact of pluralism. Both private and public discourses became increasingly more contentious, people began to realize that they were unable to convince others of the truth of their views, and so what was initially an interesting and novel phenomenon started to become a *problem*. People began to get irritated at their failure to convince others, and more generally at the failure of public discourse.

As we will see later, public discourse gradually became more political in nature, in the sense of being conducted to win an argument by force and exercise of power, and not by reason or persuasion. Some still tried hard to reason with others, to remain above the fray, to chart a middle road by strongly championing civil and reasonable public deliberation, and often tried to steer a steadying course between opposing and contentious views. However, my claim is that this approach is gradually diminishing and that it is now a cultural phenomenon in itself that reasoned discourse is regarded as generally hopeless, and that it is becoming common to accept that one is involved in a political and cultural battle that has no easy solution, and that one's best hope is to try to win at all costs. So those at the forefront of public discourse in democratic societies became resigned to the failure of reason to solve problems, began to try to cope with this fact, *and to try to promote their views despite it.*

Step 5. Pluralism led to incommensurable worldviews: the emphasis on freedom and the inability of reason to produce consensus paved the way for the appearance of new worldviews, the redevelopment of current worldviews, and even renewed adherence to more traditional worldviews, and many beliefs and positions in between. This in turn led eventually to a plurality of different, but also incommensurable, worldviews in the democratic state. Let us recall from our earlier chapters that by incommensurable we are referring to *worldviews that are fundamentally in conflict with each other and that cannot be reconciled with each other* because they hold opposing beliefs on the nature of reality, the human person, and consequently on moral and political issues. The presence of incommensurable worldviews leads to social and cultural conflict in matters relating to public policy and concerning which values our laws should embody—among church denominations, in academia, in social and political action groups, even in business and the work place. Almost every area of life in modern democracies is now showing some acquaintance with the problem of worldview pluralism, the problem of how to handle different and incommensurable worldviews in the same state.

One example of many is the conflict over abortion, a topic many intellectuals have written about from the point of view of how contentious a topic it is for public discourse and modern culture, and what possibly can be done about it.[3] The topic has generated a large political battle in several democratic countries already, with neither side willing to compromise, or perhaps even consider compromise. The debate exhibits all of the hallmarks of the loss of confidence in reason that leads to this kind of conflict: frustration with reasoned argument, the attempt to use strong and intemperate language to smear and label one's opponents, a fanatical unwillingness to compromise, or even to recognize the logical space for compromise, the attempt to do an end run around the democratic process, a political fight to the death if ever there was one. This is just one example but there are many, and there will be more to come, depending on which stage a particular country is at with regard to the causal chain I am suggesting is operating.

The sheer shrillness of the contemporary debates in some countries, and the contempt expressed for opposing views, is new and was perhaps difficult to foresee. It seems to have occurred as people became more politically aware, more self-assured about the absolute rightness of their views, and so they began to adopt a kind of moral superiority over those who held different views. The presumption in the democratic system that opposing views are inevitable and so should be respected (even if one does not think they are true) has been lost, and is now only usually trotted out as yet another rhetorical tactic in the attempt to win the argument at the political level. Somewhere in the social and cultural debate there occurred a transition from respectfully disagreeing with others over moral, social, and political issues to coming to regard the other side as morally wrong, and then even as morally corrupt. The views of others represented something that one might barely tolerate (to such an extent that one might start to avoid people with whom one disagreed, would not do business with them, even call for them to be shunned, or ostracized in some way). One of the casualties of such a contentious pluralism is the distinction between the person, and the worldview he or she holds. It is becoming increasingly difficult to separate the two, which leads to a tendency to define people purely by their beliefs. This quickly leads to a breakdown of the possibility of civil debate, and to a kind of political posturing becoming the main way one thinks about political disagreement and approaches matters of politics. We can debate the reasons for why people became so shrill and self-righteous, but the *fact* of it is an important part of the story and does hasten the deep level of conflict in society, and therefore puts great pressure on the democratic model of government.

My argument here does not require that it be possible to place a neat label on everyone or to be able to easily classify a person's views. It is enough that there are different views existing, for example, on religious and moral topics. This means that people within the same worldview, broadly conceived, such as Christianity, or even a specific denomination of Christianity, such as Catholicism, could still exhibit these unfortunate traits and tendencies of pluralism by holding different views on important topics, such as on abortion, education, or economic matters. It is also important to emphasize that these views are not just different; we get to a stage where we regard them as mostly *incommensurable*, views that cannot be reconciled with each other. It does not follow from the fact that people hold different, even opposing views, on important questions of life and culture that they could not compromise. This is where the notion of incommensurability is helpful because it describes well the current reality of pluralism: that compromise both at the level of theory and at the practical level of everyday living seems to be more or less *impossible*.

Loss of Confidence in Reason: Anti-Realist Views of Knowledge

The above causal sequence comes to a head, I believe, with a final step (**Step 6**)—a loss of confidence in reason. We are not referring to a loss of confidence in reason to solve everyday problems of practical living, or even more complex problems, such as deciding how to repair an electrical grid, how to improve traffic flow in a city, the cheapest way to provide more affordable housing, how best to tackle a health epidemic, and so forth. Instead, we refer to the inability of reason to help solve our differences with regard to *worldview disputes*, disputes about momentous issues of religion, morality, politics, society, culture, and life.

This loss of confidence in reason has many causes but one of the main ones is the inability by means of rational argument to arrive at a consensus on large questions that relate to the way human beings live together in society. The exact opposite in fact has occurred in many democratic countries in the Western hemisphere: a pluralism of incommensurable views has emerged, views that are on a collision course with each other, a pluralism that has led to political and social strife in public life. Pluralism leads to disagreements that only seem resolvable by anti-democratic means, and in ways that exhibit the worst form of political grandstanding and abandonment of moral principle. This unfortunate scenario has led to a crisis of confidence and a loss of meaning across Western culture, the exact opposite perhaps of what Mill thought would happen when he advocated his theory of largely unrestrained freedom. Mature democracies did not end up in a place where the truth regarding momentous questions became clear and evident to all, but instead seem to be moving inexorably toward relativism.

It is hard to be precise of course about the exact causes for this but I am trying to trace a plausible line from an initial emphasis on freedom to an end result of a loss of confidence in reason and the onset of moral relativism that is so prevalent today. But there are various trends and developments that have all played some contributory role in the undermining of reason and confidence in rational persuasion, even though it can be hard to say exactly in what way or how much influence a particular trend had. The first development we should focus on occurred at the intellectual and academic level. This is the movement of anti-realism as a general approach to knowledge that has become dominant in many academic disciplines, including my own, philosophy, and that has had considerable influence across the academic world, to such an extent that both epistemological and moral relativism are largely the result.[4]

The standard understanding of knowledge is that the human mind in the act of knowing comes to know the world as it is in itself, as it exists in a real and objective way outside the mind. This is the common sense view of knowledge, the view that the ordinary person holds and works with. People believe that when they come to know something that is true or is really the case that this knowledge describes the way the world is independently of the human mind. This view is known as realism in philosophy. Until recently, realism was the dominant view of knowledge held by most academic disciplines including philosophy, religion, ethics, history, science, psychology, economics, and so forth. All academic disciplines advocate claims that their proponents think accurately describe the real world, claims that are presented as being objectively true independently of the opinion of the person expressing them. Of course, one might be wrong about what one claims to be true, but this does not alter the fact that one understands truth in this objective sense. The pursuit of objective truth then is what is involved in the search for knowledge, and this knowledge is seen as a good thing to help human beings understand the world better, to improve our lives in both material areas such as medicine and communications, but also in deeper areas such as in politics, morality, religion, culture, and the social arrangements of society. Indeed, usually those who advocate the democratic form of government itself do so because they believe that it is an objective fact that it is morally superior to other forms of government.

However, the view known as anti-realism has become dominant in many academic disciplines and has led to the severe compromising of the possibility of finding objective truth. Anti-realism is a general approach to the question of the status of knowledge claims in philosophy that is then applied in the various knowledge disciplines. The opposite of realism, philosophically stated, it is the view that the mind *in the process or act of knowing* somehow modifies (or filters) the content of what is known. This modifying affects all aspects of knowledge, not just specific domains. Therefore, the anti-realist claims that when I come to know things in the world about topics concerning morality, religion, and politics, and even about areas that would seem to be more accessible, such as about physical objects and their properties, this knowing is somehow compromised or modified in the *act of knowing* itself. So there is a *difference* between things as they are in themselves, and things as they *appear* to me in human knowing. In addition, I do not have access to the real things themselves, to the realm of objective truth; all I know is how things *appear to me* in human knowing. I cannot get outside of my knowing structures to see what things are like *in themselves*.

I like to use the illustration of the knower as someone who has put on what we might call "knowledge glasses" in order to see the world; the anti-realist holds that the glasses cause you to see everything in a certain specific way; let us say they make you see everything in green.[5] Now suppose you did not know that you were wearing the glasses. You might think that everything really is green; whereas in reality the objects themselves are not green at all, but are modified in the act of knowing (represented by the glasses). This is a very radical view of knowledge, one subject to many difficulties, but the crucial point for our purposes is that it has become dominant in the intellectual approach to the understanding of the nature of knowledge, and is therefore extremely influential in many disciplines in higher education. Of course, it then filters down to ordinary living in ways that many people will recognize, especially in the areas of religion, morality, politics, and topics having to do with ultimate questions and the meaning of life.

There are different versions of anti-realism, some more radical than others (we will consider another version, postmodernism, in the next chapter). The anti-realist approach drives the popular view today that the "knower" always brings ideological biases to any subject under study, to any set of claims or arguments that are advanced, including about questions of morality and politics, no matter how hard one might try to avoid this. We now see this view gaining defining influence in many areas such as education (where the traditional canon and the idea of objective, rather than subjective, standards of assessment, are under great attack), in art (how do we judge what counts as objectively good art?); and so it spreads to religion, ethics, even history (where the view is becoming popular that all historical facts need to be "interpreted," and so historical research always involves significant subjective influence—that of the author, or of the dominate cultural tradition that produces the history). In short, there is a subjective dimension in varying degrees present in all claims to "objective" truth. The subjective dimension, along with our biases, influences our interpretations of the "facts," so that our results are compromised in the sense that although they purportedly describe objective reality, they fall short of this. This difficulty would afflict all areas of research if antirealism is true (and not just research that one might disapprove of). For everyone brings biases to any investigation, including *the anti-realist himself*, a relativism about knowledge that many will not find credible, notwithstanding the point that one thing we can learn from the anti-realist argument is that we should be mindful of the biases we might bring to an issue, and try not to let them influence our conclusions.

Problematic and counter-intuitive though this view is, and also the fact that it is inconsistently applied,[6] we cannot understate its influence on the state of knowledge claims as we move into the twenty-first century. It also has led to curious results, for at the same time that knowledge has been undermined in this way, perhaps more than ever in the history of ideas, it has had an unusual effect that one might not expect to see. Although it does lead to a relativism at the level of theory, this relativism has had an odd effect in practical life. One might think that it would make people fence sitters on many issues, unwilling to take a position because of their doubts about the possibilities of discovering the objective truth, and so forth. Such an approach would be disconcerting, and would surely usher in a cultural phenomenon of loss of meaning, alienation, despair, loss of hope, even nihilism. It is true that we have seen a good deal of these reactions to the abandonment of truth in recent times, but there has also occurred another clear but unusual effect. Instead of becoming moral relativists in practice, many, especially perhaps those working in academia, have actually become more entrenched in their views than ever before, more certain of their views in ethics and politics. This is despite holding at the same time that there is really no objective answer to many of the questions in dispute!

In short, the widespread acceptance of relativism has produced some alienation and loss of meaning, but it also has led to a cultural trend of people becoming even further entrenched in their beliefs, accompanied by an even stronger reliance on political struggle as the preferred means of advancing one's views. So it would not be unusual to find a philosophy professor today, for instance, who adopts the following general approach to teaching and research: that anti-realism and relativism are the true positions with regard to knowledge (and not realism and objective truth), to ignore the contradictions in this thesis, and to use the classroom as a vehicle to argue for the objective truth of a political and moral agenda (rather than as a place for rigorously exploring interesting questions in the company of the best minds in history). Some may even attempt to turn their students into political activists. None of this is unusual, even though it may seem odd. Yet, it is easy enough to understand when approached in the light of our causal argument. It only heightens the problem of worldview pluralism that we have been describing. Anti-realism is one cause for the loss of confidence in reason today. It can perhaps be described as a foundational cause, a cause at the level of theory, one with very significant influence. I am not claiming that anti-realism naturally emerges from the democratic system, though it is I believe closely connected to the practice of free expression, though hardly a direct consequence of it. But anti-realism and relativism filter down then from the academy to the general population in different ways, especially to the intellectual class who of course train many leaders and respected groups in society, such as teachers, clergy, judges, lawyers, journalists, politicians, and civic leaders. So I think it does play a formative role in many people's attitudes toward debate in the public square today, and especially with regard to expectations for what such a debate can achieve.

A second contributory factor to the loss of confidence in reason is our actual experience of the process of deliberative discussion and rational debate today. Many are now coming to the uncomfortable realization that arguments that seem persuasive to them fail to convince others; of course, at the same time, they recognize that arguments offered by others don't persuade them, so sadly everyone is in the same boat. People usually respond to this reality in one of three ways. In a public discussion, I need to consider the choices available to me. The best choice is to try to persuade those who disagree with me that I am right and that they are wrong, that my view is factually more correct than theirs, is better reasoned, is morally superior, would be better for society, and so forth. The tragedy today is that I know from experience that this approach will not succeed for the most part, or if I do not yet know it, I will soon discover it to be true! I may then be tempted to adopt a position of ridiculing or mocking those who do not agree with me as an alternative, or even perhaps trying to bully them if I have either individual or cultural control over them (perhaps through the media or the zeitgeist). I may paint them as irrational, stupid, uninformed, psychologically troubled, even mentally ill, or as possessing lots of undesirable qualities (such as being authoritarian, fascist, racist, wishy-washy, soft, weak, indecisive, or too emotional!). Many today give into this temptation, and use it at very least as a rhetorical tactic to help their case politically. But this rebuff is not productive and simply leads to more deeply entrenched views, since my ridicule is sure to provoke a reciprocal response, hasten polarization in society, and further abandonment of reasonable discourse.

A second choice is to more fully embrace the anti-realist and relativistic posture described earlier, to adopt a relativistic and cynical attitude toward life, even a nihilistic approach. One may try to convince oneself that there is actually no truth on any issue, that we are condemned to disagree strongly, perhaps that the great project of the Enlightenment that promised progress in so many areas, with its emphasis on reason and the free and open pursuit of truth, is doomed! I will say more about this view below but although some do adopt it, especially perhaps in academia, it is not widespread because people find it difficult to dispense with their strongly held convictions, especially the posture that they are right on crucial matters affecting society and culture. Moreover, it is not possible for most people to live a life without firm convictions, another strong indication that something has gone wrong somewhere, of course. The third option is the actual one that has come to be realized in contemporary pluralist culture. This is where one accepts that one will be unable to convince others, and where one also recognizes that there will be little compromise or consensus; so one settles for the strategy of forcing one's views on others whenever the opportunity presents itself. This strategy requires that one be strongly committed to the superiority of one's view. It also means that one is not inclined to engage seriously in public discourse, to subject one's views to debate and discussion, because this stage has been passed and has failed. So one becomes convinced that reasoned discourse is no longer productive.

At this point, there may occur what may be described as a significant change in a person's thinking, the transition from holding a philosophical view of life, a worldview, to holding that worldview now as an ideology, where we understand the notion of ideology in two senses, one negative, one positive. The positive meaning focuses on the political and moral implications of one's beliefs, and includes a strong inclination to promote one's beliefs politically, to promote their influence in society. This leads to individuals becoming more politically aware and more politically active, even if this is only expressed by voting for candidates based on their overall worldviews. The negative meaning emerges when one begins to regard one's opponents as morally wrong and adopts the practice of generally avoiding debate concerning issues of disagreement because one believes that debate, even if carried out reasonably and with good will, is futile. One adopts a pragmatic approach to pluralism: that reasonable discourse is fruitless, and that our differences now require us to enjoin in a political battle.

So worldviews quickly turn into ideologies, a dangerous development that threatens the foundations of democracy. We fall into the mindset of interpreting every issue from the point of view of our ideology. We are no longer willing to consider issues from the point of view of others, and from a philosophical point of view. We are generally not open to changing our minds on most topics, and so are less inclined to listen to an opposing argument or a review of evidence. Yet crucially the ideologue still relies upon controversial assumptions without which his or her position is not plausible; for example, a feminist may assume that gender is a social construction in her advocacy of certain moral, political, and social views; a religious believer may assume that the soul exists in an argument against abortion; the secularist may assume that there is no afterlife in an argument for euthanasia. The ideologue then *refuses to acknowledge* that their assumptions are either controversial or debatable, and that others may legitimately hold a different view. Moreover, every argument that is offered on the issues under dispute *relies upon acceptance of the controversial assumption*. This is the primary way that ideology operates in modern pluralist societies. It is a phenomenon that has even spread to the universities: many professors are fast becoming ideologues, even in philosophy, which is supposed to be mainly an exploratory, as opposed to a political or ideological, discipline, but the phenomenon can be found in many other disciplines (perhaps especially but not exclusively in the humanities). Philosophers routinely now describe views (particularly relating to social, religious, moral, political, and cultural topics) other than their own as irrational, as a way of drawing attention to their extreme dislike for them. Of course, in a discipline famous for the quality of its arguments and for its general rigor, this is yet another tactic; a rhetorical approach, not an argument. It is becoming increasingly difficult even at the academic level to have a rational discussion concerning very important issues of society and culture, such as on abortion, gender analysis and relations, just war, immigration, policies proposed to solve social problems, and so forth.

Pluralism as a Cultural Phenomenon

We have all experienced the emergence of pluralism as a phenomenon in Western democracies and indeed in many parts of the world. We don't just see this pluralism at the national level; it is beginning to pervade every area of life, and to become an increasing source of strife in families, neighborhoods, communities, churches, schools and universities, and, of course, in the workplace. This phenomenon is now being documented by sociologists and pollsters (as we will see in Chap. 6). We should not underestimate pluralism as a cultural phenomenon. It is quite a remarkable cultural change for many societies to experience a plethora of views on momentous topics of life, morality, politics, and culture. If one adds to this the fact of significant immigration of different nationalities and worldviews—often introducing different languages, values, and customs into their newly adopted countries—one truly has a potent mix of beliefs, traditions, and cultures that inevitable create pressures and tensions in local and national communities, in addition to the problems that simple pluralism itself raises. In one way, we are engaged in a very interesting, and perhaps also risky, experiment in the sense that, particularly when we factor immigration into the mix, we have a situation that might lead to civil and social unrest if not handled carefully. From a logical point of view, it is quite a challenge for many people from different backgrounds and with widely different beliefs to live together in harmony. This for the simple reason that the problem of worldview pluralism—the clash of incommensurable beliefs and values—is greatly heightened in such a situation.

Two temperaments can now be distinguished in democratic culture. One is reflected in a more traditional approach to democratic disagreement, which is to accept that people will disagree over difficult issues, that deliberative discussion and debate is good and can sometimes change minds, and that we resolve our differences by accepting the democratic will of the majority. The second has always existed but is becoming more mainstream, perhaps the mainstream, temperament—to begin to regard oneself as more enlightened than others, and so become impatient and perhaps even to fear the democratic process. This can lead to a temptation to suppress views, shun those one disagrees with, and to seek an end run around the democratic process, all issues we noted in the previous chapter. One hopes that it is not just a matter of time before disdain for the views of others leads to civil unrest, since it has already led to the compromising of key values of democracy, such as freedom of expression.

Coupled with the loss of confidence in reason to persuade, and the unwillingness to compromise, it is no wonder that it has crossed the minds of many that we may be in the midst of a tinder box situation. This phenomenon of pluralism means that now more than ever before one is very likely to consider oneself as a member of a worldview first, to be self-consciously aware of one's beliefs and values, and how they differ from those of others. This is opposed to thinking of oneself as a citizen first, or perhaps as a person first, who happens to hold a particular worldview! In this way, worldviews are becoming more defining of how we understand ourselves, particularly in the context of pluralism.[7] One can no longer assume or presuppose a uniformity of opinion on key matters in society, like in the old democracies. I am reminded of the Sports columnist in *The Irish Times* newspaper a decade ago who felt compelled to declare in an article about boxing that he was a Catholic, showing not just an awareness of his worldview, but also that he felt he should admit it as background to some point he was making, while acknowledging that some of his readers would hold different views. I suspect the climate in his newsroom made him self-conscious about the fact of, quite simply, pluralism. The self-conscious awareness and attitude of this sportswriter with regard to his worldview is now *common* I believe among the general population in most Western democracies. Though, it is true that some societies are more aware of the phenomenon of pluralism than others, are more ideological in how they approach disagreement (with the U.S. being perhaps the worst in this respect). *The Irish Times* sports columnist was one early, small example of pluralism becoming a phenomenon in Ireland. Since then, it is no exaggeration to say that Irish society and culture has been swept up and completely transformed by pluralism (as we will see in our case study in Chap. 6).

One might look upon the phenomenon of pluralism as an opportunity in the normative sense of pluralism, or if not as an opportunity then as an occasion to exercise some typical Christian virtues of humility, modesty, openness to others, desire to treat others well, desire to accommodate, etc. However, this is not the attitude that pluralism produces. For the fact is that most people adopt what I call the "John Stuart Mill attitude" to worldviews! One implication of Mill's philosophy of freedom is that other people are regarded initially as *obstacles*, as being in the way of the exercise of *my* freedom. I have to figure out some way of asserting myself over others, of putting myself first, and this is not easy, because our existence is complicated by the fact that other people exist, as French philosopher Jean Paul Sartre noted! In a fully developed pluralist state, other worldviews are inevitably seen as being in the way of my choices and the exercise of my freedom. They are obstacles to my way of thinking and living (as my worldview is to them). The absolutizing of freedom seems to lead to a liberal approach that is confrontational and selfish in its essence. Separatist movements in democratic nations are yet another example of this; instead of pursuing accommodation and aiming to live together in harmony, the desire is to seek a strident independence from the influence of others. Pluralism, paradoxically, encourages us today to focus on our differences rather than on what we have in common. We welcome other worldviews only as long as they agree with ours on important issues, or if we regard them as posing no significant threat to the practice of our worldview. We are accommodating as long as our worldview has the defining say on matters of law and public policy, or so long as it is possible to contain views that are contrary to ours (and so limiting their cultural influence). Indeed, we are now very much inclined not to support any initiative or action that is perceived to significantly advance another worldview with which we strongly disagree. *In general we do not look upon pluralism as an opportunity but as a problem, and "solutions" or ways of dealing with it do not involve accommodation but suppression*, or subtle maneuvers to convince others of the superior nature, both rationally and morally, of our own views. Pluralism seems to naturally separate and divide people, rather than bringing them together. We often consider other worldviews as threats to ours, rather than as complements to them; our first reaction in a developed pluralist nation is not to respect our differences but to mark out our enemies. Given that many think the future direction of society and culture is at stake, it is perhaps understandable that it is becoming difficult to respect all views that aim to shape it.

Perhaps it is possible that the phenomenon of pluralism might have taken another course (though it is hard to see how), that it might have brought people of different cultures together in a more cohesive way. It might have led to a richer view of human dignity and of the common good. And while there is perhaps some suggestion of this today, the practical effect of pluralism in the modern world has been to pit people against each other, a conflict that will likely only get worse, not better. And we cannot truthfully say that pluralism represents progress if it involves one worldview becoming culturally dominant by suppressing others against their will, since this is a clear violation of democratic principles. Is it possible to construct a type of causal argument to make a prediction about how things might play out in the future? The loss of confidence in reason could lead to intolerance and abuse (even suppression) of certain worldviews; this in turn may lead to civil unrest and violence, and perhaps to some type of (bloodless) revolution. Many of our current debates, including over abortion, gender relations, and immigration, seem to represent microcosms that foreshadow this larger scenario.

I submit that all of these developments are a sign that my earlier thesis is correct—that pluralism is becoming a defining cultural phenomenon; it is the main way many people now think about the world, and it is making people less tolerant, more entrenched, more ideological than ever. Intolerance, hypersensitivity, even fanaticism is an effect of pluralism (especially perhaps on the left side of the political spectrum) that is being passed onto the next generation. My aim in this study is not to solve this problem, but to describe it, make some observations about it in various areas, and offer (in later chapters) some suggestions for how, given the fact of pluralism, we might proceed going forward. I don't think there is any easy solution. I see only three possible ways out of the problem of worldview pluralism and crisis of confidence that is undermining the democratic system, and none seem promising or acceptable. I will come back to them from time to time in the discussion that follows but will mention them here as we bring this chapter to a close.

The first is that among the plurality of worldviews in a democratic state, one group succeeds in bringing everyone around to their view on the key issues of contention, and they do this by engaging in respectful, reasonable argument and persuasion. I think we are as far away from this solution as we could possibly be! The second is that one worldview (or some specific parts of a worldview) succeeds in bringing everyone around to the central features of their worldview, especially at the level of law, by force. Force could be applied in a number of ways, directly or indirectly. Indirect force might be imposed by those who have the power to do so through the courts, the media, the educational system, or policies governing certain areas of society, especially the classroom and workplace. This approach might succeed in practical terms and often seems to be the preferred choice of many caught up in our struggles revolving around pluralism, but it would only work by violating the foundational values of democracy and freedom. The third possibility is for each worldview to split up into different geographical areas within the same nation, and to live side by side, and in (relative) harmony (though this "solution" would only work for a while before the problem of worldview pluralism would reassert itself)![8] This is not practical in many places, but we may be seeing the beginnings of it with talk of secession in various regions of different democratic countries in recent times, talk which will likely get louder in the future. Perhaps a fourth option is that we can somehow muck along together despite our differences, living with tension, intensely partisan politics, acrimonious public discourse, and all of the other difficulties and abuses we noted earlier. Whether democratic countries can eventually resolve the problem of pluralism, or whether the problem will eventually lead to the disintegration of many current democracies, and perhaps to the end of the democratic system of government, is an extremely difficult matter about which to make a judgment. Only time will tell. But, as I suggested in Chap. 1, it is no longer alarmist or silly to consider the question.

NOTES

1. See my *Why Politics Needs Religion: The Place of Religious Arguments in the Public Square* (Downers Grove, IL.: InterVarsity, 2006), Chapter 1, which has influenced my account here.
2. There has been much fascinating work carried out on the phenomena behind social change in various countries, especially as relating to the democratic growth of freedom, religious issues, secularization, modernization, the expansion of bureaucracy, and advances in technology, and their effects on the modern mind. Much of this work has been done by sociologists; as a representative sample see the following: Grace Davie, *Religion in Modern Europe* (New York: Oxford U.P., 2000); Peter Berger, Brigitte Berger, and Hansfried Kellner, *The Homeless Mind: Modernization and Consciousness* (New York: Vintage, 1974); Shmuel N. Eisenstadt (ed.), *Multiple Modernities* (New York: Routledge, 2002); Callum Brown, *The Death of Christian Britain* (New York: Routledge, 2001); Andrew Greeley, *Religious Change in America* (Cambridge, MA.: Harvard U.P., 1996); Ahmet T. Kuri, *Secularism and State Policies Toward Religion: The United States, France,*

and *Turkey* (New York: Cambridge U.P., 2009); Tamara Trojanowska et al (eds.), *Being Poland: A New History of Polish Literature and Culture since 1918* (Toronto: University of Toronto Press, 2018); Eugenio F. Biagini and Mary E. Daly (eds.), *Cambridge Social History of Modern Ireland* (New York: Cambridge, 2017); Olivier Roy, "Another Source of Morality?: The Church Versus Modernism (1864–1964)" in his *Is Europe Christian?* (London: Hurst, 2019), pp. 43–55; Robert Nisbet, "Progress as Freedom," in his *History of the Idea of Progress* (New York: Basic Books, 1970), pp. 179–236; David Sikkink, "From Christian Civilization to Individual Liberties: Framing Religion in the Legal Field, 1880–1949," in Christian Smith (ed.), *The Secular Revolution* (Berkeley, CA.: University of California Press, 2003), pp. 310–354.
3. See Ronald Dworkin, *Life's Dominion* (New York: Knopf, 1993); Ziad Munson, *Abortion Politics* (Cambridge, UK.: Polity, 2018); Michael Sandel, *Public Philosophy* (Cambridge, MA.: Harvard U.P., 2006).
4. For a masterly account of the massive shift in Western beliefs and attitudes concerning the possibility of moral knowledge, and how such knowledge—as a publicly available resource to aid in practical living—has disappeared from our social and academic institutions, see Dallas Willard, *The Disappearance of Moral Knowledge* (New York: Routledge, 2018).
5. See my *Religion and Science: An Introduction* (New York: Continuum, 2010), pp. 66–70, for a full discussion.
6. It would take us too far from our task to provide a full discussion of the anti-realist approach. But it is a view that faces serious objections as an approach to knowledge. These include the key question of how does the modifying (or filtering) involved in the act of knowing actually work? No philosopher has ever provided a detailed answer to this question; instead an appeal is usually made to vague and unhelpful generalities of the form "language produces meaning," or "one's cultural background defines what one knows," claims that are too vague to support such a radical thesis. A second problem is one of contradiction, which afflicts the claim that "all knowledge is perspectival." Is this claim itself perspectival? If yes, then it is not objective; if no, then all knowledge does not come from a perspective. In addition, anti-realism would condemn us to extreme relativism because in its modern forms it usually proposes that each person has a different type of filter, thereby making knowledge relative to each individual, an impractical, chaotic conclusion. Finally, anti-realism is often appealed to in order to debunk tradition (usually religious and moral tradition), but the problem always is that this debunking would also apply to the view installed instead of the tradition, another contradiction at the heart of the view. For a full discussion, see Stuart Brock and Edwin Mares, *Realism and Anti-Realism* (Montreal: McGill–Queens University Press, 2007).

7. As a small example from any number one could focus on, consider the current issue under consideration in some democratic countries of whether the voting age should be lowered to sixteen. Those in political power and with a strong interest in and around politics would only support such a move if they thought it would benefit them politically; they would make a political calculation, rather than considering the question morally or philosophically. So we might say then that the issue should be decided by the electorate. However, today in our pluralist culture, the electorate is also very likely to be mainly influenced by political considerations. This is what pluralism now means in modern democracy. One of its features is to encourage us to look at every issue from the perspective of the promotion of our worldviews.
8. See the intriguing article by Sasha Issenberg exploring what might be involved in the breakup of America (into three separate countries), in terms of geographical territory, population, economy, trade, and international relations! The article may be a bit tongue in cheek, but it raises a topic that is clearly suggested today by modern pluralism. See Sasha Issenberg, "Divided We Stand," *New York Magazine*, November 14, 2014.

CHAPTER 4

Democracy and Relativism

It seems undeniable that those of us who live in the Western world are living in the age of relativism! The idea has simply "caught on" in democratic culture that everything is a matter of opinion, interpretation, or personal preference, that there is no objective truth to be known, especially on matters of morality, religion, culture, and politics. It should be no surprise to anyone, given our description in earlier chapters of democratic themes and trends, along with our causal argument, that a *culture of relativism* has been the result of the absolutist interpretation of freedom. It is a growing trend that many now approach and think about their disagreements with others through the lens of relativism. A relativistic approach is very prominent in public discourse, and it signals again our increasing awareness of our individual worldviews, and how they are rejected by others who see things differently than we do. It is emblematic of our cultural experience that everyone has a different opinion on matters of vital importance, and that there is no easy way to resolve our disagreements, no easy road to objective truth. It is no coincidence that a prominent feature of advanced democracies, especially when compared to early democracies, is that the latter are more relativistic than the former.

Relativism as a Cultural Phenomenon

One of the claims we are making in this book is that democracy has a strong tendency toward moral relativism. We have been arguing that this tendency is inevitable given the historical journey of interpreting freedom in an absolutist manner, in the way explained in the previous chapters. This journey has led to the incommensurability of worldviews and to a loss of confidence in reason to settle differences and make progress. There is surely no doubt that moral relativism has become a significant cultural force in modern Western democracies in the last thirty years or so. Our task is to understand further the ways in which this phenomenon is manifested in society, the role relativism plays in our approach to public discourse, the influence of relativism on our worldviews and attitudes toward our cherished beliefs and values, and where it leaves us with regard to the contentious pluralism in the midst of which we find ourselves.

Freedom approached in an absolutist, all-or-nothing, extreme manner has led to the undermining of our confidence in the possibility of discovering the truth. Perhaps it did not have to end up this way, as we noted, and democratic culture might have branched in different directions, but this in fact is the path it did take. No doubt there are several contributing causes to the phenomenon of relativism, including global communications and ease of travel which bring increasing familiarity with other worldviews, cultures, and ways of life, but absolute freedom is one of the main factors. It also plays an important part in the move to anti-realism, and especially in the emergence of the movement of postmodernism that we will consider in this chapter. This is because the inability of reason to settle our differences in a practical sense has two related consequences; the first is to undermine confidence in the objective nature of reason; the second is to begin to regard rational argument as itself politically compromised, as just another tactical maneuver in the political struggle that emerges when we confront head on the incommensurability of worldviews.

We shall focus mostly in this chapter on moral relativism rather than relativism in general (though we will briefly introduce the movement of postmodernism along the way). Moral relativism is a curious phenomenon, and the way it plays out in contemporary Western societies is complex, and involves subtleties that we should analyze carefully. It is also important to think about how at one and the same time individuals can become so certain, almost to the point of fanaticism, of the rational and moral superiority of their views, while at the same time urging a fallibilism and skepticism about our ability to discover objective truth! And also why, despite adopting a generally skeptical stance about the possibility of finding objective truth, we see a trend where people are more willing than ever, especially in certain circles (such as universities or parts of the media), to close down free debate, to force their views on others who do not agree with them.

Moral relativism is the view that moral values are not absolute in themselves, but are relative to some other guide or standard, such as to one's individual preferences, or to one's culture. It can be a stand-alone thesis, or can be part of a general theory of epistemological relativism about knowledge (in fact it usually gets its force from a more general relativism, even as its proponents shrink from the consequences of general relativism). Sometimes people are reluctant to embrace a wholesale relativism, but are more likely to be attracted to the view that our lack of objective knowledge applies only to the moral sphere (and perhaps also in religion, and other issues of culture), but does not apply in areas such as science, history, psychology, economics, or political theory. It is accurate to say that moral relativism is that form of relativism that has had the most influence on the thinking of the general populace.

The opposite of moral relativism, and indeed until recently the mainstream view, is moral objectivism, the thesis that moral values are objectively true and absolute and apply always and everywhere, whether people accept the values or not. The moral objectivist might hold, for example, that kindness is an objective moral value, and that everyone therefore morally ought to be kind, whether they agree or not (though people might still disagree on which actions exemplified kindness in particular cases). The objectivist would hold that slavery is immoral and that it should be illegal everywhere whether people agree with this or not. Objectivists do not always *agree* with each other about what the correct moral values are; for example, two objectivists might disagree about capital punishment, one thinking that it is a morally appropriate punishment for murder and another holding that it is not. But these moral objectivists do agree that the correct moral values apply to everyone; they do not think that one's moral judgment on capital punishment is a matter of taste, or personal opinion, or is based on subjective criteria. In addition, it is perfectly reasonable for a moral objectivist to want his or her view (at least on some matters) to be enshrined in law so that everyone in a society is bound by it, whether they accept it or not. In this way, most laws are founded on a belief in an objective moral order that can be known by reason.

A Postmodern World

Relativism is gradually sweeping through Western democratic culture, even if most people might not be aware of its deeper meaning and analysis from a philosophical point of view, or might not be able to state it formally, or even recognize that they are under its influence. But it is now in the air we breathe, is a fog we are surrounded by and are all getting caught up in, and has considerable influence over the way pluralist debate about values and the meaning of life is conducted. In the previous chapter, we considered the anti-realist version of relativism, a view which has had great influence on philosophers and other intellectuals in various disciplines, but perhaps not quite as much influence on the general population. A different version of relativism, postmodernism, has had more influence on culture, so much so that some thinkers would say that today we are living in a postmodern world.[1] We often seem now to be in the midst of a postmodern age, even if many have never heard of the movement of postmodernism.

Postmodernism is a sophisticated form of relativism that has been advanced by contemporary European philosophers Michael Foucault, Jean–François Lyotard, Roland Barthes, and especially Jacques Derrida.[2] The term "postmodernism" is itself ambiguous and hard to define, yet despite this it has been very influential in many academic disciplines, especially literature, theology, feminism, history, and multiculturalism. I like to define postmodernism as a movement whose central theme is the critique of objective rationality and identity, and a working out of the implications of this critique for central questions in philosophy, literature, and culture.[3] It is usually accompanied by one or more of the following theses, depending on the version under discussion (not every postmodernist thinker would subscribe to all of these claims): (1) *All knowledge is perspectival*: this means that even though we think we are making claims that are objectively true, we are mistaken because all knowledge claims contain biases, prejudices, points of view and influences (especially coming from the situatedness of the person making the claims), even though we are often unaware of these compromising factors; (2) *A shift away from talking about objective truth and objective facts to talking about interpretation and meaning*: the latter is understood to contain a significant subjective element. The more radical versions of this thesis hold that there is no objective truth at all, that truth is only a social construction. Truth emerges from a social consensus, and this is all there is to it; the suggestion that a social consensus could be incorrect or might not match up with reality is rejected by postmodernist thinkers.

(3) *All truth claims can be seen as inherently oppressive in the moral and political sense*: this is because what are proposed as objectively true claims are really historically situational and perspectival. While this criticism would apply to any view that makes assertions that are intended to be objective, postmodernists have particularly in mind Western culture as a whole, which they accuse of being guilty of egregiously oppressing other cultures and minority views under the guise of objective truth. (4) *An attack on dominant, influential worldviews, which postmodernists often describe as "metanarratives."* Traditional metanarratives are problematic because they purport to offer a true view of the world, yet are actually oppressive since there is no objective truth. Some philosophers extend this position to include a critique of such crucial Western subjects as metaphysics, philosophy, objective history, objective morality, objective truth in religion, even reason itself, all of which would be undermined and called into question by the postmodern approach. (5) *A special emphasis on literature, and literary texts in various disciplines*: postmodernists are well known for applying their relativistic approach to undermine the place of the author in the interpretation of meaning. Postmodernist thinkers assert that the reader always brings a perspective to the text thereby generating a reading that is unique to that individual. But the author does the same since he or she is simply working with meanings independently present in a certain cultural context, and offers one arrangement or places one particular structure on them, thereby privileging one "interpretation" over other possible ones. There are other legitimate interpretations because this is how meaning works. Meaning is always suggestive, elusive, unformed, oblique in itself, and it is up to us to invent and impose an interpretation on it, in our particular context; another instance of the wholesale relativism that characterizes postmodernism.

Derrida in particular has suggested that there are no *fixed meanings* present in a text, despite any appearance to the contrary, and despite the intentions of the author.[4] He calls into question the literal readings of texts, along with the intentions of the author, and suggests that texts need to be "deconstructed." French writer, Roland Barthes, suggests that our concern must be to look at *how* texts mean, not at what they mean.[5] This postmodernist thesis, however, is not restricted to books or art works, for texts may consist of any set of ever-changing meanings. Hence, the world, and almost any object or combination of objects in it, may be regarded as a "text." To relate all of this to the topic of worldviews—a key theme in our book—and to express these points in more familiar language, the postmodernists are saying that no particular worldview can claim to have the truth. All worldviews can be called into question (including the worldview of postmodernism itself, a point to which I will return later). This is because the meanings which are constitutive of a worldview cannot be known to be true objectively, since there is no objective knowledge. All knowledge is *contextual* and is influenced by culture, tradition, language, prejudices, background beliefs, biases, etc., and is therefore, in some very important sense, *relative* to these phenomena. But the claim of postmodernist thinkers is that the influence of these phenomena on truth or meaning is not trivial or benign; it is such that it inevitably undermines all claims to objectivity that one might be tempted to make from the point of view of one's worldview. Postmodernism itself becomes a distinctive new philosophical approach in the way it responds to this anti-realist view of knowledge, by claiming then that our job is to challenge and call into question (i.e., to "deconstruct") all claims to objective knowledge by illustrating alternative meanings and "truths" in any particular worldview, which are really there whether or not the adherents of the worldview recognize or acknowledge them. And these alternative meanings will undermine the worldview in question, because they will be different from, and often opposed to, the original, "objective" meanings claimed for that worldview. Such an approach therefore only worsens the problem of worldview pluralism because the clash of worldviews will become more severe. It also appears to present us with an intractable problem, given that there is no foundation to identify and build on, only a relativistic quicksand.

The approach of postmodernism quickly lends itself to a political agenda in the sense that worldviews are almost by definition oppressive since they privilege some (literal, dominant) meanings and marginalize others; deconstruction thus becomes the method for rejecting and debunking worldviews. It also lends itself to a political agenda because it becomes necessary to unmask the posturing of the traditional approach and its appeal to objective truth, and since it is usually the case that we are unable to see our biases at work, someone more enlightened than us will need to show us where we are going wrong (and point toward the "correct" path). So postmodernism also allows those views and readings and alternative meanings which have often been marginalized to reclaim their rightful place in the marketplace of ideas.

However, this is where postmodernism runs into trouble. For the fact is that these marginalized worldviews do not reclaim their place because they are true (for that would be to acknowledge objective knowledge), but because, since there is no objective knowledge, they have just as much claim to legitimacy as any other view. Of course, they too will have to be deconstructed in the end. (This is a point many supporters of the deconstructionist approach conveniently overlook; they frequently talk as if the marginal views are somehow *true*, and the mainstream views somehow *false*.) The implications of the postmodernist approach when taken to their logical conclusion and when applied consistently are that there are no certainties any more, especially in the areas of religion, morality, and politics, or having to do with theories of human nature and the meaning of life. Everything can be questioned; people are alone with their freedom (to borrow a theme from Sartre) to arrive at their own truth. Needless to say, this is a position which seems to invite only disorder, anarchy, loss of meaning, and nihilism.

Relativism as Rhetorical Strategy

To say that we are living in a postmodern age then is to say that we are coming more and more under the influence of the view just described in its various forms. Most readers will hardly fail to recognize the influence of the postmodernist approach in their own search for meaning. We must consider the extent of the influence of this view in modern culture, and how it actually works at the practical level of public discourse. It is helpful to distinguish between what I call *the rhetoric of relativism* and *relativism held as a philosophical thesis*.[6] In this section, I will introduce the theme of the rhetoric of relativism, and explain and illustrate how it works in debates involving a postmodernist approach. Later, we will consider how it might work in ordinary moral debates in society. For I do think the rhetoric of relativism plays a key role in the way public discourse is conducted concerning worldviews, and that it now has achieved the status of being an important strategic approach which many utilize in a way that I will attempt to illustrate.

We might approach the issue of worldview disagreement in the following way, initially. One might be tempted to think, when engaged in a public square debate about momentous issues of life and culture, and when one is confronted with the postmodernist approach described above, that, nevertheless and despite appearances to the contrary, all we have here is a simple (though deep) disagreement. We might think that A holds one particular view that he believes to be objectively true and his opponent B (who let us stipulate is taking a postmodernist approach) simply holds a different view that he thinks is objectively true. Both A and B wish to establish the truth of their respective views so that they may have influence over society and culture. A thinks B's view is mistaken in key respects, and B thinks the same about A's view. A might be tempted to think that, despite the special terminology his interlocutor, B, uses, and the philosophically sophisticated ideas employed by B, that B really does believe in objective truth after all. B is simply using the language of postmodernism as a kind of smokescreen to assert the objective superiority of his own view. Many suspect that this is really what is going on with the postmodernist style of arguing, and there is some truth to this charge, but it is not the whole story. Let us try to get a clearer picture of these interesting clashes between different views.

The official position of a postmodern relativistic approach is that the problem with A's view is that A is asserting his view as objectively true, but this is a mistake because there is no objective truth. The postmodernist also insists that *he* is not making the same mistake, because he *denies* that any view can be objectively true. Of course, the problem with this general postmodernist approach is that it would seem to leave us in confusion and disarray, because *no one* would then be able to assert a view as objectively true since there is no objective truth. So, how would society arrive at a set of values that could become the foundation for morality and law? How could we attempt to distinguish between constructive and destructive ways of living, and so forth? Moreover, this approach would also seem to undermine the moral and political agenda of postmodernism *itself*, since postmodernists would no longer be in a position to critique Western culture, for example, and to advocate an alternative!

However, I wish to suggest that although it appears that the postmodernist may be arguing this way (denying objective truth), in most cases he is pursuing a different strategy. We can illustrate it this way. Suppose a postmodernist wishes to defend a moral and political agenda and to impose it on society (which most of them do). How might he approach such a task? I suggest there are two possibilities. The first is to argue that his moral and political agenda is objectively superior to other views. But this would involve acknowledging the fact that *there is an objective order of knowledge that can be discovered by reason*, which goes against all postmodernist sensibilities. It would also involve dignifying the view one rejects in an important sense—since one acknowledges in this first approach that there is a realm of objective knowledge, one is then obliged to debate which account of it is the most accurate (the postmodernists', or their opponents'). In this way one must acknowledge the legitimacy even of views one rejects because they are based on an honest attempt to discover what is true using reason. So such views are worthy of discussion, even if they are wrong. This is how we approach standard philosophical disagreements.

The second way to approach the argument is to advance the postmodernist position and theses on the nature of knowledge described above. However, one promotes it not as a sincerely held philosophical thesis, but *as a rhetorical strategy*. This means that one denies the objectivity of knowledge, proposes the "deconstruction" of reason, commends the elevation of interpretation over truth, and so forth, *but only as a way of gaining a rhetorical advantage over one's opponent*. How does one gain an advantage? By making it appear that your opponent is appealing to objective truth, which is biased and oppressive, but you are not doing anything so crass! However, the rhetorical language of postmodernism is simply used to *mask the objective truth claims that one is in fact making all the time*. So, on this second strategy, postmodernists are not really advocating a new approach to knowledge, despite what they claim; they are simply pretending they are as a rhetorical strategy! They will then go on in the debate to assert their own view as objectively true, as the one that should shape society—all this after it appeared they did not hold any objective view. The rhetoric of postmodernist language is used very effectively to *mask* the contradiction. This explains also why postmodernism runs into contradictions and inconsistencies. I submit that many works that adopt a postmodernist approach exhibit this tendency all too clearly—they advocate relativism on the one hand, and then propose their own truth claims, understandings, and interpretations *as the true ones*.

My claim is that postmodernism is now an effective part of the rhetoric of relativism that operates in modern life, especially in philosophical and academic discussions, though it is beginning to filter down to more general exchanges, particularly those concerning ethics, politics, religion, and general matters of culture. For example, one well-known postmodernist strategy is to celebrate the notion of difference (this has echoes of Derrida's approach, with difference being opposed to "sameness"). The idea here is that we take up a positive attitude and encourage a welcoming and warm reception, toward those who are different from ourselves in some way, especially with regard to moral, political, and religious beliefs, and perhaps also including the categories of ethnic groups, minority groups, nationalities, and so on. For example, we are encouraged to go out of our way to welcome people into a discussion who practice a different religion to the dominant one, or who have different moral beliefs than traditionally dominant beliefs, and so forth. The key point here is that this is a deceptive move, part of the rhetorical strategy of postmodernism. For it might at first sight appear to be genuinely welcoming of those with different beliefs, and so those with more traditional beliefs (or any beliefs) might feel that they would be welcome as well. But they would be wrong about this. This approach is not so interested in welcoming everyone with different beliefs per se, but *only those with different beliefs than the dominant tradition*, perhaps especially those who hold beliefs that have been (according to postmodernists) marginalized. These types of beliefs have a special cachet at the table, although from the official philosophical understanding of the postmodernist approach, it is hard to see how they could have, given that there are supposed to be *no* privileged beliefs, and this strategy would seem to be privileging the marginalized beliefs. At the same time, this rhetorical strategy is a way of disparaging the dominant beliefs. For example, it is often used in theology to critique the traditional understanding of the nature of God (as articulated in philosophy and theology), and so anyone who holds the traditional view would not feel welcome at the table. Moreover, when a traditionalist in religion hears the postmodernist approach being introduced she knows that it will be used to attack her view! My contention is that this is how postmodernism usually works *in practice*.

As we noted above, the postmodernist approach is fraught with contradiction. For it is a view that is supposed to undermine the objectivity of *all* knowledge, including any objective claims postmodernists make themselves such as the claim that "all knowledge is from a perspective"! The critical question is whether this claim is itself influenced by a perspective, is compromised by the biased viewpoint of those who advocate it? If it is, then it cannot claim by its own lights to be an objective account of knowledge, and if it is not, then it is contradictory because it is undermines the very claim that all knowledge comes from a perspective. This is a devastating criticism of postmodernism, so it is no wonder that they never face up to it as honest thinkers should. Instead, they exercise a key move in their rhetorical strategy—to apply their critique of the objectivity of knowledge *selectively*. The postmodernist approach should be used to critique *all* forms of knowledge since it is a claim about how knowledge occurs (Lyotard's most influential book is subtitled "A Report on Knowledge"). However, in this instance where it is used as a form of rhetoric, as I claim, its purpose is to undermine the knowledge claims of the dominant tradition, but not those moral, political, and religious claims *favored by the postmodernist*. These latter claims are welcomed at the table *as if they are true*. When postmodernists welcome "difference" (a favored term of theirs), they only wish to welcome those views which they themselves can support, agree with, live with, or at least tolerate to some extent. They are not interested in welcoming all views to the table, despite appearances. This is because inevitably some views would go against the political and moral agenda they are promoting, and by which they wish to influence society.[7] My thesis is that this way of arguing, in a variety of forms, is rife in modern culture in the West.

Relativism therefore has a very significant foothold in modern democratic culture. Perhaps we can say that there is a kind of de facto relativism operating, even if many are reluctant to fully embrace the philosophical position of relativism. It is more obvious in some areas than others, such as religious belief, where the attitude is now widespread that one's religion is simply one among many, all of which are legitimate (a big change from the last generation where the dominant attitude was that one's religion is the true one, and that other religions, however noble and edifying in so many ways, are nevertheless false). The pluralism of worldviews, along with various attacks on the power of reason to discover objective truth, has made relativism attractive to people. It is attractive for some because of its denial of objective truth; that is to say, they are attracted to it because of its philosophical stance about the nature of knowledge. But many others are attracted to its rhetorical power because it seems to give them a way to argue in debate while claiming the moral high ground. The moral high ground (let us not forget) in a relativistic culture is where one appears to eschew asserting one's own moral and political positions in situations of contentious debate while criticizing others who are not nearly so refined, those so crass and insensitive to insist on the *rightness* of their views in public discourse! Of course, the motivation for embracing the rhetoric of relativism (rather than actually committing to the philosophical position of relativism) is that people still wish to impose their views on society, believe their vision is better than the alternatives, and so cannot let go of the realm of objective truth (in the sense in which strict philosophical relativism demands). From a practical point of view, many people think that we are stuck with some kind of general relativism in any case because we have no objective way of settling our disputes, no way of deciding which view is true. This is very unsettling to people, and so while they may talk a good game of philosophical relativism, even be quite attracted to it in some ways, they cannot quite bring themselves to embrace it. Yet, they are drawn to the rhetorical power that comes from talking *as if* they are relativists!

The spirit of relativism now hovers over the democratic political landscape, and seems to be part of its essence. It is also a significant contributory cause of the therapeutic culture we now live in which eschews reason and evidence in favor of feeling and emotional reaction. More and more, democratic culture is drawn to relativism as a philosophical theory, and perhaps the influence of anti-realist and postmodernist approaches to knowledge will eventually lead to a more widespread acceptance of philosophical relativism. Yet it remains difficult for us to accept philosophical relativism in practice even if we are inclined toward it in theory. This, I think, is why the rhetoric of relativism is widely used today. Everyone finds it hard to implement real philosophical relativism in practice, but many find it rhetorically very useful to talk *as if* they are relativists as a way of further promoting their own objective beliefs and values. The reason the rhetoric of relativism has such power is because of the influence of movements like anti-realism and postmodernism as approaches to knowledge at the theoretical level. These movements, along with the inability to draw a limit to freedom, have given strong credence to the view that there is no such thing as objective truth, so (somewhat paradoxically) it can be a good first move to begin from this starting point in moral debate, as we will now see.

Relativism in Ordinary Moral Debate

It will be helpful to show how the rhetoric of relativism functions in the kind of ordinary moral debates people engage in all the time in the culture of democratic pluralism. This will help us to understand why people find it an attractive and useful approach when faced with contentious disagreements, and also how it is easy to confuse the philosophical position with the rhetorical strategy. We saw above how relativism works at the level of philosophical debate, but the strategy has become quite common in ordinary moral debate in a variety of areas, another reason why relativism has become a commonplace phenomenon in democratic practice. The rhetoric or language of relativism in moral discussion may include such phrases as "nobody should judge the moral values of another," "nobody should impose his/her values on anybody else," "who's to say what is right or wrong?," "everyone has their own moral views," "morality is a matter of subjective preference," "one's worldview is only one perspective on reality," and so on. Why do some people talk like this if they are not really relativists? I think there are two reasons. First, these phrases are appealed to solely for their rhetorical power in a culture that is already in large measure seduced by such language, is under the influence of such language. A second reason is that modern pluralism leads to and encourages this kind of rhetorical approach because of the loss of confidence in reason. One of the effects of a low view of reason is a new appeal to rhetorical strategies, for a variety of motivations: as a way of coping with incommensurability, as a way of avoiding an argument, as a recognition that reason has failed, as a tactical way of advancing one's views even though they are unconvincing to others.

The appeal to the language of relativism is becoming more prominent in everyday moral discussion and enables its proponents to achieve three things: first, it is quite a significant aid in getting one's beliefs and values a hearing and even in their possibly having some cultural influence, *all without having to argue the substantive content of those values.* Avoiding debate over substantive matters of disagreement in the pluralist climate described in Chap. 3, while at the same time still being able to influence public discourse, is a considerable advantage for a worldview. Second, by avoiding engagement with views one rejects, it further allows one to adopt the position of *not dignifying* such views by refusing to take them seriously. If one does not even engage with ideas then one conveys the impression that they are not worth taking seriously, and so one can (perhaps) win the argument by default rather than by honest, substantive, rational argument and discussion. Third, since this is only a rhetorical strategy and not a philosophical position to which one is truly committed, one (later) gets to assert or at least imply that morality is not relativistic after all; that, in fact, one's own views are objectively true! This last might sound like a stretch, but it is common practice today.

How does all of this work at the level of concrete debate and discussion? Let us illustrate with an example from American current affairs. In recent years in the U.S., several states have voted on proposals to legalize marijuana, and some, including Colorado, California, Michigan, and Maine, have done so. In some states more than others there was a public debate before the general populace went to the polls on the issue. I noticed during many of these debates the rhetoric of relativism in action. It was frequently employed by those who were arguing that marijuana should be legalized. This sounds as if it would involve complicated moral maneuvering, but our example will show how it can work smoothly enough in practice. Suppose one takes the position that marijuana should be legalized, and one is invited to participate in a public forum to debate the topic with a member of a group opposed to its legalization. There are two ways in which the proponent of legalization could approach the debate. The first is the obvious, indeed the traditional, logical, way. One might argue that smoking marijuana is a positive good, that the euphoria or feeling of well-being it produces relieves stress, and gives one a break from the difficulties of life! One might add that it has at least the potential to make certain types of people more creative, more productive, and so forth! On the negative side, one could suggest that the bad effects of taking the drug are exaggerated, that it does not lead to the deterioration of brain cells, does not lead to increased anti-social behavior, to an increase in crime, to more dysfunctional behavior overall, that it is not a gateway to harder drugs, all arguments one knows one's opponent is likely to raise. In short, one might adopt the approach that overall the drug is good for some people, and that any harms associated with it are exaggerated.

However, arguing along these lines leaves the pro-legalization position vulnerable in a couple of senses. One is that listeners will hear a good debate—assuming both sides do a capable job of expressing their best points—and may be persuaded by the other side. This is because even though the proponent of legalization thinks he has good arguments, he admits that the other side has too. The arguments being presented against his view are plausible and not ridiculous non-starters (he also knows that, whatever he may think of these arguments, they resonate strongly with the general public). The second point is that by engaging with your opponent in this way you *dignify* his position simply by listening to his arguments and trying to refute them. This by itself gives your opponent's view good status in the discussion (even if some are not persuaded by it).

However, there is a second strategy the proponent of the legalization of marijuana might pursue. This one involves *avoiding* as much as possible any discussion over the substantive content of the topic and so avoiding any possible dignifying of your opponent's view. It may perhaps also involve, depending on how the debate develops, preventing or discouraging your opponent from stating his views clearly, and putting any meat on his argument in a way that might resonate with listeners. So one avoids any claims that suggest that marijuana is good for people, and avoids debating the scientific or empirical validity of problems with marijuana use, such as the factual question of whether it leads to deterioration of brain cells, to an increase in crime, and so forth. Instead, one deliberately moves the debate to the abstract level and tries to keep it there. This is done by appealing to what I am calling the rhetoric or language of moral relativism. How is this possible? In this second strategy, the supporter of marijuana keeps the discussion at an abstract level by arguing that people have different views on whether marijuana should be legalized, and that no one should be able to impose their views on others. Why should some get to decide this matter for everyone? If one does not wish to use recreational drugs, then of course one will not be forced to, but one should not try to make these drugs illegal for all. One may opine that in a democratic society citizens should be free to make up their own minds on issues of this kind, and so forth.

I am sure this second strategy will sound familiar to most readers, since it is now a commonly used feature of democratic public deliberation. It was often adopted in the recent debate that took place in some U.S. states concerning the legalization of marijuana. It may sound like an odd way of arguing, since it never engages with actual issues of content. Yet, it can be a powerful rhetorical tactic in a culture that is already under the sway of moral relativism. (If one doubts this, I invite readers to test it out for themselves as a strategy the next time one is involved in a moral debate!) Those defending the practice of abortion at the level of public discourse also frequently adopt the same rhetorical strategy; indeed, I believe this is now the preferred way to defend the legalization of abortion. It is seldom we hear a public square debate today with regard to the topic of abortion in which the substantive question of the moral status of the embryo is even discussed. The discussion is deliberately kept at the abstract level concerning such abstract topics as the "right to choose," that it is wrong to force your opinion on others, that abortion is between a woman and her doctor, that good health care should include abortion. People know that this kind of strategy can be very effective in our (relativistic) culture.

Characteristic of this strategy is that those who adopt it talk as if they hold the position of moral relativism right at the beginning of a moral discussion, even though they are not moral relativists. This move puts their (usually unsuspecting) opponent immediately on the defensive, since because of the loss of confidence in reason and the general move toward relativism, there is a stigma in contemporary democratic culture that comes with the attempt to impose one's moral values on others (we must qualify this, of course, to restrict it to certain types of issues, and even there we run into lots of contradictions and problems which is why moral relativism is not a viable philosophical position, a point to which we will return in the next section). In terms of whether genuine moral knowledge is possible or not, those who engage in the rhetoric of relativism are approaching the matter as if they are denying the possibility of moral knowledge at all, and so relativism is the default position. So a consequence of this view would be that everybody gets to make up their own minds on key moral questions, such as regarding the morality of marijuana or abortion. The reality, however, is that our rhetorician is not a moral relativist in the philosophical sense. He believes that it is possible to discover objective truth, and he himself has in fact discovered it on various issues, including with regard to marijuana! He believes that drug taking is a moral practice, and this is why he wants it to be legal. So I think it is best here to describe relativism as a rhetorical strategy or as a device to "win" the argument without debating the content.

Here is another example to illustrate the same phenomenon. A theologian might wish to criticize the traditional teaching of Christianity on this or that issue because she thinks this teaching is wrong. She further believes that her own moral view on the issue in question is correct. Rather than debating the topic with regard to substantive issues of content, she might adopt a more general strategy. She might argue, for instance, that all major theological decisions made throughout history are political, meaning that they are arrived at as the outcome of a political struggle. The implication is that if the political struggle had gone differently, the outcome of the moral discussion would also have been different, and so the moral teaching would be different. Key theological teachings are, therefore, politically and historically arrived at, and so should not be regarded as objectively true. It would follow from this that all theological claims in traditional Christianity are subject to the same difficulty, and so this position, if developed to its logical conclusion, would be tantamount to a kind of cultural relativism, and to the denial of objective moral truth. But arriving at a conclusion of moral relativism is not the aim of our theologian. Her aim is to undermine the tradition so that her own moral and political views then come to be asserted as the true ones! It sounds like the theologian's intent is to undermine all theological and moral knowledge initially, but this is not what she wishes to do. She is undermining it only for rhetorical purposes. This is deemed better than arguing that the tradition is wrong and she is right, which is the other logical alternative for how she might approach the topic. If she argues this way, her view is easier to debate and therefore refute—because her critics will simply argue that she is wrong and the tradition is right on this or that issue. This is an argument she may lose; this approach also requires her to engage in debate if she is interested in an honest search for the truth, and it is also one that automatically dignifies the other side. People are attracted to the rhetorical strategy because it seems to allow one to reject a position without actually debating it; one seems to be taking a morally high ground and to be in superior position in some formal way to one's opponents, who are engaged in the unseemly practice of trying to impose their views on others!

Problems for Relativism

Although I am taking a mostly descriptive position with regard to relativism in this book, trying to discover how it originated and to describe its influence in modern democracy, we would be remiss if we did not also bring out its considerable problems. The problems are serious and reveal inconsistencies and contradictions all over the place, which irritate many, yet they do not seem to diminish the power of the rhetoric of relativism, especially at the political and cultural level. Many people are in an odd position today with regard to relativism in that they either accept it as a philosophical position, or work with it in its rhetorical sense, but nevertheless in both cases continue to make objective judgments, and often with a certainty that brooks no argument! This reveals our inability to live without appealing to a realm of objective truth, including moral truth, but it also may explain why moral debates today, especially those which invoke or rely upon some element of relativism, have become so shrill. One may be more inclined to cling in a extremist fashion to one's view if one believes that there is no objective way to ground it than if one thinks that open discussion and debate, against a backdrop of objective knowledge and reason, is the best way to understand reality. If there is no truth, there is no real point to rational debate because there are no common standards, and so there is little hope of success. So adopting an entrenched position may seem to be the most expedient option.

One of the difficulties illustrated by the above discussion is that relativism seems to be a near impossible thesis to actually live by. It is very difficult to function without making moral judgments at the practical level of everyday interaction with others. A true relativist could not criticize a person for lying to him, for defrauding him in a business deal, could not condemn racism or oppression, could not condemn a terrorist attack. This is also why relativism falls into logical problems of contradiction, because it is a commonplace for the relativist to claim that there are no objective values and then to assert objective values himself! Those drawn to relativism routinely advocate tolerance of other beliefs, and often condemn moral objectivists, both positions that involve appeal to objective moral values. Relativists also cannot meaningfully talk of moral progress: cultures and individuals may *change* their beliefs, for various reasons, from time to time (such as from pro to anti-slavery) but this cannot be because they came to see that their previously held beliefs were objectively wrong. Moral reformers are similarly anathema to relativism; people like Socrates, Jesus, Gandhi, Sojourner Truth, Martin Luther King, and Mother Teresa are misguided because they made the mistake of thinking that there are objective moral values which can be known, and of trying to impose specific values on societies which rejected them.

Sometimes those inclined toward relativism will attempt to suggest that one can be an objectivist about some values and a relativist about others. This way, it may be possible to have the advantages of relativism while avoiding the disadvantages. However, this position is also very problematic for a number of reasons. First, there is no agreement about which values would fall into which category, and so the moral debate cannot be avoided (often one of the main attractions of relativism). Second, an extension of the first point is that once one acknowledges that there is a realm of objective moral knowledge, one must enter into debate with other moral objectivists who disagree about which values fall into that category. In this way, moral relativism loses much of its force because one loses the two things that give it its power—the total denial of objective moral knowledge and the attempt not to dignify the opposing view by debating issues of moral content. There is also, third, a serious risk that such a view may fall into extreme relativism eventually because if one denies that moral truth can be known objectively about some values, it is perhaps inevitable that this argument will eventually be extended to all values (a trend we surely see in modern democratic culture).

Disagreement, Incommensurability, and Relativism

It is an interesting question as to how far democratic society has gone down the road of philosophical relativism. It seems that once we acknowledge the fact of the incommensurability of worldviews, the practical effect is that we are stuck with some form of relativism in fact, if not in theory. A way forward based on consensus and compromise becomes harder to envisage. Moreover, the movements of anti-realism and postmodernism have gone a good way toward contributing to a general loss of confidence in reason to know the truth, especially if we accept that these are dominant ways of approaching the question of knowledge in many academic disciplines. Of course, we can make a distinction between holding that one's view is true, and all others are wrong (which is not relativism), and thinking that all views are just as good as each other (which is closer to relativism). Modern democratic culture generally moves between these two positions; perhaps our societies are gradually moving toward the latter. But because of the attack on reason, many no longer think that they can get anywhere in a contentious debate; we also have the worry that reason can become so supple that it can be invoked to justify any position at all! This leaves us with the problem of how to proceed with our disagreements, especially with the problem of how someone who takes a strong relativistic approach, perhaps embraces full philosophical relativism, can engage in dialogue with a moral objectivist. So it is helpful when considering the debate between worldviews to distinguish the following three types of possible disagreement.

A. Between an objectivist and an objectivist: This is where we start out: both sides hold different and (increasingly today) incommensurable views, which, respectively, they believe to be objectively true. We still have many disagreements of this type, perhaps the majority, and they are far from easy to revolve. We are showing in this chapter only how relativism is influential in modern society, not how it has taken over, though it is fair to say that we are moving closer to a wholesale relativism.

B. Between an objectivist and a relativist: This type of disagreement needs to be handled carefully. A first step is to make sure that it is actually present in a particular case. For we have just seen how a moral dispute can *appear* to belong to this category, but in fact belongs to the first category because one side is simply giving the appearance of relativism by using the rhetoric of relativism (but is really advocating objective truths). But genuine disagreements of this type constitute a very difficult problem because the parties disagree over the status of moral knowledge itself (keeping our focus on ethical relativism). One side is very influenced by the spirit of relativism that surrounds judgments about morality and brings this spirit to the table, and the other side rejects relativism and holds an objectivist position. The dispute is grave because the main disagreement is over deeper foundational issues which leads to further clashes about practical moral questions.

C. Between a relativist and a relativist: This is perhaps the hardest disagreement to resolve because there is no objective standpoint from which to approach a solution. It is the problem that liberal political theory is grappling with, as we will see later. It is also perhaps that place toward which democratic society is regrettably (and worryingly) moving, because it is a position which seems to invite anarchy (since there is no truth) and/or tyranny (since those views that get to shape law and society will do so because their advocates have the most political power, rather than because they are true, or even believed to be true).

Yet, even if we clarify which of these three types of dispute we may be dealing with in individual cases, it does not seem to help us very much. The positions described in B and C appear hopeless from the point of view of making any kind of reasonable and practical progress. And even if we are working with a more straightforward dispute between two objectivists—who at least agree about the status of moral knowledge—we are still left with the problem of the incommensurability of worldviews. Given this, we can suggest the following guidelines for how to proceed given these very difficult problems. These guidelines will help us to see more easily the role that relativism plays in modern democratic nations, to distinguish between relativism as a philosophical position and the rhetoric of relativism, and to at least understand more clearly what is going on in various moral debates. This is not to say that our suggestions here will solve our problems, because (as I have been arguing) these problems are severe, and are precipitating a crisis in the democratic system of governing.

1. Discern which type of disagreement is involved: When involved in or analyzing a moral or political disagreement, we should be aware of which type of disagreement it falls into, A, B, or C (above). Is it a debate between two objectivists, a relativist and an objectivist, or between two relativists? This essential point will help one know what exactly the disagreement is about, and how to approach it. For example, if the debate is between an objectivist and a relativist, one must settle the question of the status of moral knowledge first before one discusses the actual moral issue (how does one go about *doing that*, however?). This move is helpful, though, because the morality of the issue can be obscured if one fails to realize that the dispute is primarily about the nature and range of moral knowledge. Similarly, if it is a dispute between two relativists, one can see that it would be odd for one side to be insisting that her view is true and the other false, and so on. So, knowing which category the dispute falls into can itself bring clarity, if not a solution, to the disagreement.

2. Establish one's own views clearly before engaging in moral and political debate at the level of public discourse: This does not just mean knowing what you believe on specific moral issues (such as abortion or how to tackle the problem of homelessness). It also involves knowing where one stands on the question of objectivism versus relativism (and indeed on the general question of realist versus anti-realist views of knowledge). Do you believe that all moral values are relative in some way, that there is no objective moral order? If so, do you still make objective moral judgments yourself, and how do you justify them? If you don't make such judgments, do you think that anything goes in ethics? Many are wishy-washy about such questions, and don't face squarely up to the consequences of what they believe. But this process of discernment is enormously helpful for clarifying where one stands with regard to one's worldview and its role in a democratic pluralist state.

3. Discern your own position on whether incommensurability means for all practical purposes relativism: This point is an extension of the above point. A holder of a worldview needs to settle on a position with regard to this crucial matter. Do you think the fact that others hold worldviews different to yours means that no worldview can be said to have the truth? If so, how do you think we should proceed with regard to the making of laws and public policy? Admittedly this is a very difficult question, one we are working through in this book. But participants in a democratic society need to decide where they stand on it. If one thinks, on the other hand, that one's view is the objective truth, and that other views are wrong, how should we then proceed? Another difficult question; we consider how to address both as our work unfolds.

Notes

1. For a helpful overview of the meaning and influence of postmodernism, see Walt T. Anderson (ed.), *The Truth about Truth: De-confusing and Re-constructing the Postmodern World* (New York: Putnam, 1995).

2. For some representative works, see Jacques Derrida, *Writing and Difference*, trans. by Alan Bass (Chicago, IL.: University of Chicago Press, 1978); Roland Barthes, *Mythologies* (New York: Hill and Wang, 2013); Paul Rabinow (ed.), *The Foucault Reader* (New York: Pantheon, 1984); Jean-François Lyotard, *The Postmodern Condition: A Report on Knowledge* (Minneapolis, MS: University of Minnesota Press, 1984).
3. See my "Postmodernism, Derrida and *Différance*: A Critique," *International Philosophical Quarterly*, Vol. XXXIX, No.1 (March 1999), pp. 5–18, which influences my exposition here.
4. See Derrida, *Writing and Difference*, pp. 112–122; also his *Margins of Philosophy*, trans. A. Bass (Chicago: University of Chicago Press, 1982), pp. 21–25.
5. As described by John Sturrock in *Structuralism and Since*, ed. John Sturrock (Oxford: Oxford U.P., 1979), p. 58.
6. See also my *Why Politics Needs Religion*, pp. 239–244.
7. See the discussion between Gary Gutting and John Caputo for a readable example of the rhetorical strategy of postmodernists; Gary Gutting, *Talking God* (New York: Norton, 2017), pp. 38–54.

PART II

Secularization and Political Liberalism: The Exclusion of Religion

CHAPTER 5

Religion, and the Rise of Secularism

One of the themes we wish to highlight in this book is that secularism is becoming a major worldview in contemporary Western democratic societies. This fact has two significant consequences. The first is that it makes the problem of worldview pluralism (identified in Chap. 1) much worse, and perhaps intractable. The second is the effect it has on our understanding of the religious worldview, and on the relationship between religion and politics, in particular. It changes the debate between religion and politics in a fundamental way so that the conventional wisdom about their relationship in secular democracies (a term we have to define very carefully in what follows) is no longer adequate and needs to be re-envisioned. These consequences are closely related to each other, and present challenges for democracy that we need to work through carefully, and as clearly as possible.

One of the problems we face is that these concerns are often obscured in contemporary political debates, and can become shrouded by rhetoric on all sides. Sometimes the rhetoric of relativism (discussed in the previous chapter) dominates the conversation as people attempt to advance their political and moral agendas, and so a clear understanding and analysis of the topic can be hard to obtain. Arriving at a good understanding of what is admittedly a complex topic and providing a careful analysis of the key questions, issues, and concerns is part of our job in this book. We will begin in this chapter with a brief overview of what we mean by religion and by secularism, so that we know what we are referring to. Although secularism is becoming very influential, it is still a worldview that many may be somewhat unfamiliar with, especially with regard to its defining beliefs and philosophical foundations. So it is helpful to clarify this view in a more formal way, especially its philosophical structure. The remainder of the chapter will offer some further reflections on secularism, and consider a serious attempt at a philosophical defense of this approach in the work of philosopher of science, Philip Kitcher. The next chapter will then expand on our understanding of secularism, distinguishing it from the process of "secularization" and from the concept of "the secular," and will illustrate further the role secularism plays in contemporary democratic culture.

The Worldviews of Religion and Secularism

I am assuming that most readers will be thoroughly familiar with what we mean by religion. We will work with Christianity as the religion that will be of primary interest to most readers with regard to the pluralist debate in Western democracies. Though, it is important to emphasize, as we will from time to time, that our arguments apply to all religions, indeed to all worldviews, that come into contact with the democratic state. The presence of other religions and worldviews that command significant numbers in democratic societies (e.g., Islam, atheism, and those who fall into the grouping often labeled "spiritual, but not religious" or the "nones"—those who claim no official or formal religion) is a development that is also very germane to our arguments in this book. Indeed, the emergence of different religious perspectives and worldviews that gain the allegiance of a considerable number of citizens strengthens my overall argument because it clearly contributes to the difficulties that this kind of pluralism presents for modern democracies.

The Religious Worldview: In this section, I wish simply to remind ourselves of what we mean by religion and to capture the salient points that are most relevant for our discussion. Many different definitions of religion have been offered, and they each capture something fundamental to its essential nature. We don't need to have an exact definition, just an overall understanding of it that captures its main features, the essential attributes in so far as we can identify them, since we are concerned with more general, foundational issues, rather than with the finer points of religious teachings, doctrines, or religious morality. We need to emphasize in thinking about religion the salient points: that it is a complex system of beliefs, that it is life-regulating (it influences how we live), that it has an ethical theory, is expressed in certain types of rituals and practices, and is based in significant part on a belief in a sacred, transcendent (unseen) reality. We might also specify that it usually includes belief in God, or in a Supreme Reality or Power, that is responsible for the existence of the universe, and the moral order. It is, however, true that one can find religions that do not contain one or other of these features, but we do not need to get into a debate about the set of necessary criteria for deciding what counts as a religion, because (although fascinating) this matter would take us too far off track. Emile Durkheim understood religion as "a unified system of beliefs and practices relative to sacred things," while William James draws attention to the moral dimension, when he says that religion involves "the belief there is an unseen order, and that our supreme good lies in harmoniously adjusting ourselves thereto." Noted scholar of various religious traditions, Ninian Smart, gives a fuller and perhaps more useful definition: religion is "a set of institutionalized rituals with a tradition and expressing and/or evoking sacral sentiments directed at a divine or trans-divine focus seen in the context of the human phenomenological environment and at least partially described by myths or by myths and doctrines."[1] These definitions provide an overview of the types of features that are generally accepted as belonging to religion, and also remind us that there is really no standard definition.

With this general understanding in mind, let us consider Christianity from the point of view of identifying some of its main beliefs. With regard to what we might call metaphysical beliefs (or foundational philosophical beliefs), Christians believe that God exists, and possesses the characteristics (or attributes) identified in traditional Western theology and philosophy (often called classical theism). God is eternal, omnipotent, omniscient, all good, all merciful, and so on. God created the world and all that exists, including all life, according to a particular design. Human beings occupy a special place in God's creation. God is also understood to be three persons in one Being: Father, Son, and Holy Spirit. Jesus Christ was God incarnate. A fulfilled human life is one where we love God and one another. There exists an objective moral law or order, closely linked to human nature, and it is grounded in God's law and God's plan for humanity. The moral law is discoverable in part by a mixture of reason and experience. As a result of being created in God's image, each human being is unique and has a special dignity and integrity that ought not to be violated. Human beings are by nature social beings. Human beings are made up of body and soul. Human beings may, through God's grace, enjoy happiness and eternal life with God, resurrected as body and soul.

The main guiding text for this view is the Bible, which is regarded as God's revealed word to man. The Church as an institution helps to model, explain, and promote the worldview in a public way. Christianity, as I will show later, does have a political side to it, which means that some religious beliefs have something to say about political issues, and so Christianity would have some role to play in politics (the extent of this role is controversial and much debated, of course, and will be a major focus in later chapters). However, in general the various branches of Christianity are committed to a principle of the separation of church and state in one key sense: that no particular denomination should seek to become the official established religion, the official worldview, of the state. With regard to the political system of democracy, most Christian churches accept the basic principles of democracy, such as popular sovereignty, freedom, equality, justice, and natural rights, though what each of these values means will often be understood by reference to some of the main beliefs of the specific worldview in question. This does not mean, however, that Christianity endorses the democratic system as the official political theory of Christianity, nor does it mean that Christianity could not work in other political systems. In this sense, Christianity is independent of any political system, and also of any economic system. Any political or economic system can be evaluated morally by Christianity, based on its foundational beliefs, and no political or economic system is a necessary part of, or consequence of, Christianity.[2]

It is also necessary to say a little about the reasonability of the religious worldview, and about the relationship between various religious worldviews and their sacred or revealed texts, again using Christianity as an example, though the general argument applies to most major religions of the world. The first main point is that Christianity is not simply based on uncritical acceptance of biblical revelation. Ever since the beginning of Christianity, it has been accompanied by an attempt to develop a philosophical, theological, and historical defense of it as a reasonable view of reality. This is only to be expected as reasonable, indeed highly intelligent, people reflect on their beliefs. There is a 2000-year history of deep philosophical thinking and analysis of every aspect of what we might refer to as the Christian philosophy of life. We do not need to rehearse this here, or to evaluate its success, we only need to note that it exists, and that it is a key part of Christianity. (In any case, in evaluating its success in a democratic context one could only speak for oneself, and, crucially, not for others, on this matter.) But it is essential to realize that Christianity is a theory of ultimate meaning, a philosophy of life and the human person, an ethical vision, that is defended by philosophical argument. It is a response to the ultimate questions that speak to the inner person and concern matters of the soul and the spiritual dimension of experience. It is true that the attempt to show the affinities or coherence between the philosophical vision and scriptural revelation is an important topic that has generated much debate, and indeed disagreement. It includes disputes about both the content and the reliability of scripture. In this way, the Christian worldview involves scripture but it is not completely based on it; there are versions of it that stick very closely to scripture and versions that have little contact with scripture. There are also contentious disagreements over the correct account of Christian teachings, over scriptural interpretations, and over moral and other issues.

We need to acknowledge, second, that some versions of Christianity are more philosophically based than scripturally based, though they would likely still have a strong affinity with scripture. Indeed, today I think it is accurate to describe many people as *philosophical Christians*, meaning that their understanding of, articulation of, and defense of their belief in the worldview of Christianity is based primarily on a rational, analytical, philosophical approach, rather than on appeal to scriptural support (and indeed many philosophical Christians often dispute traditional interpretations of scripture, or sometimes bypass them altogether). All of these versions of Christianity are *a reality* in democratic pluralist nations—this is the key truth from the point of view of the problem of contentious pluralism. The origins of these views are perhaps of less importance. What we might call philosophical Christianity is a view that many subscribe to today, even if no official or particular Church holds or promotes it. It is a worldview that is freely chosen by many of our contemporaries from among the alternatives.

All of this is par for the course in *any* worldview, religious or secularist. We can make the same two points, I believe, about at least the major religions of the world, that they are grounded in a philosophical vision, which is related to, but may not be based exclusively upon, a tradition of scriptural revelation. Some may object that my view of religion is too Christian or too Western. I accept this point with the proviso that any view that wishes to influence politics is subject to the arguments I lay out in this book, no matter what beliefs it holds or what the structure of its worldview is. In this sense, my view includes every religion, every worldview, as long as it accepts the democratic system and democratic values. Each tradition has its major thinkers (often some of the great minds in history) who were engaged in the attempt to develop the strongest philosophical articulation and defense of their worldview. Of course, each religion must be judged individually on these matters, from a rational point of view. Moreover, the *disagreement* between major world religions, and between religious worldviews and secularist worldviews (and indeed among secularists themselves), on such matters as the nature of reality, the human person, and moral and political values, is a fact of life. Nothing can be deduced from the mere fact of disagreement that would help us in any way to discern which of these visions of reality is the correct one, or more likely to be correct.

The Secularist Worldview: Turning now to the worldview of secularism, again we only need a general overview, while recognizing that there are different forms of this worldview, just as there are different religions. We need to focus on what is common to most versions of it—the salient features of the view—in the discussion concerning modern democratic societies. Secularism shall refer to the view that holds that all of reality is physical in nature, consisting of some configuration of matter and energy.[3] This claim also applies to the human person, and to all living things. The secularist worldview places a large emphasis in contemporary times on science, because science is the method for studying the physical realm. Proponents of secularism sometimes hold that every feature of reality can be explained by science, at least in principle, though it is important not to confuse secularism with science, since most scientists are not secularists. Understood this way, secularism is a philosophical theory about reality. As such, it will need to have philosophical accounts and explanations eventually for all aspects of reality, including morality and politics. So in addition to holding a more metaphysical or philosophical account of reality, secularists will also propose moral and political theories, and perhaps eventually even an economic theory. (Secularism is sometimes known as philosophical secularism, secular humanism, humanism, naturalism, materialism, scientism, or philosophical atheism, though the term secularism is more descriptive of the current version of it, and so the most accurate and appropriate term to use in this book.)

It is helpful to note that in the past this type of secularist view was usually expressed in a negative way. In more recent times, there has been a transition to expressing it in an ostentatiously more positive manner, and so to promoting it as a serious alternative to the religious worldview in the contemporary world, especially in democratic societies. In the past atheism generally was primarily a *negative* position in the sense that atheists understood themselves mainly (and oddly perhaps) in terms of what they did not believe, by what they rejected, rather than in terms of what they accepted as true in a positive sense. So, for example, the atheist denied the existence of God, rejected the Bible and religious morality, the authority of the Church, and so forth. Their general position was negative in two other ways as well, psychologically and in terms of the intellectual defense of their view. From a psychological point of view, atheists often saw themselves as outsiders, as a group whose members did not believe what most other people believed. When called upon to defend their view, they also usually did this by attacking religious belief, for example, by critiquing the arguments of the philosophers for the existence of God, or by challenging the reliability of the Bible. They adopted this negative approach rather than offering (positive) evidence and arguments for their (positive) claims—that all of reality is physical in composition, and that we can arrive at (secular) independent accounts of morality and politics that would be capable of guiding individual and societal living.

In the latter half of the twentieth century, as the debate between atheists and religious believers has become more intense, not least in the disagreements at the political level in democratic societies over moral and social issues, *all of this has changed.* Atheists came to realize that they needed to develop and express their views in positive terms. If one wishes to expand one's philosophy of life and take it to the next level, instead of just criticizing the beliefs of others, then one needs to develop a more serious and sophisticated case. And so contemporary atheists have worked hard individually and collectively to apply themselves to this task. They have focused on what they believe and wish to promote in the place of religion, and some thinkers, such as Richard Dawkins, have embarked on campaigns aimed at diminishing allegiance to, and the influence of, religion in society.[4] Secularists have also begun to sharpen their moral and political antennae in public and social debates. So they have turned to the positive claim (one that states what is true, or what they believe, rather than what they deny or reject) that all of reality is physical in nature, and that science will eventually unravel the mysteries of the universe. They then turn to current scientific theories, such as those in evolution, genetics, and cosmology, giving them an atheistic spin (and a bad name to boot among many theists[5]) to support their views with positive arguments, rather than simply attacking the arguments of their opponents. This more positive approach, of course, if true, would entail that the religious view of the world is false, that there is no God, no soul, no revelation, no religious morality, and so forth. *What we have seen in the twentieth century is a gradual shift from the negative worldview of atheism to the positive worldview of secularism.*

Secularism therefore, due to such developments, is now becoming a more clearly defined worldview, and is more recognizable in the modern world, though it is not nearly as popular as religion, and is still confused by many with "the secular" (rather than clearly identified as secularism, a distinction we will address in the next chapter). Nevertheless, the influence of secularism is growing; secularists are becoming more outspoken with regard to social and cultural matters in various countries. It is also true that the general public is beginning to recognize the presence of this worldview in various areas of life, and in public debates (and we also see a noticeable increase in publications and discussions of secularism in the contemporary literature). So this is what we mean by secularism in our discussion; it is not to be confused with positions that are similar to it but different, and which the term is sometimes used to describe, such as that the state should be neutral between worldviews, or neutral between religion and non-religion, that the state should be free from religion, that there should be separation of church and state, that the state should allow freedom of conscience, welcome "free thinkers," and so on. (We will come back to such views and their contrast with secularism in later chapters.)

It is of the utmost importance, I think, in this crucial debate for our times that we recognize that secularism is a growing and influential worldview. Many recent surveys of religious affiliation and practice show both a significant decline in the number of people who belong to an organized religion and a significant rise in the numbers who describe themselves as having no religion or as atheists or agnostics.[6] Atheists and secularists were perhaps once reluctant to make positive claims about reality, the nature of the human person, and morality, in the sense noted earlier. Sometimes this reluctance is inspired by a desire to "contain" (or perhaps placate) religion, rather than defeat it. So one might hold that religious beliefs should not be discussed in a school science curriculum, or should not influence public policy on stem cell research, and offer as the reason that, although one has nothing against religion, it should really be a private matter. This could be a political move to mask one's real view which is that religion is false and should have no influence on society. I think some secularists did initially adopt this kind of tactical approach, and some still do so today, in the debate with religious worldviews.

However, this is changing, and secularists are now more open about what they believe (and about what they reject), and about promoting secularism in society. They are less likely to claim that their position on key questions is "neutral,"—or that they don't have any belief system or worldview themselves, or that the state should be "neutral" between different views. Secularists will now insist that their view is the *correct* one, and that it should be the philosophy that guides society. Secularists in the university setting are quite aggressive and "in your face" about this, but I think it is a feature of modern life that is now showing up in other public areas, such as media discussions, popular books, legal judgments, and in politics. This trend is also due in part to the crisis of religion that has occurred in some democratic countries, a crisis that has created a space for people to look for alternatives, one of which is secularist. This space also enables those who are already secularist to advance their worldview in the vacuum that is forming because of waning religious influence, especially in public discussions.

Secularists are also trying hard to change their image! Secularism, and any form of atheism, is still looked upon unfavorably by the general public in many countries, mainly because they regard it as primarily anti-religious, especially as being against religious authority and religious morality (for instance, in sexual matters), rather than regarding it as a benign alternative worldview (the attitude many now adopt toward other religions). There is also perhaps a typical "secularist persona" that often accompanies the view, which many frown upon. Religious believers often perceive with some justification that secularists cultivate a supercilious attitude, thinking and acting as if they are smarter or superior to religious people. All of this inevitably puts secularism on a collision course with religious belief. In this sense, the problem of worldview pluralism is perhaps worse than it might be otherwise, notwithstanding the fact that there will always be a clash between religion and secularism because of the gulf between their foundational beliefs about reality, the human person, and the meaning of life. However, it is an important part of the persona of secularism, if we might put it like that, that it is often defined and perceived as much as being against a worldview (religion), as it is in promoting a worldview (secularism). In the next chapter, I will discuss this phenomenon a bit more, when introducing the notions of mature and immature secularism.

Areas of Disagreement and Some Qualifications

It is helpful to bring out a contrast between the religious worldview and the secularist worldview with regard to their respective positions on the nature of human beings, their understanding of what it means to be a human person. Many of the clashes between secularism and religious belief can be traced back to differences over this central topic, one that has been given much attention by many of the greatest thinkers in history. The religious view of the world (staying particularly with Christianity) holds what is sometimes referred to as the traditional view of the human person (especially as developed in the thought of the tradition of Aristotle and St. Thomas Aquinas). This view says that human beings are created by God for a particular purpose. It holds that all human beings share the same nature and that other differences such as racial, ethnic, and cultural differences are secondary. Human nature may be understood as a set of traits and characteristics that all human beings share, that are not merely biological since they are part of the human soul, and that have special relevance for morality. These characteristics would include reason, free will, our spiritual dimension, and morality, particularly understood as the development of human virtues. Virtues, as Aristotle argued, are understood as human excellences, whose proper development expresses what it means for a human being to live a good and fulfilled human life, the sort of life that a human being ought to live in order to bring out the best of one's nature or essence.[7] Human beings are also social by nature (rather than primarily individuals), and are at the top of the evolutionary tree by design, not by chance. Of course, there are nuances within this view depending on which denomination of Christianity one is dealing with, or which Christian thinker one is reading. The underlying point is that it is a fact that these versions of Christianity are part of the mix that is contemporary pluralism.

The secularist view is largely the opposite to this account. Since proponents of the secularist worldview hold that all of reality is physical in nature or structure, and everything that exists consists of some configuration of matter and energy, they naturally also hold then that the human being is a completely material being. This means that there is no soul, and for many secularists it also means that there is nothing non-biological in our human characteristics, including in our higher level features of consciousness, reason, morality, and free will (the existence of the latter is denied or at least questioned by some secularists). Consequently, there is no afterlife.

Secularists also hold that the existence of the universe occurred by chance, as did the existence of all life on earth. They generally think that the process of evolution operates with a large element of chance, and that this played a significant role in the emergence of every species, including *Homo sapiens*. A consequence of this view is that there is no overall purpose to human life, no end to which human life is striving. Secularists also typically hold that human beings are primarily individual beings first, and social beings second.

When it comes to the democratic political system, and politics more generally, most secularists in the West hold that secularism has a role to play in the public square, that is, appeal to its truths and values is appropriate in public debates, and also can be an appropriate guide when passing legislation on some matters. Secularists also generally hold that religious views should have little or no role in politics, because of the democratic principle of the separation of church and state, but primarily because they hold that the religious view is false. Their attitude toward other worldviews not their own is that these other worldviews are more or less right insofar as they agree with secularists' beliefs and values, wrong if they do not.

Secularists normally articulate their worldview within the context of democracy, and so place a high priority on democratic values, such as natural rights, freedom, equality, and justice. The worldview is not *necessarily* committed to the democratic form of government (some secularists might be Marxists or socialists of one kind or another; nor are they, like religious believers, committed to any particular economic theory). Secularists need not be left wing politically; there are many people who are conservative in general attitude and who subscribe to a secularist outlook as well. Nevertheless, when we think about secularism in the context of the debate we are concerned with, and its influence in Western societies, we tend to associate it with the views of Mill (mentioned in Chap. 2), especially with regard to an almost extreme emphasis on freedom and appeal to the harm principle. These ideas play a large role in the way the secularist worldview is articulated and understood in the West. Secularists place significant weight on the idea of the rational autonomy of the individual, and are inclined to look down upon any decision that is not arrived at in this way. In fact, they often regard the highest form of life as one that is chosen freely, even if an individual chooses wrongly; this is preferable to imposing a (correct?) view upon a person!

We also tend to ally it with a utilitarian theory (also coming from the thought of Mill) which puts the emphasis on maximizing the amount of good in society. The meaning of life is often understood to involve increasing the amount of happiness, where happiness is understood as the fulfillment of and the maximization of pleasure, as well as keeping pain to a minimum. Yet, none of these beliefs are essential to secularism. There can be many shades of secularism; they qualify as being secularist as long as they contain the main foundational beliefs listed and the broad view of the human person we have noted. A secularist, for example, could support a constitutional monarchy, or a conservative view along the lines of that held by Edmund Burke, which sought to balance individual liberty with a role for tradition and authority and the collective wisdom of past societies in the governing of the state. A secularist might be conservative or liberal with regard to economic policy; secularists also might disagree among themselves on the correct moral values; one might support abortion and another reject it, and so forth.

We need to acknowledge that we have been painting with broad strokes in this section. Although this is adequate for our purposes, it does not reflect the many different shades of worldviews *that actually exist*. We must acknowledge that there are many diverse worldviews within our categories, with distinctive foundational beliefs, different approaches to some of the important issues we have mentioned such as the human person, one's political system, one's view of morality and the meaning of life. For example, there are many versions of Christianity, and although we would expect that they would have much in common, they also have differences, and some of these can be quite significant. Christians might disagree over which particular Christian doctrines are true, for instance, or about the nature of God (such as the disagreement between classical theologians and process theologians), about how to interpret the Bible (in general, and/or in specific cases), about whether the Bible is divinely inspired, about the correct account of Christian morality. Today, we can broadly distinguish between traditional Christians, liberal Christians, and philosophical Christians. All of these positions have adherents in modern democratic states.

Moreover, there are different religions which have even more fundamental differences, for example, more radical differences over the nature of God, or over which religious text is divinely inspired, or over other issues of doctrine, morality, and the path to salvation. There are also diverse versions of secularism. These differences among worldviews, however, do not affect the main points we are making here. Our key point is that an individual needs to know what their worldview is, how best to defend it from a philosophical point of view and when challenged by others, and what role it can properly play in democratic politics. One should also know something of how one's worldview differs from others on central issues. These are the essential things to know at the concrete level of living and functioning in a pluralist state from a moral and political point of view (in later chapters we will look at some concrete examples of public square debates concerning different worldviews).

It is not quite true to say that there are as many worldviews as there are people (since millions of people often share the same worldview), yet there are many diverse expressions of the familiar, dominant, and culture-shaping worldviews, especially in our increasingly individualistic and fractious society. Actual life and practice with regard to worldviews is now quite complicated. We must also appreciate that in our modern pluralist context we need to be extra careful about saying that there is a "religious position" on a question, or a "secularist position," if this is meant to suggest that all religious believers or all secularists hold the same view on a particular topic, or even with regard to the foundational beliefs of their worldview. We know that this is not true; indeed it is one of the reasons it can be so hard to give a general definition of these respective worldviews, and is the reason why we have to settle for an overview of general, salient beliefs. It is appropriate nevertheless to speak of "the religious view" on a topic or "the secularist view" in some contexts (e.g., when we say that secularism is becoming more influential in modern culture, or that secularists wish to keep religion out of politics). But it is also essential to keep in mind that if we had a completely secularist country, or world for that matter, we would still have the problem of worldview pluralism because there would inevitably be different versions of secularism that would clash with each other, particularly with regard to political structures, economic approaches, and moral issues.

Secularism and Western Societies

When compared with the religious worldview in general, secularism is not nearly as popular, nor does it have as large a number of famous thinkers and promoters. Certainly, it has no well-established tradition when compared with religion (though it does have a tradition). However, all of this is slowly changing. Secularism today does not lack for contemporary spokesperson, some of whom are very well known and are the authors of bestselling books on the subject. The list of representative contemporary thinkers would include philosophers Daniel Dennett, Philip Kitcher and Thomas Nagel, psychologist Steven Pinker, scientists Richard Dawkins, Jerry Coyne, and the late Carl Sagan, and writers and thinkers from a variety of other disciplines, including Sam Harris, Ann Druyan, Alex Rosenberg, and Louise Anthony.[8] Secularism was also often advanced historically, though sometimes under a different name. The list of influential thinkers from the past who supported it would include Julian Offray de La Mettrie (1709–1751); John Stuart Mill (1806–1873), Karl Marx (1818–1883), Oliver Wendell Holmes (1841–1935), Friedrich Nietzsche (1844–1900), and John Dewey (1859–1952).

Although the secularist worldview is becoming influential in modern democratic culture, it still does not have *official* institutions that have significant cultural authority, nor does it have official spokespersons, nor too many formal associations that prospective secularists could seek out and join (though there are secularist societies in most democratic countries). This is in part because it is not yet sufficiently organized, nor does it have a unified set of beliefs, especially moral and political beliefs, to which all secularists could subscribe. Though, even this is changing. More people today do describe themselves as secularists, and they are taking their secularist views into politics. Some politicians are even beginning to promote a secularist agenda in various countries, another significant step in it becoming influential with regard to public policy. Official secularist groups that gain significant public influence surely cannot be far behind. And it is important to observe that secularism does have self-appointed spokespersons that have many followers, and who make no bones about the fact that they are trying to promote the secularist worldview over the religious worldview as the best way forward for modern democracy. One of the most famous (and most notorious) of these spokespersons is the Oxford biologist, Richard Dawkins, though he is not the only one. Others would include Sam Harris, Steven Pinker, and Philip Kitcher (whose view we will consider in the last section).

There is no real need to document the phenomenon of the growth of secularism, especially in Western democracies (though in the next chapter we will consider in more detail the fascinating process of *secularization* that has contributed to the growth of secularism in Western countries).[9] We are more interested in the philosophical and political debate provoked by the expanse of secularism: the attempt to justify it philosophically; its attack on the religious worldview (which is currently part of its identity); its dispute with other worldviews within the context of pluralism; in addition to its effects on society and implications for other related questions (such as the role it should have in education, and so forth). I do think that it is reasonable to suggest that secularism as a worldview, through its advocates, promoters, and fellow travelers, wishes to have considerable influence on Western society. Its supporters wish for it to be the presumptive worldview that most impacts the lives of people and culture, and that has most authority with regard to political, social, and moral issues. There is no coordinated strategy for this, and it is carried out at present by a small cadre of individuals and groups, often working in a piecemeal fashion. Promoting the idea that religion has no place in public life, and attempting to relegate it to a private sphere of living and decision-making, is one strategy that aids in the spread of secularism. This is an interesting strategy because it does not require that a religious believer become a secularist; it needs only for religious people to defer to secularism on moral, political, and cultural matters, that the secularist view gets to shape law and culture (we will come back to this and other related points in the next chapter). Indeed, secularism can perhaps be more effective if it is presented subtly or even introduced by stealth, than if advocated in a direct way. If secularists are more open about their beliefs, their hopes and plans for society, they are more likely to be challenged and to meet resistance than if the general populace is not really aware of what they are doing! This is the way it was in the recent past, I believe, because secularists were mindful of the power and influence of religion so they were usually cautious about taking it on directly. But that situation is changing. Secularism is becoming a more overt movement, and so is beginning to provoke a more contentious debate in Western societies, a situation that exacerbates the clash of worldviews.

Secularism is more political in its general orientation than most religious worldviews tend to be, and so more aimed at change at the political or societal level. It is less concerned with the personal development or transformation of the individual, especially in a spiritual or moral sense, one of the most challenging, but also one of the most attractive, features of the religious worldview for many. This can be partly explained by the fact that secularism focuses on the material world and denies the realm of the transcendent. So it places little emphasis on self-reform in a moral sense, though there is some indication that it values personal reform in a material sense, perhaps in the areas of looks and health. It also places less emphasis on community life than religion. The emphasis on personal reform, and on community living, gives religion, I believe, a great advantage over the secularist worldview, and is one of the reasons it is a superior view in terms of leading to human fulfillment, and providing overall meaning and purpose in life. This is why so many find it both emotionally and rationally extremely satisfying (a point Kitcher honestly struggles with, as we will see in the next section.) In a way, this is why secularists tend to look more to public life as the most effective standpoint from which to influence society, though it is an interesting question as to whether secularism can eventually develop (as Kitcher will suggest) either a coherent argument for the necessity of the moral development and even perfection of the human person, and a specific program of moral exercises and virtues that would aid in bringing this about. The close relationship between modern Western secularism and the freedom embodied in the thought of Mill has tended to promote a selfishness in the individual person, characterized by the fact that others (as noted earlier) are often regarded as obstacles to the exercise of my freedom. There is a tendency to initially regard other people as those who are in my way, rather than as people whom I can assist or to whom I can be of service. In the past, it was true that secularists did not wear their worldview on their sleeves in as obvious a way as religious believers tend to, but this is changing. Signs of this change can be found everywhere now in Western democracies (one small example of many is the number of "humanist" wedding and funeral services that are becoming common in Western countries).

It is noteworthy that a religious believer need not become a secularist for secularism to have an important influence on religion, and therefore on society. It is surely inevitable that if a major worldview held by many is on the wane that any new worldview that begins to earn people's allegiance will produce a cultural phenomenon where many people come under the influence of both worldviews at the same time! This is why it is important to note that many religious believers may adopt part of the secularist worldview into their religion for a variety of reasons. Changes in allegiance to worldviews are usually gradual, not abrupt, and are brought about by cultural changes, that may involve, among other things, people being no longer engaged by expressions of religious teachings and values. In this way secularism can have influence even though it might not significantly dislodge the religious worldview. While bringing about the demise of the religious worldview is the aim of most secularists, it is hardly a realistic goal, so a strategy of keeping religion in the background can work just as well in terms of which worldview gets to have more influence on society.

So we should not be surprised that many people will not fit into neatly defined categories, such as the ones we provided above for the purposes of laying out clearly the contours of the debate and the philosophical disagreement. Indeed, sometimes it can be difficult to classify a person, and it may be that some people will have feet in both the secularist and the Christian camps. Some may be confused about their own beliefs, holding strongly for instance to their religious worldview, but also being impressed by some secularist arguments to the extent that they might follow a secularist position when it comes to social policy. For example, one might be a strong religious believer, but become convinced by the secularist case for the legalization of euthanasia or abortion. These tendencies confirm the arrival of secularism on the scene as a significant cultural player; many people who were raised in a religious worldview are coming under the influence of secularism and are adopting some secularist beliefs. This is a trend in contemporary democracies. There is also a growing phenomenon of people *reinterpreting* their religion so that it coheres with secularist positions on various topics.

It can be helpful to consider the origins or source of a particular belief if one wishes to assess which worldview is being influenced and which is doing the influencing. Did the belief originate in secularist thought initially, and some religious believers are now going along with it, or did religious thinkers first suggest a belief (or a practice) and then persuade society, including secularists, to adopt it? This can be a good test for gauging the influence of a worldview at the level of society and culture. With regard to this question, the secularist worldview is clearly in the ascendency, and it is accurate to say that secularism is gradually pushing religion out of public life, out of public and social policy, and this is generally how secularists do interpret it. And for many the process is not fast enough, though the influence of secularism is truly astonishing if one takes into account how few people actually subscribe to this worldview in its full philosophical expression. All of this means that the time is now upon us when we need to be more proactive about what we believe, to check the consistency of our beliefs, and to be familiar with how to defend our beliefs philosophically. Then we are ready for pluralist engagement with other views, and to participate in public deliberation.

Case Study: Philosophical Secularism in the Work of Philip Kitcher

It is appropriate before we conclude our discussion in this chapter to consider an illustration of the secularist worldview as defended by a serious philosopher, Philip Kitcher. Kitcher attempts to consider carefully the issues that arise out of holding (philosophical) secularism, the challenges such a view faces, and the role of secularism in society. I believe his work represents one of the most sustained, honest attempts to articulate a secularist alternative to religion. Moreover, his treatment of the topic is noteworthy for its lack of self-righteous smugness and intemperate ranting with regard to the religious worldview that is so typical of this literature, and also for its seriousness of purpose in trying to come to terms with the difficulties that face his own view. He is very aware of the challenges of life, and of our need to find a theory of meaning that can handle them. His approach is a mixture of negative critique of religion, and an attempt to sketch a way forward for a secularist option. Although I find Kitcher's defense of secularism weak overall, I am not so much interested in that topic here, but mainly wish to consider how this philosophical view is expressed by one of its most responsible contemporary proponents. However, along the way some of the difficulties facing his view will emerge, most of which he himself acknowledges, since the question of the overall rationality of secularism versus the overall rationality of the religious worldview is relevant for the topics of this book. In considering Kitcher's position, we gain a valuable insight into the nature of this influential contemporary worldview, a worldview that is now competing hard with various religious worldviews in many democratic countries.

We will mainly consider Kitcher's views as defended in his book, *Life After Faith: The Case for Secular Humanism*, and to a lesser extent in his earlier work, *Living with Darwin: Evolution, Design, and the Future of Faith.*[10] We can approach the analysis of the secularist worldview from a consideration of questions relating to the following four topics: 1. The ultimate origin of the universe; 2. The ultimate origin of life; 3. The origin and foundation of ethics, especially of an objective moral order; and 4. The meaning of life. Kitcher does not discuss the first topic, except to criticize the religious answer (though, unlike many contemporary secularists, he does not deny the importance of the question). He acknowledges the great difficulties in coming to any scientific position on the second topic, in his general account and defense of an evolutionary explanation for the development of life in his earlier work, *Living with Darwin*. He addresses topic 3 in detail, and discusses topic 4 more briefly. Kitcher explains why he rejects the religious worldview in Chap. 1 of his book, *Life after Faith* (a topic he had also addressed in the last chapter of *Living with Darwin*). His approach is similar to the shriller voices on his side of the divide in one key sense: his discussion of the case for and against theism (and so for secularism) is superficial and often uninformed; as a result it is unlikely to come across as convincing. When one engages the debate between atheism and theism fully, and with due regard to the best arguments on both sides, one thing is clear: that it is an *open question* which view is true, that there are no arguments that clearly show that one side is very likely the correct position, and the other side is false. At very least, this is what one learns from an open, honest, and thorough analysis and discussion. My own position is that the theistic (or religious) worldview is the most rational position; further, I think one can struggle to show how secularism can be rational. Be all that as it may, and it is not our task here to assess the respective merits of these two general views, one thing that is very obvious from much of the literature from the atheistic side is that these thinkers do a poor job of discussing the topic fairly and facing up to the issues fully. As a result, I think it is a fair criticism that secularists very often come across as uninformed, superficial, even sometimes quite sophomoric, as in the work of Dawkins in particular.[11] Though, one must again acknowledge that in this respect Kitcher's arguments and his general tone in the discussion are reasonable, and his position is not only very well expressed, but also challenging and insightful.

Kitcher does at least make an attempt to defend his critique of religion. He offers a few reasons for why he does not find religious belief convincing, for why he regards all religious beliefs as "almost certainly false," and for why he thinks there is no evidence to support the reality of the transcendent.[12] A main reason he offers is that there are many different religions which often contradict each other with regard to their positions on theological matters, the path to salvation, and on morality. Of course, this is true but does it follow from this observation then that all religious beliefs are false? Might not some of them be true, and others false? Indeed, Kitcher's objection would apply also to secularist beliefs, and indeed to any category of beliefs, say concerning philosophical theories, theories of law, economic theories, or political theories. Yet, we do not conclude from the mere fact of disagreement that all such theories must be false. Kitcher points out the strong influence culture has on religion, that one usually holds the religion of one's culture, that culture has a huge influence on the religious beliefs one is likely to accept as true. He believes this is a strong argument against the truth of any religious worldview.[13] He is also not impressed with any appeal to religious experience as a justification for religious belief, even though he accepts that many such appeals are completely sincere, but he thinks that the wide discrepancy between the content of religious experiences, particularly as reported in different religious traditions, is a strong argument against them being revelatory of any transcendent dimension. He also offers a critique of any claims concerning revelation from a Supreme Being. Taking Christianity as an example, and, appealing to recent biblical and historical criticism, he argues that canonical texts cannot be regarded as reliable, and are very likely the result of human creation. He adds to his case by appealing to a version of the problem of evil—the problem of why would a benevolent and perfect deity allow so much pain and hardship in the world—especially when we take into account the vast array of suffering that the history of evolution suggests.[14]

With regard to the philosophical case for God's existence, and the rationality of religious belief more generally, including considering responses to issues like the problem of evil, the diversity of religions in the world, and so forth (what philosophers refer to as the area of natural theology or philosophical theology), Kitcher does not consider any specific arguments from this general area of research. We can be sure he rejects the arguments for the existence of God that have been advanced by many philosophers but he offers no discussion of them. The only point he makes is that many of them seem to presuppose a religious tradition, which he thinks undermines their claims to be independent logical arguments. I suspect he is not familiar enough with recent work in philosophy of religion, which adheres to the strictest standards of philosophical method and rigor. Kitcher's position in the opening chapter of *Life after Faith* is probably close enough to the position of many contemporary secularists who seem to reject the religious worldview simply *as a matter of policy*, rather than as a reasoned to position. In short, they simply assume the truth of secularism and proceed from that starting point. Later, they will be called upon to explain why they are rejecting religion, and their rational case will require a (hasty) revisit, and this is where secularist thinkers can come across as superficial and uninformed.

Kitcher defends what he calls a "soft atheism." This is an atheism that has some respect for religion, accepts the bare logical possibility that in the future there could be a justified acceptance of the transcendent (though currently this looks extremely unlikely), recognizes the good that the religious way of life contributes to the world, and the practical utility it has for many millions of people. However, he admits that his argument is meant to prepare the way for the eventual disappearance of religion. Along the way, he acknowledges that secularism (or secular humanism) will have to develop substitutes for many of the advantages or positive points of religion. He also introduces the notion of what he calls "refined religion," a position that has both a negative and a positive meaning. It is quite hard to discern what the positive meaning is supposed to be, though I do think he has correctly described the views of a large category of people today who are not quite sure where they stand regarding the religious worldview. The negative meaning is that those who belong to the category of refined religion reject all the transcendent and supernatural claims of traditional religion, so for all intents and purposes they are secularists with regard to the existence of God or a Supreme Being, the existence of an afterlife, and God as the author and ground of the objective moral order. The positive meaning is best understood as "a commitment to values that are external to (independent of) the believer, and indeed to all human beings."[15] These values are grounded in a kind of commitment to a transcendent moral order, and are embedded in religious practices, even though one holds that there is no literal transcendent dimension. Moral experience that revolves around such values is often accompanied by profound human emotions such as awe, humility before something greater, an experience of "something larger and grander."[16] Those in this category believe that community life is a vital part of living and of ethical striving, and Kitcher acknowledges that religious communities can play a large contributory role in promoting this way of life. As examples of those thinkers who have subscribed to some version of refined religion. Kitcher includes (controversially) Robert Bella, William James, Paul Tillich, and Martin Buber.[17] As one would expect, some secularists are inclined to regard the notion of refined religion as an appeal to mysterious nonsense, but Kitcher believes it has a valuable role to play because it can make us "feel at home in the universe."[18] This form of religion, he suggests, can have a productive exchange and dialogue with his version of secularism or soft atheism.

I think Kitcher has described an attractive approach for many people today, especially those in two minds about religious belief. A telling feature of the concept of refined religion is that one seems to decide on or specify its content by appealing to liberal moral and political values, and presumably one has arrived at these values in some independent (philosophical) way, *before* one comes to consider the question of religion. It other words, many people who subscribe to some version of what he calls refined religion, have, like Kitcher himself, a liberal moral test of what can count as acceptable even in an understanding of religion that is largely metaphorical. Although those who hold to a refined view of religion are often unsure about what exactly they believe, they usually do have a moral agenda that they have arrived at independently (a liberal moral agenda, in short), and they use this moral approach to determine which religious beliefs (and so which Church or religious denomination), they could subscribe to, even if their religious beliefs are mainly understood metaphorically. This is probably the best way to characterize the notion of refined religion. There are also many believers who subscribe to a quite liberal moral view (meaning they reject most of the moral teachings of traditional religion) but who are also traditional religious believers in the sense that they accept many of the supernatural claims of religion. Yet even members of this group often use their liberal moral beliefs to dictate how they should interpret their religion, so perhaps Kitcher's notion of refined religion could be extended to include them as well. Although secularists usually ridicule the notion of refined religion, he suggests that they should make common cause with it to promote the cause of social justice (another example of his general approach, because this would seem to require that we be able to arrive at an account of morality, including what counts as social justice, antecedently to and independently of religion).

This raises one of the most perplexing questions facing Kitcher: how to arrive at a theory of moral values that is truly objective and independent of religion? Unlike many secularists who downplay or ignore this problem, Kitcher acknowledges that it is a serious difficulty for the secularist view, one that involves two connected problems, in fact. The first is that secularism struggles with providing an objective grounding or foundation for ethical values; the related point is that human life appears to have no overall meaning or purpose from a secularist perspective, and that this can lead to alienation, loss of meaning, even a certain nihilism. Kitcher wrestles honestly with these difficulties (unlike Dawkins, e.g., who in many of his discussions willfully ignores the difference between practicing one's moral values in one's daily life {which is one thing}, and then justifying these values philosophically {which is quite another}).[19] Kitcher does not engage in such obfuscation; as a result the problem he is honestly facing up to comes across as a near fatal one for secularism (which he seems to admit).[20]

Kitcher explains that one appeal of the religious worldview is that the existence of God provides an objective grounding for the moral order. This means that the objective moral rightness of the values that human beings try to practice comes from the moral order put in place by God (based on his nature which is one of perfect goodness, according to Christianity). So we are justified in practicing these values because they have an overall meaning and purpose. Of course, one must believe in God for such a view to carry force, and from the philosophical point of view, one must argue that belief in God is rationally acceptable. The religious believer does believe that this position is rationally acceptable, and so thinks he has a coherent and defensible, if not proved, position. The question is: if we get rid of God, do we not also thereby get rid of the objective grounding for the moral order? Kitcher is especially honest in facing the troubling question posed by the Russian novelist, Dostoevsky, in his famous statement that, "If God does not exist, everything is permitted."[21]

In an attempt to avoid this very unpalatable conclusion, Kitcher tries to develop an evolutionary account of ethics, the view that any objective moral order we settle on must have originated from the process of evolution, just as everything else originated in this way (including, according to Kitcher, the origin of life). Such a view inevitably must be speculative since we barely have any idea of the course of evolution with regard to biological and other material properties, let alone with regard to defining human characteristics, such as morality. Although holding very few cards because of the nebulous nature of the subject matter, Kitcher weaves an interesting account of how we arrived at our current set of moral values from an impersonal and unsupervised evolutionary process. He believes that a key development in the progress of group behavior may have been what he calls *responsiveness*, a capacity to "promote cooperative projects and accommodations that reduce social tension,"[22] a tendency we can still detect, he claims, in the behavior of chimpanzees and bonobos. He suggests that the capacity for responsiveness itself grew out of fear of the consequences of failing to express the capacity.

He acknowledges that his secularist view entails that the universe and life have no overall purpose or end, and are governed largely by chance, and so any objective values we eventually settle on must also have originated through a process of chance, and *so could have been quite different than they are*. He is facing the same problem that French philosopher, Jean Paul Sartre, faced when he abandoned God and suggested that human beings are alone with their freedom—we seem then to be free to choose any scheme of values to regulate our lives, and the scheme would be justified. Kitcher's response to this problem is similar to Sartre's. Sartre had suggested that ethics may be likened to aesthetics: the artist's work comes out of her experience, which appears to limit it, even though in theory it is true that her paintings could have taken any form (since she is quite free to choose the topic and the form).[23] Moral judgments are the same. As an example, Kitcher points to the public reaction to Charles Dickens' novels. One of Dickens' themes was the depth of poverty in London; Kitcher notes that readers could not but recognize the truth of the social situation Dickens described, which gave rise to a moral imperative to try to do something about it. He acknowledges that this reaction, however, appears to be an accident of our evolutionary history. If evolution had gone differently (and it could have[24]), our attitude to poverty and the plight of our fellow human beings might have been quite different. Moreover, why could we not recognize the fact of poverty, but concede that since there is no overall meaning to life, no overall purpose, we are not morally required to do anything about it? This is a central problem that Kitcher agrees his view faces. Even if such a judgment would be *psychologically* very difficult for most of us to make, it would not follow that there is a *moral* imperative with regard to this or any other moral issue. Indeed, philosophers such as Frederick Nietzsche have explored the view that we need to get over our psychological hang-ups with regard to morality because they make us weak (a position it would seem that Kitcher from a logical point of view could just as easily defend if he so wished). Indeed, there exists a small subset of (Nietzschean) moral nihilists, who can be genuinely dangerous, who subscribe to a view very similar to Kitcher's about the origins (and so, in their mind, lack of force) of (conventional) morality.

Sometimes secularists will object to this line of reasoning by pointing out that religious believers appear to face the same problem. Don't religious believers have to work out which moral values they will subscribe to in their religion? Many religious believers appear to decide first on independent grounds what they will believe about morality and then "read" it back into their religion, rather than the texts, teachings, or tradition of their religion dictating which values they will hold. This is true, but nevertheless it is not the same problem as the one that faces the secularist. The reason is that as long as the religious person believes that God exists and is the objective ground of the moral order, then he or she believes that moral values have an objective grounding that gives them their authority. In addition, religious believers do not just rely on a rational analysis of biblical texts to discern the correct moral code, they also rely on their view of God, which has been arrived at philosophically as well, and often consider whether such and such a reading of scripture would be compatible with God's nature. Even though we could be mistaken about what the moral order consists in, about which moral values are the right ones, this question of content is secondary and separate from the fact that the moral order must have an objective ground. It is this grounding that the secularist is lacking. It is one thing to disagree about which values God has ordained as part of the objective moral law, it is quite another to think that there is no objective ground at all for our moral values. This is the position the secularist is in, the one to which Kitcher is trying to formulate a response.

Another way to bring out what is at stake is to ask what is it that grounds the objective moral order that one lives by? This helps us to see more clearly the distinction between practicing objective moral values and the grounding or foundation for these values, a distinction that Dawkins in particular always seems to overlook. The question is not would you practice the objective moral values you are committed to if you did not believe in God, or did not believe these values had an objective grounding, the question is what is the *objective justification for the moral values that currently guide your beliefs and actions*? And although it is true that *most* of us psychologically would be unable to stop practicing our objective moral code if we came to believe it had no objective grounding, some people would, and it is surely the case that there is a clear link between not believing in a grounding for one's values and finding it more difficult to practice them. There is, in short, a lot of truth in Dostoevsky's claim. And the reverse may also be true: the fact that we are unable to stop practicing objective moral values might be because we realize that they *must* have a (transcendent) objective ground, as Kant argued, as part of his moral argument for God's existence.[25]

The same point applies to the question of the meaning of life. There is often what philosophers call a *reductio ad absurdum* form of argument working here, a form of argument that relies on showing that some position cannot be true because it leads to absurd or unbelievable consequences. If one can show that a position leads to an absurdity, then there must be something wrong with that position! The form of the argument in this case is: we know from our experience that life has meaning; life cannot have meaning on a secularist view; therefore, the secularist view is false. This is a version of the moral argument for God's existence that undergirds the above discussion about morality. A distinctive version of the argument takes this form: morality is meaningful (we know this from our experience), morality cannot be meaningful on a secularist view, and so secularism is false. Kitcher is trying to respond to these problems.

Kitcher agrees that on the meaning of life question, religion has advantages over secularism because it fosters strong communities which play a key role in people's lives; it also offers a critique and a corrective to a crass materialism, which secularism often seems to promote.[26] Indeed, few doubt the accuracy of the general principle that material comforts cannot bring happiness. There is a worry surrounding secularism that it could lead to cultural collapse, especially in moral terms, because it is often accompanied by loss of meaning and nihilism. Sometimes people see economic prosperity as the only thing worth living for, and if a society fails to deliver this, it can lead to social unrest. This point is often expressed by saying that there is a spiritual dimension to human experience (perhaps the most important feature of human life), that, crucially, secularism ignores (perhaps even suppresses) with the consequence that our lives are impoverished. Kitcher accepts all of these advantages of religion as long as they are not understood as being grounded in the literal truth of religion, the existence of God, who created a real and objective moral order, an afterlife, and so forth. He argues that while secularism might struggle with these difficulties at present, it can probably develop in the future secular substitutes for the advantages of religion. He believes that there can be fulfilling meaning in secular lives, even though there is no overall purpose to life,[27] and agrees that human beings have a need for structure, meaning, and comfort, and that it will be incumbent on secularism eventually to provide this. He is honest enough to make this claim in a quite tentative way, noting that we are in a transition from religion to secularism, and that building secular substitutes will take time. He is worried by the approach and the tone of most contemporary secularists, who regard themselves as superior and who do not make an adequate attempt to acknowledge these challenges for secularism, and whose voices, "are hectoring, almost exultant that comfort is being stripped away and faith undermined; frequently, they are without charity. And they are almost always without hope."[28] Kitcher notes that religion has been essential to most people who have ever lived, and that we need to work hard to offer an alternative if it comes to that. (There are some signs in Western democracies that secularists are trying to establish secularist "spiritual" communities, such as the Sunday

Assembly movement in London, though it is not clear that these will catch on.[29])

Is Secularism Rational?: It will be helpful before we bring this chapter to a close to raise the question of whether the view we have just considered is a rational or reasonable view? Although we are not focusing so much on that question in this book—on which view is the most rational between secularism and religious belief—it is appropriate to introduce the question. It is important when it comes to the political, legal, and social decision-making in a pluralist state, the question of which views have a right to contribute to society in a democratic context. Kitcher obviously thinks that secularism is a rational view, more rational than religious belief, so much so that although he believes that religion adds value to life and community, his position is that arguments like his are preparing the way for its eventual disappearance. My view is the opposite to this. I believe that the secularist view that he has defended is irrational. Not only does it have the problems with regard to ethics and the meaning of life noted, but it is largely (as Kitcher acknowledges) an untested view, and it does seem to have destructive tendencies that could be very bad for individual happiness and fulfillment, and for the good of society as a whole, in the long run. It fails because of its view of human nature (or rather denial of human nature) and its incorrect understanding of the path to human fulfillment, irrespective of the question of the transcendent. The problem about lacking an objective ground for moral values is surely of the utmost importance for the moral behavior of people as we move into the future.

It is important to note also that many, perhaps the vast majority of, people, think that the secularist view defended by Kitcher and others is not only false, but very difficult to believe—irrational, in fact. Many also think that secularism is primarily motivated not by logical arguments and evidence (despite pretensions to the contrary) but by psychological reasons, in particular, a deep rooted desire, founded on hubris and arrogance, to reject any authority (such as God) to which secularists would have to answer. Secularists are very reluctant to submit to a moral order that threatens their autonomy, which they (mistakenly) regard as the highest of human values (as we noted in Chap. 2). Again, Kitcher acknowledges the dilemma for secularists in reconciling individual autonomy with recognition of any transcendent purpose to human life; as he puts it "transcending finitude is purchased at the cost of autonomy."[30] This is another reason why the vast majority of people are not persuaded by, and indeed are often suspicious of, the case for the rationality of secularism.

Be all that as it may, there are two key points to note as we conclude our reflections here. First, the view defended by Kitcher cannot be regarded as the default view. While it is interesting, fascinating, and developed carefully and honestly by Kitcher in so far as he is able, it is by no means a view that is obviously true. In a logical sense, it would simply be folly to regard it as the default view from the point of view of seeking the truth about life and the universe. Crucial parts of it are based on speculation and promissory notes, which leaves its truth as much an open question as the secularist is inclined to attribute to the religious worldview. This is particularly true when we see both views in the context of human history, and the fact that so many have regarded the religious view as the default view. But from the perspective of the question of which worldviews should have a role in the modern democratic state, it is by no means obvious that the secularist philosophy of life should be regarded as the default position. This makes our discussion in the rest of the book all the more urgent. The second point is that it is a fact that secularism is now a major worldview in contemporary democratic society, and is one worldview among many others, most of which are religious. And the question that inevitably presents itself is: as we go forward, what role should these worldviews have in politics and society, in the shaping of culture, morality, and matters that affect human fulfillment and happiness? As we discuss this question in the following chapters, we must be clear on the differences between *secularism*, *secularization*, and *the secular state*. We will also see that responding to this question does not depend on our settling which worldview is the most acceptable from a rational point of view, or it being necessary to establish which worldview has the truth. That avenue is no longer productive in the context of pluralism, and in light of the problem of the incommensurability of worldviews. We need to pursue other avenues, and so it becomes necessary to radically rethink our approach to these matters in the modern democratic state.

Notes

1. See Irving Hexham's, *Concise Dictionary of Religion* (Downers Grove, IL: InterVarsity Press, 1993) for this brief survey of definitions of religion; also John Haught, *What is Religion?: An Introduction* (Mahwah, NJ.: Paulist Press, 1990).
2. See my *Why Politics Needs Religion*, Chapter 1, for a fuller overview of the Christian worldview.

3. The term "secularism" was first introduced by the English atheist and secularist, George Holyoake (1817–1906) in 1851. Holyoake ran several newspapers promoting the secularist worldview and critiquing religion.
4. As an example, see the *Atheist Bus Campaign*, which Dawkins, Grayling, and other secularists supported financially. It attracted widespread attention and support from around the world.
5. See my *Evolution, Chance, and God* (New York: Bloomsbury, 2015), Chapter 1, for further discussion of this approach.
6. Recent surveys and opinion polls reveal that religious affiliation and practice is declining in many countries and that some version of secularism is on the rise, though it would obviously be a mistake to identify the former with the latter. Belief in Christianity has declined significantly in many European countries, such as Belgium, Holland, France, and Britain with church attendance down to single digits in some cities. There are declines also, though not as sharp as in these countries, in Canada, America, Australia, and Ireland. At the same time, there is a noticeable rise in the number of people who classify themselves as atheists or secularists or who report " no religion" or "nothing in particular." That number is now 26% in the U.S., a 9% rise in a decade. The Irish census of 2016 had 10% reporting "no religion" (up 5% from 2011). Meanwhile, the number identifying themselves as Catholics declined from 93% to 78% in ten years. In France, almost one-third identify as having no religion. For helpful reporting and analysis of data in a number of countries, see D. Pollack and D.V.A. Olson (eds.), *The Role of Religion in Modern Societies* (New York: Routledge, 2007); also "Fewer Catholics, while 'no religion' up 74%,", *RTE Television* (Ireland), Oct 12th, 2017 at https://www.rte.ie. For data on France, see Pew Templeton Global Religious Futures project, at http://www.globalreligiousfutures.org. For the U.S., see the Pew Report, "In U.S., decline of Christianity continues at a rapid pace," Oct 17th, 2019 at https://www.pewforum.org.
7. See Aristotle, *The Nicomachean Ethics* (New York: Oxford U.P., 2009); also Julia Annas, *The Morality of Happiness* (New York: Oxford U.P., 1995); also Ralph McInerny, *Aquinas* (Cambridge, UK.: Polity, 2004).
8. Some representative works include Richard Dawkins, *The Blind Watchmaker* (New York: Norton, 1987); Jerry Coyne, *Why Evolution is True* (New York: Penguin, 2010); Steven Pinker, *How the Mind Works* (New York: Norton, 1997); Louise Anthony (ed.), *Philosophers without Gods* (New York: Oxford U.P., 2007); Sam Harris, *The Moral Landscape* (New York: Free Press, 2011).
9. See Endnote 6 (above) for an overview of recent data.

10. See Philip Kitcher, *Life after Faith: The Case for Secular Humanism* (New Haven, CT.: Yale U.P., 2014) and *Living with Darwin: Evolution, Design and the Future of Faith* (New York: Oxford U.P., 2007).
11. See Richard Dawkins, *The God Delusion* (New York: Houghton Mifflin, 2006), for an egregious example, especially his discussion of the arguments for God's existence (pp. 77–109).
12. Philip Kitcher, *Life After Faith*, pp. 7ff, p. 19.
13. See ibid., pp. 3–15.
14. These latter two arguments are laid out in *Living with Darwin*, pp. 123–131; pp. 132–140.
15. Philip Kitcher, *Life After Faith*, p. 64.
16. Ibid., p. 90.
17. See ibid., p. 72.
18. Ibid., p. 87.
19. See Dawkins, *The God Delusion*, pp. 226–233.
20. See Kitcher, *Life After Faith*, pp. 154ff.
21. See ibid., pp. 149ff.
22. Ibid., p. 32.
23. See Jean Paul Sartre, *Existentialism is a Humanism* (New Haven, CT.: Yale U.P., 2007 ed. [original: 1946]).
24. Even if evolution could not have gone differently and must reach certain outcomes by necessity, given the initial starting conditions in the universe, its eventual outcomes would still be a matter of chance. This is because these outcomes are determined by the nature and makeup of the initial conditions, which, according to the secularist view, are themselves a matter of chance, since there is no designer or design plan responsible for the makeup, and hence the direction, of the process.
25. See Immanuel Kant, *Critique of Practical Reason*, trans. W.S. Pluhar (Indianapolis, IN.: Hackett, 2002), pp. 155ff.
26. See Kitcher, *Life After Faith*, pp. 121–122.
27. For more on secularist attempts to address the question of the meaning of life, see Thomas Nagel, *The View from Nowhere* (New York: Oxford, 1986), pp. 208–231; Kai Nielsen, "Death and the Meaning of Life" in E.D. Klemke, *The Meaning of Life* (New York: Oxford U.P., 2000 2nd ed.), pp. 153–159; Julian Baggini, *What's It All About?* (New York: Oxford U.P, 2005), pp. 23–29. See also Louis Pojman, "Religion gives Meaning to Life," in Louis P. Pojman and Louis Vaughn (eds.), *Philosophy: The Quest for Truth* (New York: Oxford U.P., 2019, 11th ed.), pp. 680–684. Pojman argues that theistic religion gives special meaning to life that is not available in secular worldviews. He also argues that the autonomy secularists prize so much is not significantly diminished in the religious way of life. See also Charles Taylor, *Sources of the Self* (Cambridge, MA.: Harvard U.P., 1989),

pp. 515ff, where he discusses the question of the justification of the objective moral order.
28. Kitcher, *Living with Darwin*, p. 155.
29. See the website of the Sunday Assembly movement for non-believers at https://www.sundayassembly.com.
30. See Kitcher, *Life After Faith*, pp. 105ff.

CHAPTER 6

Secularizing Society

The secularist worldview described in the previous chapter is widely held in some form by many people across many democratic countries. We see its presence everywhere now, but particularly in political, moral, and cultural discussion, and in areas such as law, education, and the arts. Public awareness of pluralism has obviously increased, as democracies become more divided, as has public focus on the debate between secularism and religion. The language, ideas, and approach of secularism are now more familiar to people. Indeed, the pluralist reality concerning worldviews is now increasingly in the air we breathe in democratic societies. Many questions that society must face in the future, such as, for example, the ethical questions raised by developments in scientific research relating to cloning and genetic engineering, will drag us inevitably into what will turn into a debate concerning worldviews. These debates will raise all of the issues of this book! So it is helpful in this chapter to examine some of the features of an increasingly secularized society, and the way secularism actually plays out in practice, and its influence on contemporary life and culture. Our identification of various forms of secular language will not only further illuminate what is involved in the clash of worldviews, but will also lead naturally to recent liberal political theory (which we will come to in the next chapter).

Secularism and Secularization

The term "secularism," and the language, ideas, attitudes, and approach of the secularist worldview, have become much more familiar in recent decades. At least in intellectual circles, people know generally what is meant by secularism, and recognize that it is not only a subject that might be of academic interest, but is one that plays a much larger role in society and culture than it once did. However, there is still some confusion surrounding the correct understanding of the term "secularism," and related terms that have a similar but different meaning. We also need to bring out how secular terminology relates to the religious worldview, and to other matters that concern democracy and politics. So in this section it will be helpful to distinguish carefully between various terms commonly used in the discussion surrounding secularism, not only to indicate the way we are using them, but also to help us appreciate and have some clarity about what is being referred to when these terms are introduced into pluralistic debate in modern democracy.

With regard to the term "secularism" itself, we only need to recapitulate our explanation from the previous chapter. When we use the term secularism, we are referring to the philosophical worldview we described earlier, the key claims of which are that everything that exists is made up of some configuration of matter and energy, that there is no ultimate cause of the universe, that life originated and developed on earth largely due to chance, that life is purposeless, and that we must develop secularist accounts of morality and politics. Like most worldviews, secularism has foundational beliefs, beliefs about the human person, moral and political beliefs, representative thinkers and advocates, influential literature, and so forth, and its adherents wish for it to play some role in democratic politics. This is also a worldview which will require philosophical justification by those who hold it. As I noted, it is becoming a more popular worldview, but of course it is also rejected by many.

It is important not to confuse secularism with the concept of "the secular," of which more in a moment. As noted in the previous chapter, it is especially important not to confuse secularism with other views that the word is often misleadingly used to describe, such as the view that the state either should be, or is in fact, *neutral* between worldviews, or that the state has (or should have) no official religion, or that religion should have no influence in public life. Sometimes these latter positions are described as secularism. While such meanings may have had some use in the past, our argument is that this way of talking is now out of date, creates much confusion, and needs to be dispensed with. The term *secularism* most properly captures *the philosophical worldview of secularism*, and should not be confused with the view that the democratic state should be neutral between worldviews, with the view that a secularist state is one that is free from religious influence, or one that allows freedom of conscience, and so forth.

Let us now consider the term *secularization*. Today, it is common to hear that we are living in a secularized world; many suggest that the societies of Western Europe or the U.S., or perhaps of Australia, or even of South America, are becoming more secularized, that "secularization is sweeping the country," and the world, that religious perspectives are losing ground to the forces of a secular society, and so forth. When one describes modern France, for instance, as a country that has become considerably secularized in recent times, this way of talking is not meant to convey the point that secularism understood as a distinctive worldview is becoming more common. No, it is meant to describe a cultural change where the religious way of looking at things is losing its influence, where people do not appeal to their religious worldviews to make important decisions in their lives in the way they used to, that some secularist beliefs and attitudes are now replacing in a piecemeal fashion some religious beliefs and attitudes, especially on moral questions. We might describe this as a *process of secularization*; it is taking place in many countries, especially in the West. It is often not carefully defined in the discussion concerning democracy and pluralism, and indeed can be quite hard to describe as a phenomenon.

Secularization usually refers to cultural trends and attitudes in areas such as consumerism, materialism, the use of technology, the worry that there is too much focus on pursuits of this world (such as wealth, good looks, material possessions, healthy eating, the development of the body but not the spirit) that are gradually pushing to the background the spiritual and even the moral life. The religious and spiritual aspects of human existence are being squashed in favor of more worldly pursuits, and religion then has less influence on contemporary living. Charles Taylor has argued that there are three marks of secularization: that from a positive point of view, contemporary society emphasizes maximum freedom of conscience, the freedom to exercise it, and freedom of religion. These features of contemporary society taken together would put pressure on religion and convey to people the message that they are free to reject religious views if they wish, that religion has no special place in the state, can claim no special allegiance. Taylor has also identified three trends in the process of secularization (what he calls types of "secularity"): the withdrawal of religion from public spaces; a decline in religious belief and behavior; and the fact that religion is now regarded as just another preference among several alternatives.[1] As Mary Warnock has put it, today religion "is no longer compulsory."[2] Yet, these are probably more symptoms of secularization than they are causes. Indeed, the causes are not easy to identify and are hotly debated, but there can be no doubt that secularization has become a significant trend in the latter half of the twentieth century, especially in Western societies.[3]

The Secularization Thesis

Sociologists have debated the "secularization thesis," the view that as societies become more modern in terms of economic development, scientific advancement, and political progress, they become less religious.[4] The debate is over the causes of the diminishing effect of religion, and of the secularizing processes. Did the decline in religious belief and practice occur just because these societies developed too many tempting alternatives that had a deleterious effect on the influence of religion (e.g., in the areas of consumerism, entertainment, medicine, travel)? Such enticements can encourage materialistic lifestyles dominated by comfort, escapism, the pursuit of novelty, even hedonism, all of which can be a seductive distraction from the life of the spirit. Some post-liberal theologians have argued that for these reasons modern liberal society verges toward a moral corruption that weakens religious practice, but does not really engage with the essence of religious belief in any metaphysical or deep philosophical sense. Such trends also reveal dangerous fault lines in democracy itself.[5]

The sociologist, Steve Bruce, has argued that modern secularization is a result of several historical developments that had a number of unintended consequences. Bruce understands secularization to include some or all of the following phenomena: the diminishing of the realm of the supernatural in our understanding of religion; this worldly rewards becoming more important than the afterlife; the therapeutic side of religion beginning to replace the worship of God; an emphasis on individualism and a corresponding rejection of external authority; major religions ceasing to claim sole access to the will of God and becoming increasingly ecumenical; the state no longer enforcing religious conformity; religion becoming less relevant in many areas of life and to fewer people; religion becoming more private; and so forth.[6] This is a good description of some of the features of the process of secularization; a key question is how did such trends come about? Bruce believes they were the result of unintended consequences stemming from various earlier philosophical and social developments. These include the development of the concept of the modern state from Locke onward, with related ideas of tolerance; the principle of the separation of church and state; a focus on the value of freedom and autonomy, and consequently on individualism, that we see after Mill. Add to these developments, which took place over a long period of time, the increasing diversity of populations, in addition to the growth and influence of science and technology, and we get a new attitude toward religion which is an important aspect of what we mean today by "secularization." Such developments, Bruce contends, support his central thesis concerning the "displacement of religion from public life."[7]

Some sociologists, such as Rodney Stark, take the view that secularization was caused primarily by the growth of science, which pushed religion and the supernatural back from everyday living.[8] Many secularist thinkers are also often quick to jump on this explanation. It is also a thesis held by Christian Smith, who has argued that at least in the United States, there was a deliberate move in a number of disciplines, including sociology, philosophy, psychology, anthropology, and the sciences to advance a secularist agenda, mainly through our higher educational, and other elite, institutions, a movement that would eventually have a significant influence on society at large.[9] Bruce, however, rejects this view and holds that secularization was not the result of a deliberate agenda, but happened in a piecemeal fashion over time as a result of the above-mentioned trends that were not deliberately aimed at undermining religion, although they did in fact come to have this effect. Perhaps, depending on the country or area of life one is talking about, both views are partially correct. Bruce does not believe that the reason for increased secularization is that there is a strong cultural debate between religious worldviews and secularist worldviews, and that the secularist worldview is winning.

Whether Bruce is correct that the process of secularization is irreversible is quite another matter. Another key claim of his is also quite contentious: that even though secularism (advanced as a philosophical worldview) is not responsible for secularization, secularization gradually leads to secularism—to the abandonment of religious belief and conversion to secularist beliefs—rather than only to abandonment of going to Church and loss of interest in religious institutions, but not loss of religious belief. Needless to say, this claim is hotly disputed.[10] He is surely right though that secularization leads to some increase in the number of secularists. This is a fascinating discussion from the point of view of the future of secularism. It is obviously significant whether secularization does or does not lead to secularism, just as it is important whether Bruce is correct that the debate between secularism and theism is not the main driver of secularization. If the growth of secularism is not responsible for the process of secularization, then it might be possible for religious worldviews to mount a successful cultural counter-attack, especially if it is correct (as I suggested in the previous chapter) that secularism is an untested worldview that faces severe difficulties (as we saw in our overview of Kitcher's argument) in providing an alternative to the type of fulfillment and meaning that people find in religion.

We might understand secularization to mean: 1. People no longer practice their religion as much as they once did, at least in the sense of going to Church (they may still pray, however, and look at the world "in a religious way," as described by Wittgenstein, among others). 2. It may also mean that eventually a significant number either no longer believe in God, or the supernatural order (which is what Bruce claims), or (which I think is more likely) are not quite clear concerning what they believe about religious matters (they may be lapsed religious believers, or immature atheists—meaning they have no coherent alternative to religion, and are uncertain about key aspects of their worldview). But, 3. It does not follow from any of this, of course, that the religious worldview is false, especially if the causes of secularization and indeed secularism are not philosophical, but mainly driven by materialistic and hedonistic impulses. 4. Bruce seems to think that because the process of secularization is irreversible, that religion will die out in the future. I am not convinced. I don't think enough people under the influence of secularization become atheists, although I do acknowledge that a lapsed religious believer is usually quite unsure about what he or she believes. But it seems correct to say that if people do not become secularized for philosophical reasons, but mainly due to materialistic and even selfish reasons, then this will affect whether or not the process of secularization is permanent, and it must also affect our assessment of religious belief as an essential dimension of the human condition.

Many thinkers have held that human beings are naturally religious, a thesis which, if correct, would mean that secularization is likely to be a temporary blip in the history of religion rather than a permanent new state of affairs. We might be living in the "age of sin"—the view that it is largely for sinful reasons (as Churches would have described it in the past) that secularization has gotten a grip on society, not for philosophical reasons! One of the reasons that secularism, at least in the abstract, is attractive to people is because it is very permissive; it is a philosophy of life that requires few restrictions on living, compared to the demanding strictures of religion. As noted in the previous chapter, it also generally tends to put little emphasis on personal striving for moral reform and moral excellence, essential features of many religious worldviews. So people may find it attractive in a contest with religion, once the stigma of accepting it is removed. It can be seen as a worldview that appeals to the weaknesses of people; indeed this may be a motivation for promoting it. British social historian, Callum Brown, has argued that religion in Britain was in a good and healthy state until the 1960s, when it was then seriously undermined by a permissive culture.[11] Some also hold this view about Irish society— that a permissive culture, driven especially by media and TV shows in the 1980s, and other trends, undermined Catholic values. This is at least an alternative interpretation of the causes of secularization that we should consider, and it is not irrelevant to the question of whether the process can be reversed.

Another possible cause of secularization is a crisis of faith that we see in many Western countries, such as Belgium and the Netherlands. In addition to Church scandals and institutional failures, as well as dissatisfaction with traditional Church teachings, another contributory cause of this crisis is rampant consumerism and materialism. This is in addition to modernizing tendencies such as an emphasis on freedom and moral relativism which have promoted the view that one religion is as good as another, or that one does not even need to follow a religion. These reasons are interesting in an important sense: it is not philosophical arguments for the superiority of secularism that have led to its influence on culture; it is not always because people think that the secularist worldview is better or more rational on certain issues, than religious worldviews, but rather that society seems to drift into a secularizing mindset because of all of the distractions from the life of the spirit. Perhaps some of this is inevitable given the increased wealth in modern societies which leads to a preoccupation with material comfort, the pursuit of consumerism almost as a hobby or avocation (including an alarming increase in cosmetic surgery), an obsession with becoming one of the "beautiful people," a preoccupation with sports, all pursuits that either distract from or provide some kind of (inferior) substitute for religious expression. The religious worldview after all rouses one's conscience about the inadequacy of such pursuits for attaining a moral and happy life.

We can recognize that secularization is the *process*, as described above, and that *secularism* may be *one* result of the process. An important thinker on these matters, Jurgen Habermas, has suggested three causes for the process of secularization. First, advances in science prompt us to approach all issues from an empirical standpoint, because science has made enormous progress in explaining things in empirical terms, so there is less need for religious explanations. Second, the rise of secular liberalism in politics has resulted in religious institutions and churches losing their influence over life and culture, with the further consequence that for many religion becomes more of a private matter, which in turn feeds the view that it should have very little influence in public life. Third, greater economic security and control over one's life has led to less need for a faith in a higher power to make sense of, and to better cope with, the contingencies of life.[12] Habermas also notes that in the past in some countries a lot of property was owned by the Church, and that gradually we can understand the decline of Church power in a state as part of the secularizing process, along with secularism emerging in opposition to religion. This trend further encouraged the decoupling of religion from the state; it was accompanied also by a gradual insistence on the superiority of some form of secularism from the point of view of running society.

All of these trends and tendencies contribute to the secularizing process, and so eventually to the growth of secularism, since some who become secularized in the way they live their day-to-day lives eventually become secularists in terms of worldview, as we have noted. So secularization contributes to secularism in two senses: a weaker sense where people remain religious but allow secularist beliefs and attitudes to influence their own lives, along with law and culture, and in a stronger sense, where some become secularists, and see secularism as the way forward for democratic society. Perhaps the eventual outcome of a sustained secularization process is a *secularist* state. While the processes of secularization are fascinating in themselves, they are of lesser significance to our discussion, except to highlight the point that it is important not to confuse secularization with secularism. Our primary concern is with philosophical secularism, its influence on society, its place in public life, and its disagreements with other worldviews, especially religious ones.

Reflections on the Concept of "The Secular"

Let us now turn to the ubiquitous, overly used, but sometimes elusive, term *secular*! The concept of the secular is a difficult one to characterize, and we need to take care to capture its meaning as accurately as we can. It is generally used in a negative sense, but can have a positive meaning as well. We see the word "secular" employed in phrases such as: "the modern state should be secular in nature," "in a secular state, religion should have no place," "members of government are secular officials," "the democratic state should provide a good secular education," and so on. What does the word mean in these statements, what is it describing? The main meaning, I suggest, is *negative*. It is meant to convey a non or even antireligious point; it refers to what should not be happening in the state (and by extension to what secularists and some religious believers reject, or do not approve of). So to say that government officials, for instance, are secular officials is to convey that they do not represent any particular religious worldview (and usually also to *imply* that the religious worldview in general should have no role in political decisions). A good secular education would mean one from which religion is mostly absent.

The word "secular" (from the Latin *saecularis*) literally means "of or relating to the world," and this is how we would explain its positive meaning. Yet, traditionally the word was used to describe a turning away from religion in varying ways, to convey the point that if something is of or relates to the world, then it does *not* relate to the supernatural, religion, the Church, the clergy, and so forth. However, today, it has mostly a negative, even tendentious, connotation. The phrase "a secular state," when used today, mostly means a state that keeps religion out of public life, or at least aspires toward this outcome. A secular piece of music is one that does not feature religious themes or references, and so forth. A secular university is one that has no religious affiliation. So in today's usage the word mostly describes what people reject, not what they affirm. If we were to describe the president or the prime minister of a country as a "secular official," this would mean not that he or she is a secularist, but does not represent any particular religion in the official state office. The term is sometimes used in this way to convey the negative meaning that the state has no official religion, as in when we describe a state as a secular state.

The idea of the "secular state" is also often meant to convey the point that the state is neutral (or should be neutral).[13] Neutral in what way, or about what? Neutral with regard to worldviews, specifically with regard to taking sides on this matter. However, this understanding runs into obvious logical difficulties. We might say that the notion of a neutral state can be understood in two ways: first, that the state has no official worldview; the second is that the state takes no position on any issue, and so does not favor any worldview in particular. This second meaning is what is usually intended when the phrase is invoked. But this understanding is problematic and cannot be realized in practice (as many thinkers have pointed out, including Roger Trigg).[14] This is because as soon as the state passes a law with regard to any issue, it is immediately taking a side against the opposite view! It is a common move in modern liberalism for the supporters of a position to argue that one of the reasons we should legalize a practice (such as abortion) is because the state should be neutral between the positions of different worldviews on the matter. However (as Amy Guthman has pointed out about the area of education, and as I would point out more generally), it is not possible for the state to take a neutral stance, since if the state sanctions (or forbids) a practice it is not being neutral on *that* issue (even though it may not be taking a position on the truth or falsity of any worldview *as a whole*).[15]

In general, I wish to insist that this way of talking—describing a state as a secular state or as a neutral state—is now out of date. It is based on an outmoded approach of putting all religious worldviews in a special category and treating them differently. Such an approach may have been useful in the past, but in the modern age, when secularism is now an influential philosophy of life, it is no longer appropriate. To treat religion differently in the modern democratic state is now automatically to privilege secularism. This way of thinking is no longer sustainable in our changing times. It is also no longer fitting, as we will see, to speak of "secular values." This phrase again was mainly understood negatively to express a rejection of religious values. For instance, one might agree to accommodate religion as long as it supported "sex equality" in the state, and then define sex equality to include a right to an abortion, a view which therefore would not be "neutral." So the secular values that would replace the religious values are contentious since not everyone accepts them, or perhaps more accurately, agrees about how they are to be understood, about what they mean. On my view, it is better to insist that *there is no such thing as a secular value*, only secularist values or religious values, or values from whatever worldview we are considering. Perhaps the best way to put this point is to say that any values that guide the state are being asserted as true, and their opposites as false, and those who hold the opposite values are therefore regarded as wrong, and out of luck! (This point raises a question about that general set of liberal values on which the state is founded, values that we all accept in some form, a key issue that we will discuss in Chaps. 7 and 8. We should also note that to insist that a state should be neutral between worldviews is itself to make a value judgment.)

This is why it is best to describe anything to do with the worldview of secularism as secularist, rather than secular (where the word is intended to have a positive rather than a negative meaning) because the word secular can be misleading. So if one wishes to assert the argument that we ought to keep religion out of modern democratic politics, we should not say things like "we need a secular state" to convey this point, but rather "we need a secularist state." One may use this phrase thinking that the state can be neutral between all worldviews, religious and secularist, but this is a mistake, as we have noted. Sometimes people will say that the law should be "secular." This means that religious beliefs and values should play no part in making laws, but then we need to ask which beliefs and values are allowed to play such a role, why they should have this privileged position, and how they are justified? The key point is that such values would not and could not be neutral between all worldviews. So it is less confusing and more accurate for us to say that this or that (or all) religious values should have no place in the making of law, *but these other values should have*, than saying the law should be "secular." But this type of argument then must engage the debate over pluralism we have been describing.

Does the word have a positive meaning? I hold that in modern pluralist culture it does not (or, more accurately, that it is better to think of it only in a negative way, because it avoids confusion). We are much better off focusing on its negative meaning and confining our understanding of the word to that meaning. We might compare the idea of a "secular state" to the idea of a "secular university." We noted above that a secular university is one that has no religious affiliation; we might go further and say that religious beliefs, values, and attitudes play no part in its educational philosophy, programs, or curricula. Nevertheless, a secular university cannot simply define itself negatively; it must have a positive educational philosophy as well, a set of values and beliefs it wishes to promote to students. What are these? We don't need to go into them here, but the crucial point is that whatever values such universities infuse throughout their educational programs will exclude their (religious) opposites, to some degree. And so a secular university can be said to be promoting a positive view in opposition to religious views, at least to some extent. It is true historically that secular universities largely defined themselves in opposition to religious universities (i.e., as not offering what religious institutions were offering), but this is changing. Secular universities, I contend—like secular states—are now beginning to, and logically must, face the question of what it is that they are promoting, and when they do this it becomes clear that they are moving in a *secularist* direction, just as the modern state is. This analogy is very helpful I believe for our understanding of recent developments in the democratic, pluralist state.

Sometimes it is suggested that the concept of the secular can be used in a positive sense to describe a state that is politically neutral between the worldviews (as noted above), not one that is directly promoting secularism, or moving in a secularist direction. And we must clearly acknowledge that some may wish to promote what they call a "secular state" who are in no way hostile to religion, and without wishing in any way to promote secularism. This is an important point that we need to be clear about because one of the reasons that the word "secular" is misleading is that while it is often used as a synonym for secularism, sometimes the word is used where the intention is not to refer to or to promote secularism (at least not in a direct sense).[16] For example, if parents say they wish for their children to have a secular education, they may just mean that they don't want to send them to a religious school, but not that they want them to be educated in a secularist worldview. So in this case, they might simply be motivated for whatever reason by dissatisfaction with religious education. This way of talking was, I believe, easier to understand in the past when religious worldviews were more dominant, but it is becoming less appropriate for the simple reason that people are now more aware that one cannot simply reject religion but must give some thought to *what will replace it*. In practical terms, this means one must consider which values and outlook on life children will be brought up to believe.

Modern approaches to education in many democratic countries include providing alternatives to religious education for school children in response to the growth of secularism, and of multicultural communities in many areas, and also because of parental demand. Such schools are still working out which values and outlook on life they wish to inculcate in children as an alternative to religion. One such example is the phenomenon of the "Educate Together" network of schools in Ireland that were set up over the past two decades to offer an alternative to those who did not want a Catholic education. Sometimes characterized (perhaps unfairly) as being anti-Catholic, these schools have developed a positive curriculum in which they will teach about (but not advocate) religion and also teach ethical values, all indications that they are adopting a positive position on what is true with regard to these general topics. In the U.S., private schools (which are usually religious) and public schools are often seen as a rebuke to each other, while public education also serves multicultural populations in urban areas in a more practical way than private religious schools can. While it is important to note that being anti-religious is not the same thing as secularism, there comes a time when people have to choose what they believe in a positive sense, and *which values* they wish to inculcate in their children. So the confusion between secularism and the secular is, unfortunately, widespread. But from now on, I am advocating that we should be very careful to distinguish them. I am claiming that i) it may have been common and acceptable in the past to conflate them (when almost everyone subscribed to a religious worldview), but that ii) today this conflation only leads to confusion (and is also often misleading, sometimes deliberately so), because iii) many today are advocating not for a secular, but a secularist, state. Moreover, iv) some may not be clear that *this* is what they are advocating, but their views are moving society this way, since eventually some belief system will have to replace what they are abandoning (such as in Ireland), since there can be no such thing as a state that is neutral between the incommensurable worldviews that are characteristic of modern pluralist societies.

This brings us then to the term "secular liberalism," often used to describe the modern democratic state. Recall our point in Chap. 1 that the term "liberal" is properly used to describe a state based on the five key values foundational to democracy: freedom, equality, justice, popular sovereignty, and natural rights; this is what is meant by a "liberal democracy," and a "liberal" is someone who supports this view of the state (though, as we have pointed out several times, there will be considerable disagreement about how these abstract values are to be understood in the concrete and how they should be implemented in practical situations). A liberal democracy, therefore, as we understand the term is one in which these liberal values are accepted by all and where it is also agreed that disputes about their interpretation and application are to be settled through the democratic process after a public debate. (This is why there are "conservative liberals"; indeed, most conservatives are liberals—i.e., subscribing to liberal democratic theory {*of course*} and {*not but*} holding conservative positions on most topics.) This classical meaning should be distinguished from the term "secular liberalism." The latter is sometimes presented as meaning that while the state is "secular" and "liberal," it is not thereby secularist, and so can lay claim to *neutrality* among the worldviews. Although secular liberals are usually moving in the direction of secularism, it is correct to say that not all secular liberals are secularists. However, all secular liberals today usually have one thing in common: they want to restrict *certain* religious beliefs and religious values from participating in public discussions, and they hope that these restrictions will result then in these particular religious views *playing little or no role in public policy*. So the term would usually include secularists, liberal religious believers, and those others who think that certain religious beliefs should have no place or be severely restricted in public discourse.

Yet we must go further, for it is a fact than secular liberalism is much more robust than just involving the rejection of certain specific religious views in public deliberation; it usually promotes an unmistakable ideology. In practical terms, it hardly differs from the philosophical liberalism we mentioned in Chap. 1. Most forms of it usually include (sometimes covertly but increasingly overtly) the beliefs that freedom is the highest good, that there is no human nature, that liberal values should be interpreted *in certain definite ways that are not open to debate* in a free society, as well as the belief that religious arguments are not appropriate in politics, that one's religion should be a purely private matter. The problem with these beliefs is that there are many who subscribe to the theory of democracy—who are classical liberals that accept the foundational values referred to above—*but who disagree with all of these claims*. So to pursue only this understanding seems to favor and to allow to flourish only one worldview or family of worldviews, and the moral, political, and social culture that flows from them, and to exclude others, especially certain religious types. Yet another argument against the position that the modern state is "neutral" with regard to the issues that are in dispute between the worldviews in that state. This is why although they are conceptually distinct secular liberalism and secularism are often in practice the same, or very similar.

Once laws are passed, they will favor the values and beliefs of some worldviews and exclude others. It is usually secularists, or those who are pursuing some political goal in society, who advocate for any positive meaning of the term secular, for obvious reasons. In modern democracies, the state is as a matter of sociological fact becoming more secularist, though it is obviously possible for a state to emphasize values that are primarily religious (as many have in the past and some still do), and such a state would be moving in a religious direction. But in neither case is the state completely neutral between worldviews, nor logically can it be, though it might not favor any particular worldview on many issues that affect the state (indeed, many issues of governance, law, and society do not directly require taking a position on worldview questions).

What about the argument that a secular state might be understood as a state that is neutral *with regard to religion*, neither favoring nor disfavoring it? The problem with this view is that it is not possible to justify singling out religion for this kind of special treatment, and indeed discrimination (e.g., in public school funding). Nor (as we have just seen) is it possible for a state in practice to neither favor nor disfavor any particular worldview (or subset of worldviews). This is because *some* values are going to guide social policy on many topics, some are going to be enshrined in law, and these will exclude their opposites, as we have seen. Some thinkers suggest that the modern state should accommodate religion, but not favor it. This, however, usually means that values antecedently built into what is meant by "the state" would place a limit on the influence and practice of religion, and this is fine as long as we acknowledge once again that such values must be justified not assumed, that they exclude their opposites, and promote at the level of the state the worldview of which they are a part. This will turn out to be problematic from the point of view of freedom and pluralism (as we will see in our discussion of Rawls' view in the next chapter). It might be suggested that religion can be singled out as a worldview from which citizens need special protection because it has a tendency to force itself on others and that secularism and other non-religious worldviews do not have this tendency. With secularism becoming a force in modern democracy, however, this claim is no longer believable. In the context of a quite fractious modern pluralism, there is only one appropriate positive meaning that can be given to the word "secular"—that it be understood to mean *secularism*—as described above, and this brings us right back to the problem of worldview pluralism once again.

Using these terms correctly and understanding their distinct meanings, as well as their relationship to each other, is of the highest importance. So *secularism* refers to the worldview of secularism which I am arguing is a distinctive worldview in itself, is becoming more widely held, is openly asserted and promoted, and is having increasing cultural influence in modern democratic societies, often in opposition to religion. It need not necessarily be completely hostile to religion, though it usually is. It could in theory be quite accommodating to religious perspectives, as long as (from the point of view of its supporters) it remains the preferred, the default, worldview in the modern state (meaning a secularist perspective would be arbiter over those values that ultimately get to guide state policy on matters affecting life and culture).[17] *Secularization* describes the process of democratic society becoming less religious, a process that has a number of causes, and the process itself leads to the spread of secularism (though it must be distinguished from secularism). The *secular* refers to what is not religious, and in the context of democratic pluralism usually also means that religion should play no role in public arguments, as a guide to policy, and in the making of laws. *If* the word is used in a positive sense, it is most accurately understood as meaning secularism. Finally, the term *secular liberalism* is best understood as referring to that view that wishes to deny religious arguments a place in public deliberations, and that also is committed to the robust understanding of liberal values, described earlier.

Passive and Active Secularism

We might helpfully distinguish between a kind of passive secularism and an active secularism.[18] Passive secularism might describe the position of a religious believer who is very influenced by secularization trends in society that distract him from his religion, for example, he goes out for a convenient and expensive breakfast on Sunday morning instead of going to Church! Gradually, this secularization trend, which is sometimes accompanied by secularist values and beliefs, begins to affect (or infect) his religious views, and so influenced is he by these trends that he starts to adopt secularist values and attitudes. For example, he may support the legalization of abortion, even though it is against his religion. This is not always because he has changed his mind on abortion; it may also be because he is going along with the flow of fashionable beliefs, or for selfish reasons, or because he fears the reaction of his peers. It is a complicated matter as to how new trends in a culture influence the general populace but it is not always because people change their minds on a topic. I believe that this passive type of secularism plays a big role in the spread of secularism in society. Passive secularism is not (yet) atheism (or philosophical secularism)—it describes the situation where a religious believer is influenced by the beliefs of secularism. To become passively secularist is to start to adopt some of the beliefs and attitudes of secularism. The process of secularization could be going on in a society for a long time without any move to philosophical secularism, yet it is probably inevitable that many will adopt the secularist worldview eventually. Many democratic societies seem to have had a longish period of secularization before secularism began to take hold; as we noted, this topic is of much interest to sociologists, with a number of different positions and explanations being advanced. The phenomenon of passive secularism is interesting because both the religious worldview and the secularist worldview could compete for the allegiance of passive secularists in social and political debates.

We can contrast this trend with an active secularism where people are very aware of their secularist worldview, make a conscious decision to hold it and promote it, usually in opposition to religion, and wish it to be the main influence over society and politics. Active secularists will deliberately promote their worldview as a way of shaping public life, influencing government agencies, or educational programs. We may see politicians openly advocating, even running for political office on, a secularist agenda, and so forth. One of my claims in this book is that this form of secularism is becoming more dominant in modern society. We might characterize modern democratic society as a society in which active secularism is now a serious cultural force.

Many secularists are now quite clear and open about wanting to influence society according to their beliefs and values. Often these influences are in opposition to religion, and so secularism still carries with it a strong connotation of being anti-religion. It is for this reason that the word "secularism" is still somewhat regarded as a bad word in some Western countries! Many people still hear its negative connotation when they hear the term, and it evokes for them certain attitudes—that secularists are hostile to them and their beliefs, and are likely to exhibit a supercilious attitude toward religion and religious believers. When some religious believers hear the words "secularist" or "secular," they often interpret them to mean that their views will be discriminated against, that such language is invoked to exclude religious views from the discussion. In other countries, like India (the world's largest democracy), the words "secular" or "secularism" often have a more positive connotation for many because they convey the idea that the state will protect minority religions from a Hindu theocracy; such terms can be a kind of code for the view that all religions have a place at the table in the democratic state, whereas in Western countries they are often code for the view that religions should be excluded from the table.[19] But the key point is that in India the term does not refer to the worldview of secularism, it refers to the position that the state shall have no official religion, not the view that religious views can have no influence on the state.

Case Study: Republic of Ireland

My home country, the Republic of Ireland, is a very interesting nation to study with regard to the process of secularization at work, and with regard to the relationship between religion, secularism, and politics in the modern democratic state. It is one of the most fascinating recent examples of the phenomenon of secularization that one will find anywhere. The transformation of Ireland from a serious and devout Catholic country to a secularized society, with a very significant and very influential secularist strand to it, in less than a generation is quite astonishing. It is also a clear indication of the power of the process of secularization to transform a culture. While it would be by no means accurate to describe Ireland as a secularist state, the country has become in less than thirty years a state in which secularist ideas and trends are almost dominant over religious values and themes. Whether this is a good thing or not, of course, depends on your point of view, depends on your worldview. And the role of young people in the process is also of great interest since they are growing up in a society that is changing and tend to embrace the worldview and trends of the moment, and not necessarily as a result of a period of reflective deliberation!

Our concern is not with how to assess the changes, but with the more descriptive question of how did they came about, and so quickly, and also with the way such changes illustrate some of our observations and arguments in this chapter. It is obviously of great interest to consider how a society can change so fast from embracing one worldview held very strongly by the vast majority of the people, to an almost totally opposite worldview that has great influence not only over how people think, but also over their behavior, and that has cultural effects that are easy enough to observe and document (such as marital breakdown). Of course, it is notoriously difficult to try to pin point the causes of social change, especially change on such a large scale over so short a time, but I think we can identify several factors that at least played some role in the process of secularization in Ireland. Some will be common to other countries that have experienced, or are currently experiencing, their own secularizing process (such as Poland), though one would be hard pressed to identify another society that changed so quickly.

Change began to happen slowly in Ireland during the 1970s, especially after Ireland's entry into the European Community in 1973, which put pressure on the Irish government to modernize its equality laws. Modern media and cultural forces during this period, especially in music, films, and TV shows, also had a significant effect on Irish attitudes and behavior. Many felt that the Catholic Church, slow to modernize during the 1980s, was becoming irrelevant to everyday life. But it was with the loss of credibility of the Catholic Church beginning in the late 1980s and all through the 1990s, due to the child sex abuse scandals, that cultural change gained rapid momentum. The Church scandals have been extensively reported on and documented so there is no need to rehearse the sordid details, but they were a strong contributory factor to the decline of the influence of the Catholic Church in Irish society, for a few different reasons. The obvious one is the fact of the abuse itself, and its perpetration by the most trusted and revered members of Irish society. The exposure of this abuse led to moral outrage among the people of Ireland, most of whom were weekly mass-going, practicing Catholics. In addition, many people were rightly sickened and disappointed with the way the Church covered up the scandals, moving priests from parish to parish and putting children in harm's way. They lost confidence in the institution and also at least partly in its teachings. The latter reaction is not perhaps a logical reaction, since it does not follow from the sins of an institution that its teachings are wrong, but it is understandable from a human point of view, and many close to the scandals or directly affected by them turned against the Church, some for good. Third, the scandals gave young people, in particular, the excuse to stop attending mass and practicing their religion. It was a temptation for young people to skip mass in Ireland when they reached their teen years, especially when faced with the many distractions of modern life, but it was often difficult to do so because of family influence and authority, and parents were usually strict about passing on the faith. But the scandals weakened the resistance of parents with the result that mass attendance began to fall sharply, especially among the young. Another development was that sections of the Irish media used the occasion of the scandals as an opportunity to attack the Church; they had been waiting for an opportunity for a long time. Like everyone, they rightly deplored the abuse, but given the fact of it, they not only reported on it, but used the occasion as an opportunity to often ridicule and reject Catholic beliefs.

This is not to say that the Catholic Church in Ireland was not open to criticism—it was, and much of the strong criticism aimed at its leaders was thoroughly deserved. But given that the Catholic Church behaved very badly and let a lot of people down, and worse, engaged in criminal behavior, sections of the intelligentsia and the media took advantage of this fact, and used it to attack the Church culturally as much as they possibly could. Some believe they went even further than this, and allowed the scandals to be the occasion for the release of a kind of hatred for the Catholic Church that they had kept pent up for a long time! This hatred, often expressed in the way and to the extent that reporters and news outlets covered news stories about the scandals, and items about the Church generally during this time, likely played some role in turning many against their religion. It also gave rise to a kind of irrational, emotional, anti-Catholicism in the country that still exists today and that a significant segment of the population has not yet gotten over. Perhaps this is understandable to some extent, but it is still important to note from a sociological point of view that this anti-Catholic reaction plays some part in cultural change in Ireland, and is driven by an emotional hatred rather than by the development of a reflective, substantive alternative position (of which more a bit later). The loss of the moral authority of the Catholic Church was one of the big catalysts for social change in the country. Such change may have happened anyway (and was happening to some extent), but it was hastened by the Church's loss of credibility. The scandals forced the Church to take a back seat in subsequent cultural debates thereby leaving the field open for secularist and other liberal views to dominate.

A few other obvious trends can be mentioned that contributed to social change in Ireland, as well as in many countries. Indeed, many of them are marks of the modern world, and have transformed societies across the globe. One is a great increase in immigration that occurred in Ireland, particularly during the economic boom years of the 1990s, exposing the Irish people to a variety of cultures, religions, and ways of living, a phenomenon that contributed to the growing pluralism in the country (the population increased by more than 40% in just over a generation).[20] Another was the availability of low cost air travel, especially to other European countries, initially through Ryanair, which began as a modest budget airline in the 1980s and has grown to become the biggest airline in Europe. Other airlines were forced to follow suit in terms of prices and numbers of flights in order to compete. Irish people began to travel like never before, usually to European destinations, not particularly on cultural holidays but often to sun destinations (such as the beaches of Spain, the south of France, the Canary Islands, and the Greek islands)! They gained further experience, even if limited, of how other people lived. How did they live? The fact is that citizens of Spain, France, and Italy (to take some specific examples of traditional Catholic countries) were living increasingly secular lives.[21] In what way? Particularly in the areas of sexual morality relating to living arrangements (such as living together instead of getting married); these societies were beginning to liberalize laws on such issues as divorce and abortion, and such practices were becoming increasingly common. These were areas of Irish law that were still under the control of Catholic belief and teaching.

Another quite significant reason for the transformation of Irish society, and one that goes hand in hand with many of the other changes, was the explosion of economic growth and business development in Ireland. Ireland went through an economic boom (often referred to as the "Celtic Tiger") in the mid-1990s until the economic collapse in 2008. It was not predictable in advance and the causes for it are still being debated, but what we do know is that the economic transformation in a fairly short time was nothing short of astonishing—the country went from a significant rate of unemployment to virtually full employment in less than a generation. There was a tremendous boom in the property and financial sectors, and also large pay rises for civil servants, teachers (who are paid by the state), increases in pensions for the elderly, and seemingly unlimited amounts of money for improvements in infrastructure and the arts! The resulting prosperity transformed Irish society and lifted many people from a working-class environment into the middle class, which brought with it an increasing amount of disposable income (keep in mind that only a hundred and fifty years ago two-thirds of the Irish population lived in mud houses, and up until the 1970s most families had barely enough income to get by).[22]

Unfortunately, this new-found wealth was often accompanied by widespread greed and irresponsible economic and social behavior, as the Irish people got caught up in a consumerist culture for the first time, which put pressure on them to meet its economic demands. The country saw much reckless behavior across all aspects of Irish society including in Ireland's largest banks, leadings businesses and corporations, among government officials, as well as in the behavior of ordinary individuals. Many were encouraged to borrow irresponsibly to finance a material lifestyle neither they nor the economy could afford (primarily houses, property, cars, and foreign holidays). This shortsighted, irresponsible behavior thus led to the economic collapse of the country in 2008, which, among other things, saw the imminent failure of Ireland's two biggest banks (which had to be rescued by the government in early 2009). Many people were ruined financially, and Ireland had to be bailed out by the E.U. and the

International Monetary Fund, as the government was forced to implement a strict austerity regimen. In the general election of 2011, the governing Fianna Fail party suffered a total rout, with only twenty members of the outgoing government of seventy-seven retaining their seats, including only half of the cabinet, the worst defeat for a political party in Irish history, and among the worst ever in any European country. These personal and financial failings did not only affect Ireland, of course, but were worldwide and led to severe economic distress everywhere, including in the U.S.

However, that period of rapid economic expansion was very significant for Ireland. It moved the nation from being a second world country to a first world country, a quite remarkable achievement and one that should perhaps also be regarded as an indication of the success of capitalism. Its effect on Irish society, especially in terms of attitudes and living, is what we are interested in. Again, we must be somewhat tentative, but more money and prosperity leads inevitably to more emphasis on the material life and a move away from the life of the spirit, as we noted earlier. It led to Ireland rapidly becoming a consumer society with an emphasis to an unbelievable degree on fancy houses, big cars, foreign holidays, investment in domestic and foreign property, new businesses, and all of the excessive choices and material crassness that often accompanies such changes. All of these developments had an effect on Irish attitudes. The society became more secular in the sense that religious values began to take a backseat to the complexities of modern living. The sexual revolution in particular took off in Ireland at this time, fully abetted by sections of an increasingly secularist press and Irish television. It came to Ireland quite late, but it hit it with force!

Coupled with the legalization of divorce in 1995, one of the obvious effects of secularization on Irish society is the extreme pressure on marriage as an institution. Ireland went from a very low breakdown rate after the introduction of divorce to a quite significant breakdown rate (though still low compared to some other countries) in a very short period of time, astonishingly short.[23] Indeed, the institution of marriage is one of those areas where the effects of the secularization of Irish society has been most obvious with marital breakdown now much more common, and becoming normalized, like in many other countries that have undergone a similar process. It is also one of those areas where the destructive force of secularizing tendencies is evident, and the spinoff effects on society are very severe, since an increase in many social problems can be attributed in some significant causal sense to the breakdown of the family. And, as many countries have discovered, alleviating these problems has become extremely difficult, almost intractable; indeed in many secular societies in the West these problems appear to be getting worse. In some sense an increasing number in Ireland are now living the kind of life depicted in the soap operas that have become a staple of TV watching in many households, particularly as regards marriage failure, relationship difficulties and breakdowns, child custody disputes, greed and irresponsible financial behavior, and so on! This is a massive social change in a society that was fairly exemplary in terms of avoiding such problems less than a generation ago.

Another trend is the phenomenon of young people living together before marriage, a phenomenon that was almost unthinkable even thirty years ago, and for which the social penalties in terms of ostracization were high. Thankfully, we have moved beyond that era of harsh moral judgment but our interest is in how this change came about. How did a society in which sexual abstention before marriage was the norm and co-habitation before marriage rare go from that to one where living together before marriage (and usually getting married later, after having children) became normalized? The answer is that the process of secularization, described earlier, is responsible for it, along with the collapse in moral authority of the Catholic Church. But the influence of the media, TV shows, movies, music, exposure to other cultures, in addition to the role of cultural reformers, in changing people's attitudes cannot be underestimated. People's attitudes on these matters *were changed for them*. Most people are too busy living to make these kinds of culture-changing judgments themselves; they are usually encouraged to do so by activists, social reformers, and a very powerful and influential media who wish to change society in the light of their moral vision. Young people especially are not usually so political, and often manage with a jumbled set of beliefs. Indeed, many people don't have a clear view on each issue, or a vision of how topics fit together. So they are very much under the influence of cultural reformers and media voices (one reason for the widespread phenomenon today of "helicopter parents," parents who are anxious to protect their children from cultural influences that are often too strong for young people to resist).

We also see in contemporary Ireland some politicians and some influential journalists taking that extra step amid these secularizing trends and arguing for a *secularist* nation, now openly advocating secularist policies, and attempting to move Ireland toward a secularist, not just a more secular, society.[24] This is perhaps a trend to be welcomed because it *brings the key differences between people out in the open, and moves the debate to the level of worldviews, where it must now be.* It is also a move that confirms the thesis of this book, that secularism is becoming more widely held, more widely practiced, and is seeking to influence society and culture, usually at the expense of religious views. It is surely healthier to have the debate out in the open so that everyone knows where everyone stands. Ireland took further steps toward a secularist society in recent years with the legalization of same sex marriage (2015), and the removal in 2018 of the Eighth Amendment from the Irish Constitution (which had protected the life of the unborn), paving the way for the legalization of abortion. A referendum was also passed in 2019 clearing the way for the government to ease restrictions on divorce. Such moves were simply unthinkable in Irish culture until quite recently, and are further evidence of the seismic shift in Irish attitudes in the last two decades. One interesting side note is that all of these issues were decided by referendums, and not by the government or the Courts, which is a strong vote of confidence in the Irish democratic system (pun intended!). Unlike in several countries where the elites could not be sure of popular support, such as in the U.S., these measures were not introduced by the Courts in opposition to majority opinion. After a public debate, the Irish people voted "yes" on all measures by significant margins. (A referendum to legalize divorce was passed in Ireland in 1995 by 50.28% to 49.72%; the referendum in 2019 to allow the government to pass legislation to liberalize the law, particularly to reduce the required waiting period, passed by 82% to 18%, a clear indication of the dramatic shift in Irish attitudes.) Some modern political philosophers, like Grayling, would not have agreed with the way these issues were settled, having no time for referendums: "Representative democracy should have no truck with referenda. A referendum is an opinion poll, in which the profile of sentiment in the population, as it stands on the day of the vote, is measured."[25] He has more confidence in representatives making decisions, naively holding that they are not subject to the same weaknesses as the electorate. He does not explain how general elections would not be subject to the same criticism.

To conclude our case study of Ireland, we should reflect briefly on the question of whether Ireland could now be classed as a secularist society? Our question is asking whether most people in Ireland now subscribe to the secularist worldview, whereas previously they had subscribed to a religious, usually Catholic, worldview? Sometimes Irish intellectuals will say things like: "we have gotten rid of Catholicism but have not replaced it with an alternative." (The "we" presumably refers to those who have abandoned Catholicism, and to the establishment who move public opinion in this direction.) We should keep in mind that a society could be secularist in fact, if not in name. Or is it more accurate to say that the Irish people are influenced by strong secularist tendencies, while mostly retaining their religious worldview? The latter is the correct answer, although many have in fact embraced the secularist worldview, as we have noted. It is interesting to observe that most of the children in Ireland are still baptized, and continue to make their First Communions and Confirmations, and so remain Catholics, even though mass attendance and general religious devotion and practice has fallen off sharply. This is especially true of young people, and the number who describe themselves as something other than Catholic has increased by a large percentage; there has also been a big increase in the number of civil weddings and, to a lesser extent, humanist funeral services.[26] There is also a significant minority who exhibit a strong hatred for the Catholic Church and Catholicism. The important point, though, is that many came under the influence of secularist thinking, especially on moral issues and in education. It would be no surprise if this social revolution were to continue in the near future, perhaps with a vote to allow the legalization of euthanasia, which would be another rejection of a bedrock teaching of Christianity.

The changes in Irish society and culture we have described were noted in a speech at Dublin Castle by the then Irish Taoiseach (Prime Minister), Leo Varadkar, on the occasion of Pope Francis' visit to Ireland in August 2018. Noting the radical transformation of Irish culture, the Taoiseach told the Pope that Ireland would need a new relationship between church and state, one in which "religion is no longer at the center of our society, but in which it still has an important place."[27] His message to the Pope, although expressed somewhat vaguely and with respect for his Holiness, was nevertheless clear: Ireland is now a secular democracy, and while not a secularist society, secularist values will be presumptive over religious ones whenever the two clash. The default view on many issues is fast becoming secularism and not Catholicism, as it was in the past.

Immature and Mature Secularism

I think it can be helpful to distinguish between immature and mature secularism, especially in the context of modern Ireland, but the distinction would have application in many countries. Irish society is a good, perhaps even extreme, illustration of the phenomenon. One must keep in mind that the people of Ireland did not consciously adopt a secularist perspective; rather, secularist trends caught on in society for the reasons we described above. Partly for this reason, Ireland is undergoing a process of what I think we can accurately describe as immature secularism. This is characterized by hedonistic tendencies, strong anti-religious sentiment (especially anti-Catholicism) almost to the point of bigotry (the Church is now often afraid to advance its views on various topics due to severe elite backlash), a disdain for views other than one's own especially if they are Christian views (though the hatred and anger toward the Catholic Church is understandable as a human reaction to the child abuse scandals, and also as a reaction to the overall power the Catholic Church held over Irish society). These attitudes are marked by a kind of stubborn, extreme, in your face shrillness, revealing a strident dogmatism with regard to secularist ideology, a reminder that we are often dealing with true believers who brook no argument (though their influence in Ireland is still somewhat tempered). Randal Rauser has perceptively described the contemporary "village atheist" as being characterized by lacking critical reflection, as unresponsive to criticism, as caricaturing the opinion of others, as promoting tribalism among themselves, as exhibiting a hostile backlash approach to issues of life and culture.[28] This attitude is becoming common in Ireland and in parts of other countries.

The immature secularist exhibits the same kind of certainty, the same kind of dogmatic attitude, the same way of treating moral and political disagreement, that was often attributed in the past to extreme religious views. It is the same mindset, the same fervor, the same sense of self-righteousness leading to moral blindness, the same certainty concerning a set of unquestionable beliefs—just a different ideology. The phenomenon of political correctness can be regarded as another manifestation of this mindset. Indeed, the hysteria surrounding political correctness generates the same type of fear people used to experience in the past if they were judged to be challenging traditional religious orthodoxy. The phenomenon of "cancel culture" is another example. Indeed, the term "liberal fundamentalism" has become quite common in these debates, and at very least the term does describe how the liberal mindset is *perceived* by those on the receiving end of it—the same way that some liberals perceive certain types of religious attitudes. Perhaps, however, even immature secularism can serve a purpose by keeping religion on its toes with regard to the integrity of its beliefs and actions.

We can understand mature secularism to describe a situation where a society has embraced secularism, is comfortable with it, and has largely forgotten what it replaced, and so is not much exercised by its rivals. Mature secularists are no longer concerned with, and so are no longer reacting to, what they reject. There are few societies, if any, currently in this position. Most societies still exhibit immature secularist tendencies (including, e.g., France, where the term "militant secularism" is often used to describe current attitudes[29]). Indeed, it remains to be seen whether there will ever be a mature secularist society—a key philosophical question, because it would involve a whole society coming to accept the overall rationality of secularism. Perhaps secularism must remain immature almost by definition, and will never get to a mature stage. The average secularist today often exhibits an immature approach to cultural debate, motivated by a "chip on shoulder" attitude toward religion! This is why although secularism is becoming more recognizable as a philosophical thesis, it often starts with the view that there is no God, or with a rejection of religion, or is at least still perceived this way by many citizens. Indeed, much of secularist literature (both academic and popular) now reads like old religious literature (indeed worse): supercilious, pious, patronizing, intolerant, dogmatic, and dripping with certitude. Secularism in theory is one thing, a position the academics can discuss with great interest. The practice of secularism is quite another, say in a country like Ireland, where, despite its advantages, it does come with unattractive elements, and often exhibits destructive tendencies not only for people personally, but also for the family and by extension for society.

Notes

1. See Charles Taylor, *A Secular Age* (Cambridge, MA.: Harvard U.P., 2007), pp. 1–22; also Charles Taylor, "Western Secularity" (pp. 31–53) and José Casanova, "The Secular, Secularization, Secularisms" (pp. 54–74), both in Craig Calhoun et al., *Rethinking Secularism* (New York: Oxford U.P., 2011).
2. Mary Warnock, *Dishonest to God: On Keeping Religion out of Politics* (New York: Continuum, 2010), p. 159.

3. See Christian Smith, *The Secular Revolution* (Berkeley, CA: University of California Press, 2003); Joseph Ratzinger and Jurgen Habermas, *The Dialectics of Secularization: On Reason and Religion* (San Francisco: Ignatius Press, 2007); Charles Taylor, *A Secular Age*.
4. See José Casanova, *Public Religions in the Modern World* (Chicago: University of Chicago Press, 1994); Peter Berger, *The Sacred Canopy* (New York: Anchor, 1967); David Martin, *A General Theory of Secularization* (New York: Harper and Row, 1979).
5. See the essays in John Milbank, Catherine Pickstock and Graham Ward (eds.), *Radical Orthodoxy: A New Theology* (New York: Routledge, 1999); also Stanley Hauerwas and Romand Coles, *Christianity, Democracy and the Radical Ordinary* (Eugene, OR.: Wipf and Stock, 2008).
6. See Steve Bruce, *Secularization* (New York: Oxford U.P., 2011), p. 154.
7. Ibid., p. 2.
8. See Rodney Stark and R. Finke, *Acts of Faith: Explaining the Human Side of Religion* (Los Angeles: University of California Press, 2000), p. 61.
9. See the essays in Christian Smith (ed.), *The Secular Revolution*.
10. See Steve Bruce, *Secularization*, pp. 57–78 for a full discussion.
11. See Callum Brown, *The Death of Christian Britain*.
12. See Jurgen Habermas "Notes on a Post–Secular Society," at http://www.signandsight.com/features/1714.html
13. The topic of state neutrality has been widely discussed. As examples, see Stephen Macedo, *Liberal Virtues* (New York: Oxford U.P., 1990); George Sher, *Beyond Neutrality* (New York: Cambridge U.P., 1997); Amy Guthman, *Democratic Education* (Princeton, NJ.: Princeton U.P., 1987); R. Merrill and D. Weinstock (eds.), *Political Neutrality: A Re-evaluation* (New York: Palgrave, 2014); Cécile Laborde, *Liberalism's Religion* (Cambridge, MA.: Harvard U.P., 2017); Christopher Eberle, *Religious Conviction in Liberal Politics* (New York: Cambridge U.P., 2002); Peter Simpson, *Political Illiberalism: A Defense of Freedom* (New York: Routledge, 2015).
14. See Roger Trigg, *Religion in Public Life* (New York: Oxford U.P., 2007), p. 112.
15. In her book, *Democratic Education*, Guthman makes a similar argument about the field of education, that it is not possible to have a neutral educational curriculum because it would require an educational philosophy devoid of moral principles and there can be no such thing (see especially, pp. 3–47). Guthman goes on to defend the position that the disputes that arise with regard to education in a pluralist context should be settled democratically.
16. To add to the confusion, the term "secularism" is often used as a synonym for "secular." This usage seems to be common in the UK; for an example,

see Andrew Copson, *Secularism* (London: Oxford U.P., 2017); see also the discussion of the French version of secularism, *laïcité*, in Jean Baubérot, "The Evolution of French Secularism," in Ranjan Ghosh (ed.), *Making Sense of the Secular* (New York: Routledge, 2013), pp. 44–54. However, as I have been arguing, it is now vital that we keep both terms distinct as the debate about modern pluralism moves forward.

17. Charles Taylor is thinking along similar lines with his distinction between a closed and open secular society, where the former is hostile, but the latter open, to a place for religion in the modern state; see his *A Secular Age*, pp. 541ff.
18. I owe this distinction to David E. Campbell and Geoffrey C. Layman in their insightful paper, "The Politics of Secularism in the United States," in Robert Scott and Marlis Buchmann (eds.), *Emerging Trends in the Social and Behavioral Sciences* (John Wiley On Line Reference Work, 2017), pp. 1–13, though I am using the terms in a slightly different way to these authors. One of their conclusions is that active secularists are much more likely to be engaged in (the promotion of left-wing) politics in the U.S., while passive secularists are more on the sidelines politically.
19. I owe this point to my late colleague and friend, Fr Noel Sheth, S.J.
20. For an overview of statistics, and a discussion of the effects of immigration on many aspects of Irish life and culture, see J.V. Ulin and H. Edwards (eds.), *Race and Immigration in the New Ireland* (Notre Dame, IN.: University of Notre Dame Press, 2013).
21. For an interesting discussion of recent secularizing trends across Europe, see Olivier Roy, *Is Europe Christian?* (London: Hurst, 2019).
22. See Cecil Woodham-Smith, *The Great Hunger: Ireland 1845–1849* (London: Penguin, 1992), p. 20.
23. For an overview of recent data, see the report from the Irish Central Statistics Office, "Census of Population 2016—Profile 4 Households and Families," at www.cso.ie.
24. For an overview of the current discussion, see Joseph Ruane, "Secularization and Ideology in the Republic of Ireland," in Paul Brennan (ed.), *La sécularization en Irlande* (Caen, France: Presses universitaires de Caen, 1998), pp. 239–254 (article available at books.openedition.org).
25. A.C. Grayling, *Democracy and Its Crisis*, p. 166.
26. See note 6 in the previous chapter for an overview of recent data; also "How Ireland has changed since the last papal visit," *Irish Independent*, June 17th, 2018.
27. Speech of An Taoiseach, Leo Varadkar, T.D., on the occasion of the Visit of Pope Francis to Ireland, Dublin Castle, August 25th, 2018, available at www.gov.ie.

28. See Randal Rauser, "Why more atheists need to speak out against village atheism," at randalrauser.com
29. See "Secularism with a slightly militant edge," *The New York Times*, March 23rd, 2015 and "French Minister warns of militant secularism," *Yahoo News*, May 31st, 2015.

CHAPTER 7

Secular Liberalism and the Exclusion of Religious Worldviews

We have been examining the problem of worldview pluralism and recognizing the serious difficulty it presents for modern democracy. This is especially true for advanced democracies such as those found in Western countries, but it is a problem that all democracies will likely face if the arguments I have presented in earlier chapters are correct. Most democratic countries will surely end up with a number of incommensurable worldviews that clash with each other on vital matters of morality, politics, law, and culture. These nations will also experience a phenomenon of relativism (described in Chap. 4) and will struggle with the challenge of how to place a limit to freedom in the democratic context, and enforce it consistently and non-arbitrarily. So the question now facing us is: given that this is the situation in modern democracy in its evolved forms, how will such a society function going into the future? We don't just mean to ask how can such a society remain stable, but how will it be possible for such a state to govern at all? The problem is indeed a stark one: how is it possible for the democratic form of government to promote progress and fulfillment for its citizens with regard to defining questions of morality, politics, law, economics, and culture, if the citizens in that democracy disagree sharply about these issues? Moreover, how can such a society operate if its citizens and institutions have lost confidence in one of the main tools of educated people to solve disagreement, reason? And, in addition, if they have also lost confidence in the ability of the political process of public debate and reasoned deliberation to arrive at either truth, a

© The Author(s), under exclusive license to Springer Nature Switzerland AG 2021
B. Sweetman, *The Crisis of Democratic Pluralism*,
https://doi.org/10.1007/978-3-030-78382-2_7

consensus, or a compromise on central questions of life and culture. Democratic civilized society must take a stand on such questions if it is to govern well and move forward. This is the situation in which democracy finds itself.

In this chapter, we will develop our understanding of the problem, provide an overview of some of the assumptions that democratic theorists have tended to work with when faced with this vexing modern predicament, and then consider one now standard solution, offered by political philosopher, John Rawls. In the next chapters, I will present and illustrate a tentative proposal for how we should proceed, especially with regard to public deliberation and arguments. My view will involve a rejection of the conventional wisdom of secular liberalism. Because the problem of worldview pluralism is severe, I don't think we can reach a solution that is guaranteed to produce sweetness and light. However, I believe my position is the fairest, most plausible way forward and has the best chance of success, compared to the alternatives.

Assumptions of Modern Secular Liberalism

There is a conventional wisdom among many thinkers concerning the general topic of how we should proceed given the problem of disagreement in current democratic states. The standard approach to our contemporary predicament involves working with a number of *assumptions*. These assumptions gradually became a feature of liberal democratic theory from Locke onward, but they were crystallized very well in the work of Rawls and to a lesser extent Jurgen Habermas, and we will consider their approach in what follows. Rawls is so influential that he has defined how many think about the debate today, so it is necessary that we consider his view, and (later) explain why it should be rejected. His approach is also widely regarded as being hostile to religious worldviews. Rawls' approach is based on the acceptance of several assumptions, and it is quite remarkable how many thinkers now work with the same assumptions. These assumptions are thought-provoking and influential, but not without controversy, and there is much dispute about how his view is to be understood and implemented. The fact that they are assumptions is also significant because it seems to mean that it is not necessary to defend them philosophically; we can just accept them—so we need also to consider if we would accept them, what accepting them means, and how we might proceed if we did not accept them.

Rawls' view (and similar views) are often referred to as "secular liberalism," a term we introduced in the previous chapter (other terms used to describe this general position are liberal theory, liberal political theory, or political liberalism). Many readers of Rawls believe that it might be more accurate to describe his position as secular*ist* liberalism, though it is hard to judge whether this is fair or not, since he makes a point of saying that he is not advocating secularism, even though he is commonly read this way. He often insisted, without being very convincing, that he was not trying to sideline or contain religion, because his general approach was similarly restrictive of secular*ist* views. Supporters of Rawls, however, usually advocate an interpretation of liberal political theory that would severely restrict the role of religious beliefs in public arguments, and therefore in the major democratic decisions that affect life and culture. I think that for Rawls himself and most of his strongest supporters the most accurate interpretation is that their aim is to promote a secular*ist* state (as we will see when we elaborate this view).

The first assumption of secular liberalism is that the emphasis on freedom (discussed in Chap. 2) that is part of the essence of democracy means that *an individual citizen should be free to choose his or her own worldview.* Even though most people are brought up practicing a particular worldview, it is still the case that one must eventually decide whether or not to stay with this worldview. This is especially true in modern democracies which are now often characterized by a rejection of traditional worldviews, especially if these worldviews are religious, coupled with an emphasis on living authentically, which is usually understood to involve, among other things, choosing one's worldview for oneself, making decisions on the key questions of life for oneself. So given the general direction in which modern democratic culture is moving, the problem of worldview pluralism will likely become worse as time goes on, as society splinters further into incommensurable and competing worldviews.

However, it is important to note that, under the first assumption, those who stick with traditional worldviews, or some version of these worldviews, are just as entitled to hold such views, and to expect that they will play some role in the future direction of society and culture. This is a consequence of individuals being encouraged to choose their worldviews for themselves. In actual practice what is likely to happen is that we will have many people who subscribe to traditional religions, along with a significant number who subscribe to some kind of modern religious view (this group would likely include those who describe themselves as "spiritual but not religious," those who hold some version of what Kitcher referred to as "refined religion," and those who are what I called in Chap. 5 "philosophical Christians" as well as philosophical members of other religious traditions). There will also exist a significant and growing secularist view (as I have been arguing), as well perhaps as an increasing number who are rudderless in the sense that they are unsure of what they believe on the defining questions of life (some, indeed, may have no firm convictions because of the influence of relativism on their thinking). So these are the types of worldviews that will be present in democratic society going forward, and indeed we can see the beginnings of such groupings in almost all Western countries. The relationship between the worldviews will also be significant because it seems to be inevitable that worldviews will often clash with each other; some worldviews may look down on others, attempt even to discriminate against rivals, and so forth. A sharply pluralist society of this type will not necessarily be one that generally welcomes different worldviews. It will not automatically encourage and promote an attitude of respect toward philosophical differences, one that regards pluralism as an occasion for exposure to fruitful new perspectives rather than as a situation that precipitates personal distress and social strife!

The second theme and assumption to consider is the *theme of religious freedom*. We must understand this broadly, and in both a negative and a positive sense. Indeed, these points will reveal the difficulty that confronts us when we try to put our aspirations about religious freedom into practice. Religious freedom is often regarded as one of the founding motivations of the democratic form of government. *Today, it is necessary to expand the idea to include the freedom to subscribe to any worldview, and also to practice it to some extent, whatever that worldview is, religious or secularist.* Given that we are moving away from the religious worldview in many democracies, with a corresponding increase in the number of people who subscribe to some form of secularism, then we must extend the idea of free practice to *every* worldview, not just religious ones. (Indeed, I will argue in the following chapters that talk of *religious* freedom in the modern context is becoming out of date, and that we need new language to describe the idea of being free to select, hold, and practice one's beliefs and worldview.)

There is another important facet to the notion of religious freedom. It includes the idea that people are free to practice their religion without interference from others or without significant penalty for doing so, though this meaning is under attack today.[1] The negative understanding of the term, then, is the presumption that one should be left alone to practice one's religion, that one is free to accept and commit to a religious view (or any worldview, as we have noted), and also free to practice it in society (within certain limits, as we will see later, and which will, inevitably, cause difficulties). The positive meaning includes the attitude that the freedom to practice one's religion is seen not only as a strength of a democratic society, a commendable moral feature of that society (when compared to societies that do not allow such freedom), but also the fact that one is positively encouraged in mature democracies to select one's worldview with the understanding that one will be free to practice it. It is, I think, an important feature of mature democracies that they encourage, rather than just accommodate or tolerate, different views; indeed, the presence of different views undermines by itself any one worldview that might claim to be privileged in an objective sense, a feature of pluralism that many welcome, as we noted in our discussion of relativism. But we noted a problem facing this approach as well: it has the effect of *undermining one's own claims to truth* (moral or political), claims that one is always tempted to make! So religious freedom means that I am free to practice my worldview without interference (negative meaning) and also that I should feel very welcome to choose or even develop my own worldview (positive meaning), in the modern democratic state. Built into the notion also is the understanding that one's worldview is entitled to respect, even if many do not subscribe to it, and indeed believe that it is false. Anyone who severely criticizes or ridicules a worldview or discriminates against people based on their worldview should be frowned upon, according to the conventional wisdom in democratic pluralism. Of course, it is not so easy to put this understanding of religious freedom into practice, as we know only too well. It runs into difficulty especially concerning the limits to both religious freedom (are there any worldviews one should not subscribe to?), and respect (are there worldviews we should not respect?). In addition, who would decide such questions and using what criteria, all fascinating but very challenging questions to answer, and about which to maintain consistency. These are questions not just academics and intellectuals, but ordinary citizens, struggle with now on a regular basis.

    A further assumption is that *the notion of religious freedom goes hand in hand with the notion of the secular state.* As noted in our previous chapter, the notion of the secular state is often understood to mean that the state is somehow neutral between worldviews. This is supposed to mean that the state does not favor one worldview over another, nor one religion over another. In addition, it means that the state is not founded on one particular worldview or religion in preference to others, but is supposedly somehow neutral between worldviews, to be capable of accommodating all worldviews. Obviously, this cannot mean that we must have a neutral state, since a state must have laws, and these laws will be based on moral principles, and these moral principles will favor some worldviews and not others. It is not clear how the modern democratic state logically could really be neutral between all worldviews. It is true that it is an important part of democratic theory that no particular worldview serves as the official worldview of the state, though this fact would not rule out a particular worldview (including a religious worldview) becoming dominant if enough of its values were strongly influential in the shaping of law and culture. This understanding would also, however, support the concept of religious freedom because one would be free to practice one's religion in the expectation that the state would not promote an official religion. Nevertheless, it is inevitable that one would not be able to practice every aspect of one's religion even on this understanding because the state could outlaw a practice that one's religion regarded as moral (or *vice versa*). Of course, this applies to any worldview in the state, religious or secularist, and underscores once again the impossibility of a state being neutral in any clear sense of that term.

Finally, it is important to consider briefly before we go on to examine the views of Rawls and Habermas on these matters the notion that in a modern state there is an emphasis on the consent of the governed, along with absence of coercion. This means that, whenever an attempt is made in law to coerce or force citizens into doing something, or to stop them from doing something, we make these decisions by consent of the majority; for example, if the state passes a law allowing the practice of abortion or forbidding the practice of the death penalty. *A second aspect of consent is that there is an expectation that laws and practices that are coercive to citizens are supported with good reasons, and are arrived at only after a process of public deliberation.* These notions are meant to reflect the approach that a democracy will refrain from coercion of the citizenry unless necessary, because of the sphere of personal freedom that is part of the essence of a democratic order. The conventional wisdom of contemporary democratic theory strongly emphasizes the importance of consent—that state coercion must be supported with a convincing argument for why such coercion is justified. This point is often expressed by saying that any argument for coercion must satisfy the requirements of *public reason*, or the test of public reason. This requirement is very controversial because it raises the notoriously difficult questions of *which arguments satisfy this test, and who decides?* It is not just any old argument to which one can appeal to justify a coercive law, or an argument that some people might find convincing but that others might not—it is supposed to be an argument that satisfies stricter conditions, a special type of argument. One of the main conditions often proposed is that public reason requires that arguments begin with premises that *every reasonable person could accept*, and go from there. Obviously this condition raises many questions which we will consider in detail in what follows.

Before we look at Rawls' view, we need to clarify whether the above assumptions are assumptions of modern secular liberalism in general, or are they unique to Rawls? We can say that they are assumptions of liberal political philosophy in general, with some qualifications. I think it is true that most of those who support democracy would likely accept all of these assumptions in some form. But it would not be true to say that everyone today is a secular liberal, as some political philosophers occasionally put it. This is because although most would accept the above assumptions, *there is still considerable disagreement about how such liberal policies and assumptions are to be interpreted.* Moreover, the notion of public reason is very controversial and much debated. There is also little agreement about what a process of public reasoning can achieve. Rawls' philosophy is generally read as advocating a certain understanding of secular liberalism, in the sense that he (or perhaps especially his disciples) interprets the assumptions to mean that his own worldview, secularist liberalism, will dominate, as we have noted. But if we do not read him this way, and entertain the possibility that other worldviews, such as religious ones, could have strong influence, then we may be back where we started with regard to the problem of how to proceed in the public square. Let us recall that officially Rawls' view is not supposed to be a secularist view, even though the general upshot of his view is the exclusion of religious views for the most part from having influence on society. But he seems to think that at least officially the secularist too cannot introduce his worldview into the public square. Yet, as Thomas Nagel has honestly pointed out, it is just that when you apply Rawls' principles and adopt his general procedure, secularist positions will prevail on every issue![2] So this is why it is not accurate to classify all supporters of democracy as "secular liberals"! Many *accept* liberal democratic principles but do *not* agree that such principles must lead inevitably toward secularism when it comes to the making of laws.

Reasonable Pluralism in John Rawls

John Rawls has been a pioneering and extremely influential thinker on the problems of modern democracy and pluralism over the last fifty years. It is important that we have an overview of his general approach and of some of his main themes as we work through this part of our argument. Rawls introduced a number of interesting ideas as he developed his own theory of justice for democracy, and whether one agrees with him or not, his ideas are justifiable regarded as brilliant, extremely helpful, and as adding much insight to a very difficult set of problems. Yet, it is astonishing how much the general foundations of his theory are universally accepted among academics (especially in the U.S.). The reason for this unanimity, I suspect, is because it *favors* their own worldview, as we will see. This is a constant worry about Rawls' approach—that it is structured to privilege his own worldview, no matter how hard he tries to avoid this outcome. It is helpful to provide a brief overview of the general themes in Rawls (and Habermas), before going on to discuss in more detail the notion of public reason which features in both of their positions. We do not have space to provide a full analysis of either view, and indeed that would take us away from our present task. Our concern is not with a debate over the correct exposition of Rawls' view, but with its implications for the questions raised in this book. Rawls' theory, often referred to as "justice as fairness," is presented in a number of works, the most important of which are *A Theory of Justice* (1971) and the more recent *Political Liberalism* (1993), as well as in his later essay, "The Idea of Public Reason Revisited."[3]

Rawls begins with a point that was initially raised by some of the earlier thinkers about the nature of democracy, and which was well stated in Federalist Paper No. 10, by James Madison, that it is inevitable in a democratic society, where individuals have a great deal of freedom, that many different opinions and viewpoints (what I have been calling worldviews) will eventually emerge. Rawls' own term for worldview is "comprehensive conception of the good," and he acknowledges that many of these conceptions are *incommensurable* with each other. He makes a further very important point: that many of these worldviews will be *reasonable*, which seems to mean that even people who reject a particular worldview can appreciate how others might accept that worldview. It also means that adherents of a comprehensive conception *accept the political values latent in the culture* (comprehensive conceptions that do not do this are "unreasonable"). Rawls calls acceptance of these principles and assumptions "reasonable pluralism."[4] Of course, these claims are controversial because there could be some worldviews, or certainly sets of beliefs or parts of a worldview, that one might not regard as reasonable (even as somewhat irrational), so it is not so easy to define exactly what reasonable pluralism means. It cannot mean that we think, or should think, that *every* worldview is reasonable. However, perhaps it could be understood to mean that our fellow citizens have worldviews different from ours, which they arrived at freely, and there is at least a presumption that they have arrived at them honestly and in good faith. Moreover, they are entitled to hold them, and also entitled to some measure of respect, as citizens exercising their freedom and their reason in a free society, just as we are. As Rawls puts it, "Political liberalism counts many familiar and traditional doctrines—religious, philosophical, and moral—as reasonable even though we could not seriously entertain them for ourselves."[5] Even with this softer definition of reasonable pluralism, it will likely be difficult for it to work smoothly in actual real life cases (and, unfortunately, modern democracy, has moved far beyond this situation, where the norm is fast becoming to regard those we disagree with as *unreasonable!*).

The notion of reasonable pluralism makes an underlying appeal to another reality—that it is very difficult to arrive at objective truth in a democratic society, and so we must settle for something less than this, according to Rawls. Worldviews are not like scientific theories, where we can use the scientific method to arrive at near certain truth (or at least unanimity) in the restrictive domain of the physical. The best we can do is to support our beliefs in a reasonable way, reasoning as honestly and carefully as we can and taking account of objective evidence as much as possible, while acknowledging that others may very well look *at the same arguments and evidence*, develop them in a different direction, and come to a different conclusion. To put the point negatively, we assume that the disagreement that emerges in a democracy is not mostly due to citizens simply being irrational, uninformed, selfish, or prejudiced. So Rawls' position relies on a general skepticism about obtaining objective knowledge regarding key issues of worldviews, such as about the nature of reality, the human person, and moral and political values. Those who disagree with him about this skepticism will be outside the loop. Such skepticism will haunt his theory, since it will undermine any (objective) foundational values on which his theory may rely. Rawlsian liberalism struggles constantly with the fact that, according to its own lights, others may question any such values (or, more accurately, *a particular interpretation* of them), and also be regarded as reasonable. These considerations are also extremely relevant when conducting arguments in the public square with our fellow citizens according to the procedure of "public reason," as we will see.

Rawls believes that the job of political philosophers is to seek a way to accommodate as many as possible of the values and views about which citizens disagree. He develops this position by suggesting that what we need is an agreed-upon structure or a procedure for regulating political and moral disputes. He proposes an ingenious way of arriving at this procedure. He argues that we can seek the principles for the regulation of public discourse not from within the comprehensive conceptions, but from *within our (shared) political culture*. He suggests that the political culture of a liberal democratic state has principles latent within it that most people accept, and that carry implications for how public deliberation should be conducted. These principles can be made explicit and developed, and then become part of what he calls an "overlapping consensus." Rawls refers to these shared values as a "political conception of justice"; it is one which is latent in our Western democratic culture, accepted in some form by all. Members of society can hold different, and conflicting, comprehensive worldviews, and yet, he believes, *still agree* to the political conception which is the foundation of the basic structure. What does the political conception consist of? He emphasizes the foundational values for dealing with disputes that arise in a pluralist society: the key notions are the *freedom* and *equality* of citizens, and a willingness to have *reasonable* standards of public discourse, consistent with freedom and equality.[6] This seems to mean that a reasonable citizen is willing to provide arguments that he thinks others could reasonably accept from their perspective—this is fair and respects others as free and equal; people are also entitled therefore because of the presumption of freedom to good reasons for the exercise of coercive power over them. So to be reasonable in Rawls' sense seems to involve both a commitment to the latent political values, and to *a certain way of arguing* in public deliberation, and perhaps the latter is required by the former.[7]

Of course, it would have to be spelled out more clearly what these abstract values mean, and how they are to function in the actual process of reasoning involved in public debates (a topic we will return to in detail). But Rawls argues that the political conception is not just to be regarded as what he calls a *modus vivendi*, a practical compromise that people with different comprehensive conceptions might agree to for the sake of living in harmony in society, but which they are uneasy about, and do not really support. Instead, these values are latent in democratic political culture, and all (reasonable) worldviews in a particular society can therefore be said to agree to them. So the question of what they mean in the concrete, and how they function in actual public disputes, is a crucial one. Rawls tries to develop a defensible way of thinking about these matters in his fascinating theory that is designed to alleviate the problem of worldview pluralism.

With regard to the question of how the values are justified, one wonders if Rawls is simply saying that these values are part of our culture, and so this makes them acceptable (not necessarily true) because we are all members of the same political culture, a view that sounds a bit like cultural relativism? Rawls describes the political conception as "freestanding" by which he means that it is not presented as a part of, nor derived from, any worldview or comprehensive conception of the good (including Rawls' own). However, it could be justified by appeal to principles and values that are in fact part of many comprehensive doctrines. He is undoubtedly right that most people in modern democracies would accept in the abstract most of the values he lists as making up the political conception of justice. He goes on to suggest that it is a consequence of the political conception that we must offer "public reasons" when taking part in discussions and disputes in the public square; we should not offer reasons that appeal to or rely only on the truth of our comprehensive conceptions (our worldviews). What is a public reason? We will return to this topic in greater detail in the next section, but for now we can say that any argument we present should appeal to reasons that we sincerely believe all other citizens might reasonably accept. While this is still extremely vague, it does lead to what has become a core principle of liberal political philosophy: that public reason will not normally include arguments that come from comprehensives conceptions of the good *that are religious in nature.*

Rawls himself is not so much concerned with how public reason works, or in the role of religion in a pluralist society, though his theory relies crucially on a conception of public reason being particularized and implemented, and it also clearly has serious implications for religious worldviews in a democracy. He is primarily interested in how principles that relate to the issue of *justice* in such a society can be arrived at using his method. To develop this part of the theory, he introduces a very clever device called the "original position," a kind of imaginary bargaining conversation, where all of the participants in society voluntarily place themselves behind a "veil of ignorance." Citizens are conceived first as having two moral powers: "a capacity for a sense of justice and for a conception of the good."[8] Citizens then engage in a conversation designed to arrive at the principles of justice which will be used to govern and regulate society. Due to the veil of ignorance, citizens (or perhaps representatives of various worldviews) in the original position do not know their talents and abilities, social class, race, gender, financial position, level of education, nor, most significantly, their comprehensive view of the good. This starting point is fair and just because one is more likely to agree to principles that benefit everyone, and that we can all regard as fair and reasonable, if one bargains from this position, so argues Rawls. In this way, the notions of freedom and equality, and of reasonableness, are latent in the original position, but this is acceptable because these values are also latent in the political culture (and we are presumed to all agree with these values).

Under these circumstances, Rawls believes we would agree to two principles. First, that each person has an equal claim to a fully adequate scheme of equal basic liberties and rights, which is compatible with the same scheme for all (roughly corresponding to the scheme in the U.S. Bill of Rights); second, that social and economic inequalities would have to satisfy two conditions; one, they are to be attached to positions and offices open to all under conditions of fair equality of opportunity; and two, they are to be to the greatest benefit of the least advantaged members of society (this is called the difference principle). Although, this part of Rawls' theory is very original, of great interest, and has generated extensive discussion, it is not our concern here. As noted above, most of the discussion about Rawls has tended to accept his starting position and his understanding of reasonable pluralism, and the other assumptions, and to focus on whether the original position would work, whether it is fair to all citizens, whether we would agree to the principles of justice that emerge from it, whether they are fair, and so forth. However, our concern is not with the second theme concerning issues of social justice or fair distribution of goods, but the first concerning the political values that we all accept and that make up the political conception of justice. Rawls tells us that the scheme of latent political values is similar to values found in the founding documents of American democracy (and indeed most democracies). These include the foundational values of justice, freedom, a scheme of equal basic rights, ideals concerning the distribution of income, a just system of taxation, and so forth.[9] Those who live in a democratic system accept these values, at least as stated abstractly (we do not all agree about what they mean, or how they are to be applied, in concrete cases). But acceptance of such values is what Rawls means by saying that democratic society is based on fair terms of cooperation, where citizens understand themselves as free and equal citizens, where they accept "reasonable pluralism," and where they recognize that coercion, especially in law, should be justified with "good reasons."

RAWLS AND HABERMAS ON PUBLIC REASON

Before we look at Rawls and Habermas on public reason, we should say a little about what we mean by reason itself, since it is such a crucial notion. We are using the term in its ordinary common sense meaning, with some qualifications. We can make a number of points that it is good to always keep in mind. First, reason is to be understood as thinking in a logical way, as trying to be objective, as seeking good arguments, as willing to consider evidence, as willing to listen to constructive criticism and analysis of one's views. A good argument is an argument where the premises and case being made show good support for (not necessarily prove) the conclusion, and is also one that takes serious account of any available evidence that is germane to a topic. Second, our position is that reason understood in this sense is objective, and that all human beings should strive to be reasonable, especially when it comes to discussing questions of great importance, such as those concerning worldview disagreements. (Philosophers have debated whether or not this second point is true, as we saw in our earlier discussions of anti-realism and postmodernism, and there are even arguments among Rawls' followers about whether the process of reasoning can be objective, but we will take the position here that *reason is an objective part of human nature*. Rawls himself identifies judgment, principles of inference, rules of evidence, along with standards of correctness and criteria of justification as belonging to "common human reasoning."[10]) Third, in a pluralist context this means that one should offer arguments in a public forum for one's conclusions in an attempt to persuade others of their truth or reasonability.

Fourth, this approach to reason means that we should make a distinction between *justification* and *persuasion* in the sense that, from a logical point of view, an argument that is reasonable and well justified might not persuade everyone! This may be because the audience is unreasonable, but it might also be because *there is room for disagreement* about the structure of the argument and the appraisal of the evidence. Many arguments, debates about evidence and what the evidence shows, and judgments about what we can plausibly believe, seem to fall into a gray area between the reasonable and the unreasonable. Similarly, an argument could persuade people, even though from an objective point of view it might not be reasonable or justified. (Which arguments would fall into this category?; a question that once again highlights the vexing problem of disagreement in pluralist democracy.) Fifth, as we noted in Chap. 2, all of this means that although I may hold that many of my views are objectively true, I would have to acknowledge that at least in some cases I could be wrong, but I would still advocate my beliefs politically because I believe they are true. So individuals will accept a certain amount of fallibilism, but do not fall into relativism or skepticism. Sixth, our earlier points raise another question: is there any particular way then that we should reason in the public square in a liberal democracy? Rawls and Habermas have a special interest in this question.

From the point of view of pluralism, and the clash of worldviews in a democratic context, and so the urgency for dialogue, discussion, debate, and perhaps cooperation between worldviews, one of the most interesting features of Rawls' view is the notion of public reason. It is an important notion that is supposed to address directly the problem of worldview pluralism—the clash of incommensurable worldviews in the modern democratic state—and help toward a solution that would allow us to make progress and reach some kind of harmony. Aware of the potential for conflict and severe disagreement, Rawls argues that when we wish to propose laws that are based on our worldview, values, and philosophy of life (our comprehensive conception of the good), we are required to present arguments in public to support our position. Such arguments must be based on public reason. The idea of public reason is thought to go back to such thinkers in the democratic tradition as Hobbes, Locke, and Kant, though it is not easy to discern the notion in their work. Perhaps Kant's attempt to derive moral principles from a process of pure reasoning might come closest, and one of the central ideas behind Kant's categorical imperative—treating others the way I would like to be treated myself—seems to play a large role in liberal anxiety about people asserting their worldview beliefs at the political level. Nevertheless, the idea has become a central one in modern political theory.

Rawls explains that public reason is public in three ways: "as the reason of citizens as such, it is the reason of the public; its subject is the good of the public and matters of fundamental justice; and its nature and content is public, being given by the ideals and principles expressed by society's conception of political justice, and conducted open to view on that basis."[11] The requirements of public reason, he adds, "do not apply to all political questions but only to those involving what we may call 'constitutional essentials' and questions of basic justice."[12] The former include questions relating to the structure and running of the government, and the second refers to the basic rights of citizens such as the right to vote, freedom of conscience, thought, and association (what Rawls often refers to as "our basic rights and liberties"). While this criterion is obviously a very controversial one, and raises as many questions as it answers, Rawls has particularly in mind instances of coercive legislation, such as laws restricting abortion, an appropriate example to use to illustrate his view, and also to bring out some of the difficulties with it. Public reason applies to politicians, legislators, judges, candidates for office, and citizens who wish to participate in debate concerning matters of basic justice and constitutional essentials.[13] (Recall that matters of basic justice are supposed to be based on the intuitive ideas of political liberalism latent in the culture, and not on Rawls' own view of what basic justice involves, a distinction political liberalism has never been able to maintain.)

While we will subject the notion of public reason to a more detailed analysis in the next chapter, we need to bring out the main meaning here: that if one wishes the citizenry to follow rules and laws, then one must provide a justification for this coercion. But it has to be a special kind of justification—Rawls' claim is that it must be based on a form of argument that reasonable people would assent to in a liberal democratic society. A liberal democratic society, let us recall, is one that is committed to the basic liberal political values, that assumes that people are free to come up with their own views, and one where, if we wish to coerce people into a certain view or path (e.g., banning gun ownership), we should give them reasons or justification for doing so. The obvious problem, of course, is that we might offer people reasons that we think are reasonable, but nevertheless they might reject these reasons. Does this then count as a good justification—if I present to you what I sincerely think is a good justification for a position but you reject it? We recognize also that most legislation will be coercive in some way, so Rawls is hardly saying that we cannot pass any legislation until everyone is convinced of its rationality and thereby consents to it—this would be an impossibly high and impractical bar to the running of society.

Rawls elaborates by suggesting that one should not base one's justification on one's comprehensive conception of the good, because this is likely to be rejected by others in a pluralist society, and so appeal to it would lead to conflict immediately.[14] In making this argument, he seems to have in mind in particular *religious* comprehensive conceptions of the good. He later modifies his view to say that perhaps one could base a public argument initially on a religious comprehensive conception, as long as one was prepared later to justify the view by appeal to public reason (this is called the "proviso"), with the implication being that if one could not do this, then the argument would be illegitimate, and with the further implication that most religious arguments cannot meet this test.[15] So the questions whether we should accept the notion of public reason, and also *how it would work* in terms of deciding whether a particular argument for a particular conclusion met its "test," are obviously crucial ones. This general approach led to the frequent accusation that his proposal discriminates against religious worldviews, and is "rigged" to favor secularist worldviews, concerns that we will come back to later.[16] Rawls adds that "As far as possible the knowledge and ways of reasoning that ground our affirming the principles of justice and their application to constitutional essentials and basic justice are to rest on the plain truths now widely accepted, or available, to citizens generally."[17] One problem with Rawls' use of the notion of public reason, one common to many subsequent discussions of the topic, is that he never considers clear and detailed examples to illustrate how the notion is to be applied.

Let us consider the example of abortion to help illustrate Rawls' interesting proposal. According to Rawls' conception of public reason, one should *not* present the following type of argument to support the view that abortion is immoral and should be illegal in a democratic society: an innocent human life has an absolute value because it has a soul, the embryo has a soul, therefore the embryo has an absolute value…and so the practice of abortion is wrong, and should be illegal. Of course, a citizen could introduce an argument of this sort because she or he would have a right to freedom of expression, so Rawls would not outlaw it, but he is saying that one *should not* introduce this argument into public discourse. Why not? The reason is because a fundamental part of the argument involves the claim that the embryo has a *soul*. The problem with this claim is that it relies on the truth of a religious view of reality. What is problematic with relying on the truth of a religious view of reality? The difficulty seems to lie in the fact that it is a view rejected by some citizens. It also seems to be an essential part of Rawls' position that their rejection of this view is reasonable (this is what reasonable pluralism means). So if we wish to argue against abortion, we would need to give an argument that did not rely on any appeal to controversial claims (from the point of view of disagreement in a pluralist society) about the soul.

It would be acceptable to Rawls to reframe this argument by appealing to considerations other than the existence of the soul to support the claim that the embryo has value; for example, to the fact that the embryo has value by virtue of being a member of the human species, or because of its special properties (such as a unique DNA and consciousness), or potential properties, and so forth. What is different about this second argument? It seems to be based on premises that all people in society could rationally accept. But is it an argument that everyone *would* accept? No; so presenting an argument that appeals to premises that are acceptable to all rational people does not mean that all rational people actually accept the conclusion of the argument. What does it mean then? It is open to a number of interpretations but it seems to mean for Rawls that *everyone starts from the same place, even if all do not arrive at the same conclusion*. Working through several examples, we will explore this matter fully in the next chapter. Here, we simply wish to get an idea of the interesting notion of public reason, and to show that it does seem to be framed to discriminate against religious views and to favor secularist views, in the sense that some worldviews (i.e., religious ones) appear to face restrictions that others do not face (i.e., secularist ones).

A similar idea is developed by Jurgen Habermas. While Rawls is writing primarily from an American perspective, Habermas approaches the topic from a European perspective. Impressed by the model of the European Union, he addresses a number of issues in his complex body of work, including the nature of democracy, international politics, pluralism, and the topic in which we are interested—the notion of how arguments are to be conducted today in the public square, assuming pluralism and a democratic context.[18] There is a strong Marxist influence evident in Habermas' ideas, especially in his early work, expressed in his concern that people should be able to discuss ideas free from economic or social pressures, that we should treat each other as equals, and try to reach a consensus. To this end, he adopted a pragmatic approach rather than what we might call a metaphysical approach to what public argument could achieve. He was initially less interested in whether public discourse can arrive at *truth*, understood as corresponding to external reality, and more in whether it can arrive at *consensus*, reaching tentative conclusions to which all citizens in a public discussion could assent. Though, in his later career he refined his view to address more directly the question of truth.

Habermas devoted a good deal of time to developing the circumstances and conditions for the type of discourse that should characterize public, political discussion. He developed initially a view known as the ideal speech situation, but modified it over the course of his work. The details of his very complex approach would take us too far afield, but the basic idea is that he attempts to conceive of the conditions for public discourse as it would occur ideally, if these conditions were met, rather than of how it might actually occur in a specific concrete situation, under less than ideal conditions. Habermas goes on to propose what he calls *the discourse principle*: this states that a law or principle is valid only if all of those affected by it would accept it after a reasonable discourse; as Habermas puts it, only "those action norms are valid to which all possibly affected persons could agree as participants in rational discourse."[19] This discourse principle carries the idea that people must consent to a law, for example, that is to be imposed on them, so it applies to disputes involving worldview topics.

Public discourse applies, Habermas argues, to the sphere of what he calls "communicative action." This is where people engage in rational discourse with the aim of persuading others of the truth of their position, with the hope of getting others to adopt it. Because of the fractious nature of modern pluralism, Habermas thought that the more practical aim of most discourse was consensus, since this was more realistic to achieve. He distinguishes communicative action from strategic action; the latter describes the position of various interest groups and action committees that operate in politics, such as environmentalist groups, who hold a non-negotiable political position, and whose members are not generally interested in dialogue or consensus.[20] Of course, it is not easy to keep the line clear between the two types of discourse. This problem draws attention once again to the complexities of modern pluralism, and to the care we must exercise in trying to frame procedures and develop criteria by which to regulate public argument, and the all too real danger of rigging the debate in favor of (and against) certain views.

Although both Rawls' and Habermas' views are often vaguely stated and too abstract to give much guidance for how a public debate would actually be carried out in practice, Habermas does offer a few practical guidelines. He argues that in any public discourse between parties in a pluralist setting, for instance, one should presume that the speakers are sincere, that there is some kind of objective truth, and that we want to respect each other as mutual participants (so there is a moral dimension to an intersubjective dialogue). He notes also that the difficulty often arises because it is not possible to give deductive or certain arguments that settle definitively most of the issues that are in dispute between worldviews. The conclusions of arguments often go further than the premises; some claims are based on a preponderance of evidence and argument that require one's best rational judgment. The difficulty is that different individuals judge the same evidence and arguments differently, and this allows for a subjective element, which we must take into account, while trying to avoid any kind of relativism. This has turned out to be an almost insuperable problem for pluralism and is one of the reasons that both Habermas' and especially Rawls' views seem to presuppose a kind of skepticism about knowledge in general.

Nevertheless, when these thinkers say that an argument should be submitted to the test of public reason they mean that, as Habermas puts it, we should have a dialectical process of reasoning. This is where one subjects one's views to the test of public debate, where this debate involves presenting one's case in a rational way, listening to objections, engaging in a critical analysis of the evidence, and so forth. Habermas also lays out some sensible conditions to help lead toward true consensus: these include the provisions that no one who is capable of making a relevant contribution has been excluded from the discourse, all participants have an equal voice, are free to present their honest opinion without deception or self-deception, and that there are no sources of coercion built into the process and procedures of discourse. Those who contribute to public discourse should also be consistent, including using terminology consistently, sincere, and are free to discuss any topic.[21] These conditions can be used also to *assess* public arguments, which, he correctly observes, are often actually conducted in far from perfect circumstances (indeed, most of his conditions are routinely flouted in contemporary democratic discourse, especially in the two areas where they seem most essential, politics and the media).[22]

In general, many of these points seem sensible guidelines for how to conduct public arguments between people who hold different and incommensurable worldviews. We will see in the next chapter, however, that they are far from easy to apply in practice, due to difficulties of both interpretation and overall justification. Before that, however, I wish to provide an overview of how this account of public reason, which has become widely accepted among contemporary political philosophers, has been used as the foundation for the exclusion of religious worldviews from the public square in a secular liberal democracy.

Audi on Excluding Religious Views from Democratic Politics

The Rawlsian understanding of the notion of public reason has become a dominant way of thinking about political discussion in a pluralist context in a modern democracy. It is especially welcomed and adopted by secularists and by liberal religious believers. At least in Western countries, as mentioned in Chap. 5, we can usefully divide worldviews into three groups, especially with regard to the topic of whether religious worldviews should have a role in politics. Working for simplicity sake with the example of Christianity, the first group would be made up of traditional Christians, which we understand as including those who accept most of the traditional teachings of Christianity, including on moral issues. The second group would be liberal Christians who, though still religious believers, reject many of the traditional teachings of Christianity, especially on moral issues. The third group would be secularists (who are also usually hostile to religion).

We should make two additional points of clarification. First, religious believers in the first two groups would not always or simply appeal to the Bible as an authoritative text to justify their views on various issues; they will also appeal to philosophical and theological arguments, or rely on the tradition of such arguments (if one is unable to present such arguments oneself). (We drew attention to the philosophical and theological tradition in Chap. 5.) Second, it is, however, true that many in the second group and many in the third group *will almost always assume or adopt the working approach* that the views of those in the first group are based on an unacceptable and simplistic appeal to biblical or church authority. Either out of ignorance or as a deliberate tactic, they will rarely acknowledge any other kind of argument that might be used to support the positions of those in the first group (this is even true in the scholarly literature on the topic of public reason and justification, as we will see in the next chapter). While we are working with Christianity here as an example, and while this overview of different views describes the situation in some Western countries quite well, it would also I think fit with religious and secularist worldview disputes in non-western countries and would even fit, *mutatis mutandis*, with other religions that have a significant presence in some Western countries, such as Islam.

Given this classification of different views, the Rawlsian approach has very strong appeal to those in the second and third groups. This is because it forbids the introduction of religious views in public arguments, and so treats the views of those in the second and especially the third groups as presumptive. It also justifies this exclusion by arguing that the views from the first group *fail the test of public reason*—because these views are based on arguments that other people could not reasonably accept. This is why it can be tempting to portray *all* arguments that support religious views one objects to as failing the test of public reason; it is also why many liberal religious believers and secularists in Western political culture are so enamored of Rawls' general approach. (It is rare to find a religious believer and follower of Rawls who wishes to invoke the Rawlsian approach *to restrict his own strongly held religious beliefs* from having political influence; he is usually concerned with restricting the political influence of religious beliefs with which he disagrees. Even if a religious believer who is a strong advocate of the Rawlsian approach does accept that his own religious beliefs are also restricted, it is usually the case that the end result is the one he seeks—his own *moral and political views* are still the ones that get to prevail in public policy.)

While many religious believers, both traditional and liberal, would still have reservations about the Rawlsian approach, it has a very strong appeal to secularists, especially those that reject religious belief altogether. This group is greatly attracted to liberal democracy of the Rawlsian variety because it gives them a way to exclude and marginalize religion from culture without the necessity of having to engage religious believers in public deliberation. It can hide behind the argument that the liberal procedure is neutral and is based on values that we all share, values that just so happen to entail the conclusion that religious views should have no place in politics. I suggest, however, that secularists in this camp nearly always work with caricatures of religion, are ignorant of the philosophical case for religious belief, and would just as soon be rid of it if possible. Defining public reason is hard enough, but in the present climate of a difficult pluralism it is simply risible to believe that all of these thinkers have made an assessment of the religious worldview on the basis of evidence and argument, and have found it wanting in a rational sense! It is much more likely in this age of relativism and anti-realism that they have simply rejected the religious worldview and wish to find a rationalization for this rejection at the political, as well as at the individual, level. Nevertheless, I don't insist on this point. We can simply note it as a likely motivation, and work with the secular liberal approach at face value. Yet, there is a sense in which the whole idea of reasonable pluralism may be more hospitable to religion, despite the fact that it has been mainly developed in a way that is hostile to it. This is because if applied fairly it would give religious views that are presented in a rational way—*that satisfy the test of public reason*—a place at the table, as we will see later in our discussion. So from this perspective, the concept of public reason *can* be—even though it usually has not been so interpreted—a positive one for religious people.

I think we can place thinkers like Rawls, Dworkin, Nagel, Bruce Ackerman, and others, into the third category—those who reject religion altogether and wish to keep it out of the public square, or seriously reduce its influence, contain it, as it were, thereby opening the way for the secularist worldview to dominate.[23] But the philosopher whose views I wish to consider here, Robert Audi, belongs to the second category above. Audi is one of those thinkers who has discussed the issue of religion in public life in some detail and who has worked out a sophisticated and thorough position. It is a position I reject, but I think a consideration of it will be very helpful, and will set us up well for our discussion in the next chapter.

Audi is an American philosopher and a religious person who seems to want to restrict certain religious views from public square deliberations. Indeed, the practical effect of his view would likely be to exclude millions of citizens from the process of public deliberation in U.S. society. He opens his discussion with a particular concern about what he describes as religious fundamentalism and the situation in contemporary American society, in particular. Here, he appears to have in mind certain evangelical Christian groups whose main justification for their political positions is an appeal to biblical revelation, and who wish to make illegal such practices as abortion and physician-assisted suicide, practices Audi believes should be legal. We will keep these kinds of examples in mind throughout because they help to highlight the differences between positions very clearly. Audi seems to think that it is fairly obvious that the human embryo is not entitled to protection in law and so he develops a sophisticated and somewhat convoluted argument to attempt to restrict religious views from the debate, especially those that come to a different position on the issues of the day than he does. In a way, he could be said to adopt a typical liberal approach: he believes that a certain type of religious approach is wrongheaded, cannot be defended according to the standards of reason (which may be a roundabout way of saying that it is irrational), and so devises a system, heavily under the influence of Rawls, to restrict it in the public arena. His task then is to show why the views of religious believers have no place in democratic politics without it simply being a matter of him *not agreeing with* their political conclusions, and so just another way of *privileging his own political views* and ensuring that they get to shape society.

Audi appeals to the notion of "secular reason" in his thinking on this matter. This is not quite the same thing as public reason, which he believes can be corrupted, or distorted, and is often far from perfectly applied in real life. Secular reason is higher-level reasoning, a form of reasoning that is envisaged as operating with no prejudices, biases, or imperfections. As long as one defines public reason in the same way (as Rawls and Habermas are often inclined to do—to consider it in a more idealized form, rather than in an actual form in a concrete situation of disagreement), then secular reason and public reason can be taken to be the same.[24] Audi is particularly worried about situations of legal coercion—where laws are passed that coerce people in the state into some activity, for example, if abortion or smoking were outlawed. His view is that all of those subject to the coercion must assent to it, and this means that they must be presented with adequate secular reasons that they find persuasive. This sounds like a vague, and indeed unrealistically high, bar but Audi is clear that it will *not* include religious reasons because these are not persuasive to all citizens.

Audi is very helpful and much clearer that Rawlsians are about which reasons are not acceptable. He rules out arguments based on the following sources: scriptural revelation (such as the Bible); religious authority (such as a particular Church, the Pope, or an influential religious leader); private religious experiences; and religious traditions (such as the Christian tradition).[25] (Like us, Audi focuses on the Christian tradition, but his argument applies to any religion operating in a democratic context.) His point is that arguments based on any of these sources will not be persuasive to people from other worldviews; for example, a secularist would not be persuaded by an argument that appealed mainly to Biblical revelation. If a religious believer were to object that he *should* be persuaded by such an argument, that the reason he is not persuaded is because he is misguided, uninformed, morally blind, and so on, Audi asks how the religious believer would like it if a similar criterion was used to coerce him into activity he did not agree with?

While there is something to this argument in a free society, and we will come back to it later, Audi offers two criteria that an argument must satisfy in order to be introduced legitimately into the public square, the principle of secular rationale and the principle of secular motivation.[26] The principle of secular rationale proposes that anyone who introduces a religious argument into politics must also have an adequate secular rationale for it, and must present this rationale in a public argument. This would be an entirely secular argument to support a position. What kind of argument is that? It is an argument that appeals to reason, and argument and evidence in a familiar sense, and that *does not appeal to religious content in its premises*. So an argument against abortion could not appeal to the Bible or Christian tradition as part of its premises, since these sources of justification are rejected by others in a pluralist society. It must appeal only to reason, to premises and evidence that are available to and accepted by everyone. As Audi puts it: adequate reasons must be "in a certain way accessible to rational adults…appraisable by them through natural reason in the light of facts."[27]

What if a religious believer holds that abortion should be illegal because of a scriptural argument but realizes that it is best from a pragmatic point of view to present the type of secular argument Audi calls for while engaged in a public exchange in a pluralist context? In this case the religious person may believe that the secular argument is sufficiently motivational for some, say for secular liberals, even though she does not find it motivational herself. (Secularists could offer religious people similar religious justifications for their {secularist} views that they do not themselves find persuasive, but that they think the religious believers might find persuasive.) But Audi does not think this is adequate. He introduces the principle of secular motivation as a stricter check on sinister religious arguments working their way insidiously into politics! This principle stipulates that the person presenting the argument must find the secular argument convincing themselves; they must agree that the secular argument by itself provides adequate justification for their position, and not just be developing it for pragmatic purposes in the context of a difficult and contentious public discussion. So, for example, if a person thinks that the reason abortion is wrong is because the embryo has a soul (an appeal to religious content, according to Audi, and so not allowed) but decided to present the argument publicly by saying that abortion is wrong because it is the killing of an innocent human being (and not mention the soul, the real reason she thinks innocent human life has great value), this would fail the principle of secular motivation.

Audi seems to think that the latter argument is much weaker if we leave out the premise about the soul and just argue that the embryo is an innocent human life, an issue he thinks reasonable people can disagree over. This is similar to Rawls' "proviso" (noted above) where the religious arguments must be translated into secular arguments, and if one can do this the secular arguments are all that is necessary, and if one cannot, the religious arguments by themselves are not legitimate. This may be a case of his own moral views influencing the debate too much. He does not really consider carefully cases where (i) a person argues for the overall rationality of religious belief, and then applies it to various moral and legal issues—this kind of argument would appear to satisfy the principle of secular rationale, and (ii) cases involving a purely secular argument *against* supporting the legalization of abortion. There is also the position (iii) that simply rejects the two criteria outright on the grounds that no consistent, coherent account of secular reasoning can be given that does not *pre-judge* the issue being debated. We will come back to all three of these fascinating scenarios in our detailed development of the notion of public reason in the next chapter.

Audi recognizes that one is free in a democracy to advocate any argument one wishes in public debate, since this is what it means to have freedom of thought and expression, something liberal thinkers in particular have usually interpreted in an absolutist sense, as we have been arguing. So there would be something incongruous about holding this view and then discouraging Catholic bishops, for instance, from putting out a statement calling for the government to improve programs to alleviate poverty because each person is a child of God, and it is part of the divine moral order that we are our brother's keeper. Audi is aware that many will find his restrictions on religious views illiberal and undemocratic. So, he acknowledges that while religious believers are free—legally, because they enjoy freedom of expression—to present any public argument they wish, they *should not* (à la Rawls), however, present arguments that do not satisfy his two criteria. In other words, they are acting as bad citizens if they present purely religious arguments on contentious issues because they would not be treating their fellow citizens the way they should be treating them in a democratic context.[28] So even though they can present such arguments from a legal point of view, morally they *should* not do so, according to Audi. Despite holding moral and political views like everyone else, they should hold their tongues in public.[29] The irony of course is that a public deliberation dominated by purely secular arguments will settle nothing, since people disagree about secular arguments as well. So it appears that the restriction on religious arguments does not help. It ends up discriminating against religious worldviews, but does not settle any issues. It seems to be just a way of keeping religion out of politics, and is a tactic that will end up promoting secularism, and many secular liberals do interpret it this way. That is to say, they think that if one cannot present religious arguments for abortion, then automatically abortion must be made legal.

Audi notes that his view is different from Rawls' because Rawls wishes to keep comprehensive views out of the public debate, and allows only an appeal to the "overlapping consensus" of shared values. Audi's view does allow us to bring our comprehensive views into the public square debate (including religious views), as long as one adheres to his two principles, but in practice both views are very much the same. On Rawls' view the "overlapping consensus" has the consequence that one should not bring arguments taken from one's comprehensive religious views into the public square, and on Audi's view one will not need the religious arguments because one is required to have adequate secular argument and motivation. This is why we must be careful when appealing to any notion of shared values to ensure that they are not defined in such a way as to settle in advance substantive foundational, moral, and political questions that are disputed by the various worldviews in our pluralist society. We will consider this and other key issues in our next chapter, where we subject the liberal position to a more detailed critical analysis, illustrating with a more extensive consideration of practical examples of public debate.

Notes

1. Historian Michael Burleigh has noted that secularists have quite a history of hostility to religious freedom; see his *Sacred Causes: The Clash of Religion and Politics* (New York: Harper Perennial, 2007).
2. See Thomas Nagel, "Moral Conflict and Political Legitimacy," *Philosophy and Public Affairs*, Vol. 16, 3 (Summer 1987), p. 217.
3. Along with works already mentioned, see John Rawls, "The Idea of Public Reason Revisited," *The University of Chicago Law Review*, Vol. 64 (Summer 1997), No. 3, pp. 765–807. See also, Thomas Pogge, *John Rawls: His Life and Theory of Justice* (New York: Oxford U.P., 2007).
4. Rawls sometimes distinguishes between "the rational" and "the reasonable," though the distinction is unclear in his work. The basic idea seems to be that being rational could be used to describe taking a logical approach to advancing my own self-interest and my own worldview, whereas being reasonable seems to require that I take others into consideration with regard to public policy matters, and involves a recognition of "reasonable pluralism." In our discussion, we shall ignore this distinction and use the

terms synonymously to refer to their ordinary, common sense meaning; see *Political Liberalism*, pp. 48–54.
5. John Rawls, ibid., pp. 59–60.
6. See ibid., pp. 3–46.
7. I am following James W. Boettcher's excellent analysis in his "What is Reasonableness?," *Philosophy and Social Criticism*, Vo. 30 (5–6), pp. 597–621; see also Paul Weithman, *Rawls, Political Liberalism and Reasonable Faith* (New York: Cambridge U.P., 2016).
8. Rawls, *Political Liberalism*, p. 19.
9. See, Rawls, "The Ideal of Public Reason Revisited," p. 776.
10. See Rawls, *Political Liberalism*, p. 220.
11. Ibid., p. 213; see also, pp. 212–254.
12. Ibid., p. 214.
13. See Rawls, "Reply to Habermas," *Journal of Philosophy*, Vol. 92 (3) 1995, p. 140.
14. See Rawls, *Political Liberalism*, pp. 224–225.
15. See his "The Idea of Public Reason Revisited," p. 776, where he refers to the example of Martin Luther King, Jr. Rawls thinks King could have given a secular argument for civil rights instead of a religious argument, even though he did not in fact do so. We discuss King's argument in detail in Chap. 9.
16. See Marilyn Friedman, "John Rawls and the Political Coercion of Unreasonable People," in Victoria Davion and Clark Wolf (eds.), *The Idea of Political Liberalism* (New York: Rowman and Littlefield, 2000), pp. 16–33; also Miriam Galston, "Rawlsian Dualism and the Autonomy of Political Thought," *Columbia Law Review* 94, 6 (October 1994), pp. 1842–1859.
17. Rawls, *Political Liberalism*, p. 225.
18. Habermas' main works on these matters are: *Moral Consciousness and Communicative Action* (Cambridge, MA: MIT Press, 2001); *Between Facts and Norms* (Boston, MA: MIT Press, 1996).
19. Habermas, *Between Facts and Norms*, p. 107.
20. See Jurgen Habermas, *Moral Consciousness and Communicative Action*, p. 58.
21. See Habermas, ibid., pp. 65ff.
22. See also Iris Young, *Inclusion and Democracy* (New York: Oxford U.P., 2000), who argues that there is a worry that social power can sometimes prevail over reason, and that deliberation should include more than reason.
23. In addition to the thinkers whose work we have already referred to, see Bruce Ackerman, *Social Justice in the Liberal State* (New Haven, CT.: Yale U.P., 1980).

24. Rawls rejects any identification of public reason with secular reason, but his argument is confusing. He defines secular reason, not as a particular form or way of reasoning, but as a process that reasons to *secularist* conclusions, and because (understood this way) it appeals to a (secularist) comprehensive conception of the good, it is not appropriate in public argument. Perhaps this is just a matter of terminology, but he seems here to conflate a *form* of arguing with the *conclusions* to which one argues. For more on this latter distinction, see our next chapter.
25. See Robert Audi, *Religious Commitment and Secular Reason* (Cambridge: Cambridge U.P., 2000), pp. 116ff.
26. See ibid., pp. 86–100.
27. See Robert Audi, *Democratic Authority and the Separation of Church and State* (New York: Oxford U.P., 2011), p. 70; also, *Religious Commitment and Secular Reason*, p. 123.
28. Audi attempted to nuance his view in response to objections, but the practical result of his view remains the same; see his *Democratic Authority and the Separation of Church and State*, p. 65; p. 89.
29. One might even argue that a logical consequence of such a view is that religious believers should be strongly discouraged from *voting*, especially if they are inclined to vote based on their religious beliefs! If one should not bring one's religious beliefs into public deliberations, it is not such a big step to suggest that perhaps religious people should not vote either. Of course, discouraging people from voting would violate a basic principle of democracy, but then so does preventing a certain type of view from contributing to public debate. Just as secular liberalism attempts a rationale for the latter exclusion, so perhaps it could do the same for the former.

PART III

Reasonable Worldviews and Public Deliberation: The Way Ahead

CHAPTER 8

Public Reason

The notion of public reason is obviously crucial in modern political theory as it tries to come to terms with pluralism. It likely should play some role in political deliberation in a pluralist democracy, if all is not assumed to be lost as society becomes more splintered. In this chapter, we will examine the concept carefully in order to further our understanding of how it should be applied, and whether it can work as an effective strategy in contemporary democratic society. We will see that although there is something to be said for the notion, it also faces vexing problems of interpretation and of application, and even concerning whether it has any clear sense. There is, moreover, the crucial question as to whether participants should accept the notion as a guiding procedure for public deliberation. Even though there is an extensive literature on the concept of public reason, there is little agreement on three main questions provoked by the notion: what does it mean or how is it understood; how is it supposed to work in actual concrete cases; and why should anyone agree to abide by it? Sorting through every view on this topic would require a book-length study, but it is unnecessary for us to get bogged down in exhaustive analysis of this kind, analysis that risks losing the meaning of the concept in a thicket of (tedious) minutiae (an unfortunate tendency in some areas of contemporary philosophical research). We are primarily interested in where the idea would lead us in democratic deliberation in a pluralist setting.

Many people are quite suspicious of Rawls' notion of reasonable pluralism. Let us recall that this is the idea that people hold different worldviews, with irreconcilable positions on matters of culture, law, and society, and yet somehow all or most of these views can be said to be *reasonable*. This means that not only do I regard my own worldview as reasonable, but it also seems to mean that I must regard my neighbor's worldview as reasonable, even though it is different than, and often opposed to, mine. An obvious problem with this proposal is that I may not regard my neighbor's worldview as reasonable! We should distinguish between regarding my neighbor's worldview as reasonable and regarding it as true. It probably makes sense to say that I might recognize a worldview different from my own as reasonable, yet I would not regard it as true; for example, if I am a secularist and my neighbor is a Hindu. However, there is a limit to this because in some circumstances I might regard my neighbor's worldview as unreasonable, depending on what she believes, and on my assessment of the reasonableness of her beliefs on this or that topic. And which worldviews fit into this category in our divided society would depend on whom you ask! For example, I might regard my neighbor's Hinduism as reasonable (but false), but a Richard Dawkins-type may regard it as unreasonable, since Dawkins is inclined to the view that all religious views are unreasonable. There are also many religious people who think that every version of secularism is unreasonable, so to them Dawkins' view is unreasonable! Of course, I may think that a particular worldview is reasonable on some issues but not on others, and even that it is correct on some issues (those where it agrees with my views, for instance). My neighbor, and others in society, will have the same attitude toward worldviews that agree or disagree with *their* worldview, and so we are right back in the middle of the problem of pluralism once again.

Reasonable Pluralism and Interpretations of Public Reason

So we need to try to be more precise about what reasonable pluralism could mean, more clear-cut than Rawls and his followers are. One way of thinking about reasonable pluralism is that we might recognize that others arrived at their worldview the way we arrived at ours. We appealed to reason, argument and evidence, and engaged freely in an honest, fair, and let us say thorough inquiry. And so we assume that others followed roughly the same approach, but arrived at different conclusions. In this sense, we would have to agree that their views are honestly arrived at. This is surely correct, but does it follow that we should regard their views as reasonable? That is obviously a controversial claim since two things could have occurred: others might not after all have engaged in a thorough and honest inquiry, but may have been guided by cultural influences, selfishness, prejudice, or bias of some sort, by human desire, or some other impulse that compromised their reasoning, and led to irrational or mistaken views. Second, they may have made some errors or mistakes in reasoning (in *our* judgment, remember), such as giving too much weight to certain premises in an argument, drawing a conclusion that the premises do not support (again in *our* judgment), exaggerating the weight of evidence, or perhaps not giving enough consideration to an important factor relevant to the topic, and so forth, and so arrived at a position that (*in our view*) is not reasonable. Needless to say, *we* may have made some of these mistakes in arriving at *our* views, at least from the perspective of others! And let us not forget that from the point of view of pluralism there is no independent standpoint, no objective "God's eye" view, from which to judge these matters; we must settle for an individual person's judgment of another's motives and the quality of their arguments in arriving at worldview beliefs. So, even if we assume goodwill on the part of those we disagree with, it does not seem to follow that we have to regard their views as reasonable.

There is obviously some sense in which I would regard other people in society as reasonable in general. But it does not follow that I would regard all of their personal beliefs in the area of worldviews as reasonable, and this is the crucial point. For example, I might regard others as reasonable in the sense that I would trust them to do a job well at my place of business, or I would be guided by their judgment in a local matter, say in assessing a person's character or with regard to financial or civic issues. Yet, I still may regard their worldview, or parts of it, as irrational. So even if a person's *worldview* is judged to be irrational, it does not follow that the person is completely irrational, or that they could not be relied upon to use common sense reasoning to solve a problem! Do I regard my neighbor as reasonable? Yes, if this means that I think she can complete a task competently, knows how to budget responsibly, can offer good advice on the best schools in the neighborhood, or about the best way to think about a policy of the city government. But if you ask me if I think her worldview is reasonable, and was arrived at reasonably, well that depends on what her worldview is, and how she arrived at it. Surely this is the key question?

With regard to the meaning of pubic reason and how it would work in practice, Rawls proposes a kind of definition of a reasonable person. A reasonable person is one who accepts two understandings of reasoning in a pluralist society. The first is that we agree that we should offer a type of *public justification* of our view in a way that others can reasonably accept, and also that we are willing to consider other views; the second is that a reasonable person accepts what Rawls calls the *burdens of judgment*, which he defines as the many "hazards involved in the correct (and conscientious) exercise of our powers of reason and judgment in the ordinary course of political life."[1] These burdens of judgment include being aware of the following facts: that (a) empirical and scientific evidence is often complex and conflicting; (b) we may reasonably disagree about the relative weight of different considerations; (c) concepts are vague and subject to hard cases; (d) the way we assess evidence and weigh values can be shaped by our total life experience; (e) different normative considerations on different sides can make overall assessment difficult; and (f) the number of values any social institution can incorporate is limited.[2] It is important also to add a third point: that a reasonable person within the context of democratic pluralism accepts the political conception of justice, the shared political values in our democratic culture, as we noted in the previous chapter. Among other things these values require us to give those that would be subject to coercive legislation public reasons to justify this coercion.

Rawls thinks that the burdens of judgment explain how it is that reasonable people can disagree fundamentally about vital matters concerning worldviews, ethics, and the meaning of life. But his main point is not that people disagree, but that a reasonable person accepts the reality of these burdens of judgment and so recognizes that people can disagree and still be reasonable. This means, therefore, that whenever we offer arguments to support moral and political positions, *we should present reasons that all people can accept*. This is especially true if the topic under discussion proposes legislation that would be coercive. This seems to be Rawls' understanding of public reason. As noted in the previous chapter, Rawls' discussion of public reason is often vague, and suffers from a lack of detailed, clear examples (a characteristic of this literature in general). He defines public reason in three ways: it is of free and equal citizens; concerns questions of fundamental political justice; and its nature and content are public, being expressed in public reason by a family of reasonable conceptions of political justice reasonably thought to satisfy the criterion of reciprocity.[3] He says that use of political power must fulfill a *criterion of reciprocity*: citizens must reasonably believe that all citizens can reasonably accept the enforcement of a particular set of basic laws. Those coerced by law must be able to endorse the society's fundamental political arrangements freely, not because they are dominated or manipulated or kept uninformed. He notes that: "The idea of political legitimacy based on the criterion of reciprocity says: Our exercise of political power is proper only when we sincerely believe that the reasons we would offer for our political actions—were we to state them as government officials—*are sufficient, and we also reasonably think that other citizens might also reasonably accept these reasons.*"[4] He elaborates further: "Public justification is not simply valid reasoning, but argument addressed to others; it proceeds correctly from premises we accept and think others could reasonably accept to conclusions we think they could also reasonably accept. This meets the duty of civility."[5]

Appealing to the duty of civility, or what is often called civic virtue, Rawls gives the example that if we were to deny someone religious liberty we must give reasons that a free and equal citizen might reasonably accept. *He adds that the criterion of reciprocity is normally violated whenever basic liberties are denied.* So, as noted in the previous chapter, to judge a citizen as reasonable seems to mean two things: acceptance of the latent political values in modern liberal culture, and an actual way that one is required *to reason* in public argument. To satisfy this latter requirement, a citizen must present reasons that he sincerely believes others could accept. A problem with this proposal is that it lacks specifics because Rawls does not explain or illustrate the type of reasoning that would be involved (say in a discussion about whether abortion should be legal or illegal), so we are left to guess at how an actual argument based on appeal to public reason would go. His suggestion that the criterion of reciprocity is normally violated whenever basic liberties are denied suggests that it is the values themselves, those latent in the political culture and which we all accept (one of his assumptions), that somehow function as the criterion by which we judge whether the reasons presented in an argument are acceptable to all (even if not all are persuaded by them).

Let us recall that the latent political values include justice, domestic tranquility, freedom, a scheme of equal basic rights, equality, ideals concerning the distribution of income, a fair system of taxation, and so forth. So Rawls seems to be extending the notion of public reason to refer not just to a particular way of reasoning but to involve *a particular interpretation* of the latent political values in democratic culture, in the sense that we may need to show how our arguments do not violate (a particular interpretation of) the latent political values. He seems to want these values to *constrain* what one can argue. At one point he uses the not very helpful phrase, "the political values of public reason,"[6] which seems to conflate latent democratic political values with the actual way one reasons and formulates public arguments within a democratic setting. Is Rawls suggesting that we have only to look at the latent political values (e.g., the value of equality) and we will "see" that a certain type of public argument is unreasonable? Perhaps he means that a general value, such as equality, requires us all to present a certain type of argument in public. Which type of argument? We might say minimally one that everyone can recognize as a genuine attempt to argue for one's view by appeal to reason, logic, facts, and evidence. As a general stipulation, I think most people would agree to this, since it is the type of argument we ourselves require whenever someone presents us a justification for a public policy proposal.

Yet this approach seems unworkable, for it is surely not as simple as this. This is because of two important points: the latent political values are subject to differences of opinion concerning their interpretation and application, and these differences can hardly fail to come back to differences in comprehensive conceptions of the good.[7] This is why Rawls' disciples do not present differences over interpretation and application (say, on whether religious schools should be funded by taxation, or whether abortion should be legal) as legitimate differences of reasonable opinion in a democracy; they nearly always present them as one side being in violation of the political conception of justice. Rawls himself may not do this, but most of his disciples do.[8] Nobody, for example, would deny that all human beings are equal, a key value latent in our political culture that we all accept. But we do disagree about its range of application. For example, some think that certain categories of life do not qualify as people, such as the unborn. Some believe we have a moral duty to future generations, while others do not. These are differences at the level of our comprehensive conceptions. In the tension over interpretation and application that exists between the political conception, and one's comprehensive conception, one's comprehensive conception always plays a role in how one thinks the tension should be resolved. Rawls talks as if we can easily divorce the two, but surely this is not so. Perhaps we should say that this divorce would not be a problem for those whose comprehensive conception is the same or nearly the same as the political conception, which is just to say that the Rawlsian view favors secularism. In general, Rawls is too sanguine about the political conception and what it can achieve, especially about the fact that it can avoid influence from comprehensive views. Though, we do need to be careful to distinguish between what Rawls actually says, and what his disciples say, which tends to define how he is generally understood. For example, Rawls himself appears to suggest at times that the political values are open to interpretation, that one may be able to introduce religious views into public deliberation, and admits that the (latent) political values are moral values.[9] His disciples are often harsher, suggesting that one cannot bring religious views into politics, that the political conception is "neutral," and so not open to interpretations, or that their interpretation is the only legitimate one.[10] Indeed, it seems to be an essential part of Rawlsian liberalism that its advocates be allowed to define what counts as "reasonable."

We do not seem to be much closer to knowing what kind of reasoning public reasoning would require, or whether it is even possible to practice it. The notion of public reason at first glance might just sound like what we mean by democratic consent—the idea that you give people a voice with regard to legislation that shapes society, and then the majority decides on the way forward. However, the idea of public reason goes further—it seems to require the consent of *everyone*, not just giving people a voice. That is the main difference, and the problem. It goes beyond the usual understanding of consent in democratic theory which is that while everyone has a say, not everyone will agree, but we vote on policy matters and those who lose out agree to abide by the majority judgment. Rawls himself does concur that in the end our disagreements must be settled democratically, noting that "From the point of view of public reason, citizens must vote for the ordering of political values they sincerely think the most reasonable."[11]

The suggestion that we should base our public arguments on reasons that all people could agree to is probably a standard that most people would not regard as realistic, and would therefore reject, as Jeffrey Stout has also noted.[12] What it means to give people reasons they could agree to needs also to be spelled out. On its face, it seems to mean that *everyone* would have to accept the reasons I present in support of my position. This would surely result in many arguments never getting started, let alone having a chance of convincing others! We suggested another way to read it in the previous chapter, that it means that we all start from *premises* that everyone could accept, but not that we all must end up in the same place at the end of an argument. Such premises would appeal to matters of sense experience, common sense,[13] widely available and accepted evidence, scientific and matters of fact, and so forth, and to reasonable argument and careful inferences, given the evidence. (We must also recognize that it is possible to reach the same conclusions and so agreement, to some practical extent at least, by means of different rational routes. So it would not be necessary that everyone have exactly the same argument for a shared conclusion that commanded widespread agreement.) The pattern of logical inference allowed in an argument from premises to conclusion would also be based on the objective standards of reason and logic, which we can stipulate we all agree to. However, even with this understanding of public reason, we can see that it would not lead to arguments that everyone could accept. Some would surely dispute the premises of any argument offered, even if such premises were based on sense experience, factual matters, and appeals to common sense, since they would judge these matters differently. Others would dispute the logical inferences made in an argument; still others would deny that the weight of the conclusion was supported by the premises, and so forth.

How Would Public Reasoning Work?

One of the vexing problems facing the notion of public reason involves specifying how the process is supposed to work, and also the range of issues to which it applies. Recent scholarship has been less than effective at addressing these matters. It has tended to keep the discussion at an abstract level without much detailed consideration of concrete cases, so that it is hard to get an idea of how one might appeal to public reason, even whether it can work.[14] This literature cries out for discussion of issues that are in dispute, on a case-by-case basis with focus on specific arguments. Rawls himself, as we have noted, suggests that public reason applies to matters of constitutional essentials, the rights and freedoms of citizens, and to the question of the distribution of wealth, one of his own main concerns.[15] We might think that it should apply to all forms of coercion (even laws against actions widely regarded as criminal), but again this is hardly realistic. Maybe it should only concern those issues about which there is a serious dispute in society, but again one can see problems with this proposal. Rawls and his followers generally seem to have in mind serious disagreements that arise among the worldviews and that require some kind of legislation, concerning topics such as abortion, euthanasia, sexual conduct, public funding and displays of religion, animal welfare, economic proposals, and other similar issues.

Those who believe that religion has a role in politics, such as Philip Quinn, look upon the notion of public reason with suspicion and argue that it would lead only to at best a standoff in the public square.[16] Others go further and suggest that the notion is something of a sham, a procedure carefully crafted with the express aim of targeting religious beliefs with which many liberal theorists disagree.[17] Religious thinkers often suspect that secular liberals never really believed that religious views emerging from reasonable pluralism were reasonable at all, or if they did once, they no longer do! Many religious thinkers feel belittled by the "philosophical, objective" arguments offered by secular liberal thinkers for excluding religious believers from public discourse, and regard such arguments as a form of secularist bigotry. While I am greatly sympathetic to such criticisms, I do agree with the Rawlsian liberals on two points—our general commitment to liberal political values and the need to try to support one's public political proposals with rational arguments. Almost everyone agrees with the first point (though how the values are to be interpreted and applied does not command, nor require, universal agreement, on my view), but the second is more controversial among Christian thinkers. Some thinkers, such as Paul Weithman, advocate a broader category of what can count as acceptable religious beliefs in public.[18]

I disagree with secular liberals who often seem to sail very close to advancing the view that religious beliefs are not rational. More often than not they work with caricatures of the religious worldview, and try to pass off their disagreement with certain religious positions as "procedural," a maneuver that always involves their own usually secularist worldview becoming the de facto, "default" worldview in modern liberal democracy. Some are quite strident in their articulation of this outlook, such as Ackerman and Stephen Gey, others are more subtle, like Dworkin, but even those who are more sympathetic to the perceived discrimination against religious worldviews, like Cécile Laborde and Gerald Gaus, are not unaffected by these problems, as we will see.[19] For these reasons, we will go through some examples of public arguments as we examine various problems with the notion of public reason and consider whether it can deal with them. Nagel is aware that many people of good will hold misgivings about the concept, for the obvious reason that the restraint it calls for with regard to the use of state power always seems to favor secularist worldviews. So it is no wonder than many suspect that secular liberalism is a disingenuous theory, rigged to restrict religious morality in favor of promoting a secular, individualistic, indeed libertine, alternative.[20]

One of the immediate difficulties facing the notion of public reason is the fact that almost all legislation and government policy is coercive in some form, and so it seems to be unrealistic to say that in order to justify such legislation one must give people reasons they can accept. Legislation is coercive in two ways. The first is the most obvious way: where one is required to follow the law on certain issues, for example, one is forced to pay taxes, to maintain the upkeep of one's residence, to send one's children to school, to respect the property of others, and so forth. This is a direct form of coercion in the sense that one will be prosecuted if one refuses to obey such laws. These laws represent the views of others (or of society perhaps) on particular matters; for example, it is because people think that all children should be educated to a certain level that we require by force of law parents to send their kids to school, whether they agree or not. So this would be a law that one would have to justify with public reasons—reasons that parents could reasonably accept. These types of laws are usually passed by a majority support in a representative democratic context, so they can be said to have the support of a majority of citizens. However, in some democracies, notably the U.S., laws are sometimes passed by the Courts and imposed coercively on citizens, and these are obviously more controversial, since not only are they not arrived at through the democratic process but they often do not command majority support.

There is, in addition, another more subtle form of coercion. This is where a law is passed in a society allowing a practice that many find morally abhorrent, such as slavery in earlier times, or abortion in our times. Although the practice is not forced on people directly in the sense that no one is forced to have an abortion, people are forced to live in a society that permits what they regard as a morally abhorrent practice. It is also true that when a practice becomes more common in a society, which often happens when it has been legal for a long time, it gradually contributes to the zeitgeist that has such a formative influence on attitudes and behavior. Many accept it simply because it is established in the culture, and not because they have arrived at a rational, considered decision that the practice is moral. So this also amounts to a (more subtle) form of coercion. This type of subtle coercion is an important reason that people are concerned about the "common good" in their society; parents everywhere are always worried about the impact of the zeitgeist on their children. A couple who had moved to Ireland because the country did not permit abortion noted recently, after a referendum aimed at legalizing the practice was passed, that they were leaving the country. Many held a similar view during slavery times, and indeed one occasionally hears the same view expressed today related to discussions about current affairs in the U.S., especially concerning immigration, and other government policies that many strongly object to (though it is unclear how many people have actually left the U.S. to live in Canada, but the sentiment is enough to affirm our point here!). One cannot justify this type of coercion by arguing that it is okay to force the legalization of abortion, for instance, on society for the reason that abortion is moral. This is because one is then forcing one's moral views on others, and if this is justified for one worldview, then it is also justified for other worldviews. So then one might be tempted to invent some argument that shows that overall *my view* belongs in fact to a better class of view, and so should have a privileged position in public debates! This is the position of Rawlsian liberalism, at least according to its critics! Secular liberalism as a philosophical approach to morality and politics often refuses to acknowledge this kind of coercion, mainly because its existence poses a direct challenge to the very individualistic view of the human person characteristic of the overall liberal approach to ethics (the idea that a person's autonomous decisions affect only the individual making them and have no effect on others, even when these actions progressively change society).

Let us turn then to the idea that in public debates we should present arguments that everyone can accept. It seems to me that this can be understood in two ways, about which liberal political philosophers are not clear, but both of which face some difficulties. The first understanding is that when advocating a public political position I attempt to present others with reasons that they regard as reasonable, but which they may not (and often in fact do not) accept. While others agree that my case is reasonable, they do not accept my conclusion, and so reject my view as wrong (and perhaps we must also say that *in some sense* they must see it as unreasonable). I will work with an example from (radical) feminist theory to illustrate. One of the key claims of radical feminism is that gender is a social construct, the view that masculine and feminine traits are largely due to social and cultural forces and not to biological characteristics. Many others regard this belief as both false and irrational, holding the view that gender is a biological fact that is mostly determinative of its expression, and that little of it is socially constructed. We don't need to settle this issue here; just to note that there are different positions on it (and perhaps that the radical feminist view is a minority view), and also that any argument proposed by one side is likely to be rejected by the other side! Now, suppose one wishes to argue that in general women are more suited to, and so better at, raising small children than men, and that families should be given tax relief if the mother stays at home to raise the children when they are very young. Or suppose one opposes the introduction in schools of any curriculum material that presupposes that gender is a social construct, and so forth. In public arguments about these matters, I may interpret the requirement of giving people reasons they can accept as meaning that I offer arguments which others will *recognize as reasonable even though they do not accept them*, that is, do not find the arguments convincing. Let us agree that, as mentioned above, I strive to begin my public argument from premises and evidence that is openly accessible to all from the point of view of ordinary reason, experience, and common sense. I am appealing to what Audi calls "secular reason" and Rawls calls "public reason." So others with different worldviews regard me as reasonable, even if wrong, but I may (perhaps) command a certain amount of respect from them!

Is it possible to give people arguments they might regard as reasonable, but that they do not accept, or are very unlikely to accept? I think this might be possible, for some issues at least. Perhaps one such issue is the death penalty, where I will just stipulate that there are good arguments on both sides. It might be that I am familiar with the strongest case against my position, and when I hear it presented in the public square I honestly believe that the person has a reasonable argument, even if I don't find it convincing. My opponent may make the same assessment of my viewpoint. As Rawls noted in his point about the burdens of judgment, people can disagree about the weight of various considerations, and also, of course, about whether a supporting argument and body of evidence really does justify a particular conclusion. However, a clear problem is that there is no objective position from which to settle these disagreements, a conundrum facing liberalism in general. No one can come in and pronounce definitively that my suggested approach works well for the death penalty because, yes in fact, the reasons for and against the practice are indeed finely balanced. I can only say that *I* find the moral issues finely balanced but (crucially) *I cannot speak for others* with regard to this matter. Others may find the death penalty abhorrent and obviously morally wrong, and believe there is no reasonable position on the other side (and *vice versa*). So when they hear an argument for the other side they immediately dismiss it as unreasonable, even irrational.

But the point I want to make here is that I don't think there is any argument on the topic of our present example, gender, that one could give to most radical feminist theorists that they might regard as reasonable, and *vice versa*. This is because the divide between people on this issue is too wide, and *involves too many deeper assumptions and arguments concerning the nature of the human person*. In earlier, less ideological and more collaborative times, it was still the case that one believed that one should make a good effort to try to convince others before one proceeded, but one of the effects of the loss of confidence in reason is that we no longer believe we have to do this. Many people see themselves as so far apart on foundational issues of life and ultimate meaning that they no longer think they must convince others before proceeding; they believe that they cannot convince others, but must proceed anyway! The discussion over gender is but one instance of this general problem. We cannot settle this dispute by insisting on a particular interpretation of the latent political values, because any such insistence seems to be just another way of insisting on the superiority of one's worldview, the rightness of it, without any argument for it. That is the problem. Suppose one were to argue that our liberal commitment to equality requires that we must accord equality in matters of gender which means that gender must be regarded as a social construct? The problem with this is that it assumes an answer to the very issue that is in dispute. There is no built-in answer that settles these contentious matters, as I am sure we can see. So with regard to this particular topic, I do not think this first interpretation of the notion of public reason can be satisfied. Perhaps I am wrong about this, but I don't see much hope of a meeting of minds on this question.

We should also add that there is an unfortunate tendency in liberal democracies of late to adopt a general position that one cannot reason with one's opponents because they are irrational and their positions are stupid and ridiculous, to label positions immediately as not worth discussing (the tone of the contributions at even the more respectable, serious intellectual blogs on the internet is a good example). One even sees this tendency in academia, where the professors should know better! This is a consequence of the problem of worldview pluralism and of the loss of confidence in reason. Often our first response is not to argue or question or defend but (particularly if we have some authority or political power over those with whom we disagree) to attack them, as a way of bullying them into silence, ending the discussion, and thus staking out our own positions. If this general attitude persists as a feature of public and even academic debate it will make it much harder to present reasons to people that they regard as reasonable, let alone that they accept! So while the test of public argument as a check on beliefs that often seem surrounded by hysteria rather than reason now appears to be vital, it seems to be harder to put into practice than ever before.

The second interpretation of the notion of public reason is the one that a literal reading of Rawls' view would suggest (it is also the position proposed by Audi): that *everyone* who is subject to proposed coercive legislation or practice ought to be given reasons to justify this coercion *that they can accept* (not just that they find reasonable). This seems to mean that in terms of fairly formal and sophisticated arguments one must accept both the premises of an argument, including any data and other considerations used to support them, and also that the conclusion follows from the premises, or that the conclusion is reasonable given the premises (though this latter requirement likely would not be sufficient if we agree, as we have just discussed, that one could regard an argument as reasonable, and yet still reject it). The problem with this more literal interpretation is that it imposes a criterion that simply cannot be met, as many have pointed out, including Nicholas Wolterstorff. Wolterstorff has noted that not only is it not realistic but that it is more reasonable to believe that as soon as one person presents a public argument for any view in our current pluralist climate the first thing that will happen is that someone else will immediately reject it![21] This is clearly true, no matter what kind of common sense approach one adopts. One could perhaps soften this interpretation to require not that everyone needs to accept an argument, but only a majority. This might be more realistic and would require a democratic vote or at least a vote of government to support coercive legislation, but it would have the consequence that those making public policy would have to present arguments that they know will not be accepted by everyone, which means that they cannot present an argument that fulfills Rawls' criteria.

Could we interpret Rawls' view to mean that I should give people reasons not that they actually accept but that it would be unreasonable for them not to accept! This is a subtle, interesting formulation of the concept. The problem is that I have to judge whether others are being unreasonable if they reject my arguments, and I am back to the cases described above, back where I started, in fact. (I am deciding which arguments people should accept, not them.) It is true that we do treat people this way all the time, adopting the attitude (as we noted in Chap. 1), that others would accept my view *if only* they were not so mistaken, uninformed, naive, blind, irrational, stupid, stubborn, biased, prejudiced, and so on. This is a very dangerous approach, however, because we cannot speak for others on the topic, and we may not be as fully rational as we think! We may have logs in our own eyes, be biased toward our own view, motivated by selfishness, a desire for power, even a sincere desire to tell others what *we think* is best for society (thereby usurping *their* freedom, according to liberal political theory). Perhaps we may encourage people to be cautious in a free society in asserting that their view is objectively true, but the dilemma is that we cannot maintain such a position consistently. Even if we try to restrict imposing our true beliefs on others in cases of coercive legislation, this only works if we define coercion in the way secular liberals do, where it is understood as preventing a person from engaging in an activity, but not as practices and behaviors that shape society and so form the attitudes and beliefs of the general population.

This brings us to another difficulty with the notion of public reason. One might be wary of it because one does not trust others to be reasonable. This is in fact an acute concern in the context of current pluralism (this is the reason why Audi introduces the notion of secular motivation, because he does not trust religious believers to argue honestly in the public square). However, I think we must admit that there is enough mistrust to go around, and that we have ample reasons in the contemporary climate *not* to trust our opponents in an argument! This seems to me to be particularly true at this time in the history of pluralist democracies when people have lost faith in reason to settle disputes, or to work through difficult worldview disagreements, to arrive at the truth. Concomitant with this, our disagreements are getting more shrill and political by the day. When one sees the field of academia infected with these vices from the point of view of good civic behavior in a democracy, where there is a growing tendency to attack one's opponent as an initial response rather than to engage in debate, to regard one's academic discipline not as one that explores difficult topics in an attempt to arrive at truth, but as a political endeavor that can aid in the promotion of one's political agenda, and where some are openly arguing for a redefinition of free speech in order to exclude certain views, then one is fully justified in not having much confidence that those one engages with in public deliberation will be reasonable! One might be inclined to think just the opposite—that they will be motivated primarily by their settled political certainties, not reasoned argument.

Thinkers interested in the concept of public reason are aware of some of these worries, and sometimes they propose as a way of dealing with them that we think of public debates not as they actually do take place but as they might take place *under ideal conditions*. This refers to the way these debates would take place *if citizens acted as ideal reasoners* and were not subject to the vices we mentioned above (Habermas' ideal speech situation is an attempt to outline criteria for how this might work, as we saw in the previous chapter). Ideal conditions might include having access to full facts and information, reasoning perfectly, or with great care and precision, being very honest and open, and so forth. Yet, this proposal comes with a worry that any account of what should be involved in the ideal conditions might be biased toward what certain thinkers regard as "reasonable." One's own worldview may play a decisive role in what counts as "good reason" under ideal conditions. Setting this worry aside for now, how would people reason under ideal conditions? Minimally, we would support our positions with reasons that everyone could accept, according to those who suggest we pursue this approach. What kind of reasons would these be? And herein lies the difficulty! We are unable to say anything about these reasons, are hard-pushed to give examples of what these reasons would look like. Any example (or set of criteria) offered of an ideally rational argument may be judged by others as unreasonable, in the way we have suggested! And then it seems to me that we are back facing the same problem yet again. Any argument one offers might be rejected by those who appraise it; some may reject the premises as unreasonable, or as not supported by the evidence, as not as obvious as some think they are, or the conclusion as not reasonably drawn from the premises, and so forth. Some may object to how we interpret certain facts or the weight we give to them (which may crucially depend on some of our other beliefs, particularly the foundational beliefs of our worldview), the kinds of things that Rawls identified in his notion of the burdens of judgment. The point is that even an "ideal" argument would not persuade others, and it is not enough to object that others would (or should) accept my "ideal" argument if only they were reasoning as well as me! The bottom line is this: *even if we were all ideal reasoners, we would still disagree.*

Rejecting Public Reason?

There is a deeper worry that might make us suspicious of the notion of public reason, for why one might, in fact, reject it altogether. One might be skeptical because one does not think it adds anything new to a public discussion. One might see it as simply an appeal to rely on reason, argument, and evidence in any public deliberation. But if one already accepts this restriction, then one might think that the notion of public reason does not add much by way of new criteria or a new insight for how to make progress in a pluralist democracy with regard to settling contentious issues among the worldviews. Let us recall that secular reason was supposed to be a way of bracketing out, or setting to one side, contentious forms of reasoning (and the worldview of which they are a part) in a democracy and debating according to *common sense standards of reason* (although it is generally interpreted as applying only to the bracketing out of religious worldviews). Why do we need to bracket out comprehensive views? There are two reasons: the first is reflected in a general understanding of what Rawls called reasonable pluralism—that we recognize that others arrived at their worldviews the same way we did, and though these worldviews differ from ours, we must accept that in some sense they are reasonable. So we should set our comprehensive views aside in public deliberation because it is not reasonable to ask others to subscribe to our worldview. The second reason is not often stated clearly, though it is assumed in Audi's principle of secular rationale. Some ways of arriving at a worldview are not reasonable, such as, for example, those based on scriptural revelation—especially from the point of view of pluralism—and so we should not introduce these approaches into a public discussion. This is not just because we know that such arguments will not persuade others, let us recall, but it is also because if we accept reasonable pluralism, then we should recognize (so the argument goes) *that it is not reasonable for us* to present these kinds of arguments (arguments based on questionable sources such as revelation or Church authority) in the public arena.

I think we can recognize that these are all good points, even though the notion of reasonable pluralism itself has been dismissed by many in this age of anti-realism and relativism. As we noted, the view is now quite prevalent that it is very difficult, perhaps even impossible, for people to reason in the way that Rawls and others promote. This is because of the influence of culture, biases, prejudices, privilege, language, conceptual schemes, all of those mechanisms that are supposed to play a role in compromising the mind's ability to know objective reality, to arrive at an objective, rational argument. We are living in a postmodernist and anti-realist age, an age dominated by the spirit of epistemological and moral relativism, and given this, the chances of even *being perceived* to be presenting and appraising arguments and evidence in a rational, objective, honest way are becoming more remote. Moreover, if the whole notion of public reason initially requires taking a particular stance on a philosophical theory of truth, or a commitment to the objectivity of logic and truth, even though from the point of view of common sense there seems nothing wrong with this, those who hold anti-realist theories of knowledge would argue that this commitment is part of one's comprehensive view of the good.

Of course, many of us reject these postmodernist tendencies and strive for objectivity. Many will accept the general liberal point that we should try to present reasonable arguments in a public debate (as well as accepting the democratic system and its values). What kinds of arguments would these be? It cannot be an argument that all people must accept. It cannot even be an argument that everyone regards as reasonable, as we have seen. No, let us say that it is a kind of minimalist standard. It means only that we present an argument that is based on reason, that appeals to evidence and common sense facts, in the manner noted earlier, to premises that are based on as much openly available, objective common-sense-type support as possible, to "secular reason." To put the point in the negative, it would mean that we would *not* present an argument in a public forum, especially one in support of coercive legislation, that was based on an appeal to biblical revelation, or, to take a secularist example, that was founded on appeal to the tradition of the Enlightenment. This is because neither revelation by itself nor the fact that something was a tradition at a certain time, is a rational basis upon which to try to persuade those who reject the revelation source or the tradition. Stated more clearly as a logical objection, we can always ask why we should accept this or that source of revelation, or this or that tradition as our guiding authority? Note also that *this argument is itself a rational argument*—grounded in an appeal to objective standards of logic and reason, for why one should not offer a public argument based on revelation! There is a pragmatic reason also for not basing public arguments on texts, traditions or authorities, or indeed personal experiences or testimonies (religious or secularist) that are not widely shared. There is considerable disagreement over which texts, traditions, authorities, or testimonies to consult or rely upon, a problem there seems no practical way to get around, and so there is no chance of constructing an argument from common premises in these cases.

I think it is sufficient for introducing an argument into the public square that *the person presenting it believes that it is reasonable*. This is really all that matters. It then satisfies the test of reason. let us stipulate (that the person is not being dishonest, etc.). It is not realistic, as we noted, to insist that it must be an argument that *all* rational people would accept, because this standard is too high. Few arguments concerning worldview-type issues could pass such a test. It is enough for a person in a pluralist society to be allowed to present an argument in the public square to her fellow citizens if she honestly regards the argument as reasonable. This is a minimum requirement. It is not acceptable to object that one should not present an argument if others do not think it is reasonable. This means that you are giving to yourself veto power over what others regard as good arguments, and this goes against the principles of democracy and free speech (and indeed against what Rawls has called the burdens of judgment and reasonable pluralism). While one is free to make one's own assessment of the rationality of an argument, one is not entitled to speak for others on this matter. And indeed, one hopes that public square discourse will be *a test of the rationality of arguments*, though perhaps this is an unrealistic hope when many have lost confidence in reason itself. Perhaps also one might assume foundational or key beliefs in the public square debates, and provide the justification for them elsewhere, such as academia. It only matters that such arguments be available. For example, radical feminists may assume in their pronouncements on gender, law, and society the foundational belief that gender is a social construct, but rarely argue for this view in actual public debates (relating to educational programs in schools, e.g.), but assume it there and argue for it elsewhere. Needless to say, the academics and the politicians might work together on some matters—the professors supplying the rationale for the positions that the politicians, activists, and special interest groups pursue politically. So, the idea of public reason does not seem to add much to the requirements of *rational* debate that did not apply before we started talking about the notion. Let us develop these points further by consideration of concrete cases.

Case Study: Arguing About Abortion in the Public Square

To illustrate the notion of public reason more concretely, let us consider a disagreement concerning the morality of the practice of abortion in a democratic state, and how, in particular, the public debate over the issue should be approached, given that there is a plurality of views on the topic. Abortion is a very serious, very controversial and much debated topic, one that involves clearly the incommensurability of worldviews. It is, therefore, an appropriate topic with which to illustrate our points about the notion of public reason. Unsurprisingly, given the strongly held positions on the issue as well as its cultural significance, it is also one that has been given considerable attention by philosophers interested in pluralist debate in a democratic setting. Most thinkers who have written on these topics in the context of public deliberation usually do so in general terms. It is important, I think, that we move beyond generalities, and examine the actual arguments in concrete detail. That way we can get a good insight, I believe, into not only the topic, but how public reason is supposed to, and actually does, work. We will also see how foundational worldview beliefs are influential in how we present arguments and in how we assess the rationality of certain views, even if we do not always realize they are playing a role.

We shall imagine the case of an educated and informed citizen, Anne, who is committed to the basic values of a liberal democracy (to the latent political values, to use the terminology of Rawlsian liberalism). Anne also believes that abortion is an immoral practice and wishes to make it illegal in the democratic society in which she lives. We need to consider, as we work through this example, how she would, could or should argue for her view to her fellow citizens in a public setting. We will specify that the public setting involves presenting an argument to the general public in some way, say by writing a newspaper article, or presenting an argument on a TV show, or in a radio discussion, or at a meeting arranged by the government to hear the views of the public, or in political canvassing, and so forth. Anne may or may not be a member of a political action group aimed at promoting political positions in society, and may or may not support such groups financially. Although Anne is not a public official, political liberalism of the Rawlsian variety asks her to regard herself as such, as if she were making an argument to all citizens, so this is also how a public official should reason in public.

Suppose that Anne's basic case for the immorality of abortion is that an innocent human being has a fundamental value and so has a right to life. This stance is required by the basic values of a democracy. She also holds that the embryo is an innocent human life, and since abortion would be the ending of that life, then abortion is wrong and should therefore be illegal. In addition, she believes that it is the possession of a soul that gives a human life its fundamental value, a soul that was created by God. She also believes there are additional arguments against abortion, but this is, in her view, the best argument, the one she finds the most convincing. Let us say that Anne has elaborated her argument into this form following several discussions with friends who agree and disagree with her position. She is unable to handle questions concerning the argument for the existence of the soul, but she knows there is a long tradition devoted to this topic, which she studied somewhat in college, and she refers those interested to the works of philosophers in this tradition. Such arguments appeal to the distinction between the body and the mind (such as arguments appealing to properties such as intentionality, qualia, and other peculiar features of mental life), and arguments from that branch of philosophy of religion known as natural theology (which includes the famous, and in her view, impressive arguments for the existence of God; other arguments that appeal to latest scientific evidence in cosmology; and various theories of theodicy). These are the types of arguments developed by some of the greatest minds in history for the rationality of a theistic worldview, in general. So Anne accepts that there are strong arguments in favor of the existence of the soul, and of God, and so she thinks that her general theistic worldview is reasonable, even though she cannot do justice to these arguments herself. But overall she is convinced that she has a reasonable argument against abortion, one, moreover, that it is legitimate to present in public deliberations about abortion.

Anne acknowledges that many people do not accept that the embryo has a soul, and a smaller number do not agree that all innocent human life has a fundamental value; an even smaller minority hold that even though the first two claims might be true, they are outweighed by other considerations, and so, at least in some cases, the deliberate ending of an innocent human life is morally and therefore legally justified. Anne disagrees with these positions, regarding them as profoundly misguided, and is glad of the opportunity to debate her view in a public setting to try to persuade others and to influence public policy. Let us also say that Anne was impressed by one of the arguments on the other side at an earlier time—that because pregnancy is a heavy burden for a woman, this burden might outweigh the embryo's value, and be a sufficient reason to justify abortion. Anne, benefiting from public debate, considered this argument seriously for a time, but eventually rejected it.

An objection is often raised against Anne's view that is aimed not at disagreeing with this or that premise of the argument, or with the conclusion, or with introducing other considerations, but with suggesting that this type of argument is not appropriate to introduce into a public discussion of abortion. This would be the stance of Rawls and Audi, and many liberal political philosophers. There is something "wrong" with this type of argument. The problem stems from the fact that it is a *religious* argument. What does this mean? It means that the argument makes an appeal to *religious content* in its premises; it makes an appeal to the truth of (religious) beliefs, specifically to the truth of the belief that the embryo has a soul, and also that God exists, and other (religious) beliefs. According to the theory of liberal democracy, as developed from Rawls onward, this form of argument is not acceptable in the public square. Why not? One can see that an obvious reason one might be tempted to offer is not convincing, the one that says that some people do not agree with these religious claims. We saw above that this is too high a standard, and that it seems to be true of any claim one introduces in any kind of public argument. Audi has also suggested, as we have seen, that the *source* of justification for religious arguments is often suspect. But this critical point does not apply in Anne's case because her argument is not based on one of the sources he singles out: revelation, authority, tradition, or personal religious experiences. Anne's argument is, instead, justified by appeal to *reason*. So it does not fall under Audi's list of suspect sources for public arguments.

To explore these points further, it is helpful to consider an equivalent argument for the *legality* of abortion. Let us consider an argument that has no religious content, such as the following (stated in abbreviated form): abortion should be legal because the embryo is not fully a human being. Robert, who proposes this argument, is also pushed by his friends to state it in a more formal and detailed way. So he reformulates the argument in this manner: the possession of certain qualities is required to qualify as a human being; the embryo does not have these qualities; therefore the embryo is not a human being. The extended argument would then be: only practices that deliberately end the life of an innocent human being are immoral and should be illegal, abortion does not end the life of an innocent human being; so abortion is not immoral and should not be illegal. And so on. The argument can be structured in several different ways (e.g., in a form that argues the embryo is a human being but not a human person, and only *persons* have value) but for our purposes the general argument is the same. The question is: is this an argument that a religious believer could reasonably accept? Also, where does it fare according to Audi's two principles, and the general understanding of public reason we have been looking at?

To help us think through this example, we might distinguish two questions. 1. Is Robert's argument a philosophical, rational argument; an argument that appeals only to secular reason? An argument that appeals to common sense reasoning and premises that are generally available to everyone? 2. Is it an argument that appeals to *the truth of secularism* in its premises (even if it might not do so explicitly)? Does it appeal to Robert's "comprehensive conception of the good" (in Rawls' language)? If we agree that it is a philosophical argument, an argument that appeals only to secular reason, then we also have to allow that the argument Anne presented above is an argument based on secular reason *in the key sense that she provides a rational argument for all of her claims, including the claim about the human soul*. The argument for the existence of the soul begins from facts and premises open to everyone; the end of the argument is the inference that the soul exists (it is not an argument based on appeal to religious scripture; it is a philosophical argument, familiar in the Western philosophical tradition in the work of any number of thinkers). Arguments for the existence of God have the same form. Some will be tempted to reply that even if Anne thinks she has a reasonable argument for this conclusion, they disagree. *Yet the judgment of others on Anne's argument seems to be irrelevant.*

I submit that it does not matter whether this argument is convincing to others; what is relevant is that Anne finds it convincing, and that it does not appeal to any sources where the question of their reliability, reasonableness, or truth is assumed, bypassed, or ignored, such as revelation or private experience or church authority, and so forth. Indeed, Anne could begin her argument with the claim that all human beings consist of body and soul, that embryos are human beings, and so forth. Anne need not even be a religious believer to hold such a view, and we might not even regard such an argument as "religious." (It might be understood as similar to the more anthropological arguments to be found in Aristotle, or twentieth-century philosopher, C. J. Ducasse.[22]) We can say that her religious beliefs are supported philosophically—meaning that they are all backed by reasoned argument. Her religious beliefs would then pass the test of public reason. Religious arguments that are not based on reason in this way would not pass the test and would be inadmissible into the public square because their sources of support can always be legitimately questioned.

It is also not acceptable to insist that Anne's argument is not reasonable because it does not respect liberal political values. Why might one say this? One might suspect that Anne is not respecting reasonable pluralism, but this is not so. Anne is respecting liberal values because she is not requiring that everyone commit to her worldview, that everyone should become, say, a Catholic. It is difficult to see how in this context *a reasonable argument* could go against liberal values. One may object that not everyone finds her argument reasonable, but I have noted that this is irrelevant—for otherwise, one would be forcing the religious believer to accept someone else's judgment of what is reasonable, and so violating reasonable pluralism oneself. Moreover, everyone who argues for a particular view of public policy is doing the same thing as Anne—they are arguing that we should accept *some truth* of their worldview, even if not the whole worldview. Anne is arguing rationally to the truth of a view on abortion but not requiring one to adopt her comprehensive view of the good, *nor crucially does one need to adopt a comprehensive view to see that the argument is intelligible and reasonable, in the liberal sense*. An argument that required everyone (however subtly) to be a secularist or a Catholic would violate liberal values, and so would be unreasonable in this context, but Anne's is clearly not an example of such an argument.

Turning to the second question of whether Robert's argument *assumes the truth of secularism* (or at least of a controversial metaphysical belief), I think we can say that it usually does assume this in most contemporary forms (though perhaps it need not). That is to say, most people who advance this argument *already assume that there is no soul*, that whatever qualities we are using to pronounce judgment on the value of the embryo, having a soul is not one of them. They rule out the existence of the soul in advance, according to their worldview, so the argument would be a conversation stopper to a religious believer. They may rule it out simply as an assumption of their position, or they may believe they can back up their claim about the non-existence of the soul with rational arguments. The question is whether Robert determines the value of the embryo in part by ruling out that it has a soul, and so whether his overall argument is an instance of sectarian secularism? He does seem to be assuming a position on the truth of the question concerning the existence of soul in his argument. This becomes clear if we consider an objection that Anne might raise. She might point out that he has overlooked a property that is constitutive of the identity and value of the embryo, the soul. In this case, Robert would then be obliged to engage the debate over the existence of the soul, and so the metaphysical views of both sides (not just the religious side) would become more obvious. In this way, Robert's argument would fail Rawls' and Audi's test of public reason because it (subtly) appeals to a belief that could reasonably be rejected by the religious believer. His argument depends on accepting the truth of a central belief of the secularist worldview. It seems obvious that one's secularist beliefs will influence one's moral and political commitments, particularly with regard to a crucial issue like abortion.

The fact that Robert may believe that he can provide a rational argument against the existence of the soul would not be enough to place secularist arguments in a more worthy, "better" category than religious arguments. Suppose Robert replied that people do reasonably disagree over whether or not there is a soul, and given this we should not appeal to the soul in public arguments on abortion. It is true that people perhaps can reasonably disagree over this issue, but this does not seem to be enough to rule talk of the soul out of the abortion argument. This is because if one rules it out, then one is arguing *as if there is no soul*, and this is to favor one particular view in the debate, in the way that we have seen. It would mean that one would have to be a (confessional) secularist not to find this argument objectionable! This restriction would also appear to apply to *any* belief that people disagree over, which would make public argument virtually impossible. It is also important that the same conclusions can be drawn against whatever version of the argument for the morality of abortion that may be advanced. Indeed, Robert's argument does not have to be an argument that assumes the truth of any *particular* worldview. The point is that it will be based on the *truth* of *some belief* that will be part of *someone's* worldview (even if the worldview is a religious one), and it will exclude its opposite, and so we cannot claim a privilege for this worldview that is at the same time denied to other worldviews that are a party to the same discussion. This is why it is important to make secularist premises and assumptions explicit in arguments of this kind, to become clearly aware of them, indeed to be on the lookout for them. We need to avoid a common mistake that besets public arguments of the kind advanced by Robert—to think that such arguments are really "neutral" due to the fact that the secularist premises are not obvious or cannot be discerned so easily. This confusion makes it look, incorrectly, as if it is only the religious believer who is relying on her comprehensive view of the good. The temptation of liberal political theory to rig the debate is obvious here, but it is also unjustified.

The Reasoning Process Versus the Conclusions of Reason

Cécile Laborde has some observations which are interesting to consider in the light of our present discussion, especially as regards what counts as a public reason. Laborde agrees with Audi that some arguments are problematic because they are not accessible to "common reasons." For example, she thinks any argument, similar to Anne's above, that appeals to a religious claim that life is a gift from God "is not shared nor subjectable to common standards."[23] But Laborde's explanation for what common standards refers to is weak. It is true that Anne's view about the soul is not shared, but is it true that it is not subjectable to common standards? I don't see how, since Anne backs it up with reasoned arguments. And, we have noted clearly, just because some may not share a view, or think it reasonable, is not sufficient justification to exclude that view from public deliberation. Laborde elaborates by briefly considering a different type of argument to the one above. Suppose someone like Anne appeals to a weighing of values in her argument concerning abortion; for example, if her argument suggested that there are two competing values at play in a consideration of the issue—the value of the unborn human being and the freedom of the mother—and that she weighs the value of the unborn human being higher. Another person, however, might weigh the freedom of the mother higher. In this case, Laborde thinks that Anne's argument is acceptable as a candidate for public deliberation; even though some will reject it, this form of the argument, according to Laborde, does appeal to "common standards" and so is entitled to respect from others in the democratic state. Why is this? It seems it is because the argument is based only on an appeal to those liberal political values that we all accept (in Rawls' formulation), and so the thought seems to be that although people disagree about how such values are to be weighed in relation to each other, they can see where another is coming from, understand the argument, and accord it some respect. Yet, Laborde's suggestion for excluding religious beliefs from the public square is far from convincing.

There are two points to make. Anne weighs the values differently because she thinks the embryo has more value (as we noted above), and she thinks this because the embryo possesses a soul. Robert holds that the embryo has less value, in part because he thinks there is no soul present. Second, it seems to me to be obvious that Anne's argument for the existence of the soul *is* based on "common standards," which Laborde later elaborates to mean (agreeing somewhat with Audi) an argument that appeals to reason and natural facts. She suggests that a reason can be intelligible but not accessible to public standards but does not explain how Anne's argument is not "accessible," other than to say that some reject it.[24] Even though she acknowledges the distinction between intelligibility and accessibility, she seems always to mean by non-accessible "unintelligible." This is illustrated by her remark that "It is one thing to be coerced in the name of reasons one does not understand (such as that life is a gift from God) and quite another to be coerced in the name of reasons that one does not agree with but can engage with."[25] The problem here is that Anne's argument is perfectly understandable; anyone who says they don't understand what it means for the soul to exist and for the soul to be created by God is being willfully disingenuous, or, just as problematic, is assuming that secularism is true. Even worse, they may be adopting the stubborn mindset of some of the old logical positivists who adopted the posture that *they* just could not understand what religious language referred to! It is one thing to reject a view because you don't think it is well argued or true, it is quite another to claim you don't understand it! I think it is accurate to observe that some in our culture may have trained themselves to regard religious beliefs as unintelligible, or may be so out of touch with the religious dimension of human experience, that they have little time for a religious perspective on things. However, surely that is their problem, and not Anne's? Moreover, it is not a serious cultural problem, since it is confined to a quite small minority. We must be careful not to define comprehensibility, intelligibility, and accessibility as describing beliefs we happen not to agree with! I think it can sometimes be hard for philosophical liberals to consider religious arguments fairly, remaining free from anti-religious prejudice.

I think that Laborde fails to distinguish clearly between the *process* and the *conclusions* of reason, between a specific instance or path of reasoning and the conclusions that reason reaches, a confusion that is common in literature on this topic. Laborde and others in the discussion sometimes confusingly use the word "reasons" to refer to the conclusion of an argument, rather than the logical process that was employed to reach the conclusion. If we say that religious *reasons* are not acceptable and we mean by "reasons" *the claim* that the soul exists, this is a confused use of the term "reason," especially in the context of a discussion concerning how public reason should be understood and how it works. A claim about the existence of the soul is not a reason in the sense of the process of reasoning; it is a conclusion of one argument (the argument that tries to show that the soul exists) and a premise in another argument (the one that tries to show that the embryo has value). One may not be convinced by an argument that the soul exists, but this is not a sufficient justification to rule any argument that appeals to the existence of the soul out of public deliberation, as we have seen. Sometimes, however, Laborde seems to be referring to the process of reasoning, to those factual claims based on common sense, logical inferences, and argument structure that *lead* to the conclusion that the soul exists. In that case, as we have been emphasizing, an argument such as Anne's is a proper one because it does not appeal to any of the problematic sources we mentioned earlier (such as revelation, authority, or personal experience). It appeals only to ordinary, common sense, logical reasoning. (Indeed, let us not forget that all of the arguments for the existence of God in natural theology begin and proceed this way.) Consequently, it is not sufficient to exclude Anne because you don't think her process of reasoning is a good one. One cannot *define* the process of reasoning itself as requiring any kind of prior commitment to a comprehensive conception, or to some set of substantive metaphysical beliefs that are still in dispute in a pluralist society. There is a distinction between reasoning understood as accepting the truth of a worldview, and reasoning understood as the actual process itself, the way an argument is structured, how a reasonable case is presented and fits together. In any case, if one were to rule out a definition of reasoning because it required commitment to a worldview, this would have to apply to all worldviews, not just religious ones. Similarly, the process of general reasoning *is* available to everyone, just as scientific and mathematical forms of reasoning are. It is important to remind everyone (though we should not need reminding), that religious people use the same process of reasoning as everyone else, the same logic, the same pattern of inference, the same general ways of judging the rational case advanced to support a position.

These points concerning the nature of arguments for religious conclusions are pretty obvious, and having to insist on them reminds us once again not only of the special pleading involved but also of the general ignorance about religion that is present in the literature of secular liberalism. This literature is often only too happy to appeal to caricatures that rely heavily on portraying religious claims and by extension religious people as unreasonable. Religious believers should not be constantly faced with such a shallow approach, and continually called upon to respond to the ignorance and prejudices of liberal political philosophers and other intellectuals. Too often, secularists and secular liberals intentionally work with the caricature that religious claims are irrational, and often portray them as being based on "faith," in the sense of being based on a (blind) commitment, and on a (blind) trust in a certain scripture or religious tradition. "Faith" is here understood to refer to a view that is not based on argument or evidence, or at least that is not concerned with them.[26] Now, it is true that some religious beliefs *are* held in this way, and some are often represented as being held in this way (though it may only be a shorthand way of assuming but not making explicit a philosophical argument, as we have already noted). Yet our point here, however, is that a religious person can present a rational, analytical, philosophical, argument for his or her beliefs that is appropriate to introduce into public square arguments. So while we might rule out beliefs that are based on "faith," in this pejorative understanding of the term, we cannot rule out reasonable arguments. Indeed, we should be careful to distinguish between what individual religious believers might do, and religious beliefs themselves. It is the latter whose rationality we are concerned with! It is also very important for secular liberals to have an adequate understanding of views they reject. This means they have to talk more to people who disagree with them, make an honest effort to study the literature in the philosophy of religion, and approach it with the same professional attitude as they adopt toward any other area of research. This also seems to be required by a reasonable pluralism.

We should also point out that it is not only religious believers who hold beliefs on faith in the sense of a blind trust, and in the sense of not being particularly concerned with the evidence. Secularists do this too, as indeed do worldviews of every stripe. It is simply a fact of life that the subject matter of worldviews, the nature of reality, the nature of the human person, and the nature of moral and political values, does not admit of any kind of rational proof or scientific demonstration, and so at some point we must *commit* to the truth of our beliefs, as I have argued elsewhere.[27] There is always *an element of faith involved in our commitment to the main propositions of our worldviews.* Of course, it should be a reasonable commitment, one backed up by a rational argument insofar as one can do this, given our discussion above about the difficulties of convincing others of the truth of our beliefs. One example of a secularist belief that is accepted on a blind faith is the belief in and commitment to a range of natural human rights. We noted in earlier chapters that secular liberals of all stripes have found it very difficult to defend the scheme of natural rights that are among the foundations of secular liberalism (and kindred worldviews, such as secularism), and many thinkers who appeal to them in their moral and political arguments will routinely agree that they have no way to provide an ultimate justification for them.[28] Jeremy Bentham famously pronounced that appeal to rights talk was akin to "nonsense on stilts," since in rights theories of ethics rights claims are simply laid down by fiat, and lack ultimate justification (this general approach to natural rights is *very familiar* to us today). Alasdair MacIntyre has argued that the belief in human rights is like a belief in unicorns![29]; not only do many liberal thinkers admit that they have no general theory of philosophical justification for them, but it seems very difficult to see how, given their worldview commitments (especially concerning lack of purpose in nature), there could ever be an objective, as opposed to a cultural, justification for rights (a point that came out in our discussion of Kitcher's view in Chap. 5). Nicholas Wolterstorff argues that human rights can only be justified within a theistic framework.[30] Indeed, no issue shows the disagreement concerning what people regard as reasonable more than the debate about what should be included in the scheme of natural human rights.

Although Laborde, unlike many secular liberals, does consider the long tradition of philosophical argument to support religious belief (but only in an endnote), she does not think it produces arguments that are acceptable or accessible to others who disagree. Why is this? It is because: "Detailed accounts of the will of God (of the type 'If God exists, this is what he demands') are intelligible only within self-contained traditions of thought, but not broadly accessible."[31] I think one can see that this is not a satisfactory response on such a vital matter, and it is a weakness of her otherwise excellent study. The topic of the philosophical defense of religious belief requires much more attention than just one or two cursory remarks in an endnote. This is another instance where she seems again to confuse the process of reasoning with the conclusions the process arrives at. She is wrong if she thinks philosophical arguments for various religious claims are unintelligible outside of "a self-contained tradition of thought." The phrase "self-contained tradition of thought" is itself unclear; it seems to mean that only if one accepts a particular religion would one accept an argument within it but this is surely just another way of saying that she doesn't think religious conclusions arrived at after this process of reasoning are reasonable. Not only is her personal assessment of these arguments irrelevant, but it is unsatisfactory to pronounce on the reasonability of arguments for religious conclusions without discussing the actual arguments directly. We know that any direct discussion of the arguments, however, will simply show that the reason why one thinks these arguments are not "accessible" will always turn out to be because one thinks the arguments are not convincing, and not that they come from an unacceptable source (since their source, reasoned argument, is the same one that she is using herself!). That seems to be the problem that bedevils these kinds of rejections of religious arguments, in general. If a citizen like Anne is to keep her religious views out of politics, she is going to need a much better argument for doing so than Laborde's. Otherwise, liberal put-downs of religion seem to amount to little more than that Anne should keep out of politics because secular liberals disagree with her, which sounds like nothing more than discrimination toward religious views, and perhaps is even indicative of an animus toward them. These attitudes may unsettle citizens like Anne, but she does not have to take them seriously and is justified in ignoring them. It is one thing to reject a religious philosophical vision— but it is quite another to refuse to recognize it. This is an unfortunate attitude to adopt and it treats religious people with a disrespect that flies in the face of the democratic practice of civic virtue.

This leads to an important point about so-called liberal neutrality. Some thinkers, such as Jonathan Quong, have suggested that the official position of secular liberalism should be understood to mean that the state should be neutral between worldviews, advocating neither a religious comprehensive worldview nor a non-religious (i.e., secularist) comprehensive worldview.[32] The idea behind Quong's interesting argument is that when debating a topic like abortion we cannot appeal to the existence of the soul because people disagree about this, and presumably we also cannot appeal to its non-existence for the same reason. Quong suggests that we appeal just to liberal values when debating these issues, which would be a fair, neutral starting point, according to him. Yet the deeper problem facing a view like Quong's is that even if we agreed to his suggestion, it would not lead to a neutrality between the various worldviews. This is because of the fact that we decide how to interpret, apply, and weigh liberal political values *according to our worldviews*. This is inevitable: how else would one decide that the life of the unborn weighed more than the mother's (and father's) right to end that life, or *vice versa*? So if Quong decides that abortion should be made legal, he would be appealing to his own worldview, and his pretense at worldview neutrality would be gone. But even more deeply than this: his proposal, as Laborde correctly points out, to frame the problem this way—that it would be *wrong* to appeal to our comprehensive conceptions when weighing values—*itself reflects his own secularist worldview*. It requires that Quong take a position on moral truth, for instance. Besides, neutrality is an ideal one will not be able to keep because one will always end up insisting that liberal values support *one's own views* on the issues under dispute! This seems to be how modern liberal political philosophy works.

As Laborde notes, in order to draw a boundary between our comprehensive conceptions and the liberal political values latent in our democratic culture we must appeal to our own worldviews.[33] Moreover, others may feel that when weighing liberal values, we not only do, but should, appeal to our worldviews. This is in part why there is a dispute about how liberal values are to be interpreted and applied. Such values do not come with built-in answers to the difficult philosophical and moral issues of the day, despite the way many liberal thinkers talk. Liberal political theory seems to continually confuse the role of the shared political values that we all are said to accept, with the form or manner of reasoning that public reason requires. So, whenever there is a disagreement concerning whether public reason would reach this or that conclusion, liberal philosophers usually want to settle it by appealing to their own interpretation of the shared values, thereby smuggling in, and illegitimately appealing to, their own comprehensive view of the good.[34]

Within the context of which view is reasonable, which view is intelligible and accessible, Anne might also claim that it is very significant that religious views on many of these topics are the default views in history, more significant than is usually acknowledged by liberal political culture. For instance, the religious claim about the soul is the default view both historically and today in the sense that the vast majority of people think that some version of the religious worldview on the matter of the soul, and many other matters, is *the most reasonable view*. Given this fact, people *are more likely to be convinced* by a rational argument for the existence of the soul than by one against it, and surely this fact should play some role in making a decision about what people might *reasonably* accept, and whether overall a particular view is to be regarded as reasonable (and so "accessible") or not? It is true that Anne acknowledges that from a secularist (or secular liberal) point of view one would regard her view as wrong (not necessarily unreasonable), but does it follow that her view is not intelligible and that she should not then present her argument in a public debate? It does not seem so, even given the reality of reasonable pluralism. More generally, if most people regard secularism as false, even irrational, surely this fact places the onus concerning reasonability on the secularist more than on the religious believer? At very least, it seems to swing any worries concerning the intelligibility or accessibility of arguments over to the secularist camp.

Notes

1. John Rawls, *Political Liberalism*, p. 56.
2. As summarized by Jonathan Quong in "Public Reason," in the *Stanford Encyclopedia of Philosophy* (on line reference work); see also Rawls, *Political Liberalism*, p. 56.
3. See John Rawls, "The Idea of Public Reason Revisited," *The University of Chicago Law Review*, Vol. 64 (Summer 1997), p. 767.
4. Ibid., p. 771 (emphasis added).
5. Ibid., p. 786; see also *Political Liberalism*, pp. 137–138.
6. Rawls, *Political Liberalism*, p. 217.
7. Robert Talisse agrees that disagreement over the content of the ideals of liberal values is one of the things that democratic citizens are divided about; see his *Engaging Political Philosophy*, p. 151.
8. A good example is Ronald Dworkin, *Taking Rights Seriously* (Cambridge, MA: Harvard U.P., 1978); also Bruce Ackerman, *Social Justice in the Liberal State*. For further on this point, see Thomas Nagel, "Moral Conflict and Political Legitimacy," p. 223.
9. See Rawls, "The Idea of Public Reason Revisited," p. 781; pp. 783ff.
10. For a good overview of the discussion, and the literature, see Cécile Laborde, *Liberalism's Religion*, Chapters 3 and 4. See also my *Why Politics Needs Religion: The Place of Religious Arguments in the Public Square*, Chapter 6.
11. John Rawls, "The Idea of Public Reason Revisited," p. 797.
12. See Jeffrey Stout, *Democracy and Tradition*, pp. 67–68.
13. See Rawls, *Political Liberalism*, pp. 221–222.

14. Examples of discussions that would benefit from a detailed consideration of cases, similar to ones we discuss in this chapter, that use real life examples of religious and secularist arguments, making explicit their premises and conclusions, rather than relying upon abbreviated arguments and vague abstractions, include those to be found in the work of Stout, Laborde, Ackerman, and Rawls himself (all mentioned elsewhere in this chapter).
15. See Rawls, *Political Liberalism*, pp. 221–222.
    See Philip L. Quinn, "Political Liberalisms and their Exclusions of the Religious," in Paul Weithman (ed.), *Religion and Contemporary Liberalism*, pp. 150ff; see also, Robert P. George and Christopher Wolfe (eds.), *Natural Law and Public Reason* (Washington, DC: Georgetown U.P., 2000).
16. See Kent Greenawalt, *Private Consciences and Public Reasons* (New York: Oxford U.P., 1995), esp. Chapters 6 and 7; and Christopher Eberle, *Religious Conviction in Liberal Politics*, pp. 109–151.
17. See Paul Weithman, *Religion and the Obligations of Citizenship* (New York: Cambridge U.P., 2002).
18. For various perspectives on the issue of religion in public life, and the question of justifying secular liberalism, see, in addition to works already mentioned, Michael J. Perry, *Religion in Politics* (New York: Oxford U.P., 1987); Richard John Neuhaus, *The Naked Public Square* (Grand Rapids, MI.: Eerdmans, 1984); Gerald Gaus, *The Order of Public Reason* (New York: Cambridge U.P., 2011); Gavin D'Costa et al. (eds.), *Religion in a Liberal State* (New York: Cambridge U.P., 2013).
19. This point has been made by Thomas Nagel; see his "Moral Conflict and Political Legitimacy," p. 217.
20. See Robert Audi and Nicholas Wolterstorff, *Religion in the Public Square* (New York: Rowman and Littlefield, 1997, p. 99.
21. See C.J. Ducasse, *A Critical Examination of the Belief in a Life After Death* (Whitefish, MT: Kessinger, 2010; orig.1961).
22. Cécile Laborde, *Liberalism's Religion*, p. 120 and p. 121.
23. See ibid., pp. 120–121, and pp. 278–281.
24. Ibid., p. 122.
25. For several egregious examples of this phenomenon, see the work of legal scholars Stephen Gey and Suzanna Sherry, discussed in Francis J. Beckwith, *Taking Rites Seriously: Law, Politics and the Reasonableness of Faith* (New York: Cambridge, 2015), pp. 18–52.
26. See my *Why Politics Needs Religion*, pp. 38–41.
27. See Roger Trigg's criticism of A.C. Grayling on this point in his *Equality, Freedom, and Religion* (New York: Oxford U.P., 2012), p. 15.
28. See Alasdair MacIntyre, *After Virtue* (Notre Dame, IN.: University of Notre Dame Press, 1984), pp. 68–70.

29. For Wolterstorff's extensive defense of this view, see his *Understanding Liberal Democracy* (New York: Oxford U.P., 2012), pp. 177–226.
30. See Laborde, *Liberalism's Religion*, endnote 31, p. 280.
31. See Jonathan Quong, *Liberalism without Perfection* (New York: Oxford U.P., 2020), pp. 198ff.
32. See Laborde, *Liberalism's Religion*, pp. 96–97.
33. This point is demonstrated convincingly by Jean Hampton in her "Should Political Philosophy Be Done without Metaphysics?", *Ethics* 99 (4), pp. 791–814; see also on this point, Michael Sandel, *Liberalism and the Limits of Justice* (New York: Cambridge U.P., 1998); Seyla Benhabib, *The Claims of Culture: Equality and Diversity in the Global Era* (Princeton, NJ: Princeton U.P, 2002).

CHAPTER 9

Worldviews in Politics, and the Failure of Liberalism

Where does our analysis of the concept of public reason leave us with regard to the notion of reasonable pluralism? How should we respond to the fact that people hold different worldviews? Surely our fictional character Anne (and Robert), for instance, must recognize that others have different worldviews? The fairest way to approach this situation seems to be to consider things from the point of view of others (who disagree with us) in our pluralist society, *yet* it is not clear that doing this takes us any further toward any kind of liberal understanding of public reason. Anne will acknowledge that although she believes her position on abortion is true, she could be wrong. However, she does not believe it is false; at the very least she believes that it is reasonable, and also the most reasonable, position on the matter. Now the question is: is this scenario enough to make her hold back from introducing her view into public arguments? It is not clear why it should. Those who subscribe to other worldviews (like Robert) are in *exactly* the same position. Any restriction on Anne's arguments in public discussion would apply also to them, and so there is no good reason for excluding religious views that would not apply also to secularist views, as long as we respect the general restriction that arguments put forward should be reasonable, in the sense explained in the previous chapter.

Religion in Politics

It might be thought to follow from this that someone like Anne could also introduce a belief into the public square that is justified primarily by an appeal to biblical revelation. Let us say that she is much impressed with Billy Graham's argument that Jesus teaches that we should give special attention to the plight of the poor based on the many biblical passages that address this topic. Graham explained that later in his career he made a study of the numerous times Jesus talked about the poor throughout the Christian scriptures, and as a result began to address this topic more in his preaching.[1] According to Audi, Rawls, and liberal political theory, Anne (and Graham) should not introduce an argument of this form into the public square as a reason for helping the poor. But on the view we have been developing, she could do so as long as she was prepared to give a rational justification for the reliability of Christian revelation, perhaps something similar to the one offered by John Locke, who, now that she has been reading him, has greatly impressed her with his arguments for the reasonableness of Christianity![2]

Of course, these kinds of arguments are disputed; some think they are good arguments, others are not convinced. We can readily imagine that secularists and members of other religions would reject arguments like Locke's (and similar contemporary accounts, such as those from scholars Luke Timothy Johnson, N.T. Wright, or Gary Habermas). But is this enough to keep these kinds of arguments out of the public square—the fact that some disagree with them? One way to try to forbid them is Audi's—to suggest that they do not come from a legitimate source on which to base public arguments. However, this objection does not apply here because these arguments do come from the right source, *reason* (i.e., the reliability of scripture is presented as part of a rational case, and not simply assumed). Moreover—and many writings on democratic political theory today and on public reason overlook this point—many Christians introduce religious arguments into politics today because *they are convinced of the rational case for the reliability of scripture* (this is especially true of many Catholics). So this is not simply a theoretical discussion. Nonetheless, we do not need to insist on this point, but perhaps only that we should leave it on the table as a possibility. Some version of it might be appropriate in the public square, though not a fundamentalist version, but one where there is a fruitful and dialogical interplay between biblical revelation and philosophical argument.

Our main argument is that the general religious approach to reality can be shown to be reasonable, and so we can agree for current purposes not to appeal to arguments based on scriptural revelation, or some of the other problematic sources mentioned in our consideration of Audi's position, in public arguments. As we explained in Chap. 5, the religious understanding of reality is a philosophical view, based on a long tradition of philosophical, theological, and historical argument. It is a vision of ultimate meaning and value, which is backed up by reason. It is not based first and foremost on an appeal to scriptural texts. It is true that it involves some relationship with revelatory scriptures, but there is an independent line of philosophical argument to back up the broad vision outlined in Christian scriptures, even though there are often difficulties with how to reconcile the two, or even about whether they can be reconciled. This is not a critical matter for our argument. All we are interested in is the position that the religious worldview is a reasonable worldview, and can be appealed to independently of scripture. One may be tempted to reply that the fact that there is a plurality of world religions counts against the view that any tradition could present a rational case for the reliability of their scriptures (a point made by Kitcher in Chap. 5). But we noted there the problem with this claim: it applies equally well to *any* view, religious and secularist, that claims to be reasonable among the wide range of worldviews that are a feature of modern pluralism.

So we are back once again to the objection that some people disagree with the case being made—but who decides whether a person has a reasonable argument that is worthy enough to present in the public square? Surely this is itself a public issue, rather than someone deciding in advance that a certain form of reasoning is inadmissible? Who would have the authority to decide this? Anne may realize that in the present democratic context it is particularly contentious to introduce religious arguments into public discussion, but this means not that it is unreasonable but that some people with different views than hers on the issues of the day think her arguments are not reasonable. That is the problem—she thinks her views are reasonable but others do not, and there is no independent way to adjudicate between the two. The problem with an approach like Audi's is that he appears to want to use *his own worldview beliefs* to control what can count in a public argument, a move which would rig the debate in his favor, a problem that bedevils the whole of liberal political theory. Audi's view relies upon our accepting *his* metaphysical position with regard to Dostoevsky's question about whether morality can be justified (not known) independently of God, so it does not meet his own test of public reason. It is not a metaphysical claim he has convinced people of by offering reasons that all can accept, but an essential claim of his worldview we are required to agree to in advance in order to proceed in the debate. Moreover, it is a claim that plays an influential, if not decisive, role *in settling the very issue we are supposed to be debating*. Audi also appears to accept the position that secular reason *cannot* arrive at *religious* conclusions. Anne disagrees, but *Audi's judgment on this matter* seems to be the one that must regulate the public discussion.

Perhaps because of these concerns might not Anne consider adopting Audi's principle of secular motivation after all, or something close to it? She may see that many of her arguments are contentious in our pluralist society (which has a bit of a prejudice against religion, especially Christianity, in certain intellectual and elite circles) and so decide instead to offer an argument to support her view that does not make appeal to or rely upon the truth of any religious content. In this sense, she plays along with the rules proposed by secular liberalism in terms of the structure of her public arguments. So, for instance, with regard to her argument that abortion is immoral, she may try to develop it in a way that makes no reference at all to religious content, even content supported by reason. However, there are several problems with Anne adopting the principle of secular motivation, even for pragmatic purposes. One is: does she *believe* the argument that makes no appeal to religious content? Does she find it convincing? She may hold, as many religious believers do and indeed many philosophers too, that morality cannot be justified apart from God, and so she is not convinced by any argument for a moral conclusion that is not grounded in God's nature.[3] She is simply being pragmatic in appealing to a kind of secular argument because she knows that it is more likely to resonate with those who are not religious, though whether it would persuade them is another matter. As we noted, there is an old and very respectable argument in philosophy and theology that God may have given us a secular, rational route to correct morality, as well as a way through the scriptures. However, let us suppose that Anne is familiar with this tradition but is not convinced by it. Then it seems that Audi's advance argument (an advance argument for why one should not introduce religious arguments into political discussion) cannot be allowed to prevail because it is not fair—it relies upon our acceptance of an important claim of *his worldview* (that morality can be justified independently of God), a claim that Anne rejects.

A second problem is that the pragmatic argument is fundamentally dishonest in the sense that Anne is presenting a secular argument but is really motivated by a religious argument. This is in part why Audi introduces his principle of secular motivation. He seems to think that religious believers perhaps will be dishonest or disingenuous when they engage in public arguments. Giving him the benefit of a charitable reading, he thinks that they may deceive themselves into insisting on the force of their secular arguments because they are already committed to the conclusion for religious reasons *based on the questionable sources of support* that he rejects (such as scriptural revelation). For example, he thinks they might develop a non-religious argument against abortion that relies on the claim that the embryo has supreme value because it is a human being from the moment of conception. But the real reason they think the embryo is a human being from conception onward is because they believe it has a soul (though they do not mention this point, and may not even realize the part this belief plays in their public argument, for they are not really thinking about their motivation). So although their argument satisfies the principle of secular rationale, it fails the principle of secular motivation. Audi's principle wishes to exclude this possibility, and he seems to think that there will then be no good secular arguments for many of the views that religious believers wish to introduce into politics (e.g., on abortion—this is why when secular liberals insist on prohibiting arguments with religious content from public discussion they believe the result will be that religious arguments will not be able to play a role in public deliberation). Of course, we have noted that others will disagree; we saw that religious claims can also be backed by (secular) reasons. We should also note that there is always enough distrust to go around, that no side is morally pure. Robert (in our example from the previous chapter) would fail the principle of secular motivation if his motivation in defending abortion is a desire to give freedom the last word (and not his belief that the embryo is not human).

However, with regard to the present point, Anne may be acting dishonestly if she presents a secular argument of which she is not fully convinced. Perhaps her position is somewhat acceptable since we could say that there is nothing wrong with being diplomatic even in a public argument if it helps the discussion, that one shouldn't introduce contentious arguments if one can avoid doing so (especially in the current climate), but should work with whatever will help to get you to your conclusion. We can imagine a politician adopting this strategy. Anne might in fact believe that there *are* good secular arguments for her position—that it can be justified in a secular way that is sufficiently motivational, even though perhaps the full justification of it requires appealing to the reasonability of religious claims in the end. Many moral views are like this—their full justification takes us back to foundational beliefs of a particular worldview, even though we could give a good argument for them that would be sufficiently motivational without having to go back to the foundational beliefs. This is perhaps why many people from different worldviews can hold the same moral beliefs, but justify them differently (a point made by Jacques Maritain).[4] But surely Audi's suspicions about the motives and attitudes of religious believers would apply also to liberal secularists or even liberal religious believers?

It is perhaps worth reflecting for a moment on the general topic of motivation and honesty in the process of public deliberation. When it comes to the issue of motivation, one can easily imagine that someone like Anne may have particular difficulties with liberal approaches in general, especially on the topic we are considering, abortion. Anne may find it difficult to trust liberal secularists, particularly in our contentious pluralist climate (they often have the same attitude toward Anne and her kind)! She thinks they act quite irrationally, even in an age of pluralism, by adopting the stance that it is just obvious that everyone should agree with their views. (This is why more than one philosopher has suggested that the notion of public reason may be something of a sham.) Anne may have a lot of experience in engaging in contentious arguments with secular liberals on abortion, and is inclined to think that it is part of the essence of their position to be hypocritical in the sense that they continually insist on others following principles and procedures that they do not follow themselves. She is inclined to regard their appeal to principles as a tactical maneuver. So she wonders if they would really make an honest effort to be reasonable.

So the debate is made very difficult for her for several reasons. Based on her experience, she may find it difficult to trust those who argue in favor of abortion because they often refuse to acknowledge that abortion involves a moral issue at all. She struggles not to regard them as prejudiced and irrational, even sometimes as fanatics, and she often despairs of trying to reason with fanatics. They are likely to have an animus toward any religious worldview that will affect their appraisal of the rationality of its moral positions. In terms of motivation, she might feel that secularists may also be suspect in the way Audi suggests that religious believers are. For example, Anne may believe that the ultimate motivation for their views on topics like euthanasia and abortion is because they don't believe there is a supreme being who gives value to human life, and this belief influences their final views on these topics even though they do not make this belief explicit in their public arguments. In this sense, they would fail a principle analogous to the principle of secular motivation, since these foundational beliefs are essential to make sense of their views, but assumed and not shared by all.

She may hold that, in general, secularism, with its strong emphasis on individual autonomy, is particularly hard on certain categories of people, especially the disabled and others with genetic abnormalities, and is inclined to the view that such lives are not worth living. She notes that secularists are prone to refuse to discuss the issue fairly and directly; those who favor the legalization of abortion (including academics) frequently refer to abortion as a "termination," "a medical procedure," a form of "health care," employ the term "reproductive rights," even as we are supposed to be debating whether or not abortion is a right. Even though not everyone is guilty of this approach, she finds it challenging to enter a public debate because of these worries. She wonders if liberal secularists regard her as a reasonable person, and whether they approach the debate with good will. Anne may regard the liberal mind as closed, in much the same way liberal secularists regard the fundamentalist religious mind as closed.

Getting past all of this, Anne realizes, is essential for an honest debate, but it is quite difficult to do so. In fact, she may think that day is long gone! As a seasoned participant in this debate, she knows that part of the typical liberal persona is to regard themselves as enlightened and superior to her rationally and morally. She has experienced name calling, impugning of her motives, and accusations of immorality. She is quite mistrustful of such people and thinks they are likely to run roughshod over democratic rights in their zeal. Anne has grown tired of the general liberal approach to abortion because it is dishonest and inconsistent, and would rather avoid a debate if possible, especially at the political level (thankfully, it is more responsible at the academic, especially the philosophical, level). She regards liberalism in general as discriminatory because it treats her worldview differently to other worldviews. It is also irrational because it often has difficulty in grounding its moral values. It is also hypocritical (as Stanley Hauerwas has observed[5]) because it advocates the suppression of views like hers (it is not just saying she is wrong, but that she should keep out of the debate), while at the same time preaching loudly and continuously openness and respect for other views! She also finds it quite dishonest in its deliberate tendency to represent most religious arguments as being based "on faith" (in the sense of not being based on evidence, or even caring about evidence or rational argument), or some obvious irrational foundation, and ignoring the history of the discussion, and the philosophical case both for the rationality of religious belief in general, and for the immorality of abortion in particular. Moreover, liberal approaches often wish to reshape society in their image, while all the time insisting that its position is "neutral" between disputed views. Although, it is occasionally on its best behavior, it does sometimes slip into bigotry and irrationality toward her views, attitudes she has experienced in public debates, especially in the political arena. The upshot is that Anne thinks that secular liberals are unlikely to be reasonable in public; they are more likely to be everything that is the opposite! Do Anne's opponents think much the same about her? These are yet further reasons why the notion of public reason is problematic today. While we can imagine how it might work in an idealized way, we should also consider how it is likely to work in practice. At least on the question of *motivation*, there seems to be plenty of suspicion to go around. The sad fact is that if one distrusts the motives of others, one is more likely to regard them as unreasonable.

Another difficulty with Anne accepting the principle of secular motivation is that it may weaken the influence of her view in the long run. In presenting a pragmatic argument, she may be playing into the hands of the secular liberal approach, acquiescing in the view that her religious worldview has no place in politics. This is bound to give to the secular liberal a considerable advantage, and to be to the detriment of the religious view in the end. Indeed, in modern democratic societies this has been one clear effect of the secular liberal effort to treat religion as a second class citizen; in practical terms, the result has been that many religious believers keep quiet in public debates. Even official Church organizations and influential religious leaders often take a back seat in moral and cultural discussions in which they should be involved, from the point of view of healthy democratic practice. So Anne would need to think twice before embarking on such a strategy. It might be better for the advancement of her views if she advocates religious claims openly and up front, clearly and rationally, in the public square. Not only would this strengthen her view overall, but it would also highlight the rationality of her view in the debate with other worldviews, and also perhaps show what we have been discussing—that attempts to restrict religion in public life are illegitimate attempts to give the upper hand to secular liberalism (and ultimately to secularism). It also shows more respect for others if one argues honestly, tells them what one really believes, difficult though this can sometimes be in our fractious political climate.

So it is inevitable that there would be suspicion cast toward the kind of secular liberalism that we see in Rawls and his followers because of its deliberate and sustained attempt to exclude religious arguments from political deliberation. These misgivings are fueled further by the presumption that when liberal political thinkers talk about not consulting one's comprehensive view of the good in a political argument (and, in Rawls' theory, in not having access to one's view of the good in the original position) they understand themselves, and are generally understood by everyone, to be referring to religious views. We can be even more specific, as Thomas Nagel is, when he notes that secular liberals seem as if they are trying in particular to develop a view that is aimed at restricting appeals to religious moral positions in certain areas of life, usually those opposed to a secular, individualistic, permissive morality! We see this also in Audi, who makes it clear that he does not like certain views, those he describes as coming from religious fundamentalism, being introduced into politics, and his work is a good representative of this general approach. Proponents of this outlook seldom consider cases where religious thinkers advocate political positions on health care, social welfare, the morality of war, the homeless problem, gang violence, inner city housing or joblessness, drugs and problems of addiction, or other key topics of great social and cultural significance. It is hard to avoid the impression that this is because they often agree with religious views on these questions. So they look past the inconsistency that if religious views are to be restricted in politics, this should apply to all religious views, including those that would coerce us into paying more taxes to support social welfare programs, or to developing a health care system that is guided by certain religious values, and so forth.

Most liberal political philosophers give no attention (except perhaps making occasional side comments) to secularism as a significant worldview in modern democracy in the way we have done in earlier chapters. As well as working with religious caricatures for most of their examples, they rarely if ever use secularist positions as examples of arguments that could also be excluded from the public square. Liberal thinkers continually fall into two errors that are obvious from even a cursory reading of their works: they convey the impression that secularist views are neutral on worldview questions, and they think that secularism already uses secular reason (while religion usually does not, and in the opinion of most of them, cannot, yet they do not consider the question carefully or in any detail). This is obvious from our example in the previous chapter concerning the soul—secular liberalism assumes that if you hold the view that there is no soul you are not taking a position on the philosophical question, whereas if you think the soul exists you are taking a position! Audi's work, in particular, but also most of the standard works in liberal political theory, would need to be significantly revised if forced *to consider secularism as a major worldview that is competing with religious worldviews and trying to shape culture*. This move would compel an engagement with the question whether secularist claims can pass the test of public reason. If they can, why can't religious views, and if they cannot, why would secularist views then be entitled to a privileged place in politics? Many in this camp may not wish to establish secularism as the default view in society, but they do wish to establish secularist positions on various issues as the law, or at least base the law on *their own political and moral views* (as Nagel honestly admits).

CASE STUDY: MARTIN LUTHER KING, JR. AND CIVIL RIGHTS

It is instructive to continue our discussion by a consideration of the case developed by Rev. Dr. Martin Luther King, Jr. in his fight for civil rights for African Americans in the United States. King was clearly a devout and sincere religious believer, whose religious beliefs are an integral and formative part of his personality, his character, and his political views. I suggest that this is clear and indisputable based on his writings on religious and political issues, which are of course often intertwined. His famous *Letter from Birmingham Jail* (1963) clearly offers a religious argument to support his call for equality for African Americans, and to defend his campaign of political protest.[6] I think the *Letter* can also be read perhaps as offering a secular type of argument for the same conclusion, though this is not entirely clear. But the main argument he offers is a religious one, and indeed it has a quite familiar structure. In summary form, he argues that civil rights are based on natural rights and that natural rights come from God. His argument appeals to the natural law theory of morality. He quotes several thinkers in this tradition, including St. Thomas Aquinas, not as authorities to back up his argument, but to point out that the argument is very familiar and philosophically well-established. I think he is also noting that it is widely held by all of those he is addressing, including those Church leaders who agree with his moral views about racial inequality and civil rights but who disagree with his political protest.

King replies in his *Letter* to the objection that the protests are unwise at this time (Spring 1963), that we can't accomplish everything in a short time and so he should wait because African Americans will achieve equal rights eventually, by saying that time is in fact neutral and the way we accomplish things is by being "coworkers with God." He rejects the criticism that he is an extremist, unless by that term is meant someone who wishes to put God's law into action, in which case it would include Jesus, Amos, Luther, Bunyan, and Lincoln, among many others! He notes in particular that he is disappointed in the white church for *not* introducing their religious beliefs into politics; he thinks they believe and say one thing, but fail to put it into practice in society. And he praises the Catholic Church for being an exception, because of its integration of Spring Hill College, in Mobile, Alabama. He adds that many young people have become disgusted with the Churches because of the failure of their leaders to implement their religious views into politics, and notes that if religious institutions do not engage politically they will become irrelevant (an argument one still hears today). He argues that this is the true meaning of the Gospel, to put moral law into action, and "we will win our freedom because the sacred heritage of our nation and the eternal will of God are embodied in our echoing demands."[7]

The *Letter* is a very powerful document which has had enormous influence. King acknowledged later that although it was originally written on the margins of newspapers while he was in jail, he polished it afterward for publication. It is very carefully crafted, well written, makes references to religious and political thinkers throughout history, as well as employing familiar but powerful arguments from the tradition of natural law to build a very convincing case for civil rights. King does not so much present a developed argument that natural law includes equality for African Americans. He knows that most people already accept this to be true, and will acknowledge that eventually African Americans will be accorded full civil rights. He rather *reminds* people of these points; a strong theme of the essay is that many already find his argument persuasive, and so have a duty to act on it from a political point of view. The argument is primarily religious and wishes to draw attention to the political implications of our religious beliefs.

However, that is not all that is to be said. There are at least two other significant themes in the essay that are relevant. The first is one we might refer to as an appeal to the founding principles of the United States. King more than once notes that the U.S. was founded on liberty and equality, and that these values require that all citizens be treated equally before the law. He suggests that this is part of the essence of America, and that people are being inconsistent in denying these rights to a segment of the population. Whether he also thinks that the founding of America itself is based on religious ideas, specifically Christian ideals, is not entirely clear, though his remarks could be read in this way, in which case this would be another religious argument for his conclusion. It would be a more sophisticated argument but one that some contemporary thinkers have proposed, including Michael Novak and Richard John Neuhaus, that Christianity supports democracy, and that democracy supports natural and civil rights.[8]

The second point is that if we do not read this theme in a religious way, one might read King's appeal to the founding values of the U.S. as a kind of secular argument for his main conclusion in the essay. It could be read as an attempt to apply the principle of secular rationale in the sense that he can offer a secular argument for those who are not religious or who reject the religious argument he proposes.[9] He could perhaps have left out the religious argument from the essay and simply offered a secular argument for the same conclusion based on appeal to the founding values of the U.S., and its history and traditions. The question of course is: does he actually believe in the validity of such an argument, does he find it convincing, or is it simply a pragmatic gesture (if we read the essay in this way) aimed at those who might reject, even scoff, at the religious argument? In short, it might be similar to a possible approach we considered in Anne's case (above) when she discusses abortion at the political level—to avoid ridicule or dismissal, and to be taken more seriously, she makes use of a secular argument that she thinks may have some purchase value in public discourse but one which she herself does not find convincing.

I think it is clear that King is motivated by a religious argument primarily. It is not clear that he would find the secular argument, if it is present, convincing as well. In fact, I think we would have to agree that he would not, since the whole direction of his case is so strongly religious. So King's letter fails Audi's principle of secular motivation (as well as the principle of secular rationale) and so, according to Audi, he should not offer this argument in the public square. It seems to me that King is one of those thinkers who believes that morality comes from God, and that without God, there is no justification for moral values, and so he may also believe that one cannot give moral arguments without appealing to God's moral law somewhere in the argument. For example, in his essay *Our God is Able*, he points out that evil in history soon passes away because it is against God's law, drawing attention to the constant struggle between good and evil. King also notes that God works through leaders and moral reformers, and that God has placed moral laws within the structure of the universe. In addition, God gives us interior resources to deal with the trials and difficulties of life, including those challenges that call for moral reform.[10] He tells the story of how in his campaign for civil rights he was often afraid of the all too real threats to his personal safety. He thought about giving up his work. Who wouldn't in the circumstances he was faced with? However, he appealed in prayer to God for strength. He tells us that in response he experienced the presence of the divine and gained the courage to continue.[11] This clearly shows that his motivation is religious and not secular, and I think any reasonable reading of his work must come to the conclusion that he would deny that one could even have a secular justification for morality. So if King were to offer a secular argument it would be for pragmatic reasons and not because he found it convincing.

Let us recall that a secular argument is one that appeals to reason, yet is not allowed to appeal to any religious premises or conclusions; it cannot include any religious content, or appeal to the truth of any religious beliefs in the argument. We might ask whether Martin Luther King would agree that one can give a rational argument for the truth of religious belief, in the way we suggested in Chap. 8. I think he would agree, since he bases much of his own argument on the natural law tradition and this is one of the main arguments of that tradition. Recall that Audi is skeptical that one can do this, and also argued that other sources were unacceptable as a basis for religious truth, the main one being appeal to revelation, but also including appeals to tradition, authority, and private religious experiences. King appealed to a private religious experience to explain the source of his strength to continue on with his work, though this is not quite the same as offering a private religious argument for the truth of his work. His argument for the latter is, as we have just noted, more philosophical, but no less religious in content. So although his appeal to private experience would be ruled out by liberal political thinkers, my claim is that he could offer a philosophical argument for his religious conclusions about morality and civil rights that would be legitimate in the public square.

Let us draw our points together from this consideration of the historically very significant case of Martin Luther King and his very powerful argument. The first observation is that he is clearly introducing religious arguments into political matters, and that he thinks their introduction is of the upmost importance for one's integrity as a religious believer on not only the issue of civil rights but on any issue of significance for society. He believes that religious arguments clearly have a role to play in the promotion of social justice. We have noted earlier in our discussion that some religious beliefs have clear political implications, and, in our consideration of the views of Philip Kitcher in Chap. 5, we suggested that some people even *choose* their religion based on moral and political considerations (today we shop for everything; some people even go "religion shopping"!). So the political dimension of religion is not only obvious, I would say, but growing. Second, although he does not present a developed philosophical argument in any of his works, it does seem to be the case that he thinks his religious arguments are reasonable, and he refers to great minds in history as a way of introducing an argument that he is assuming but not rehearsing in his own writings. The general thrust of his approach is more on the side of rational religion than on the side of fundamentalism; the latter approach would mostly appeal to revelation and biblically based arguments. Third, he does spend a good deal of time developing the view that some religious beliefs have political implications, and that if one does not pursue such implications, it violates one's integrity as a religious believer and makes religious belief irrelevant in the modern age.

Fourth, he thinks that religion therefore can make a worthwhile contribution to the development of society because it has profound things to say about social justice and other important matters. It can be a great motivator for people, including at the political level, to do the right thing. This is not just because we already agree with the cause of social justice; religious views can make a contribution to whatever issues society is faced with, irrespective of whether or not some people frown upon or disagree with their contribution. This is true for abortion, euthanasia, social welfare policy, how to tackle poverty, the need for an adequate health care system, responding to the excesses of consumerism, human alienation, exploitation, as much as it is for civil rights. Fifth, his political argument would be greatly diminished if his religious arguments were diminished, or ruled out of court; his position would lose much of its force, as far as he is concerned. He does not seem to think that one can even give a secular argument for his position. So can we therefore conclude that any political theory that would exclude his religious arguments from politics is on the wrong track? As King said, God "is our mandate for seeking to make a better world."[12] He also said: "Before I was a civil rights leader, I was a preacher of the Gospel. This was my first calling and it still remains my greatest commitment. You know, actually all that I do in civil rights I do because I consider it a part of my ministry. I have no other ambitions in life but to achieve excellence in the Christian ministry. I don't plan to run for any political office. I don't plan to do anything but remain a preacher. And what I'm doing in this struggle, along with many others, grows out of my feeling that the preacher must be concerned about the whole man."[13]

It seems to be a clear case of discrimination against King's religious views if he were forced to sit out the debate about civil rights. He would lose his integrity as a moral human being. He would be forced to sit out opportunities for public deliberation, even though he has very strong views on the issues, and even though he believes that his view is the objectively true view (and we can agree that from the point of view of objective morality—not just an appeal to a consensus or a majority view—King's view is *the correct one* on this matter, however difficult this may be to establish rationally in our present climate of relativism, anti-realism, and appeal to majority opinion). He would be in a particularly undesirable position, because although he has strong moral views on an issue of great significance for society, and for the practical day-to-day lives of human beings, he is being silenced because of his religious views. He is not in one of two alternatives positions that would not be nearly as personally problematic. One is where he accepts that he should not bring his religious views into politics, but because he thinks there is a good secular argument for the same conclusion, it does not affect him so much. The second is the position of a secularist who can argue for or against political issues, as he sees fit.

It is no good replying, as Audi does, with an argument that he (Audi) believes that there is a secular path to the same moral position. Audi suggests that God must have given us the faculty of reason so that we could work out moral truth on our own without appealing to religious truth or religious content (e.g., that God exists and ordains the moral order). King very likely rejects this type of argument. In any case, Audi cannot speak for him on this matter—or to put it more accurately, Audi's case depends upon this independent advance argument *being convincing to King*. But if it is not convincing to him, then Audi's view that religious views should be excluded is still supposed to prevail, but arbitrarily, because it fails his own test of public reason—it is not rationally acceptable to all on whom it would be imposed. It is also no good replying that, from the point of view of free speech in a democratic society, King is still free to contribute to political debates. This is because the liberal position is that even though he *could* contribute because he enjoys freedom of speech, he *should* not do so. He is doing something wrong from the point of view of liberal democracy if he introduces his religious beliefs into politics, even though he can do so (legally); he is, in fact, being a bad citizen, treating his fellow citizens with disrespect. This is the motivation behind the notion of civic virtue that many political thinkers advocate.[14] Civic virtue is usually a notion designed to direct the public debate into a certain channel by laying out restrictions for the ways one can argue in public discussion. And while some of the criteria are good, and rooted in common sense, some are problematic because they appear to decide substantive questions in advance of the actual process of public deliberation. For instance, it would be unacceptable to hold that civic virtue includes treating others with respect, and then to define respect as meaning that one must present them with an argument they can accept.

Assessment of Rawls and Political Liberalism

This brings us to an overall assessment of political liberalism. Although I reject all versions of Rawls' political philosophy, I recognize that it is a valiant attempt to deal with a very difficult problem, the problem of what I have been calling worldview pluralism. His theory is thought-provoking, extremely insightful, thoroughly developed, and yet seems to be unrealistic and unworkable! Sometimes I don't think we appreciate the fact that Rawls is very influenced by historical circumstances. Speaking very generally, he is writing in a certain historical situation in the Western world that influences significantly how he sets up his theory, and that also explains its strong appeal to those thinkers who share the same mindset. The historical circumstances are that in the West the religious worldview has not only been the dominant one, but the only one, for many centuries, with Christianity and specifically Catholicism the main religion of most people. After the Reformation, Christianity split into various denominations. These denominations often could not live peacefully side by side; not only did they differ sharply over matters of belief and doctrine, they also engaged in the wars of religion in various countries (though we have to be careful to acknowledge that these wars were not just about religion; all kinds of political, social, and economic matters, along with ethnic grievances and resentments, played a role in civil unrest, just as they do today). Nevertheless, it is true that in specific countries religion had a great hold on the culture, and had the power to influence the state in many areas, such as education, politics, and law. Eventually, democracy led to pluralism in the way we have seen in earlier chapters. One result of pluralism is that we ended up with significant numbers of people who rejected the religious worldview, some who thought it was irrational, and many who wished to curb its power and influence over society.

Allied with all of this was the idea of setting up a secular state. While the definition of a secular state is open to debate (as we have explained), it did at least mean that the democratic state would have no established religion, a position that gradually evolved into the contemporary understanding that religion should have little or no influence on law or politics. Moreover, we also had a growing movement of secularism which is defined as much by resentment and rejection of religion as it is by its own positive theses, though it is well on the way to being a fully fledged worldview, as we illustrated. Given all of this, a brilliant thinker like Rawls came along to tackle the problem. Rawls himself is writing specifically within an American context, a country that has always had an ambivalent attitude toward religion, and that has a tradition of treating it differently to other beliefs and values, and also with regard to its relationship to the state. Patrick Dineen has argued in fact that the American version of democracy can be read as being deeply hostile to religion, even though the opposite view is widely touted by scholars and legal experts (with the usual proviso that nevertheless religion must be kept separate from the state).[15]

Rawls is writing within this context. So from his point of view the problem is how to diminish the influence of religion on the state, how to keep religious views on various issues, especially perhaps moral issues, in the background, or at least how to contain them. A solution to this difficulty may go somewhat toward mitigating what I have called the problem of worldview pluralism. One might cynically regard Rawls' view as a version of the simple problem of how—given that we have a growing number of secularists and perhaps also of (liberal) religious believers who are irritated with more traditional religious approaches—to keep the latter views on the margins in order to restrict their influence. So Rawls devises a very sophisticated theory to deal with this problem. One can suggest that if history had been different and the roles reversed, say the exact same cultural scenario had played out with the one key difference being that secularism was the dominant view, we might now have a theory aimed at keeping secularism at bay, and allowing a marginalized number of religious believers to avoid it, reject it, and contain its influence on the state!

In this way, I think that social, political, and cultural history has had a large influence on where philosophical thinking about democratic pluralism now stands, rather than thinkers simply offering an objective rational analysis of the issues, independently of historical circumstances. We have become somewhat hampered by Rawls' approach, and perhaps it would be better to leave it behind us, and move forward. It would be more fruitful, I believe, if we would stop talking as if the meaning of liberal political values is somehow built into them, stop side-stepping the question of their philosophical justification, stop talking as if reason can only reach one conclusion, and stop taking an (inconsistent) relativistic approach to modern disagreements.

In assessing Rawls' general approach then, there are many issues we could focus on such as whether there really is "a shared political culture," and what its nature is; whether there can be an overlapping consensus; whether the original position is a realistic starting point; whether we would agree to the principles of justice if we started with the original position; whether the principles are fair; how the principles are to be weighted in relation to each other, and so forth. All of these issues have been extensively discussed by scholars. I wish to focus, instead, on the bigger picture of Rawls' view and make a few general points of criticism in the areas most germane to our discussion in this book. Rawls' notion of reasonable pluralism begins from the position that we should all accept our "shared political culture." This seems to me to mean at very least that our worldview is in some way *subordinate* to this shared political culture. But what does that amount to in practice? Does it mean that my worldview can have no role in politics? No, the best understanding of it is that whenever I propose a political argument, it must be presented in terms of public reason. The problem is that the process of public reason will turn out to generally favor secularist views. This is why it is important that many liberal political philosophers seem to *take it for granted* that religious belief is outside of reason (or at least present this stance in the discussion, as an easy way of avoiding a real debate about this matter, a debate whose conclusion they may suspect would upend their whole approach). Rawls' position has also generally carried with it the connotation that the shared political values *entail* certain political positions, for example, the legalization of abortion. While this is obviously not true, it is nevertheless an assumption of the position, which is one reason it is so attractive to those who favor the legalization of abortion.

A key question now presents itself: should a religious believer accept Rawls' political theory? I have argued that it is possible for religious conclusions to be based on reason. So one of our main criticisms of Rawls and liberal political theory is that we cannot accept the notion of public reason, at least in its current form. *The problem is that appeal to it appears to rule out arbitrarily the view that reason can reach positions that are religious in nature, that it is possible to argue to reasonable religious conclusions.* One might, as we noted, believe personally that this is the case with regard to religious views, but one cannot speak for others on this question, and so the notion cannot work. One might be intellectually blind, irrational, prejudiced, stubborn, self-interested, ignorant, engaged in self-deception, or blinded by emotion, and for such reasons as these one may not accept the reasonability of an argument that reaches a religious conclusion (such as, an argument for the existence of the soul, or for the existence of God, for that matter). Or one might follow the argument honestly and as rationally as one can, but reject it, or even agree that it is reasonable, but reject it. But *none* of these responses can support the liberal notion of public deliberation. I agree that it is more problematic if a religious believer wishes to bring an argument into the public square that is based purely on an appeal to revelation or tradition, as discussed earlier.

In defending his overall approach, Rawls appeals to ideas *latent* in our shared political culture (and so avoids appealing to *his own values*, his comprehensive view of the good). Such a view however appears to commit him to a kind of cultural relativism in the sense that he is not actually defending the truth of the shared political values, but assuming it. The problem then is that the question of their objective truth is left to one side. This move is in keeping with the general skeptical and relativistic approach of modern liberalism, and is why some argue that a main reason we should reject liberal political theory is because it is based on a skeptical view of knowledge. Jean Hampton has expressed the problem very well: "Over and over again...Rawls [and liberal political philosophy] must choose between a political theory that is morally neutral but impossible to justify apart from an appeal to what people happen to believe, or else a political theory for which there is a powerful justification but which, for that reason, cannot be morally neutral. There is no middle ground between these two choices...there is no such thing as a theoretically consistent form of 'neutrality liberalism.'"[16]

In short, to embark on Rawls' project, one has to first accept a general approach to knowledge—that objective truth is very difficult to achieve, and that a skeptical stance is more appropriate in a pluralist context. From another angle, we might all be prepared for the sake of argument to accept the general idea of a shared political culture as a clever way to solve the difficult problem of pluralism, but we face an extra difficulty—that there is no agreement on what the shared political values *mean* in the concrete. And without such agreement the view is unworkable with regard to settling issues that involve substantive disputes. Settling on what the values mean, how they are to be weighted in relation to each other, and how they are to be weighted in our particular worldviews, always involves privileging *someone's* worldview (as we noted in our discussion of Quong's view in the previous chapter). Moreover, we must acknowledge that it is even doubtful whether there is a shared *set* of political values today—people are too far apart for this to be possible. Many hold incommensurable views of the nature of the human person, so no political theory has much chance of success in today's pluralist culture if it wishes to assume from the outset a common set of human values.

A related argument offered by some thinkers as a response to these problems is that the difference between liberalism as a procedural view and other comprehensive views in the state (including versions of philosophical liberalism or secularism) is that if you legalize a practice you are not forcing it on people, whereas if you make it illegal you are preventing people from availing of it. This idea has filtered down from Rawls' view, and is often how an ordinary secular liberal might think of the matter. Making practices illegal goes against our shared political values of freedom and reasonable pluralism. I think the problems with this response are clear but they are worth bringing together in our assessment of a view like Rawls'. First, we have seen that the reason secular liberals want to make a practice legal is almost always because they think it is moral—they are hardly ever in the position of making a practice legal that they are against personally. So one suspects the argument is really a smokescreen for promoting one's own moral views! Second, when you make a practice legal you are saying two things: a. that you personally don't think the practice is all that bad, so you are permitting it. You must be saying this because if you thought the practice was morally egregious you would not permit it; b. you are ignoring the fact that when it is legal, you are forcing people to live in a society that permits what they regard as an immoral practice (recall our distinction in the previous chapter between direct and subtle coercion). Moreover, legalizing a practice carries with it the expectation that its legality will over time contribute to and strengthen the view that the practice is moral, especially in the minds of young people (in this way beliefs and attitudes often gradually fall into line after a contentious new law has been implemented). Social practices are usually contagious; cultural toleration today leads to moral acceptance tomorrow (the legalization of marijuana in various countries around the world is a good case in point). Thirdly, the question of whether or not making a practice illegal violates the value of freedom and coerces a view on people unfairly or immorally depends on the particular issue in question. We all want to enforce our views on others by law, depending on what the issue is. This is true for abortion, the death penalty, or the issue of racial segregation. When you want to make these practices illegal, you are taking a moral stand on the substantive question. So when Rawlsian liberals wish to make something legal for all, this is not a disagreement over principle—where one side wants to make everything legal and the other does not. It is a simple difference concerning the morality of the practice in question.

Nagel notes that it is much more obvious that we should coerce people in some areas like social security, education, health care, and environmental preservation than it is in other areas like abortion, sexual conduct, and other religious and moral issues.[17] This may appear to be true, but only because he has already made up his mind on the moral questions. The problem arises when people disagree about the answers to the moral questions. And the main point is that one person cannot decide the moral question for another by forcing a procedure on society that appears to answer it in advance, or channel the discussion toward a desired outcome. The only way it can be answered is democratically with all parties being allowed to contribute to the outcome. One may respond by arguing that the electorate is uninformed, stupid, and/or immoral, but we have already noted that such a response cannot work as a way to solve these types of disagreements. We can probably all agree with Rawls when he says that citizens "know that in political life unanimity can rarely if ever be expected, so a reasonable democratic constitution must include majority or other plurality voting procedures in order to reach decisions."[18]

A final severe difficulty facing Rawls' view concerns how the procedure is supposed to produce the principles of justice. My objection is not with the principles themselves, although these have been subject to considerable debate, but with the fact that in the original position one does know which worldview one holds! This will surely lead to a large tension between what one might agree to when one does not have access to one's worldview, and when one does have access to it after the veil of ignorance is lifted. It will surely be impossible to dissipate this tension, and we might ask if it would be rational to operate in this way? I think it would be reasonable only if one accepted two things: the first is that one's worldview is subordinate to the shared political culture in *two* senses (both of which one would have to accept): that whenever one's worldview clashed with the shared political values, the values would trump it, *and* that the values have a particular settled interpretation (an interpretation that privileges one's *own* comprehensive conception of the good at the level of law and society). So, one has little to lose by agreeing that one's worldview must be secondary to the shared political culture (otherwise one would not agree to this stipulation). The second thing one must commit to is a kind of overall skepticism about the subject matter of worldviews in general, in that we must believe and live according to them (at least privately), and yet they can be trumped by the political conception. This skepticism represents paradoxically a position on the nature of the good life. It also represents a position on particular political issues, for example, it would require the legalization of abortion ostensibly because the answer is unknowable and not because the liberal theorist believes the practice is moral! It would also require, more hypocritically, that the general skepticism *does not apply to the shared political values themselves*, at least in the crucial sense that one wishes for everyone to live by them and to organize society based on them.

SECULARISM, RELIGION, AND POLITICS

We now need to bring together our views on the role that one's worldview may play in politics. The central issue concerns the role of *all* worldviews in the democratic state. We should not single out the role of religious worldviews for exclusive attention, the way the topic is usually approached. I will argue in the last chapter that in the world of contemporary pluralism the old approach of singling out religion for special discriminatory treatment (or protection), and the old way of talking about the relationship between church and state, is out of date. This matter will need to be rethought in the light of changes in democratic society, especially the rise of secularism. For now, we should consider the specific roles of religion and secularism, and any other worldviews, in politics in order to bring out the implications of our discussion so far; we will also see how there is a parity between all worldviews in the modern state.

The first point to emphasize is that we accept that all views presented in public political exchanges need to reasonable. What does this mean? It does not mean that we need to give every participant in debate reasons they accept, as we have argued extensively. It does mean that we should not rely on questionable sources for our arguments, such as appealing to texts or traditions or institutions or particular individuals as authorities. This is because one can always reasonably question such sources (subject to the provisos noted in the previous chapter). Public reason can also mean, as we have seen, that we could present people with reasons that they might not accept but that they might at least see as reasonable (though we saw that even this test is hard to satisfy, especially in the intense partisan atmosphere of today). But an advantage of this approach is that those we are debating with could not simply dismiss a view on the grounds that they have not been given reasonable arguments. Others of course may not find our arguments persuasive, but this is not enough to justify the exclusion of an argument from the public square. The second point is to ask whether rational arguments can be given to support religious conclusions? And whether rational arguments can be given to support secularist conclusions? We often ask the question only about religious views, but of course we need to ask it of every worldview that wishes to contribute to public deliberation. I have argued that reason can reach religious conclusions, conclusions with religious content, conclusions that rely upon the reasonability (not necessarily the truth) of some religious beliefs. An example—this time from the field of bioethics—will help to illustrate this point further.

Let us turn to the topic of human cloning, which has attracted considerable attention in recent years, and which has raised worry and concern for many people. More than forty countries have moved to ban the practice. Here I will simply sketch various arguments on the topic to illustrate what a rational approach would look like. A full discussion of the morality of cloning is not necessary, and would probably require a book-length treatment in itself! We will start with a secularist argument against cloning, that is, an argument that appeals to the truth of secularism in its premises. We will consider the question initially from the point of view of Joe, who is a secularist (but who is a very reasonable person)! He is worried about cloning, and wishes to see the practice banned in democratic society. Joe's basic argument is that nature operates by chance, and has given us a genetic identity that is optimum for our survival. Joe believes that it is dangerous to tamper with this biological identity. It is dangerous for two reasons: it will likely have long-term deleterious effects on the gene pool, and it is also likely to harm cloned individuals, both genetically and in terms of their self-understanding and self-identity. He believes that being able to decide the genetic identity of a person is too much power for people to have. He is also worried about what it might lead to in the future, if it became commonplace, in terms of further experiments in genetic engineering, in the same way that cosmetic surgery is now becoming more ubiquitous. For these reasons, he is against cloning, and supports making it illegal.

We can consider a religious argument for the same conclusion. Such an argument might go like this: God exists and created the natural order of reproduction which in human beings involves combining half the DNA of each parent, which gives each human being a unique biological identity; this biological identity is an important, though not exclusive, part of human identity, and is part of God's design for man. Human identity involves who a person is from an objective point of view, a person's essence, as well as a person's own understanding of themselves. Cloning is an artificial process that involves removing one half of the DNA from the process of reproduction leading to a cloned individual whose DNA is identical to that of the donor DNA. This is morally wrong because it compromises the biological identity of a person, and it also very likely will compromise human identity. It is an artificial process that overly interferes in nature, which will lead to future problems concerning not only the self-identity and self-understanding of the cloned individual, but likely also with the safety of the process, risks to the gene pool, and so on. Moreover, the process allows some individuals to determine the genetic identity of others, and this is too much power for an individual to have. I believe that both of these arguments, the secularist and the religious arguments, are well-intentioned, sincere arguments, aimed at preventing harm to people that would result from the practice of cloning. Of course, some might object to these arguments.

Objections might include claims such as that artificial intervention is not in itself wrong; the predicted future problems may not materialize; biological identity is not as crucial as it seems; the benefits perhaps of overcoming problems of reproduction (relating to genetic diseases, infertility, etc.,) outweigh possible harm that may result from the process. A rejection of the religious argument in particular may involve commitment to the truth of deeper metaphysical claims (indeed, often assumed in secularist arguments in favor of cloning), such as the claim that all life on earth occurs by chance. This claim is assumed in the argument that artificial intervention is not wrong in itself. It usually relies upon the unstated premise that there is no particular way our biological identity has to be (because it was not designed or intended by an Intelligent Mind). Biological identity is an accident of evolutionary history and not a planned outcome, and if we can discover a new way to produce life, and are careful about the side effects, there would be nothing wrong with this. Or one might claim that although there is a clear biological identity, it is not necessary for human identity, another metaphysical claim. So a secularist who held this latter belief would disagree with our secularist Joe, who holds that although life originated by chance, cloning takes artificial intervention too far. These are all interesting points, and so the debate between both sides is a good one, even if it is difficult to arrive at any consensus.

We note that secularists can disagree among themselves about the issue, just as religious believers might. Secularist arguments in favor of cloning appeal to the truth of a secularist worldview in their premises and religious arguments against cloning appeal to the truth of the religious worldview in their premises. In this way, there is often a parity between the approaches, even though it is seldom recognized. I am claiming that the religious argument is a reasonable argument. The religious believer can defend the main claims in the argument, or at least knows that there is a strong defense of them available (even if he cannot give it himself, and as noted earlier, he can assume some of these claims in a public discussion, just as a secularist can and usually does assume many of his key foundational claims). But I think that in our present climate we are much more likely to think that the religious argument is making an appeal to the truth of foundational premises, but fail to recognize that the secularist argument is doing the same. They both appeal to the truth of key metaphysical points in their overall case, truths that must be defended when it comes to the overall justification of each position.

Suppose a secularist replies that she does not think the religious argument is reasonable. I don't think this matters, or makes any interesting contribution to the discussion, or is even relevant. The religious believer may not find her view reasonable either. I think the secularist view noted above in favor of cloning is not plausible because it relies on a premise I find impossible to believe: that our genetic makeup came about by accident (indeed our secularist friend Joe accepts this premise, but does *not* believe it justifies cloning in our example!). This is a premise the vast majority of people would not agree with. It is not acceptable to exclude an argument from a public discussion just because one does not find it convincing. It does not matter if someone looks at my argument and does not find it persuasive, it only matters that I find it persuasive. It obviously helps if *many others find it persuasive* as well, that way I know it is not just me, and it is a check that I am not formulating my beliefs and arguments in perhaps a blinkered, biased or irrational way! More generally, it seems to me that in our pluralist society the religious believer must be regarded as being an epistemic peer of his secularist friends. When we see the number of intelligent, perfectly reasonable people who hold the religious view of reality, how can we not regard the religious believer as having reasonable arguments? Is this not what reasonable pluralism means, and what Rawls means by the burdens of judgment? Today, in secular liberal pluralist societies, it is my contention that, in a general sense, religious persons must be regarded as reasonable. No other option makes any sense.

I may regard more generally all secularist views of reality as not just false but irrational. Is it necessary that I demonstrate that secularism is irrational, or offer arguments against this worldview at the political level? From the point of view of pluralism, I need not show that secularism is irrational; it is enough that I hold that it is, then pluralism has to deal with this fact—the fact that there exist different worldviews, and different issues within worldviews, that people disagree strongly about. It *is* necessary to defend publicly any specific position that one wishes to have influence over society. I may not be able to persuade the secularist of my views (and *vice versa*, of course), but this does not prevent me from arguing my view publicly. We are only discussing which views have a legitimate place in public debates, not which views are true, or will prevail.

Would I make secularism illegal? No, I accept that we live in a pluralist society and that a significant minority of people are secularists and believe that it is a reasonable view. To this extent, I think many would accept Rawls' notion of reasonable pluralism. And this is also a strength of a view like mine because it allows both religious and secularist views to influence politics, unlike secular liberalism which wants to keep religious views out of politics. However, I would wish to restrict those aspects of secularism that I believe to be wrong from influencing society in so far as I can (*just as secularists wish to do with religious views*). I would attempt to bring this about by means of public argument. In the end, our disagreements should be decided strictly by the democratic process; that way, people who are directly affected by new laws get to have a say in the making of them—this is supposed to be a key reason for why political freedom is a fundamental value. This is much fairer in the context of a democracy than allowing some (elite) group to make decisions for everyone, for obvious reasons.

Does this mean one's views might end up having little influence on society, especially on certain issues, such as cloning, abortion, or health care, and that culture and society might go in a direction that one finds morally objectionable? Yes, this is a risk we all run in a democracy, and is one of the reasons we have what I have been calling the problem of worldview pluralism in the first place. There is no way to avoid this. Could we end up then with very intrusive laws, or even absurd laws, in some states? It would depend on how these are defined. If a majority supports a law, then it would under ideal conditions be regarded as rational by them, even if those who disagreed thought it was absurd. But from the point of view of objective knowledge, a majority could still support laws that seem excessively intrusive from the point of view of democratic values, or absurd laws or irrational laws, since the majority can be wrong. This is perhaps one of the weaknesses of the democratic system, and is one reason why those who disagree with the majority decision often wish to circumvent in some way the democratic process (Brexit being a recent example of this). It is an increasing temptation, especially in the contentious climate of contemporary democratic culture, to attempt to thwart the democratic process if it does not lead to the outcome one favors.

Secular liberals often seem to operate with a private list of "acceptable beliefs," which come, of course, from their comprehensive view of the good, or worldview, and then use these beliefs as a kind of litmus test for the procedure they develop in a Rawlsian fashion to exclude certain other (religious) worldviews from the public square. One often suspects that their own private beliefs are used to define the procedure that will then be used to decide which types of arguments are legitimate in public. In a liberal pluralist context, moral and political litmus tests are generally not acceptable because they have not been earned, since they pre-judge the very moral and political questions that are often in dispute, and are used to direct the deliberative process along a certain channel to reach a desired political or moral outcome. Fairly or not, some interpret Rawlsian liberalism generally to revolve around a strategy that works like this: (1) We, of course, welcome pluralism!; (2) Yet we (Rawlsian liberals) wish everyone to be bound by our views with regard to at least some issues in society; (3) But, because of reasonable pluralism, it is a fact that we are unable to persuade everyone of the truth of our views (recall our causal argument in Chap. 3); so (4) We have designed a "neutral procedure" for handling such disputes, but—lo and behold!—adopting the procedure leads to the truth of our views (those of Rawlsian liberals)!

What about intrusive laws? All laws are intrusive to some extent, but what about a case of, for instance, banning traditional Christians from adopting children, as they are moving toward in the United Kingdom? Could something like this happen? Indeed, but it should only be if a majority agreed to it. It seems absurd, but it is the price of democracy, assuming the decision was arrived at democratically (which in the U.K. it was not).[19] Obviously, these worrying scenarios cannot be prevented by excluding religious beliefs from the public square, since irrational or indeed absurd beliefs could be promoted by any worldview, and indeed this example from the U.K. is largely based on a secularist worldview, and is something that has actually happened! The problem for democratic pluralist states is that there is no neutral standpoint from which to clearly and definitively distinguish between reasonable and unreasonable views, or that leads to laws that are not in some way coercive. Although we generally strive toward laws that are not too intrusive, which is in keeping with a general commitment to freedom, there does not seem to be a clear way to distinguish between those laws we regard as legitimately intrusive (e.g., against stealing) and those we regard as not legitimately intrusive (e.g., abortion?). There seems to be no way to solve this difficulty in advance, without in some way privileging our own views, without regarding ourselves as somehow more enlightened than others. We must hope that common sense and reason will prevail, but the problem is made deeper by the fact that there is an assault on the legitimacy of reason itself today. This is coupled with an increasing tendency to regard those with whom we disagree as irrational, as an initial response, even before the debate has been engaged fully and honestly.

Notes

1. See William Martin, *A Prophet with Honor: The Billy Graham Story* (San Francisco: Harper, 1992), p. 349.
2. See John Locke, *The Reasonableness of Christianity* (New York: Clarendon Press, 2000; orig. 1695).
3. For a discussion of these kinds of arguments, see C. Stephen Evans, *God and Moral Obligation* (New York: Oxford University Press, 2013); David Baggett and Jerry L. Walls (ed.), *God and Cosmos: Moral Truth and Human Meaning* (New York: Oxford U.P., 2016).
4. See Jacques Maritain, *The Rights of Man and Natural Law* (Washington, D.C.: Catholic University of America Press, 1951), Chap. 4.

5. See Stanley Hauerwas, *A Better Hope* (Grand Rapids, MI.: Brazos Press, 2000), pp. 25–27.
6. See Martin Luther King, "Letter from Birmingham City Jail," in James M. Washington (ed.), *A Testament of Hope: The Essential Writings and Speeches of Martin Luther King Jr.* (San Francisco: Harper, 1986), pp. 289–302.
7. Ibid., p. 301.
8. See Michael Novak, *On Two Wings: Humble Faith and Common Sense at the American Founding* (San Francisco: Encounter, 2002), and Richard John Neuhaus, "Proposing Democracy Anew—Part Two," *First Things*, November 1999, p. 90.
9. Rawls suggests this interpretation (as we saw in Chap. 7).
10. See Martin Luther King, in his sermon "Our God is Able," (1963), available at the Martin Luther King, Jr. Research and Education Institute at Stanford University; paper at https://kinginstitute.stanford.edu/king-papers.
11. See ibid., in King's sermon "Why Jesus called a man a fool" (1967).
12. Ibid., in the sermon "Our God is Able," (1963).
13. Ibid., in the sermon "Why Jesus called a man a fool" (1967).
14. See Audi, *Religious Commitment and Secular Reason*, pp. 145–180.
15. See Patrick Dineen, "A Catholic Showdown Worth Watching," *The American Conservative*, Feb. 6th, 2014.
16. Jean Hampton, "The Moral Commitments of Liberalism," in David Copp, Jean Hampton, and John E. Roemer (eds.), *The Idea of Democracy* (New York: Cambridge U.P., 1993), p. 310.
17. See Thomas Nagel, "Moral Conflict and Political Legitimacy," pp. 231–232.
18: John Rawls, "The Idea of Public Reason Revisited," p. 805.
19. See Roger Trigg, *Equality, Freedom, and Religion*, p. 131, p. 154; also Francis Beckwith, *Taking Rites Seriously*, p. 195; also: "Foster Parent Ban, 'No place' in the law for Christianity, High Court Rules," *The Telegraph*, Feb. 28th, 2011, and "Foster Parents defeated by the new Inquisition," *The Telegraph*, Feb. 28th, 2011.

CHAPTER 10

Re-envisioning Church and State

One of our themes is that the concept of the separation of religion from the state is no longer tenable as it is understood today, and that it is a matter of urgency that it needs a re-envisioning in the new pluralist state and the way in which this state is developing. This is true even where a strong traditional understanding of the relationship is dominant, and where there is a vast body of law (as in the U.S.) relating to the concept, not to mention frequent political and cultural skirmishing over its meaning, and how it is to be applied. It also means that the constitutions of democracies which have clauses about the role of religion in the state, or which include clauses on the separation of church and state, need to be redrawn to keep up with the times. We have seen the rewriting of constitutions in various countries on a gradual basis in the latter half of the twentieth century to reflect the fact that modern democracies are becoming more pluralist. In Ireland, for instance, the special role of the Catholic Church in the state and, more recently, the blasphemy clause were removed from the Constitution (both after referendums). Belgium amended its Constitution to acknowledge secularism as one of the officially recognized religions of the state.[1] A similar update was made in the Netherlands, and Norway has moved to loosen church-state relations. Changes like these do not go far enough. It is a first step for liberal democracy and a predictable one—that it would move to downgrade the role of either a particular religion, or religion in general, in the state in various ways. *But the next step must be to consider how all worldviews in society relate to the state, and not single out*

© The Author(s), under exclusive license to Springer Nature Switzerland AG 2021
B. Sweetman, *The Crisis of Democratic Pluralism*,
https://doi.org/10.1007/978-3-030-78382-2_10

any particular category of worldview for special mention, or indeed discrimination. This involves coming to appreciate the points we have been arguing for in this book.

RE-ENVISIONING THE "SEPARATION" OF CHURCH AND STATE

The conventional understanding of the relationship between church and state is now out of date, and is in fact holding us back! This understanding has two aspects to it, depending on which democracy we are considering. The first aspect is that a modern democracy will have no official religion, or at least will not have an official religion to the exclusion of all others. This understanding can include countries like the United Kingdom which has an established religion, Anglicanism, and which favors this religion in small ways, but has no religious requirements for holding public office, nor for most other areas of public and social life. It can probably also include Norway and Sweden where there are closer ties between the official Churches and the State. The second aspect is that liberal democracies will allow freedom of religion within the state. One has the freedom to choose one's religious beliefs (or secularist beliefs), what one believes about God, about God's nature, and about morality, politics, and law. It also includes the freedom to practice one's religion, to rear one's children in that religion, and the freedom to promote one's religious beliefs in society (because of the right to freedom of expression, even though from the point of view of liberal political theory anyone who does so is looked down upon as a bad citizen). Of course, these ideals were not always practiced in democratic countries. In Ireland, in the past, although there was no religious test for office, it was often in practice hard for a non-Catholic to be elected, and in the U.S. some politicians seem to insist on an informal (non)-religious test for being a member of the Supreme Court.

But this general understanding of the relationship between church and state no longer reflects the times because of the simple fact that many people today do not subscribe to religious worldviews. It was easy for states to write constitutional principles concerning religion when everyone subscribed to not only a religious worldview, but often the same or a very similar worldview. Today, we have considerable religious diversity, not only of different religions, but even within the same religion (where in many cases orthodox and liberal views might as well be different religions).

So we cannot presume much in common, even if in principle many religious believers would share foundational beliefs. Moreover, we also have the rise of secularism, and other versions of philosophical atheism. So it is not appropriate to approach the topic as if religious worldviews are the only ones, nor should we single them out for special mention in our laws. This is simply not tenable in what we might call the age of secularism (or the age of pluralism), where secularism has grown considerably and ostentatiously seeks to influence the culture according to its vision of morality and the good life. We must recognize also that there are many churches, each representing different paths in life. In this way, while there are important differences, when it comes to promoting political and moral views, churches are not all that different from political parties, or other interest groups. In many democratic nations, it is quite easy to distinguish between "conservative" and "liberal" religions, and they are mainly defined by their political, moral, and social views. Despite all the talk of welcoming many and varied worldviews in democratic theory, we have been very slow to adjust the democratic system and practice to reflect this reality of pluralism.

I have argued that one cannot plausibly put religious views in a different category. Many liberal thinkers make two large mistakes on this question. First, they place religious belief in general in a separate category to secularism, though they rarely defend this move, but assume it. This is often because they approach the religious worldview in terms of caricatures, and also display a serious lack of knowledge of its beliefs, themes, structure, and especially of its theological and philosophical traditions, as we noted in the previous chapter. The second mistake is that they fail to appreciate the significance of the fact that secularism too is an influential contemporary worldview, and do not give this fact enough attention or weight in the discussion. They know it is a worldview, of course; indeed, it is usually the one they espouse themselves, but they do not sufficiently appreciate the fact that it is structurally similar to religious belief. Moreover, it is also engaged in the task of shaping life, culture, society, morality, and law, and has had no small success at this task. Given this, it changes the way we should regard religious belief—one should now see it as one worldview *among many*. Strangely, secular liberals are wont to think this way about almost any other (especially novel) worldviews, and generally welcome other outlooks in the discussion as an example of healthy pluralism, Yet, they fail to do so with religious, especially traditional religious, worldviews. This failure then has the practical effect of stacking the deck in favor of the secularist views in some areas of life and culture.

One cannot place religious belief in a separate category to secularism because it is structurally the same as secularism, or at least it can be. This means as I noted earlier that one can reach religious conclusions by means of reason, and that some of these conclusions have moral and political implications, just as some secularist beliefs have (with secularists further believing that it is their duty to promote these beliefs in society). It is an affront to the integrity of religious persons to insist that they ignore the moral and political implications of their beliefs. One might say in fact that the religious worldview is the default view, since the vast majority of people (including the smartest people) who have ever lived have held it. I think this is all we need to conclude that the religious worldview is a rational worldview. (Keep in mind that there are multiple religious worldviews, as I explained in Chap. 5, and they each must be assessed, both overall and with regard to their specific beliefs relating to various matters, in terms of their rationality.) Of course, a misguided secularist (such as philosopher Daniel Dennett) might think that everyone who subscribes to a religious worldview is irrational, that somehow he has a privileged road into the truth that they have missed. Yet, this is hardly convincing! In any case, he cannot speak for others on the rationality of religious belief. Making a decision about the rationality of a worldview, and its role in society, is one of the fruits of freedom in a democratic nation. With regard to the matter of secular reason, I argued in Chap. 8 that we should present our views as reasonably as possible in public deliberations, and I believe that many religious beliefs can satisfy this test.

It follows then that when writing constitutions in democratic states it is no longer appropriate to single out religious worldviews for special attention in the law. Singling out religious views, say by including a clause that stipulates that there will be no established religion, is to discriminate against religion because this leaves it open that some secularist worldview could become the basis of law, either in whole or in part. I have described a state where secularism is either the established worldview, or where various laws and practices are based on secularist beliefs and values, as a *seculocracy*.[2] This term may also be understood to describe a state where religion is frowned upon in the sense that one should not appeal to it in many facets of life. A seculocracy may be understood further as a state where religion is banned, restricted, or so strongly discouraged that it is often ineffective in contributing to democratic deliberation. To eschew an established religion at the level of law, however, leaves open the question whether this means that religion can play no role at all in politics, or whether it means that religion can influence politics but just cannot become the official religion of the state.

On the other hand, saying that the state will permit freedom of religion also picks out religions for special mention. This notion is understandable from a historical point of view, since many states had dominant religions, and there was often persecution or oppression of minority religions, and even civil unrest if we go back a few centuries. However, these considerations should no longer concern us in Western democracies. Some may have supported the separation of church and state because they were in the minority, and some may have been suspicious of separation because they were in the majority. Today, I believe neither are defensible, principled positions. The reality is more complex—we need a way of defending separation, but broadening the notion, yet still allowing some role for one's worldview in the state in terms of logic, and because there is no non-arbitrary way of restricting some worldviews but not others, and no neutral position. That is the essence of the modern problem.

So it is not appropriate to say that members of *religious* worldviews are free to practice their worldview; we should be saying that members of *all* worldviews are free to practice their worldview. If there are laws relating to what are sometimes called "religious exemptions" or conscientious objections of one sort or another to this or that public policy, these exemptions would need to be considered in relation to all worldviews. Our changing times demand this new perspective, since not everyone is religious in the conventional sense. In this way, we recognize that we live in a pluralist state with secularist as well as religious views, and it is also to acknowledge that the secularist views have a right to practice, promote, and influence politics. Sometimes secularists, like Austin Dacey, will welcome this point when it gives secularism a place at the table, and will question why we privilege religion in our laws. But Dacey fails to realize the other point that follows: that by not privileging religion and by recognizing that we live in a pluralist state with many worldviews, some of which are religious, that religious worldviews have just as much right to influence politics as any other view.[3] We cannot consistently claim both that religion should have no special protection in our laws and that it should have no role in politics. So it would be better today in our constitutional documents and laws when referring to the fact that people are free to hold and practice their philosophies of life that we restrict ourselves to the term "worldview," and do not use the term "religion" at all. This better captures the *reality* of the modern pluralist state.

This is often why drawing attention to the fact that secularism is a major worldview in contemporary culture makes some people uncomfortable; they have been hiding behind the idea of a "neutral state," or sometimes behind the claim that they have nothing against religious belief in principle. This is especially true in a culture which either (a) approaches every issue politically (from a position of how to advance a political view in practical terms, without much regard to moral or political principles), or (b) where one adopts as a matter of policy the strategy that everything is political and there is no point in debate or negotiation. It is also especially obvious in a culture where it is routine, such as in the U.S., to only invoke the principle of the separation of church and state when religious believers oppose one's political views, but to welcome religious arguments and contributions when they support them.

One problem that comes with the freedom to practice one's worldview in the modern state is that there must be some restrictions on this freedom. For we all know that this right is not unlimited—some practices and perhaps even some beliefs will not be allowed. *This will be true for all worldviews.* The question is where to draw such a limit, how the limit is decided upon (and in the democratic context, we must also ask: *who* decides it, since we recognize that from a practical point of view no one in a democratic society can speak for everyone in that society). This was an issue Locke struggled with in his *A Letter Concerning Toleration*. He brought up the example of a religion that practices human sacrifice, or today we might say to make the point in a more general way, a worldview that wishes to promote human sacrifice, or some such vile practice. It would have to be a practice that the vast majority immediately recognized as immoral. Therein lies the problem, of course. It would require almost universal agreement across all of the worldviews for something to meet this requirement. Locke thought he could decide the issue by appealing to what he called a "universal morality," as we saw in Chap. 2. He seems to have meant that there is some kind of independent moral standard to which we can all appeal to judge individual religions. One can see the difficulty immediately with such a notion. Locke's problem about setting a limit to tolerance is one all supporters of tolerance struggle with—they have to decide how tolerant they will be, what they will permit, and what they will forbid (based on appeal to their own worldview and moral values).

However, we can say that if there is widespread agreement across most worldviews in the state that a practice is immoral, then this is a place to start. And then the practice would be outlawed through the normal democratic process. One might also say that if a practice clearly went against the fundamental values of a liberal democracy that it would be a good candidate for one that would be outside the limits of what members of a worldview would be allowed to practice. What would be in this category? That is difficult to say because, as we have seen earlier, *there is disagreement among the worldviews about what the liberal values mean in the concrete.* Some people think that the Catholic Church prohibiting women from being ordained as priests goes against the value of equality in the liberal state, or that the Muslim religion requiring women to wear burqas or hijabs goes against the value of equality, as in France.[4] Some have the same view of abortion, that it automatically goes against the liberal value of equality if the unborn are not protected by law. Many disagree with these positions. So it is not easy to decide where to draw the limits when we appeal to liberal values. However, in a democracy the (not perfect) solution surely is that we enjoy a process of public deliberation insofar as this is possible and then decide such matters at the ballot box, or through legislative bodies.

We should also consider whether there is a limit to the kinds of religious beliefs (and secularist beliefs) that one can introduce into politics? If we accept the general point that religious beliefs have a legitimate role in politics, is there any limit to the type of religious beliefs one can introduce into a public argument? In considering this question, we might helpfully classify typical beliefs of religious worldviews into three categories: foundational beliefs, beliefs that express religious dogma, and moral and political beliefs. Secularism also has the first and third of these; it may also have a category of beliefs that play the same role as religious dogma if it contains beliefs that are generally not open to question. Be that as it may, it is usually only beliefs in the third category, moral and political beliefs, that religious believers wish to have some influence on culture (though their full justification as we noted in earlier chapters would require appeal to the foundational beliefs, but not usually to religious dogma). For example, the Catholic Church's position on abortion is not a dogma of the Church, but is based on a belief about the value of life, that the embryo is a human life, that all life is a gift from God, and so forth.

I have argued that only religious beliefs that are regarded as reasonable by their proponents (after an honest discussion) can be introduced into politics, but one might worry that perhaps any religious belief could pass this test. Let us recall that one does not have to convince others of the rationality of a belief, one only has to be convinced oneself. This means then that one could offer an unreasonable argument in a public forum but maintain that one found it reasonable oneself! We must be clear here about how to understand this. It is true that from the point of view of objective reason any argument presented in public might be irrational, even if some people believed it to be rational. However, we are unable to judge a belief in any area of life from such a privileged position, many philosophers now claim, and indeed it is impossible in any democratic context. Indeed, it is a truism (a dogma?) of twentieth-century thought that reason is compromised and so we do not have access to a "God's eye" view of truth. Whatever about this being the case, it is true in a democratic context, for the simple reason that because of the value of freedom I have the right *to make my own judgment* about the rationality of a belief, but I do not have the right to make such a judgment for others. This is part of the essence of freedom in a democratic context. One cannot reply, I think it is obvious, to the position I have been defending by using the litmus test of *one's own worldview* to exclude other worldviews. This is part of the paradox of liberal democracy. The only test of a view along these lines is if it is not compatible with liberal political values, but this is often a matter of debate and interpretation. So a *democratic* solution to our disagreements is best; it is better than some privileged worldview or some elite group deciding for everyone, because at least the democratic way gives everyone that is party to the disagreements a say (even, of course, if they are wrong). To reject this seems to be an unjustifiable rejection of a key part of the democratic political system.

There is a worry about allowing beliefs into the public square in this manner. If the only condition is that the person presenting the belief judges it to be reasonable, then some might, for various nefarious reasons, introduce beliefs and arguments into public discourse that they pretend to regard as reasonable (or perhaps some might not care about the matter of rationality). Although this is perhaps an odd scenario, isn't there a risk of this? There is such a risk, but it is a risk of democracy. And given the selfish, obsessive, and often inscrutable motives of people, we might say that it is not as unlikely perhaps as it sounds! However, there are two constraints in the democratic process that might help to alleviate this risk, at least to some extent. One is public opinion. It would probably not be sufficient for just one person, or a small group, to insist that a belief was rational in order for it to have influence and even prevail democratically. Yet if large numbers regarded a position as reasonable, this would give it a certain credence in public discourse. (Secular liberalism, as a general philosophy, may not particularly welcome the constraint of public opinion since it constantly champions the lone maverick who challenges conventional and traditional mores, especially in art, literature, music, and film {and rational argument?}. Given its enlightenment airs, it often does not respect public opinion!) The second constraint is the test of public argument itself. Hopefully, the process will rebuff an argument that is not in fact rational, although it is being presented as such. Of course, we have seen throughout this book, that this is not guaranteed, especially given a general loss of confidence in reason.

It is crucial to recognize, however, that this objection does not apply only to religious beliefs. Anyone might submit a belief in the public square pretending that it is rational but have some other reason for advocating it (e.g., one might present a public argument to support the legalization of medical marijuana ostensibly to provide relief from certain medical conditions, but one's real reason may be more selfish, regarding this move as an incremental step to its full legalization, and one wants this because, although one had no medical conditions, one is a frequent user of marijuana, or hopes to be!). We hope that the test of public reason will adjudicate judiciously and sort between these kinds of arguments, and that common sense will prevail. Some may not agree with this, thinking that we have passed this by, and are now in a state of confusion with regard to how to appraise the rationality of a position, that common sense has gone out the window, and that we have lost any real hope of having intelligent, reasonable, quality public debate aimed at the discovery of truth. Perhaps so, but then we are all in this boat. If this is the case, it would affect all worldviews, and we would all be in danger of being influenced or forced to live according to beliefs we find irrational, immoral, or both. So given all of this, I would like to reemphasize a distinction I made in an earlier book between lower order and higher order beliefs.[5]

We may distinguish lower order and higher order beliefs by the amount of evidence and argument available to support them, or to put the matter another way, by the amount of faith required to believe them. Faith is here understood to refer to the depth of commitment one must make to hold a belief, after the appraisal of the argument and the evidence has been exhausted. I hold that all worldview beliefs, because of the nature of the subject matter, require a commitment to hold them. We may accurately describe it as a faith commitment in the sense that one promotes and acts on a belief that one cannot prove to be true; sometimes the belief falls far short of proof. This is a very important point because the amount of faith involved in holding a belief of this sort will obviously play a role in whether others are willing to judge the belief as reasonable or not. I mean then by a *lower order belief* of a worldview a belief which, although it usually requires faith (at least some beliefs in all worldviews require a degree of faith), it is still based mostly on reason and evidence, and so it is more likely to be regarded as reasonable by others. A *higher order belief* is one which requires a great deal of faith (or at least more faith than a lower order belief) in order for a person to subscribe to it. Lower order beliefs are more likely to be persuasive to others, and this will have important implications for the debate among various worldviews in the public square. Lower order beliefs are rational beliefs from the point of view of pluralism and of introducing them into political discussion.

As examples, a lower order belief of Catholicism would be that God exists; a higher order belief might be a specific belief about the nature of God—that he is three persons in one God, for instance. Catholic philosophers argue that one can provide a strong argument for belief in the existence of God, but acknowledge that belief in the Trinity takes more faith, and is based in part on revelation, and so is therefore more accurately described (using my terminology) as a higher order belief. Many beliefs in the category of religious dogma would be higher order. In the secularist worldview, the key belief that all of reality is physical in nature might be regarded as a lower order belief by the secularist, but he may acknowledge that the belief that the human mind and all its properties are fully physical is a higher order belief, since, as well as some evidence, it requires a significant amount of faith to believe it. Higher order beliefs can be rational if they are well tied to lower order beliefs. Thus the Evangelical Christian might argue that since the belief that God exists is reasonable, and the belief that Jesus existed is reasonable, then belief in the reliability of the Bible is reasonable, and so a belief in the Incarnation is reasonable. Similarly, a secularist might propose that since the belief that all that exists is physical is reasonable, and the belief in scientific progress is reasonable, then a belief that the human mind is physical would be reasonable too.

How do we judge if a particular belief is a higher order or a lower order belief? The answer must be that we judge this matter on the basis of appeal to objective reason, and on an objective analysis of the evidence. However, even if such an appeal is made, the proponents of different worldviews will still dispute whether a belief is lower order or higher order. We must be careful not to define higher order beliefs as those that are not rational, because while I might not think they are rational, others may so regard them. What goes into each category is not clear, and as we noted I cannot decide this matter for others. If one flips around the radio dial, one will usually come across several stations devoted to one or another religious worldview. Often the hosts of various shows will discuss moral, social, and political topics, but almost always from a scriptural or a biblical point of view. They will rarely present or discuss independent philosophical arguments for their conclusions, even arguments that reason philosophically to a *religious* conclusion. These are examples of higher order beliefs, because they are based on a source of justification, religious revelation, that many people may reasonably reject. Flip further on the dial and one will come across many secular stations, where hosts will also comment just as strongly on the same topics. What is the difference in their approach? One is that the secular stations, while not officially secularist. will usually not appeal to scriptural revelation as their sole reason to support their various positions, but will try to offer a rational argument to listeners (some of whom may not be persuaded by scriptural revelation). Though, as we have noted in some of our previously discussed examples, they will often appeal to controversial premises and assumptions to justify their points (sometimes directly, but often indirectly), assumptions they may be committed to but that will not be shared by all their audience. In this case, the radio hosts may be appealing to a secularist worldview, and will themselves accept the controversial premises and assumptions, at least partly on faith. So without a direct discussion of the argument, one might regard such appeals as appeals to higher order beliefs (e.g., if the argument relies on the claim that there is no soul, or that there is no God who designed things in a certain way, or that gender is a social construct). One might describe certain media discussions as being expressions of a secularist point of view or outlook in the way one would describe a radio station as religious—in the sense that it assumes a secularist worldview on the part of its listeners for the most part, and discusses most issues from this point of view. It does not argue for the secularist worldview, and many of its key claims would be controversial and rejected by many listeners, and the broader population.

The upshot of our discussion in this section is that we need a new phrase to describe the relationship between worldviews and the state. The phrases "church and state" and "separation of church and state" are fast losing their appropriateness. I propose that we now use the phrase "separation of worldviews and the state." This describes the official position that in a democracy no worldview will be established in law as the official worldview of the state, that no one wants to make everyone a secularist, or a Catholic, or a Presbyterian, or a Marxist (acknowledging that there may be some who do not follow this ideal). However, as I have already argued, everyone wants others to follow their particular worldview *on some issues*. The state must make a decision on these issues with regard to law, and so the views of some worldviews will prevail, and some will lose out. Nicholas Wolterstorff has argued that politicians should be able to appeal to their religious beliefs when making policy, again within a democratic process, and I would add subject to the proviso that they offer reasonable arguments.[6] If they do not appeal to their religious beliefs, what would they appeal to? And if one is a secularist politician, can one appeal to one's worldview beliefs in making policy? And if not, what would a secularist politician appeal to? Such questions, I think, show clearly that the traditional way of thinking about these questions has passed.

Democracy and Populism

A concern may be raised about the view just defended with regard to a worry about the tyranny of the majority. The worry is that although the majority has the power to impose its will on minorities in a democratic state, there are some issues where it should not do so (as we saw in our discussion of Mill in Chap. 2). Which issues these are, of course, is always a difficulty. But some might object—particularly those that do not trust the democratic system, and are seeking for ways to contain it—that a majority could decide that a certain view is rational, and so impose it on society, even if a significant minority rejected the view. This is a repeat of the familiar concern that there is a danger of "mob rule" in the democratic system. While this worry would seem to affect any view or group that wishes to have influence (including secularist views), it is often aimed particularly at the influence of religious beliefs, and also raises questions about the role of populism in a democracy. Let us tease out these ideas in this and the next section as a way of further developing and clarifying our position.

It is helpful at this stage to introduce the notion of populism, which is related to democracy, and which is now in the news again given recent electoral trends in several democratic countries, including Germany, France, the United Kingdom, Austria, and the United States, among others. Critics of these trends have appealed to the notion of populism both to explain the trends, and as a way of disparaging them, so the phenomenon of populism is one we need to consider, though we should probably not get too distracted by it, since it may be short-lived. My main claim about populism is that the notion must be handled very carefully and may have to be rethought in the light of the problem of worldview pluralism we have been discussing in this book. Populism is notoriously difficult to define, and some scholars claim that as a consequence it is not a useful political term.[7] The term was originally used in the United States by the People's Party in the late nineteenth century, and it has also been utilized to refer to aspects of Marxism. So some groups have employed the term to describe themselves, though today it is mostly used to define the views of others. The literal meaning is "of the people" or the "will of the people," and this connotation would seem to convey that in a democratic context we should listen to, or be guided by, or our (particularly our politicians') concern should be to implement, the will of the people with regard to the general direction of the nation. At first glance then the term seems simply to refer to the operation of the democratic process! Isn't the essence of a democracy that the people are sovereign, and does this not mean that the people's will should be carried out, that politicians should be guided by their constituents? So how is populism different from democracy?

However, populism has come to have a negative meaning in certain contexts, and is often used to refer in a pejorative way to the views of the majority, to the opinions of the masses, to the general will. In recent times, the term is usually employed as an accusation against a political view in an attempt to suggest that populist ideas have no place in a democracy, should not guide society (and this is why use of the term is associated with elitism). Increasingly, the term is used to reveal what one is *against* from a moral and political perspective, rather than what one supports. This negative meaning has echoes of how early democracies, including in France, the U.K. and the U.S., initially responded when the right to vote became widespread in these countries (which was not until after the 1920s) when all men and women over 18 could vote, at least in principle (earlier restrictions according to property, gender and age, and in the U.S., race, having been removed). When these countries became more democratic, the elites and those with economic and social influence began to realize that the electorate had real power through the ballot box. This gave cause for concern because it meant that the general populace would have genuine influence over the establishment. As Bernard Crick notes, initially politicians and the elites, though quite concerned about what was described as "irresponsible democracy," nevertheless thought that the views and wishes of the general populace could be "managed"[8]; all of which sounds like they feared that the people would begin—in true democratic fashion—to make up their own minds about things!

So the first meaning of populism is that the views of the ordinary person in the street, those of the populace, views which would likely have widespread support, most likely would not cohere with the views of an elite and enlightened minority. When it came down to it, the populace was likely to vote against the wishes of the elites. Naturally, the elites feared losing control over the electorate, and this is yet another reminder that in many democracies a small elite often has disproportionate influence in many areas of life, including government, economics, and the shaping of culture, and effectively runs things, even though in theory the populace are supposed to be sovereign. This is especially true if the elites get to form and have a great deal of influence over public opinion, which they often do because they usually have significant control in key areas such as education, the media, the law, and the concrete implementation of government policy. If the elites are in agreement on many issues of society and culture, and speak mostly with a single voice, then their control could be great indeed. So naturally the elites were often worried if, despite this control, the populace showed signs of not listening to them, of rejecting their views, and making decisions for themselves, based on their own judgments.

We might nuance this initial understanding of populism somewhat to suggest that the electorate is generally not well informed on the issues of the day, and so they need guidance from those who are more informed and more educated. Society should be guided by facts, knowledge, and careful thinking on topics such as climate change, the direction of the economy, social problems, and their causes, such as marriage breakdown, poverty, and addiction. The general populace needs the guidance of intelligent, well-informed experts. While any responsible form of government must surely be one that is guided by informed decisions, we know that it is not as simple as this. In many cases facts and knowledge do not settle an issue. Moreover, many issues need to be considered in relation to each other and/or in the wider context of society, for example, if the cost of a solution to a problem requires higher taxation, or if there is disagreement over the best way to combat poverty or addiction (or with regard to any other issue), as there often is. So facts and knowledge are necessary and will undoubtedly help, but where there is still disagreement it is supposed to be the people who make the final decisions, not an elite group. Moreover (as we noted in Chap. 1), it is unlikely in mature democracies, where there are developed educational, scientific, and political structures, that the *majority* would adopt a position of ignorance with regard to scientific data and factual matters. Yet, there remains a dangerous tendency today to misrepresent, exaggerate, or distort facts and evidence to support a moral or political point of view. This is particularly true the more pluralist and contentious a democratic society becomes; even academic disciplines are not immune to this vice. In some situations, settling on facts and knowledge to help us understand a topic is not as easy as it sounds.

This brings us to a more contemporary understanding of populism, which focuses more directly on its negative or pejorative meaning, an understanding that has echoes of Plato's criticisms of democracy. This is the understanding that the populace if left to themselves will often be narrow-minded, ignorant, governed by emotion rather than reason, prejudiced, even racist, in their decision-making. The general populace may exhibit such undesirable traits and motives overtly, or they might be latent (or believed to be latent by the elites), and encouraged or played to by unscrupulous politicians and charismatic leaders. It is possible for certain politicians and society leaders to have this effect on ordinary people, the elites contend, because the general populace is ignorant, stupid, fickle, and easily led. This is a special danger if leaders deliberately provoke these attitudes in political campaigns and appeal to not only the worst fears but also the prejudices, and the emotions, of the masses. To counteract such worries we may need the influence of an enlightened, elite group who are morally above such tactics and emotional appeals, and who will be guided solely by reason and the interests of society.

This approach to democracy has echoes of James Madison's point in Federalist Paper No. 10 that democracies seek to avoid factions. Although Madison struggled to define a faction—to distinguish between a faction (an illegitimate political interest) and a genuine concern that one could pursue democratically (a legitimate political interest)—he seems to have had in mind a group pursuing their own self-interest above that of the country as a whole (likely to occur with issues relating to property ownership). Madison believed that a carefully structured democratic system (with, for instance, a large number of representatives) could minimize the risk of this, but he also clearly thought that an enlightened minority would play an important role. This task would fall to our political representatives, "whose wisdom may best discern the true interest of their country and whose patriotism and love of justice will be least likely to sacrifice to temporary or partial considerations," with Madison adding that "the enlightened views and virtuous sentiments" of our representatives "render them superior to local prejudices and to schemes of injustice."[9] A system of checks and balances, where each branch of government has some real power over other branches (an important part of the U.S. version of democracy) might help to limit factions, though it serves mostly as a check on government power, not popular will. One might think a system of checks and balances would work especially well in a pluralist society, but this does not seem to be the case for the simple reason that the various branches of government check the others according to their own political interests rather than according to any democratic principles (this is especially true in the U.S. system, even in the third branch of government, the judiciary). It is also a fact that most democracies don't have a structured system of checks and balances, and get on just as well without it, perhaps better (as in parliamentary systems).

However, the appeal to the notion of populism in contemporary political debates, used as an accusation and to describe election trends in several countries, goes well beyond Madison's points. Madison's concern was with narrow self-interest; today the term is used to disparage what the elites regard as an immoral set of beliefs and attitudes. In the first meaning of populism noted above, the key idea is that one side lacks knowledge which the other side believes it has, and which they also believe is essential to good governance; but the second meaning is not about knowledge, but about morality. It is the claim that the populace is immoral at heart, or so fickle, irrational and emotional that they could easily slip into immoral attitudes and prejudices, and so they need to be led by their moral superiors, not just their intellectual superiors. (Grayling thinks the solution to populism is more education.[10]) The first meaning suggests that the ordinary man cannot be trusted because he is ignorant; the second meaning says he cannot be trusted because he is likely to act in an immoral way in making political decisions. This is an important reminder that the elites in a society, defined as those who hold power in various areas, such as finance, education, law, the arts and politics, tend to believe (as Mudde and Kaltwasser argue) that the ordinary people are "dangerous, dishonest and vulgar, and that the elite are superior not only in moral, but also in cultural and intellectual terms."[11]

One way to understand democracy is that it is public opinion in action, but one might also reasonably argue that public opinion needs some guidance, and that this is where good leaders can play an important role. This is what proactive leadership means, in part. It is also possible for a bad leader, a demagogue even, to appeal to the fears and prejudices of the general populace, assuming that the public are stupid and easily led, or morally compromised in some way. While one can see how this is all true in theory, *it is becoming increasingly difficult in the context of pluralism and fractious political and policy disputes to make these distinctions accurately.* It is increasingly hard in modern democracy to distinguish between populism (understood as the claim that the electorate and some politicians are immoral) and simple policy differences between various parties. It can be quite seductive, as Eatwell and Goodwin argue, to describe a policy position that one rejects as "populist" (in the negative sense of being stupid and immoral) in order to score political points, especially if one is already coming from a liberal perspective.[12] People can have legitimate differences over complex issues without it being the case that one side is being guided by emotion, fear, prejudice, or ignorance (with the implication being that if these vices were overcome, political views would change). As we saw in Chap. 1, if the democratic process does not arrive at policy decisions one favors, there is often a temptation to conclude that there is something wrong with the deliberative process, followed by an attempt to change or find some way around it so that it arrives at the "right (i.e., my) views"! Criticism of the system of democracy because one thinks people are stupid is fine if one is talking about factual matters (and even that is hard to decide upon), but this criticism generally does not apply if one is talking about worldviews and values! The dispute about worldviews, as a practical matter, cannot be so simply resolved at the level of reason, or by instituting a new program of education, or by restructuring the electoral system, or by tweaking the structure of the government, as I have been arguing in this book.

I think the best example of this issue playing out in a recent democratic context is the Brexit debate and vote in the U.K. in 2016. This was a classic case of a widespread political view being disparaged as "populist" by the establishment classes (who mostly spoke with one voice but lost the debate). Most of the leading experts on the issue of Britain's membership in the European Union, including those in government, academia, the media, the law profession, and many at the top of the business world, all warned in the strongest possible terms of dire consequences if Britain voted to leave the European Union (their campaign was often described as "Project Fear," and employed many of the same tactics as their alleged populist opponents). Despite this unanimity of elite opinion, the British people voted to leave (the result was a surprise, because most populist movements today don't expect to win—they aim to protest, and so provide a rebuke to and perhaps a check on, elite power). Did they do so because they were racist, prejudiced and governed by emotion and self-interest, or because of legitimate worries about the sovereignty of their country, among other concerns? I believe it was the latter motivation, whether or not one thinks these worries were justified. Much of the data shows that many thought that the EU had overplayed its hand in its interference in the national affairs of member states (a feeling that is widespread across Europe), and also because of concerns about EU regulations, bureaucracy, economic loss, and how free movement of peoples was changing British society in very challenging ways.[13] Indeed, the EU model highlights another problem with democracy—the more one can keep the process of governing as far removed from the people as possible, the easier it is to govern them against their will. The EU has done this by passing general laws in Brussels at the political level of the European Parliament, and then having the details worked out by faceless civil servants whose idiosyncratic beliefs and values are then implemented in specific policy requirements in each member country, forced upon citizens who had little or no say in them. It is commonplace for the elites in the U.K., and their supporters among the elites elsewhere, to describe the vote of the general populace in the U.K. to leave the EU in pejorative terms, as motivated by fear, prejudice, xenophobia, greed, etc., to impute the worst possible motives to the populace, and to contrast this with the superior moral attitude of the elites (this is the view of Grayling, noted in Chap. 1). This is becoming a common tactic across Western societies in the light of populist tendencies in various countries to be suspicious of, and to be no longer willing to be guided by, elite opinion.

While in the past it may have been possible to define populism in a purely descriptive way, without any negative or disparaging connotations, today populism is best understood as referring to two things together: a set of specific beliefs on specific topics (such as that there should be limits on immigration in a particular country), *and* a set of irresponsible and immoral attitudes that lead to people holding these beliefs (such as racist attitudes toward people of other cultures). Unless populism is defined to include the claim that the masses are ignorant, stupid and immoral, it is not a useful term because it is too difficult to distinguish "populist" positions from ordinary democratic disagreement and policy differences. Even defining populism as "appeal to the masses," implies that such an appeal is intended to provoke an emotional and irresponsible response, rather than a rational one. This prompts an ever more serious point: in the context of the problem of worldview pluralism discussed in this book, it is really no longer possible to distinguish between elite opinion and populism in terms of attitude or moral purity, or it is at least becoming very difficult to do so. This is especially true in a democratic society with deep divisions, and that is high on rhetoric rather than substance in political debates. Often the distinction simply comes down to political differences, and not to a difference between those who know more than others and who are morally superior, and those who are ignorant and who tend to support immoral policies.

Sometimes populism is understood to mean that a certain group wishes to undermine basic human rights, or to deny minority rights, and in this way the tendency can be regarded as a threat to liberal democracy. However, within the context of a liberal democracy, it is not appropriate to define populism in this way for two reasons: it is not accurate, and the definition is again usually motivated by simple policy differences. With regard to the first point, many "populist" movements (though not all, of course) are committed to the democratic process and the scheme of rights we referred to earlier in the book (with the proviso that some of the rights still have to spelled out in concrete terms). Eatwell and Goodwin argue that populist movements today are mainly concerned with promoting more democracy, not less, and also with the growing gap between the haves and have-nots, the disregard of powerful elites for ordinary people, the erosion of the nation state, and the effects of immigration on economy and culture.[14]

With regard to the second issue of motivation, one must be vigilant not to adopt what is really a question-begging position. For example, with regard to the topic of immigration, to adopt the view that populists are denying minority rights *simply because* they wish to restrict immigration begs the question about whether every person has such a right to immigrate to any other sovereign nation, and so comes down to a policy difference after all. Or, to take another example, if one were to argue that populists are infringing upon the right to own property *simply because* they wish to implement (intolerable) amounts of income redistribution; this begs the question at issue since this critique is based on a particular *interpretation* of the right to own property (and not solely on an affirmation of a right that others deny), a topic that is subject to continual debate in society. (This latter example reminds us that we should not overlook the phenomenon of *left-wing* populism, as expressed for instance in the Occupy Wall Street movement in the U.S., a group that was involved in violent demonstrations. Since populism is a pejorative term used mainly by the left side of the political spectrum today, it usually does not come with the same harsh moral judgment of motives when used to describe left-wing populists, for obvious reasons, further evidence that the term is often used simply to highlight disagreement over policy matters.)

Negative understandings of populism—both as involving an ignorant, fickle and irrational general populace, and a populace that wishes to deny or restrict minority rights previously agreed to—might still be accurate of course in certain cases, and do represent undesirable and undemocratic tendencies. Dangerous forms of populism are fueled today by widespread effective use of social media platforms by politicians and their followers, and often involve emotional appeals to fabrications, distortions, outright lies, rallying cries, conspiracy theories, and so forth (though it is a mistake to describe as "populist" all forms of politicking, sloganeering, and dishonest policy promises aimed at manipulating electoral opinion). But today it is becoming increasingly harder to distinguish these genuinely problematic versions of populism from simple policy differences and a desire to disparage your political opponents, especially when we are tempted to call people names when we disagree with them rather than to engage in substantive argument.[15] This is why there is a tendency to lump all versions of populism today together, to make no distinction between democratic movements in Poland, Austria, and the U.K., for example, and anti-democratic tendencies exhibited by the leaders in Turkey and Hungary.[16] Most populist movements have no intention of implementing an anti-democratic or oppressive state. One might be in favor of limits on immigration, for example, because one believes that immigration is a threat to jobs or because immigration is fundamentally changing one's society, *not* because one is prejudiced against foreigners. This is a distinction that the critics of "populism" all too often refuse to acknowledge; indeed, there are many myths about the rise of populism which only serve to detract from a responsible response to the phenomenon.[17] The fractious nature of modern democratic discourse must raise suspicions that a charge of populism may be simply another rhetorical tactic in a contentious debate, rather than a charge that one could support with evidence.

As a simple matter of logic and of human decency, one should be extremely careful about describing one's political opponents as being susceptible to demagoguery and as acting from immoral motives and prejudices.

Moreover, it is no longer feasible given the widespread *reality* of worldview pluralism for an elite class to run a democratic country, and to make decisions for the masses. Nor is it feasible from a philosophical and moral point of view for an elite class to control all the key features of a society, such as education, the media, the law, the academic world, government departments and agencies, and the civil service.[18] This is because *we no longer share the same beliefs on the key questions of human existence*. It used to be that the vast majority of people shared the same outlook and beliefs with regard to foundational issues, even if some were ignorant of how to understand, articulate, and apply them perhaps. So the elite articulated them for the society, and decided how they would be implemented, especially in the areas of education and in law. However, because we no longer have the same foundational beliefs, no longer have the same worldviews, but are firmly in the middle of a robust but contentious pluralism, the elites can no longer be said to represent the ordinary man in the street. Moreover, as we noted in Chap. 1, elite and well-educated opinion is no longer itself uniform in democratic societies, but is beginning to fracture. One of the obvious features of the contentious pluralism that we have been highlighting is that there is growing disagreement among well-educated and well-informed opinion on not only current affairs, but with regard to deeper foundational issues of life and meaning.

This brings us back then to the matter of the tyranny of the majority. In relation to populism, the argument might be that populism could turn into a kind of mob rule in a democratic context. By describing the majority as a mob, it seems to mean that they are uninformed, ignorant, stupid, prejudiced, and racist, and so it is therefore dangerous to decide issues by majority opinion. This charge does indeed seem to echo Plato's worry about democracy. The solution to containing the majority seems to be based on the belief that an elite, who know better (both factually and morally) would therefore rule better. We have seen the problems above with this approach, but it is often aimed particularly at religious beliefs, and suggests the idea that religion can have a special hold upon people, and perhaps turn them into a mob in certain contexts. It is an interesting objection, but in the context of today's democratic situation, it is not easy to see how it could be legitimate. For suppose a thinker like Audi claimed that religious beliefs should not be allowed in politics because the hold of religion on people could lead to a kind of mob rule. Sometimes he does seem to talk this way. To prevent this possibility, Audi would restrict certain religious views in politics. Our concern today must be to find a way to restrict all views that might turn into mob rule, not just religious ones. The worry about mob rule surely applies to any worldview, and is a risk of a democratic culture, notwithstanding the difficulty of distinguishing genuinely undemocratic and dangerous views from simple policy differences. Indeed, mob rule seems increasingly to be a part of liberal politics, one reason it is becoming more common to describe liberal democracy as "illiberal," as reflected in the familiar tactics of attempting to bully one's opponent instead of debating her, and of the alarming increase in attempts at censorship and restrictions on freedom of expression. In truth, this is one of the reasons behind the rise of populism. It is unfortunately true that if we allow our disagreements with others to degenerate into hatred, it can make us irrational in our thinking, and difficult to engage with since it means we will struggle to appraise matters objectively. So I think the position I have outlined in this and the previous chapter is the best one, although it is not smooth sailing by any means because of the general problems we have been laying out concerning democracy, freedom, pluralism, and relativism.

A Worry About the Tyranny of the Majority

What then of the worry about the tyranny of the majority, a worry founded on the idea that even if a majority have the power to impose a view on others by virtue of their numbers, they should refrain from doing so in some instances? Yet, there are cases where they should exercise this power. (And we have noted that in some modern democracies, such as the U.S., when certain groups cannot persuade the majority of the rightness of their position, they have sometimes found a way, usually through the courts, of circumventing the democratic process. It is something of a paradox, but seems also to be possible to have a "tyranny of the minority" in a democracy.) The question of course is which beliefs fit into which category. I am suggesting that normally imposing one's whole worldview on someone would represent a tyranny of the majority, as would forcing higher order beliefs of a worldview. However, we must acknowledge that people will often disagree about such matters. For example, is the claim that life is sacred and so the death penalty is wrong a higher order religious belief of the Catholic Church or is it a lower order belief? Is the claim that gender is a social construct and so educating children in traditional sex roles is wrong a higher order claim of secularist views or is it a lower order claim? Only society can decide in these cases, in a democratic manner. We might also emphasize that as a general rule we err on the side of freedom; we tend to permit things that we are not sure about, rather than prohibiting them. So the modern state allows *freedom of worldview*, as we might put it, and will not establish any particular worldview as the official worldview of the state.

It is within this context that we should be clear about what we mean by the notion of a theocracy or a seculocracy. These days, the word "theocracy" is much bandied about, in a pejorative way, to discourage religious people from introducing their views into politics. The official meaning of theocracy is where a state is actually run by the leaders of a religion (with the Vatican City State or Iran being contemporary examples). Another meaning is that one particular religion has a very dominant influence on the governing of a state (Ireland, in the past when it was still strongly a Catholic country, would be an example). Most members of the government would be Catholic in a Catholic state, and so their worldview would have defining influence on some issues. Neither of these meanings is intended by the use of the word today. Today, the word is frequently used to refer to *any* attempt, however small, to influence public discourse by means of religious views. It is also used pejoratively, and not descriptively, and usually only of religious views that secularists and liberal religious believers disagree with. Liberal academics, especially in France, the U.K., and the U.S. are always scaremongering about the dangers of a theocracy in a democratic setting, and usually they have in mind that some religious believers wish to outlaw abortion (though there are worries in some countries about Sharia law, with the fear being that Muslim majorities might not follow democratic values and procedures). This is partly why it is common to see the argument that I am making in this book frequently misrepresented or distorted, yet another indication of the move beyond rational deliberation and discussion. But this scaremongering is ridiculous for three reasons.

First, if it is intended to draw attention to the fact that we might end up with a law based on an argument that is part of someone's (in this case religious) worldview, this would be the case with *every* worldview, and to deny this possibility to religion is to discriminate illegitimately against religious worldviews. Second, we are more in danger of a seculocracy than a theocracy in many democratic countries because the notion of a secular state usually means in practice a secularist state, especially on topics that evince strong cultural disagreement. Third, many are in fact trying proactively to bring about a secularist state, given the rise and prominence of secularism. The worry about theocracy may have been true in the past in some democracies, but today the shoe is on the other foot. Secularism, even if it is sometimes a bit coy, is in the ascendency in terms of running society, and religion is on the retreat. Liberal political theory is widely regarded by religious believers as an arm of secularism, with its somewhat self-righteous sophisticated philosophical defense of the view that religion has no place in modern democratic politics, a formal argument against religion in principle, not an argument that involves a debate about content. This is why it is accurate to refer to a state in which some significant secularist beliefs are culturally influential on the law as a seculocracy. Indeed, a seculocracy could be described as a state where *any* law in that state is based on the truth of secularism! It is very disingenuous to define the concept of theocracy so broadly that it includes *any* reference to a religious belief or a religious value, and is something of an affront to the integrity of religious believers. It is helpful for us to distinguish clearly between (a) *appealing* to a religious belief or value in a public argument, (b) trying to *establish* one's religion as the official religion of the state, and (c) advocating a religious view based on an appeal to a revealed text or on the authority of a religious leader. These distinctions, as we noted, are critical to an honest discussion of our extremely complex topic.

It seems natural that a state where there is a majority worldview will show some favor toward that worldview. This is inevitable since values from that worldview will influence much public discussion and subsequent legislation; indeed, most members of the government might subscribe to the majority worldview. It would be impossible for them to set their worldview aside (a worldview or part thereof, on which they may have been elected), when considering and passing legislation. This is why it is crucial to recognize that secularism is now a major worldview, and becoming more so. Secularists elected to government will inevitably be influenced by their worldview, a phenomenon we now see in a number of countries, including Belgium, Ireland, France, and the Netherlands. Might a democratic state be impartial between secularist and religious worldviews? I believe the answer is no. This question is a throwback to an outdated way of framing the topic. It assumes that religious worldviews should be placed in a different category to secularist ones, and I have argued that this position is no longer plausible. It ignores the fact that worldviews all have the same basic structure, have many followers, and are trying to influence society. Given this, the state logically cannot be impartial between religion and non-religion, since it must take positions on some of the issues held by either worldview. As soon as the state adopts a law, it favors the worldview that supports that law, and disfavors the one that does not.

It is sometimes objected that historically religion has been very divisive in society, exclusivist, prone to cause social unrest, excessively judgmental, and so forth, and because of such features it is different from secularism and so may *still* be treated differently, even in a contemporary liberal, democratic culture. This description of religion as it has operated in the past is undoubtedly accurate, and nobody wants to go back to those oppressive times. However, I think that those days are long gone in Western democracies and this is no longer a serious worry, though some thinkers today often wish to insist on this understanding of religious belief (among other reasons, it makes it easier for them to promote contrary worldviews politically). British theologian, Don Cupitt, once remarked that a religious belief can be defined not so much by its content but by the way in which it is held. This might suggest that religious beliefs are held in a such a way that they are not subject to doubt, and may lead to zealotry and persecution. But Cupitt's definition doesn't just apply to or describe beliefs with religious content, and these days it would simply be disingenuous to single out religious beliefs in this way. If we are honest, we must acknowledge that any belief, including secularist beliefs, might be held with the same degree of fervor. It is surely obvious today that secularism, or secular liberalism, or whatever view is in the ascendency, can be very intrusive and judgmental, and that it is in fact a mark of modern pluralism that it is becoming increasingly harsh toward those with the "wrong views." And the social media shaming we sometimes witness today, especially from the left side of the political spectrum, can, I think, be described as a type of persecution for those on the wrong end of it. Religious believers who engage in democratic deliberations might be strongly discouraged not to make excessively harsh judgments, not to proselytize to an extreme, not to shun outsiders, because these activities and attitudes violate democratic principles. So those who wish to promote aspects of their religion in appropriate public contexts should avoid suppressing free speech, hiring people based on their beliefs, vilifying and shunning people who disagree, refusing to recognize the reality of pluralism, or holding litmus tests for public office, in short—avoid all of the tactics we have seen in the promotion of secularist or philosophical liberalism in recent times! And this is the key point, of course: that such restrictions must apply to all worldviews, and that all worldviews are capable of these wrongs, not just religious ones. Whatever about the past, that is the situation today, and the evidence to support it is everywhere around us.

There is one other important point we should make about the relationship between secularism and religion. It involves the fact that because of the type of interaction that can occur between opposing worldviews, and the fact that secularism is still developing, sometimes the *absence* of a symbol or practice can promote a worldview just as much as the presence of a symbol or practice. We can see this phenomenon particularly with regard to the role of religion in public education, which has given rise to a number of controversies in many liberal democracies. For example, in the U.S. there is often controversy concerning prayer in public schools, and perhaps even with regard to the introduction of and discussion of religious perspectives in some classroom work. In several countries the display or wearing of religious symbols, reading of the Bible in schools or in public places, religious symbols in sports, and other issues, have often provoked court cases and new legislation. The modern liberal approach is increasingly to exclude religious perspectives in these settings (Trigg mentions the case of an employee who was stopped by British Airways from wearing a Christian cross, and who lost in a court of appeal, although the airline was later forced to change its policy because of a public outcry).[19] It is important, however, to acknowledge that the absence of religious symbols and practices in certain contemporary contexts reflects a worldview as well. This is sometimes overlooked by thinkers like Audi who think that if you allow prayer in schools, for instance, you are favoring religion, but if you do not allow it you are not discriminating against religion, nor favoring any other view. This is not true, because the absence of prayer or religious activity is a significant feature of the secularist view (and if we are honest we will admit that the argument to prohibit prayer in public education is very often *motivated by secularism*, even if it is rarely expressed this way). This is why when you forbid the activities of one worldview you are automatically promoting the activities of the secularist worldview in this context, because of the fact that the secularist worldview both denies the meaning and truth of the activities, but also affirms their opposites. One reason secularists in the U.S. or those who are against a particular religion, or at least some of the views of a particular religion, wish to restrict or prohibit the influence of the religion in the public square is because of their hostility to it. Rather than being accommodating, they are hostile, trying to obstruct rather than tolerate.

I believe we must take a common sense view on many of these cases, and to allow some religious activity in public spaces. I would urge that we handle various topics that come up (such as displays of Christmas trees or other religious symbols) on a case-by-case basis. We should be mindful not to slight a worldview, insofar as this is possible; and careful not to be too quick to take offense out of personal hostility. Of course, we all reject the worldviews of others at some level, not just personally but also politically, as I have illustrated. But in cases of rituals, symbols, free practice, etc., we can be tolerant of other views, and careful not to needlessly insult people. Finally, democracies with specific bodies of law with regard to many of the issues discussed here would have to rethink them, such as the U.K. and U.S. (and, indeed, the European Union). It will not be possible to abandon their present laws or their tradition, but going forward they must look at the issues in the light of the new realities, and adapt and develop laws accordingly. The old way of thinking about these topics, as I have tried to argue here, is simply outmoded. Modern life has changed with regard to religious belief and practice, with regard to our understanding of the significance and place of religion in life, as well as with regard to the commitment to, and influence of, secularism. *So, the modern liberal democratic state must change as well.*

Guidelines for Public Discourse: Ten Suggestions

I am often asked what advice I would give to people interested in participating in public life. This is a crucial question, of course, and I have developed a response to it that will help also to bring together many of our key points in this book. It is an especially important concern for those who are working in any area that has to do with making a contribution to public policy debates, who wish to influence politicians and even the electorate with regard to bringing about social change on such issues as poverty and homelessness, job and educational opportunities, abortion, climate change, health care, and so forth. Although the question is perhaps especially pertinent for religious persons who work in the area of public policy and who see themselves as facing special discrimination in secular liberal democracies, it is relevant to any worldview whose proponents think they have a contribution to make to the betterment of society. It is not that secularist individuals and groups could, if they so wish, begin contributing to public life; the fact is that they already do, and we need to understand that their contributions are subject to the same protocols, rationale, and procedures as religious views. Religious believers may see the suggestions which follow as being especially relevant to them, and may find them interesting because the conventional (liberal, secular) wisdom in the state is hostile to their outlook, and usually wishes to exclude them from public discussion. Because current thinking favors secularism and discriminates against religion, secularists may balk at them because their implementation will contribute to a public square that is fairer and more consistent in the way it treats all worldviews. Yet, these suggestions do not favor any worldview, but apply to all worldviews, including secularism.

1. Know your worldview and make an attempt to familiarize yourself with its philosophical defense. A reminder of some important questions about one's worldview: 1. What is your worldview? (recall our three main subject areas as a way of organizing your beliefs: a. the nature of reality; b. the nature of the human person; c. the nature of moral and political values, including your political theory). 2. Is your worldview reasonable? 3. How would you defend it philosophically, especially to those who reject it, or reject important parts of it? Or if you are unsure about defending it personally, to whom do you look for guidance on this matter? 4. Which beliefs of your worldview are relevant for society, culture, and public policy; which of your beliefs and arguments do you think are appropriate in public discourse on the issues of the day?; 5. What is your attitude toward other worldviews? Which parts do you regard as true, false, rational, irrational, right or wrong, and so forth? These common sense questions will help you to clarify and come to appreciate more fully *which beliefs you hold and why, and which parts of your view are relevant for the shaping of society and culture.* One may need to engage with the work of experts, professors, and those experienced in formulating and debating worldviews for some assistance here, but this type of research can be helpful for non-experts in clarifying their position.

2. Don't be naïve when engaged in public discourse. This means that one should embrace the perspective of this book, and then everything will be more intelligible and will make sense! It will allow one, for instance, to recognize when spurious arguments are being offered aimed at excluding usually the religious worldview in a certain cultural climate, and why these arguments must be rejected and are based on an outmoded view of things. Not being naïve in public discourse involves adopting the following perspective: that religion is one worldview among many; that worldviews all have the same basic structure or form; that secularism is also a worldview; that reason can support religious conclusions; that some religious beliefs have political and social implications; that no plausible case can be made for excluding religion from politics that would not also apply to non-religious positions; that reasonable arguments can play a role in politics; that secularists do not agree on every issue. I have tried to illustrate and defend these claims in this book. Once one sees the general topic from this perspective, the whole debate is changed, and we are reminded that we need a new way of thinking about such matters as democracy moves forward.

3. Make an effort to be reasonable in one's public arguments. It is obviously helpful if your interlocutors can see that you have made an effort to develop and present reasonable arguments. This not only shows others that you are reasonable, but also puts an onus on them to debate with you, and take you seriously. In a way, the debate itself will give dignity and draw attention to your beliefs, when others might be tempted to ignore them, ridicule them or pretend disingenuously that they regard them as irrational as a way of avoiding engagement with them. Of course, others will still disagree with you most likely, as we saw in our earlier illustrations of the process of public reasoning in Chap. 8. But nevertheless I do think that being reasonable can go a long way, not only in terms of one's own reputation, but also in terms of making progress in terms of tolerance, compromise, and even occasional agreement. We should welcome debate and discussion rather than simply trying to avoid it or shut it down before it begins.

4. Treat others with respect, and not as political enemies. This is obvious moral advice though it can be hard to implement because of the fractious nature of modern politics, especially around certain issues in certain countries. It is made all the harder to practice by the phenomenon of political correctness. This phenomenon can be understood in several ways, but we can helpfully distinguish between content and style. The content refers to the beliefs that fall under the heading of political correctness, and the style refers to the method of promoting these ideas in society. The style issue is more important for our point here. It is a fact that the style associated with the promotion of politically correct ideas is as far away from treating others with respect as perhaps one can get. It usually involves deliberate bullying, vilification, discrimination, and even ostracizing of those people who hold the "wrong" views. This approach, exacerbated by the rise of social media, can make the whole task of reasonable political discourse over key issues of society and culture even harder to conduct. Some questions may be helpful: can you listen to perspectives different from your own with respect, and treat the holders of these views with respect? Do you tend to bully those whose views you disagree with as a first response, display anger toward them, call people names perhaps, attack people publicly, criticize them in such a fierce way that they might be reluctant to continue the discussion (the social censorship we mentioned in Chap. 2), or perhaps even deny them a job? If so, stop this behavior and change your attitude! It is not only wrong, but completely against the spirit of freedom, equality, pluralism, and democratic values.

5. Reconcile yourself to the reality of modern pluralism. Many people, secular liberals especially, are very good at talking a good game of pluralism, but not so good at practicing it! They welcome other views, especially those that are different from the mainstream, champion freedom of speech, and celebrate novelty and innovation in ideas. All until they hear ideas they don't like, and then they often engage in the type of severe criticism we have just mentioned, which quickly turns into social censorship. This is an unfortunate tendency of modern liberalism. It is indeed a paradox that those who seem to champion the notion of freedom the most are often the first to violate principles of free speech when their views are threatened. However, our point is that we must accept that there are many worldviews in the same state, and that we will hear all sorts of ideas that we do not like, think are false, irrational or immoral, even crazy. We may also have to live under some of these if they become law, which some will (perhaps you are already living under laws, either in society or at an institutional level, that you think deserve one of these descriptors?). We must reconcile ourselves to the fact that pluralism is not going away, and the old argument that "we would all be on the pig's back if everyone would only listen to me" is naive in the extreme! But accepting pluralism means that we should not be surprised that different people have different worldviews! Political correctness and liberal bullying are, I think, simply a failure to cope with the *fact* of pluralism, as I outlined in Chap. 3. Indeed, the notion of political correctness is simply incompatible with taking pluralism seriously. Pluralism is here for the foreseeable future, so those who wish to take part in moral, political, and cultural exchanges need to make an effort to accept this, and to work within it, despite the enormous challenge it can pose (another mark of the crisis we are in).

6. Do not resort to "pure politics." Nowadays, one increasingly sees people across a wide spectrum of society approaching many issues from the point of view of what we can describe as "pure politics." We regard our disagreements with others as political struggles, ones which we have to win at almost any cost. We do not see them as matters of philosophical disagreement, where we accept and welcome the need for honest debate, try to persuade others of our position, are open to learning from others, and show trust in the democratic process. As I have noted more than once in this book, many today regard this latter approach as having failed (to put it as charitably as possible; the uncharitable reading is that many have become cynical or malicious or manipulative with regard to matters of disagreement in a pluralist society). So, unfortunately, some think it is most expedient to take every opportunity to present their opponents' views in the worst possible light, and freely resort to devious rhetorical tricks such as misrepresentation, use of caricatures and stereotypes, inflammatory language, impugning of motives, bullying, feigning stubborn resistance, adopting the attitude of absolute certainty, ironically characteristic of Eric Hoffer's "true believer." Many who do this are aware deep down, I believe, that they are being dishonest. Unfortunately, we know that such tactics can often be quite successful in the promotion of one's views and the denigration of those with whom we disagree.

So I am encouraging us not to do this, plain and simple. Assume that any position (or person who holds that position) that you have described pejoratively, or in extremely negative terms, is being described incorrectly, and look for the actual issues of philosophical contention. Consider the strongest version of the other person's view, not a caricature of it. Don't look for psychological causes for why people disagree with you; look instead at their arguments. Refrain from the temptation to bully your opponent into silence or to intimidate them toward your side in a disagreement. Ask yourself straightforward clarifying questions such as: am I considering fairly opposing views or am I caricaturing them; am I deliberately distorting or ignoring facts? If a view sounds stupid or irrational or immoral the way I am presenting it, maybe I should assume in the first instance that I am presenting it incorrectly, and then review it carefully for accuracy. *If pluralist democracy is to make progress, this change of attitude seems to be essential, not optional.* Keep in mind too that we *agree* on a lot in the modern democratic nation. We tend to focus on our disagreements; this is because they are serious, and often come down to worldview disputes, leading to a contentious pluralism that seems very hard to get past, especially given the general loss of confidence in reason.

7. Avoid judging the rationality of arguments by your politics. An extension of the above advice relates to how we evaluate arguments that are presented to us in the public square. This is a conundrum that we have struggled with throughout our discussion—how to judge an argument objectively and honestly, and avoid pretending that we are being reasonable when we are not. We have a tendency in modern democratic states to judge an argument not on its objective merits, but by whether or not it is consistent with our politics. In other words, one has a political test (indeed a worldview test), not a rational test, for an argument. This is perhaps a subtle point, but it is important. It is a point that relies on an acceptance of pluralism above, and the reality that people will evaluate rational arguments differently because of that gray area we talked about, where an argument is suggestive but not conclusive, not certain, falling short of any kind of proof or scientific demonstration. This is where the temptation to resort to abuse, peer pressure, ridicule, personal incredulity, or consensus opinion in order to get others to see things the way I see them is strong, and comes closest to failing to respect pluralism. It is a fine line but we need to be aware always of the difference between holding an entrenched ideology, and holding a worldview that we can defend and think is the right way forward for society.

8. Agree to settle differences democratically. This is vital in modern democracies because the problem of worldview pluralism creates a strong temptation to circumvent the democratic process in various ways because of our inability to persuade a majority of the rational and moral superiority of our beliefs. It is now commonplace in some countries to try to find some other way of imposing one's views on a society that does not agree with them. One can only do this if one has the power to do so, for it is not easy to circumvent the democratic process in most countries. But one popular way, as we have noted, is through the court system, especially obvious in the United States, where the U.S. Supreme Court, and increasingly lower-level courts, decide many contentious issues, based on the political opinions of judges, and not on the law. To get away with this, it is necessary (perhaps) to have the support of a good deal of public opinion; one also needs a good deal of the media on one's side, since they have so much influence in shaping public opinion. Congress or Parliament may also take positions from time to time that do not represent the will of the people. And it is interesting to consider the Brexit fiasco in the U.K. as a case in point, the fiasco being that a democratic majority support Brexit but the government, the media, and the elites do not, and so for a couple of years there was a protracted standoff about how or whether to implement it, punctuated by regular calls for a second referendum with the hope of overturning the decision of the general public. The Brexit drama is another example of some of the problems of modern democracy. I am arguing that the fairest way to settle our differences in a pluralist state is *democratically*, keeping in mind our earlier remarks about the tyranny of the majority.

9. Re-envision your understanding of the relationship between church and state. I would encourage everyone to consider rethinking the church/state relationship in the way we have argued for in this chapter. And to approach all matters of public argument, public policy issues, political debate, and exchanges about issues of culture, law and society, from this updated, fresh perspective. Once one understands that secularism is a major worldview in itself, one that wishes to influence the state and society at the level of law, just as various religious worldviews do (worldviews that also disagree among themselves), that all worldviews must be considered in their relationship to the state, that the state must inevitably support some values over others, then one is in a better position to conduct a fairer and more accurate public debate that is true to the reality of modern pluralism. One also will have a much clearer insight into, and understanding of, the issues that affect pluralist society relating to worldviews, religion and politics, moral debates, relativism, politics and ideology, and the loss of confidence in reason. I can't emphasize enough the importance of looking at things in this new way. This is one of our main themes in this book. Some will refuse to do so for various reasons, but I believe it is not only correct but *the logical next step* in the evolution of our thinking about pluralist democracy.

10. Become a critical thinker. Our final piece of advice is one that brings together several of our suggestions, a kind of foundation to our earlier points. A modern educated citizen must be a critical thinker about the ideas and forces that contribute to the shaping of society and culture. There are a number of areas where this advice is apposite, but one of the most crucial is with regard to the media. It is simply essential to be a critical thinker with regard to the whole topic of media studies and media analysis today. We noted in Chap. 2 that one of the consequences of pluralism is that media outlets *take sides* with regard to the issues of contentious dispute, and no longer effectively do their job in holding governments to account and in informing the public. Aside from problems with handling the phenomenon of pluralism, bias, and lack of objectivity, the media is a pernicious force in modern society in other ways, especially regarding the temptation to sensationalize, misrepresent, muck-rake, attack, provoke confrontation, not to mention the undue influence of conglomerates and advertisers on the production of news and information. (And, unfortunately, there seems to be no practical way to force the media to be more unbiased and objective, or more representative; no "media watchdog" model can work in a free society.) Because of their power it is absolutely essential that one be able to engage them critically, be capable of handling them in an evaluative way; otherwise they will handle you, in terms of forming your opinion but also in terms of influence on your society and culture! Even in the presence of a critically informed and reflective electorate, they will still retain considerable power over public opinion, but at least a reflective and mostly independent-minded citizenry can contain them, reduce their influence, and mitigate their destructive effect on culture. This general point also extends to politics. One should educate oneself to have a good general understanding of how politics works. This includes not only having a good understanding of the democratic system of government, but also being able to recognize the difference between a philosophical argument and a political stunt, appreciating the distinction between political and moral motivation, and the difference between honest, principled decision-making and manipulative, deceitful political expediency and gamesmanship. It also includes being able to distinguish between rhetoric and appeals to emotion and sincere positions of philosophical substance.

It is crucial to be a critical and independent thinker in our increasingly fractious public culture. If one does not think things through for oneself, one will be unable to contribute effectively to public discourse, unable to provide insight and guidance to the society in which one lives, in which one raises one's family. One will, in fact, be leaving the running of one's country, and decisions regarding the right path toward human fulfillment, to others.

NOTES

1. See Jan Velaers and Marie-Claire Foblets, "Religion and the Secular State in Belgian Law," in J. Martinez-Torron and C. Durham (eds.), *Religion and the Secular State* (Washington: Brigham Young University, 2014), pp. 99–122; for an overview of the topic in several countries, see

J. Christopher Soper et al. (eds.), *The Challenge of Pluralism: Church and State in Six Democracies* (Lanham, MD.: Rowman & Littlefield, 2017).
2. See my *Why Politics Needs Religion*, pp. 65–66.
3. See Austin Dacey, *The Secular Conscience* (New York: Prometheus, 2008), pp. 43–57.
4. See R. Eatwell and M. Goodwin, *National Populism* (London, UK: Penguin, 2018), p. 138.
5. See my *Why Politics Needs Religion*, pp. 51–53, which has influenced my exposition here.
6. See Nicholas Wolterstorff, "The Role of Religion in Political Issues," in Robert Audi and Nicholas Wolterstorff, *Religion in the Public Square* (New York: Rowman and Littlefield, 1997), pp. 117–118.
7. See Cas Mudde and Cristobal Kaltwasser, *Populism: A Very Short Introduction* (New York: Oxford U.P., 2017), pp. 1–5.
8. See Bernard Crick, *Democracy: A Very Short Introduction*, pp. 72–76.
9. James Madison in Federalist Paper No. 10 in Clinton Rossiter (ed.), *The Federalist Papers*, p. 76, p. 78.
10. See A.C. Grayling, *Democracy and Its Crisis*, pp. 131ff.
11. Mudde and Kaltwasser, *Populism*, p. 7.
12. See Eatwell and Goodwin, *National Populism*, p. xxvii.
13. Ibid., pp. 239ff; see also Harold D. Clarke et al., *Brexit: Why Britain Voted to Leave the European Union* (New York: Cambridge U.P., 2017).
14. See Eatwell and Goodwin, *National Populism*, ix–xxxii.
15. As an example of this approach, see Jan-Werner Müller, *What is Populism?* (New York: Penguin, 2017). Muller describes the (negative) meaning of populism well, but then attributes every political development today of which he disapproves to the phenomenon. For a more even-handed approach, see Benjamin Moffit, *Populism* (Cambridge, UK: Polity, 2020; also Margaret Canovan, *The People* (Cambridge, UK: Polity, 2005), pp. 65–90.
16. This point runs throughout Eatwell and Goodwin's study in their *National Populism*.
17. Eatwell and Goodwin illustrate this point by appeal to empirical data, see, ibid., pp. 156–162.
18. Mark Bovins and Anchrit Willie have shown that educated elites are in control in many countries. They also argue that, because of this fact, Plato's ideal of Philosopher Kings running society has basically come to fruition! See their *Diploma Democracy: The Rise of Political Meritocracy* (New York: Oxford U.P., 2017).
19. See Roger Trigg, *Equality, Freedom, and Religion*, p. 130.

Bibliography

Ackerman, Bruce, *Social Justice in the Liberal State* (New Haven, CT: Yale U.P., 1980).
Anderson, Walt T., *The Truth about Truth: De-confusing and Re-constructing the Postmodern World* (New York: Putnam, 1995).
Annas, Julia, *The Morality of Happiness* (New York: Oxford U.P., 1995).
Anthony, Louise (ed.), *Philosophers Without Gods* (New York: Oxford U.P., 2007).
Aristotle, *Politics* (New York: Penguin, 1981).
Aristotle, *The Nicomachean Ethics* (New York: Oxford U.P., 2009).
Audi, Robert, *Religious Commitment and Secular Reason* (New York: Cambridge U.P., 2000).
Audi, Robert, *Democratic Authority and the Separation of Church and State* (New York: Oxford U.P., 2011).
Audi, Robert and Nicholas Wolterstorff, *Religion in the Public Square* (New York: Rowman and Littlefield, 1997).
Baggett, David and Jerry L. Walls (ed.), *God and Cosmos: Moral Truth and Human Meaning* (New York: Oxford U.P., 2016).
Baggini, Julian, *What's It All About?* (New York: Oxford U.P., 2005).
Barthes, Roland, *Mythologies* (New York: Hill and Wang, 2013).
Baubérot, Jean, "The Evolution of French Secularism," in Ranjan Ghosh (ed.), *Making Sense of the Secular* (New York: Routledge, 2013).
Bayle, Pierre, *Political Writings*, ed. by Sally Jenkinson (Cambridge, UK: Cambridge U.P., 2000).
Beckwith, Francis J., *Taking Rites Seriously: Law, Politics and the Reasonableness of Faith* (New York: Cambridge U.P., 2015).
Benhabib, Seyla, *The Claims of Culture: Equality and Diversity in the Global Era* (Princeton, NJ: Princeton U.P., 2002).

Berger, Peter, *The Sacred Canopy* (New York: Anchor, 1967).
Berlin, Isaiah, *Four Essays on Liberty* (London: Oxford U.P., 2002).
Biagini, Eugenio, and Mary E. Daly (eds.), *Cambridge Social History of Modern Ireland* (New York: Cambridge U.P., 2017).
Boettcher, James W., "What Is Reasonableness?," *Philosophy and Social Criticism*, 30, No. 5–6 (2004), pp. 597–621.
Bovins, Mark and Anchrit Willie, *Diploma Democracy: The Rise of Political Meritocracy* (New York: Oxford U.P., 2017).
Brennan, Jason, *Against Democracy* (Princeton, NJ: Princeton U.P., 2017).
Brock, Stuart, and Edwin Mares, *Realism and Anti-Realism* (Montreal: McGill-Queens U.P., 2007).
Brown, Callum, *The Death of Christian Britain* (London: Routledge, 2001).
Bruce, Steve, *Secularization* (New York: Oxford U.P., 2011).
Burke, Edmund, *Reflections on the Revolution in France* (New York: Cambridge U.P., 2014).
Burleigh, Michael, *Sacred Causes: The Clash of Religion and Politics* (New York: Harper Perennial, 2007).
Calhoun, C., M. Juergensmeyer, and J. VanAntwerpen (eds.), *Rethinking Secularism* (New York: Oxford U.P., 2011).
Campbell, David E. and Geoffrey C. Layman, "The Politics of Secularism in the United States," in Robert Scott and Marlis Buchmann (eds.), *Emerging Trends in the Social and Behavioral Sciences* (John Wiley On Line Reference Work, 2017), pp. 1–13.
Canavon, Margaret, *The People* (Cambridge, UK: Polity, 2005).
Carter, Ian, *A Measure of Freedom* (New York: Oxford U.P., 1999).
Casanova, José, *Public Religions in the Modern World* (Chicago: University of Chicago Press, 1994).
Cavanaugh, William T., *The Myth of Religious Violence: Secular Ideology and the Roots of Modern Conflict* (New York: Oxford U.P., 2009).
Clarke, Harold D., Matthew Goodwin and Paul Whiteley (eds.), *Brexit: Why Britain Voted to Leave the European Union* (New York: Cambridge U.P., 2017).
Conley, Sarah, *Against Autonomy: Justifying Coercive Paternalism* (New York: Cambridge U.P., 2013).
Copson, Andrew, *Secularism* (London: Oxford U.P., 2017).
Coyne, Jerry, *Why Evolution Is True* (New York: Penguin, 2010).
Crick, Bernard, *Democracy: A Very Short Introduction* (Oxford, UK: Oxford U.P., 2002).
D'Costa, Gavin et al. (eds), *Religion in a Liberal State* (New York: Cambridge U.P., 2013).
Dacey, Austin, *The Secular Conscience* (New York: Prometheus, 2008).
Dahl, Robert A., *Democracy and Its Critics* (New Haven, CT: Yale U.P., 1989).

Dahl, Robert A., *A Preface to Democratic Theory* (Chicago: University of Chicago Press, 1989).
Davie, Grace, *Religion in Modern Europe* (New York: Oxford U.P., 2000).
Dawkins, Richard, *The Blind Watchmaker* (New York: Norton, 1987).
Dawkins, Richard, *The God Delusion* (New York: Houghton Mifflin, 2006).
Day O'Connor, Sandra, *The Majesty of the Law* (New York: Random House, 2003).
Derrida, Jacques, *Writing and Difference*, trans. by Alan Bass (Chicago, IL: University of Chicago Press, 1978).
Dineen, Patrick, *Why Liberalism Failed* (New Haven, CT: Yale U.P., 2018).
Ducasse, C.J., *A Critical Examination of the Belief in a Life After Death* (Whitefish, MT: Kessinger, 2010; orig. 1961).
Dworkin, Ronald, *Taking Rights Seriously* (Cambridge, MA: Harvard U.P., 1978).
Dworkin, Ronald, *Life's Dominion* (New York: Knopf, 1993).
Dyson, R.W., *Aquinas: Political Writings* (New York: Cambridge U.P., 2002).
Eatwell, R. and M. Goodwin, *National Populism* (London, UK: Penguin, 2018).
Eberle, Christopher, *Religious Convictions in Liberal Politics* (New York: Cambridge U.P., 2002).
Estlund, David, *Democratic Authority* (Princeton, NJ: Princeton U.P. 2008).
Evans, C. Stephen, *God and Moral Obligation* (New York: Oxford U.P., 2013).
Fawcett, Edmund, *Liberalism: The Life of an Idea* (Princeton, NJ: Princeton U.P., 2018).
Fish, Stanley, *The First: How to Think about Hate Speech, Campus Speech, Religious Speech, Fake News, Post-Truth, and Donald Trump* (New York: Atria, 2019).
Fontana, Biamcamaria (ed.), *Constant: Political Writings* (New York: Cambridge U.P., 1988).
Friedman, Marilyn, "John Rawls and the Political Coercion of Unreasonable People," in Victoria Davion and Clark Wolf (eds.), *The Idea of Political Liberalism* (New York: Rowman and Littlefield, 2000).
Galston, Miriam, "Rawlsian Dualism and the Autonomy of Political Thought," *Columbia Law Review*, 94, No. 6 (1994), pp. 1842–1859.
Gaus, Gerard, *The Order of Public Reason* (New York: Cambridge U.P., 2011).
George, Robert P. and Christopher Wolfe (eds.), *Natural Law and Public Reason* (Washington, DC: Georgetown U.P., 2000).
Grayling, A.C., *Democracy and Its Crisis* (London: Oneworld, 2017).
Greeley, Andrew, *Religious Change in America* (Cambridge, MA: Harvard U.P., 1996).
Greenawalt, Kent, *Private Consciences and Public Reasons* (New York: Oxford U.P., 1995).
Guthman, Amy, *Democratic Education* (Princeton, NJ: Princeton U.P., 1987).
Gutting, Gary, *Talking God* (New York: Norton, 2017).
Habermas, Jurgen, *Between Facts and Norms* (Cambridge, MA: MIT Press, 1996).

Habermas, Jurgen, *Moral Consciousness and Communicative Action* (Cambridge, MA: MIT Press, 2001).
Habermas, Jurgen, "Notes on a Post-Secular Society," http://www.signandsight.com/features/1714.html.
Hampton, Jean, "Should Political Philosophy be Done Without Metaphysics?", *Ethics*, 99, No. 4 (1989), pp. 791–814.
Hampton, Jean, "The Moral Commitments of Liberalism," in David Copp, Jean Hampton, and John E. Roemer (eds.), *The Idea of Democracy* (New York: Cambridge U.P., 1993), pp. 292–313.
Harris, Sam, *The Moral Landscape* (New York: Free Press, 2011).
Hauerwas, Stanley, *A Better Hope* (Grand Rapids, MI: Brazos Press, 2000).
Hauerwas, Stanley and Romand Coles, *Christianity, Democracy and the Radical Ordinary* (Eugene, OR: Wipf and Stock, 2008).
Haught, John, *What is Religion?: An Introduction* (Mahway, NJ: Paulist Press, 1990).
Held, David, *Models of Democracy* (Stanford, CA: Stanford U.P., 2006).
Hexham, Irving, *Concise Dictionary of Religion* (Downer's Grove, IL: InterVarsity Press, 1993).
Hobbes, Thomas, *Leviathan* (London: Penguin, 1985).
Hume, David, *A Treatise of Human Nature* (London: Penguin, 1985).
Issenberg, Sasha, "Divided We Stand," *New York Magazine*, November 14, 2014.
Kant, Immanuel, *Critique of Practical Reason*, trans. by W.S. Pluhar (Indianapolis, IN: Hackett, 2002).
King, Martin Luther, "Letter from Birmingham City Jail," in James M. Washington (ed.), *A Testament of Hope: The Essential Writings and Speeches of Martin Luther King Jr* (San Francisco: Harper, 1986), pp. 289–302.
Kitcher, Philip, *Living with Darwin: Evolution, Design and the Future of Faith* (New York: Oxford U.P., 2007).
Kitcher, Philip, *Life after Faith: The Case for Secular Humanism* (New Haven, CT: Yale U.P., 2014).
Kraynak, Robert P., *Christian Faith and Modern Democracy* (South Bend, IN: University of Notre Dame Press, 2001).
Kuri, Ahmet T., *Secularism and State Policies Toward Religion: The United States, France, and Turkey* (New York: Cambridge U.P., 2009).
Laborde, Cécile, *Liberalism's Religion* (Cambridge, MA: Harvard U.P., 2017).
Landemore, Hélène, *Democratic Reason* (Princeton, NJ: Princeton U.P., 2013).
Lecky, William, *Democracy and Liberty* (Indianapolis, IN: Liberty Fund, 1981).
Locke, John, *A Letter Concerning Toleration*, ed. by James Tully (Indianapolis, IN: Hackett, 1983).
Locke, John, *Two Treatises of Government* (New York: Cambridge U.P., 1988).
Locke, John, *The Reasonableness of Christianity* (New York: Clarendon Press, 2000).

Lyotard, Jean-François, *The Postmodern Condition: A Report on Knowledge* (Minneapolis, MS: University of Minnesota Press, 1984).
Macedo, Stephen, *Liberal Virtues* (New York: Oxford U.P., 1990).
MacIntyre, Alaisdair, *After Virtue* (Notre Dame, IN: University of Notre Dame Press, 1984).
Maritain, Jacques, *The Rights of Man and Natural Law* (Washington, DC: Catholic University of America Press, 1951).
Martin, David, *A General Theory of Secularization* (New York: Harper and Row, 1979).
Martin, William, *A Prophet with Honor: The Billy Graham Story* (San Francisco: Harper, 1992).
Martinez-Torron, J. and C. Durham (eds.), *Religion and the Secular State* (Washington: Brigham Young University, 2014).
McInerny, Ralph, *Aquinas* (Cambridge, UK: Polity, 2004).
Merrill, R. and D. Weinstock (eds.), *Political Neutrality: A Re-evaluation* (New York: Palgrave Macmillan, 2014).
Milbank, John, Catherine Pickstock and Graham Ward (eds.), *Radical Orthodoxy: A New Theology* (New York: Routledge, 1999).
Mill, John Stuart, *On Liberty* (Indianapolis, IN: Hackett, 1978).
Moffit, Benjamin, *Populism* (Cambridge, UK: Polity, 2020).
Montesquieu, Baron, *The Spirit of the Laws* (New York: Cambridge U.P., 1989).
Mudde, Cas, and Cristobal Kaltwasser, *Populism: A Very Short Introduction* (New York: Oxford U.P., 2017).
Müller, Jan-Werner, *What Is Populism?* (New York: Penguin, 2017).
Muncy, Mitchell (ed.), *The End of Democracy?* (Dallas, TX: Spence Publishing, 1997).
Munson, Ziad, *Abortion Politics* (Cambridge, UK: Polity, 2018).
Nagel, Thomas, *The View from Nowhere* (New York: Oxford, 1986).
Nagel, Thomas, "Moral Conflict and Political Legitimacy," *Philosophy and Public Affairs*, 16, No. 3 (1987), pp. 215–240.
Nagel, Thomas, *Equality and Partiality* (New York: Oxford U.P., 1991).
Neuhaus, Richard John, *The Naked Public Square* (Grand Rapids, MI: Eerdmans, 1984).
Neuhaus, Richard John, "Proposing Democracy Anew—Part Two," *First Things*, November 1999.
Nielsen, Kai, "Death and the Meaning of Life" in E.D. Klemke, *The Meaning of Life* (New York: Oxford U.P., 2000, 2nd ed.), pp. 153–159.
Novak, Michael, *On Two Wings: Humble Faith and Common Sense at the American Founding* (San Francisco: Encounter, 2002).
Nussbaum, Martha, *Liberty of Conscience* (New York: Basic Books, 2008).
Ober, Josiah, *Demopolis: Democracy Before Liberalism in Theory and Practice* (New York: Cambridge U.P., 2017).

Paine, Thomas, *The Rights of Man* (London: Penguin, 1984).
Pateman, Carole, *Participation and Democratic Theory* (New York: Cambridge U.P., 1976).
Perry, Michael J., *Religion in Politics* (New York: Oxford U.P., 1987).
Piketty, Thomas, *Capital in the Twenty-First Century* (Cambridge, MA: Belknap Press, 2014).
Pinker, Steven, *How the Mind Works* (New York: Norton, 1997).
Plato, *The Laws* (New York: Penguin, 2005).
Plato, *The Republic* (London: Penguin, 2007).
Pogge, Thomas, *John Rawls: His Life and Theory of Justice* (New York: Oxford U.P., 2007).
Pojman, Louis, "Religion Gives Meaning to Life," in Louis P. Pojman and Louis Vaughn (eds.), *Philosophy: The Quest for Truth* (New York: Oxford U.P., 2019, 11th ed.), pp. 680–684.
Pollack, D. and D.V.A. Olson (eds.), *The Role of Religion in Modern Societies* (New York: Routledge, 2007).
Quinn, Philip L., "Political Liberalisms and their Exclusions of the Religious," in Paul Weithman (ed.), *Religion and Contemporary Liberalism* (South Bend, IN: University of Notre Dame Press, 1997), pp. 138–161.
Quong, Jonathan, *Liberalism Without Perfection* (New York: Oxford U.P., 2020).
Rabinow, Paul (ed.), *The Foucault Reader* (New York: Pantheon, 1984).
Ratzinger, Joseph and Jurgen Habermas, *The Dialectics of Secularization: On Reason and Religion* (San Francisco: Ignatius Press, 2007).
Rawls, John, "Reply to Habermas," *Journal of Philosophy*, 92, No. 3 (1995), pp. 132–180.
Rawls, John, *Political Liberalism* (New York: Colombia U.P., 1996).
Rawls, John, "The Idea of Public Reason Revisited," *The University of Chicago Law Review*, 64 (1997), pp. 765–807.
Rawls, John, *A Theory of Justice* (Cambridge, MA: Belknap Press, 1999).
Raz, Joseph, *The Morality of Freedom* (New York: Oxford U.P., 1988).
Robson, J.M. (ed.), *The Collected Works of John Stuart Mill* (Toronto: University of Toronto Press 1963–1991).
Rossiter, Clinton (ed.), *The Federalist Papers* (New York: New American Library, 2003).
Rousseau, Jean-Jacques, *The Social Contract* (London: Penguin, 1968).
Roy, Olivier, *Is Europe Christian?* (London: Hurst, 2019).
Ruane, Joseph, "Secularization and Ideology in the Republic of Ireland," in Paul Brennan (ed.), *La sécularization en Irlande* (Caen, France: Presses universitaires de Caen, 1998), pp. 239–254.
Sandel, Michael, *Liberalism and the Limits of Justice* (New York: Cambridge U.P., 1998).
Sandel, Michael, *Public Philosophy* (Cambridge, MA: Harvard U.P., 2006).

Sartre, Jean Paul, *Existentialism Is a Humanism* (New Haven, CT: Yale U.P., 2007).
Schumpeter, Joseph, *Capitalism, Socialism and Democracy* (New York: Harper, 1975).
Sher, George, *Beyond Neutrality* (New York: Cambridge U.P., 1997).
Simpson, Peter, *Political Illiberalism: A Defense of Freedom* (New York: Routledge, 2015).
Smith, Christian, *The Secular Revolution* (Berkeley, CA: University of California Press, 2003).
Spinoza, Baruch, *Theological-Political Treatise* (New York: Cambridge U.P., 2007).
Stark, Rodney and R. Finke, *Acts of Faith: Explaining the Human Side of Religion* (Los Angeles: University of California Press, 2000).
Stout, Jeffrey, *Democracy and Tradition* (Princeton, NJ: Princeton U.P., 2004).
Sturrock, John, *Structuralism and Since* (Oxford, UK: Oxford U.P., 1979).
Sweetman, Brendan, "Postmodernism, Derrida and *Différance*: A Critique," *International Philosophical Quarterly*, XXXIX, No. 1 (1999), pp. 5–18.
Sweetman, Brendan, *Why Politics Needs Religion: The Place of Religious Arguments in the Public Square* (Downers Grove, IL: InterVarsity, 2006).
Sweetman, Brendan, *Religion and Science: An Introduction* (New York: Continuum, 2010).
Sweetman, Brendan, *Evolution, Chance, and God* (New York: Bloomsbury, 2015).
Talisse, Robert B., *Engaging Political Philosophy: An Introduction* (New York: Routledge, 2016).
Taylor, Charles, *Sources of the Self* (Cambridge, MA: Harvard U.P., 1989).
Taylor, Charles, *A Secular Age* (Cambridge, MA: Harvard U.P., 2007).
Terchek, Ronald J. and Thomas C. Conte (eds.), *Theories of Democracy: A Reader* (Lanham, MD: Rowman and Littlefield, 2000).
Trigg, Roger, *Religion in Public Life* (New York: Oxford U.P., 2007).
Trigg, Roger, *Equality, Freedom, and Religion* (New York: Oxford U.P., 2012).
Ulin, J.V. and H. Edwards (eds.), *Race and Immigration in the New Ireland* (Notre Dame, IN: University of Notre Dame Press, 2013).
Van ReyBrouck, David, *Against Elections: The Case for Democracy* (New York: Random House, 2016).
Voltaire, *A Treatise on Tolerance* (New York: Barnes and Noble, 2009).
Waldron, Jeremy, *God, Locke, and Equality: Christian Foundations of Locke's Political Thought* (New York: Cambridge U.P., 2002).
Warnock, Mary, *Dishonest to God: On Keeping Religion Out of Politics* (New York: Continuum, 2010).
Weber, Max, *Economy and Society* (Cambridge, MA: Harvard U.P., 2019).
Weithman, Paul, *Religion and the Obligations of Citizenship* (New York: Cambridge U.P., 2002).
Weithman, Paul, *Rawls, Political Liberalism and Reasonable Faith* (New York: Cambridge U.P., 2016).

Whelan, Frederick G., *Democracy in Theory and Practice* (London: Routledge, 2018).
Willard, Dallas, *The Disappearance of Moral Knowledge* (New York: Routledge, 2018).
Wolff, Jonathan, *An Introduction to Political Philosophy* (Oxford, UK: Oxford U.P., 2016).
Wolterstorff, Nicholas, "The Role of Religion in Political Issues," in Robert Audi and Nicholas Wolterstorff (eds.), *Religion in the Public Square* (New York: Rowman and Littlefield, 1997), pp. 117–118.
Wolterstorff, Nicholas, *Understanding Liberal Democracy* (New York: Oxford U.P., 2012).
Zagorin, Perez, *How the Idea of Religious Toleration Came to the West* (Princeton, NJ: Princeton U.P., 2003).

Index[1]

A

Abortion, 67, 84, 92, 115, 136, 141, 166, 172, 177, 180, 192, 201, 202, 208–212, 221, 222, 224, 226, 227, 236–242, 247, 248, 253, 256–260, 264, 266, 270, 273, 274, 279, 280, 289, 305, 309

Academia, 33, 63, 64, 69, 75, 81, 84, 89, 91, 109, 119, 133, 165, 167–168, 229, 231, 235, 259, 297, 299, 303, 305

Ackerman, Bruce, 208, 225, 250n14

Adams, John, 10

Anglicanism, 284

Anthony, Louise, 138

Anti-realism, 61, 86–93, 98n6, 102, 112, 119, 121, 199, 207, 233–234, 267

Aquinas, St Thomas, 15, 56, 74, 134, 262

Aristotle, 8, 23, 56, 74, 134, 239

Atheism, 46, 49, 126, 130–133, 143–145, 163, 172, 285

Audi, Robert, 35, 208–212, 214n28, 228, 230, 231, 233, 238, 239, 241–243, 254–258, 261, 262, 264, 265, 267, 303, 304, 308

Australia, 12, 30, 153n6, 159

Austria, 294, 302

B

Barthes, Roland, 104, 105

Bayle, Pierre, 45

Belgium, 12, 65, 153n6, 163, 283, 306

Beliefs, 73, 130, 291

Bella, Robert, 145

Bentham, Jeremy, 246

Berlin, Isaiah, 48

Bible, 128, 129, 131, 136, 144, 206, 208–210, 233, 254, 266, 292, 308

---

[1] Note: Page numbers followed by 'n' refer to notes.

© The Author(s), under exclusive license to Springer Nature Switzerland AG 2021
B. Sweetman, *The Crisis of Democratic Pluralism*,
https://doi.org/10.1007/978-3-030-78382-2

Boettcher, James, 213n7
Bovins, Mark, 317n18
Brennan, Jason, 18, 26, 38n26
Brexit, 6, 27, 279, 299, 314, 315
Brown, Callum, 163
Bruce, Steve, 160–162, 208
Burdens of judgment, 220, 228, 232, 235, 278
Burke, Edmund, 14, 136
Burleigh, Michael, 212n1

C

Cambodia, 4
Campbell, David, 185n18
Canada, 64, 65, 153n6, 227
Cancel culture, 65, 182
Capitalism, 22, 23, 38n18, 178
Capital punishment, 16, 65, 103, 192, 228, 273, 304
Catholicism, 44, 46, 86, 153n6, 163, 168, 174–182, 211, 240, 254, 263, 268, 283, 289, 292, 304, 305
Censorship, 45, 47, 54, 64, 304, 312
Chance, 73, 134, 147, 154n24, 275
Checks and balances, 298
Children, 11, 12, 31, 49, 52, 76, 78, 168–169, 175, 179, 181, 226, 280, 284
Christianity, 13, 74, 86, 116, 126–129, 134, 136, 144, 147, 153n6, 181, 206, 254, 256, 264, 268, 281n19
Christians, philosophical, 129, 136, 190
Church, 84, 128, 153n6, 260, 263
Church and state, 34, 45, 128, 132, 135, 161, 181, 274, 283–316
    See also Religion in public life
Churchill, Winston, 18
Citizens, 74, 94, 115, 126, 171, 176, 183, 201, 220, 221, 223, 224, 226, 264, 268, 284, 315

Civic virtue, 221, 231, 247, 268
Civil rights, xi, 16, 246, 262–268
Civil service, 21, 25, 303
Cloning, 157, 275–277, 279
Coercion, 192, 199, 201, 205, 209, 220, 224, 226, 227, 230, 231, 272
Common good, 9, 26, 31, 52, 96, 226
Communism, 14
Comprehensive conception of the good, 194, 197, 200, 201, 214n24, 239, 274
Conley, Sarah, 18
Consent, 5, 8, 46, 192, 204, 223
Conservatives, 135, 169, 285
Courts, 68n18, 75, 76, 97, 180, 226, 266, 304, 308
Coyne, Jerry, 138
Crick, Bernard, 296
Crisis, 3–36, 71–72, 83, 86, 96, 120, 312
Culture, 7, 11, 22, 32, 55, 80–84, 86, 93–96, 99n7, 101–103, 111–113, 115, 116, 118, 143–144, 163, 174, 176, 177, 179–182, 194, 196–198, 201, 220–222, 226, 233, 248, 262, 269–272, 274, 285, 289, 296, 300, 301
Cupitt, Don, 307

D

Dacey, Austin, 287
Dahl, Robert, 36n2
Dawkins, Richard, 131, 138, 143, 146, 149, 153n8, 218
Deconstruction, 106, 109
Democracy, vii, 66–67, 85, 101–103, 128, 160, 166, 188, 190, 207, 223, 228, 260, 273, 294–296, 301, 315
    crisis of, 3–36, 83, 120

fledging, ix, 5, 47
foundations of, vii, 4, 6, 7, 10, 12, 19, 30, 35, 62, 78, 92, 97, 169
mature, 5, 27, 51, 79, 87, 191, 297
practical problems of, 18–29, 31
representative, 8–9, 11, 16, 21, 37n9, 180, 226, 297
secular (*see* Secular liberalism; Secular state)
See also Liberal democracy; Liberal political theory
Democratic culture, 32, 55, 60, 72, 80, 93, 101, 102, 104, 111, 112, 116, 118, 119, 126, 220, 221, 248, 279, 304, 307
Dennett, Daniel, 138, 286
Derrida, Jacques, 104, 105, 109
Dewey, John, 138
Dickens, Charles, 148
Dineen, Patrick, 269
Discourse principle, 204
Divorce, 43–44, 49, 177, 178, 180
Dogma, 289, 290, 292
Dostoevsky, Fyodor, 147, 149, 255
Druyan, Ann, 138
Ducasse, C.J., 239
Durkheim, Emile, 127
Dworkin, Ronald, 35, 208, 225, 249n8

E

Eatwell, Roger, 299, 301
Economics, 7, 9, 11, 12, 14, 17, 23, 27, 63, 78, 79, 128, 130, 135, 143, 150, 160, 164, 176–178, 198, 203, 268, 295, 296, 300
Education, 11, 14, 25–27, 31, 33, 48, 81, 86, 88, 89, 139, 157, 161, 165–169, 181, 184n15, 198, 273, 296, 298, 299, 303, 308
Elitism, 12, 17, 24, 25, 28, 31, 38, 39, 46, 50, 81, 82, 161, 180, 182, 278, 290, 295–298, 300, 301, 303, 317n18
Enlightenment, viii, 10, 12, 13, 41, 45, 50, 56–57, 91, 94, 106, 234, 280, 291, 296–298
Equality, 13, 43, 77, 78, 166, 196, 222, 229, 262–264, 289
Europe, 6, 10, 45, 176, 300
European Union (EU), 21, 30, 66, 174, 203, 299–300, 309
Euthanasia, 14, 92, 141, 181, 259, 266
Evolution, 131, 134–135, 144, 147–148, 154n24, 277, 315

F

Factions, 297, 298
Facts, 31, 39n26, 71, 88–89, 104, 208, 210, 232, 234, 239, 246–247, 296, 297
Faith, 163, 164, 175, 195, 231, 245–246, 260, 291–293
Fallibilism, 102, 200
Foucault, Michel, 104
France, 10, 47, 153n6, 159, 176, 183, 289, 294, 295, 305, 306
Francis, Pope, 181
Free will, 73, 134
Freedom, vii, 8, 9, 11–14, 17, 23, 30–32, 39n26, 41–69, 74, 78–82, 87, 107, 140, 159, 170, 189, 190–192, 196, 212n1, 263, 268, 273, 280, 284, 288, 298
absolute, 30, 57, 59, 65, 95, 102, 211
negative and positive, 48
Freedom of religion, *see* Religious freedom
Freedom of speech, 9, 25, 65, 68n18, 94, 211, 231, 267
arguments for, 52–62
Fundamentalism, 182, 208, 261, 266

G

Gandhi, Mohandas, 118
Gaus, Gerard, 35, 225
Genetics, 131, 157, 275–277
Germany, 294
Gey, Stephen, 225
God, 13, 15, 16, 73, 76, 77, 110,
    127, 128, 131, 132, 134, 136,
    144, 145, 147–151, 160, 162,
    183, 211, 237–239, 242–244,
    246, 256, 262–267, 271, 276,
    284, 289, 292, 293
Goodwin, Matthew, 299, 301
Graham, Billy, 254
Grayling, A.C., 6, 26, 37n9, 180,
    298, 300
Greece, 3, 9
Guthman, Amy, 166, 184n15

H

Habermas, Gary, 254
Habermas, Jurgen, 164, 188, 192,
    194, 199–205, 209, 213n18, 232
Hamilton, Alexander, 10
Hampton, Jean, 251n34, 271
Harm principle, 50–54, 135
Harris, Sam, 138
Hauerwas, Stanley, 259
Health care, 74, 115, 259, 261
Hedonism, 9, 44, 160
Hinduism, 218
Hobbes, Thomas, 10, 13, 200
Hoffer, Eric, 313
Holmes, Oliver Wendell, 138
Holyoake, George, 153n3
Human dignity, 15, 41, 96, 127
Human fulfillment, 12, 41, 73, 82,
    140, 151, 152, 187, 316
Human nature, 9, 11–13, 15, 16,
    39n26, 41, 52, 56, 73–75, 78,
    107, 129, 130, 134, 151, 158,
    170, 199, 227, 229, 272

Human rights, *see* Natural rights
Hume, David, 10

I

Ideal speech situation, 204, 232
Ideology, 92, 170, 182, 314, 315
Immigration, 81, 93, 96, 176,
    185n20, 227, 300–302
Incommensurability, vii, xii, 29, 31,
    62, 63, 67, 71–72, 81, 84, 86,
    102, 113, 119–121, 152, 169,
    194, 205, 236, 271
India, 30, 173
Individualism, 52, 56, 135, 140, 160,
    161, 227
Integrity, 77, 127, 266, 267, 286, 306
Ireland, 81, 94, 153n6, 168, 169,
    174–183, 226, 283, 284,
    305, 306
Islam, 126, 206
Issenberg, Sasha, 99n8
Italy, 176

J

James, William, 127, 145
Jay, John, 10
Jefferson, Thomas, 10, 50
Jesus, 118, 127, 254, 263, 292
Justice, 8, 10, 13, 14, 17, 18, 28, 29,
    78, 128, 135, 146, 169, 194,
    196–198, 200–202, 220–222,
    237, 266, 270, 273, 298
Justification, 11, 74, 75, 149, 199,
    201, 206, 210, 220–222, 238,
    246, 254, 273, 277, 289, 293
Just war, 93

K

Kaltwasser, Cristobal, 298
Kant, Immanuel, 149, 200

INDEX 331

King, Jr., Martin Luther, 77, 118, 213n15, 262–268
Kitcher, Philip, 126, 138, 140, 142–152, 162, 190, 246, 255, 266
Knowledge, *see* Objective truth

L
Laborde, Cécile, 35, 225, 242–244, 246–248
Lafayette, 50
Landemore, Hélène, 39n27
Law, 7, 8, 11, 13–15, 17, 24, 28, 32, 47, 48, 50, 52, 54–56, 66, 75–76, 96, 103, 108, 120, 139, 143, 164, 166, 167, 170–172, 177, 192, 193, 199, 201–202, 204, 208, 221, 226, 262–265, 269, 273, 274, 278–280, 281n19, 283–287, 289, 294, 305–307, 309, 312, 314, 315
Layman, Geoffrey, 185n18
Leadership, 11, 20, 24–26, 45, 297, 299
Lecky, William, 23
Liberal democracy, 16, 18, 29–31, 67, 169, 188, 193–201, 205, 207, 238, 268, 283, 289, 290, 301, 304
Liberalism, 16–18, 22, 23, 38n16, 164, 166, 187–212
  philosophical, 17–18, 31, 38n16, 170, 272, 308
  See also Secular liberalism
Liberal political theory, 29, 30, 35, 60, 120, 187–205, 231, 242–248, 254, 255, 262, 271, 284, 306
Liberal religious believers, 145–146, 170, 206, 207, 258, 269, 305
Life, meaning of, 34, 41, 48, 56, 60, 81, 88, 104, 107, 133, 136, 142, 149–151, 154n27, 219, 220, 303

Lincoln, Abraham, 263
Locke, John, 10, 11, 13, 15, 17, 23, 25, 41, 44–52, 68n6, 79, 161, 188, 200, 254, 288
Lyotard, Jean-François, 104, 111

M
MacIntyre, Alasdair, 246
Madison, James, 9, 10, 31, 37n9, 194, 297, 298
Marcel, Gabriel, 21
Mares, Edwin, 98n6
Maritain, Jacques, 258
Marriage, 43, 44, 82, 178–179, 296
  See also Divorce
Marx, Karl, 23, 38n18, 138
Marxism, 295
Materialism (consumerism), 150, 159, 160, 163, 266
Media, 26, 42, 63, 65–66, 75, 81, 91, 103, 133, 163, 175, 179, 205, 293, 296, 299, 302, 303, 307, 311, 314–316
Metanarrative, 105
Milbank, John, 38n25
Mill, John Stuart, 12, 13, 15, 23, 25, 45–59, 64, 74, 87, 95, 135, 136, 138, 140, 161, 294
Milton, John, 43
Minority rights, 8, 17, 48–49, 105, 173, 301, 302
Monarchy, 3, 4, 9, 11, 14, 136
Montesquieu, Baron, 10
Morality, 7, 20, 27, 31, 46, 53, 55, 113, 134, 146–148, 150, 177, 225, 227, 241, 261, 262, 298
  objective, 7, 46, 53, 55, 105, 120, 255–256, 264–265, 267, 288
Mother Teresa, 118
Mudde, Cas, 298

N

Nagel, Thomas, 35, 138, 193, 225, 261, 262, 273
Natural law, 15, 262, 263, 265
Natural rights, 5, 8–10, 13–18, 35, 51, 128, 198, 221, 224, 237, 246, 248, 254, 262–264, 301, 302
Natural theology, 144, 237, 244
Netherlands, 163, 283, 306
Neuhaus, Richard John, 264
Neutrality, 32, 38n16, 132–133, 158, 165–171, 184n15, 191–192, 207, 223, 242, 247, 271, 279, 287, 288
New Zealand, 30, 65
Nietzsche, Friedrich, 138, 148
Nihilism, 89, 91, 107, 146, 150
Norway, 283, 284
Novak, Michael, 264

O

Ober, Josiah, 16, 38n16
Objective morality, *see* Morality
Objective truth, 7, 9, 53, 55, 59–61, 71–72, 86–93, 98n4, 98n6, 101–112, 116–121, 195, 271
O'Connor, Sandra Day, 68n18
Oligarchy, 37n9
Olson, D., 153n6
Original position, 197, 198, 261, 270, 273

P

Peru, 12
Philippines, 30
Pinker, Steven, 138
Plato, 9, 12, 19, 23, 25, 28, 41–44, 49, 56, 297, 303, 317n18
Pluralism, 18, 29–31, 33, 34, 39n26, 59, 61–63, 65–67, 71–97, 99n7, 106, 111–113, 125, 126, 157, 187–191, 194–200, 202–205, 207, 212n4, 217–225, 233, 240, 268–270, 278, 279, 299, 301, 307, 312–315
Poland, 30, 79, 81, 174, 302
Political correctness, 64, 182, 311, 312
Political theory, 74, 103, 128, 254, 266, 271, 272, 310
  See also Liberal political theory
Politics, 27, 31, 34, 42, 53, 55, 77, 97, 99n7, 125, 128, 135, 138, 152, 164, 185n18, 203–212, 223, 225, 253–280, 287, 289, 303–306, 311–316
Pollack, D., 153n6
Popular sovereignty, 4, 10–12, 18, 24, 26, 28, 47, 71, 78, 128, 169
Populism, 6, 28, 294–304, 317n15
Postmodernism, 88, 102, 104–110, 112, 119, 199, 234
Prejudice, 6, 26, 104, 106, 209, 219, 231, 233, 243, 245, 256, 297–300, 303
Public deliberation, 17, 24, 66, 71, 83, 84, 115, 141, 170, 172, 187, 192, 196, 207, 208, 211, 213n22, 214n29, 217–252, 257, 258, 267, 268, 271, 275, 286, 289, 307
Public reason, 35, 192–194, 196, 197, 199–209, 211, 214n24, 217–251, 253, 254, 256, 258, 260, 262, 267, 270, 271, 275, 291, 311
  See also Reason

Q

Quinn, Philip, 225
Quong, Jonathan, 247, 248, 272

R

Ratzinger, Joseph (Pope Benedict), 184
Rawls, John, 35, 67, 171, 188, 189, 192–205, 207–212, 212n4, 214n24, 217–224, 228, 230, 232, 233, 235, 238, 239, 241, 242, 250n14, 254, 261, 268–274, 281n9
Realism, 87, 88, 90, 121
Reason
  loss of confidence in, 29, 32, 35, 62, 71–97, 102, 113, 115, 119, 229, 235, 291, 313, 315
  process vs. conclusions of, 214n24, 242–249
  See also Public reason; Secular reason
Reasonable pluralism, 194–199, 202, 217–225, 233, 235, 240, 245, 249, 253, 272, 278, 279
Relativism, 29, 31–32, 44, 51, 54–62, 71, 87, 89, 90, 98n6, 101–122, 163, 190, 200, 271
  problems facing, 117–118
  rhetoric of vs. philosophical thesis of, 107–112
Religion in public life, 35, 125, 128, 139, 163, 189, 193, 208–212, 214n29, 256, 260, 266, 308
  See also Church and state
Religious belief, 78, 103, 107, 111, 126–130
  rationality of, 128–129, 242–246, 259, 265, 278, 286, 289
Religious freedom, 14, 31, 44, 159, 190–192, 212n1, 284, 287
Religious worldview, 29, 34, 78, 125–130, 139, 141–145, 147, 159, 161–166, 181, 187–212, 225, 233, 255, 262, 268, 269, 277, 284–287, 289, 305, 306, 315

Republic, 8
Respect, 83, 85, 94–96, 144, 190, 191, 195, 196, 204, 228, 240, 242, 259, 261, 268, 311–312, 314
Revelation, 128, 129, 144, 208, 209, 233, 234, 238, 239, 244, 245, 254, 255, 265, 266, 292, 293
  See also Bible
Rights, *see* Civil rights; Natural rights
Rosenberg, Alex, 138
Rousseau, Jean-Jacques, 10

S

Sagan, Carl, 138
Salvation, 45, 136, 143
Sartre, Jean Paul, 95, 107, 147, 148
Schumpeter, Joseph, 17, 23–26, 28, 38n18
Science, 27, 31, 38n26, 52, 59, 87, 103, 126, 130–132, 142, 157, 160, 161, 164, 195, 220, 224, 233, 237, 245, 297, 314
Scientism, 130
Secular, 126, 132, 158, 165–169, 172, 184n16
Secular humanism, 130, 145
Secularism, 33–34, 39n30, 78, 130–152, 153n3, 158–164, 168, 172, 190, 211, 222, 239–240, 249, 260–262, 269, 276–279, 283, 285–286, 288, 289, 306, 308, 316
  immature and mature, 133, 182–183
  passive and active, 172–173
  rationality of, 142, 151, 183
Secularization, 34, 97n2, 126, 138, 152, 158–164, 172–174, 178, 179, 305–306
Secularization thesis, 160–164

Secular liberalism, 22, 37n6, 125, 169–170, 187–212, 214n29, 225, 227, 245–247, 250n19, 256, 260–262, 278, 307
  See also Liberal political theory
Secular motivation, principle, 209, 210, 256, 257, 259, 260, 264
Secular rationale, principle, 209, 211, 233, 257, 264
Secular reason, 209, 214n24, 228, 233, 234, 239, 256, 257, 261, 286
  See also Public reason; Reason
Secular state, 33, 34, 37n6, 125, 152, 165–168, 171, 181, 191, 269, 306
Seculocracy, 286, 305, 306
Sheth, S.J., Noel, 185n19
Sieyès, Abbé, 50
Skepticism, 103, 195, 200, 205, 274
Slavery, 103, 226, 227
Smart, Ninian, 127
Smith, Christian, 161
Socialism, 22, 135
Socrates, 118
Soul, 45, 73, 92, 128, 129, 132, 134, 202, 203, 210, 237–244, 247–249, 257, 262, 271, 293
South America, 5, 159
Spain, 176
Spinoza, Baruch, 10
Spirituality, 129, 134, 139, 150, 159
Stark, Rodney, 161
State, 29, 33, 34, 42, 45, 47, 81, 128, 132, 158, 164–167, 170, 192, 209, 247, 269, 283–316
  See also Secular state
State neutrality, *see* Neutrality
Stout, Jeffery, 223, 250n14
Sweden, 284

T
Talisse, Robert B., 28, 249n7
Taylor, Charles, 159, 160, 185n17
Theocracy, 173, 305–306
Thirty Years' War, 10, 45
Tillich, Paul, 145
Tolerance, 9, 45–46, 52, 55, 63, 72, 85, 96, 118, 161, 273, 288, 309, 311
Tradition, 48, 55, 98n6, 106, 110, 111, 137, 148, 190, 200, 206, 209, 210, 234, 237–239, 245–247, 255, 262–265, 269, 271, 275
Transcendent, 127, 139, 143–145, 149, 151
Trigg, Roger, 166, 308
Trump, Donald, 6
Truth, Sojourner, 118
Truth, *see* Objective truth
Tyranny of the majority, 13, 48, 56, 294, 303–309, 315

U
Unamuno, Miguel de, 21
United Kingdom (UK), 4, 6, 10, 21, 65, 184n16, 280, 284, 294, 295, 299, 300, 302, 305, 309, 314
United States (U.S.), 7, 8, 10, 20, 23, 28, 30, 47, 65, 66, 68n18, 77, 94, 113, 115, 153n6, 159, 161, 169, 178, 180, 185n18, 194, 198, 208, 226, 227, 262, 264, 283, 284, 288, 294, 295, 298, 302, 304, 305, 308, 309, 314
U.S. Declaration of Independence, 8
U.S. Supreme Court, 65, 66, 284, 314
  See also Courts
Utilitarianism, 26, 51, 74, 136

V

Varadkar, Leo, 181
Veil of ignorance, 197, 198, 273
Venezuela, 5
Voltaire, 45
Voting, 8, 12, 27, 29, 92, 99n7, 214n29, 273

W

Waldron, Jeremy, 37n6
Warnock, Mary, 160
Weber, Max, 21, 23–26, 28
Weithman, Paul, 225
Willard, Dallas, 98n4
Willie, Anchrit, 317n18
Wittgenstein, Ludwig, 162
Wolterstorff, Nicholas, 230, 246, 294
Worldview pluralism, 31, 39n26, 59, 62, 72, 78–86, 90, 93, 96, 97, 106, 125, 133, 137, 171, 187–189, 197, 200, 229, 268, 269, 279, 295, 301, 303, 314
Worldviews, 13, 28–31, 35, 51, 55, 67, 92, 94, 103, 105, 121, 129, 136–137, 166, 170, 219, 240, 248, 273, 277, 278, 283, 300, 314, 315
    clash of, 29, 31, 34, 93, 106, 139, 157, 200
    incommensurability of (*see* Incommensurability)
    questions about, 75–77, 310
    solutions to problem of, 96–97
    as transformative, 77–78
Wright, N.T., 254

Y

Young, Iris, 213n22